Other Books by David Madden

Novels

Sharpshooter: A Novel of the Civil War, 1996 (Pulitzer Prize nominee)
On the Big Wind, 1980
Pleasure-Dome, 1979
The Suicide's Wife, 1978 (Pulitzer Prize nominee)
Bijou, 1974
Brothers in Confidence, 1972
Cassandra Singing, 1969
The Beautiful Greed, 1961

Collections of Short Stories

The New Orleans of Possibilities, 1982
The Shadow Knows, 1970

Scholarly Works

Touching the Web of Southern Writers, 2005
Cain's Craft, 1985
Harlequin's Stick, Charlie's Cane, 1975
James M. Cain, 1970
Poetic Image in Six Genres, 1969
Wright Morris, 1964

Books on Creative Writing and the Novel

Revising Fiction: A Handbook for Writers, 1988 (now in its ninth printing)
Writers' Revisions: An Annotated Bibliography of Articles and Books about Writers' Revisions and Their Comments on the Creative Process (with Richard Powers), 1980.

Edited works by David Madden

Loss of the Sultana and Reminiscences of Survivors, 2005
Thomas Wolfe's Civil War, 2004
The Legacy of Robert Penn Warren, 2000
Classics of Civil War Fiction (with Peggy Bach), 1991
Rediscoveries II (with Peggy Bach), 1988
Remembering James Agee, first edition 1974, second edition 1997
Contemporary Literary Scene (with Frank Magill), 1974
Nathanael West: The Cheaters and the Cheated, 1973

Rediscoveries, 1971
American Dreams, American Nightmares, 1970
Tough Guy Writers of the Thirties, 1968
Proletarian Writers of the Thirties, 1968

Creative Writing Textbooks

The Fiction Tutor: The Art of Writing and Reading Fiction, 1990
Creative Choices: A Spectrum of Quality and Technique in Fiction, 1975

Textbooks for Literature Courses

A Pocketful of Plays II, 2005
A Pocketful of Poems II, 2005
A Pocketful of Plays, 1996
A Pocketful of Poems, 1996
A Pocketful of Prose: Vintage II, 1996
A Pocketful of Essays, volumes 1 and 2, 2000
A Pocketful of Prose: Vintage, 1992
A Pocketful of Prose: Contemporary, 1992
The World of Fiction, 1990
Eight Classic American Novels, 1990
Studies in the Short Story, 1976
The Popular Culture Explosion (with Ray B. Browne), 1972

Book about David Madden

David Madden: A Writer for All Genres, edited by James A. Perkins and Randy
    J. Hendricks, 2004

A Primer of the Novel

For Readers and Writers

Revised Edition

David Madden
Charles Bane
Sean M. Flory

THE SCARECROW PRESS, INC.
Lanham, Maryland • Toronto • Oxford
2006

SCARECROW PRESS, INC.

Published in the United States of America
by Scarecrow Press, Inc.
A wholly owned subsidiary of
The Rowman & Littlefield Publishing Group, Inc.
4501 Forbes Boulevard, Suite 200, Lanham, Maryland 20706
www.scarecrowpress.com

PO Box 317
Oxford
OX2 9RU, UK

Copyright © 2006 by David Madden, Charles Bane, and Sean M. Flory

British Library Cataloguing in Publication Information Available

Library of Congress Cataloging-in-Publication Data

Madden, David, 1933–
    A primer of the novel : for readers and writers / David Madden, Charles Bane, Sean M.
Flory.—Rev. ed.
        p. cm.
    Includes bibliographical references and index.
    ISBN 13: 978-0-8108-5708-7
    ISBN 10: 0-8108-5708-1 (pbk. : alk. paper)
    1. Fiction—History and criticism. 2. Fiction—Technique. I. Bane, Charles, 1971–. II. Flory,
Sean M., 1976–. III. title.
PN3353.M25 2006
809.3—dc22   2005033522

Printed in the United States of America

⊚™ The paper used in this publication meets the minimum requirements of
American National Standard for Information Sciences—Permanence of Paper
for Printed Library Materials, ANSI/NISO Z39.48-1992.

For my students and my teachers.
—David Madden

To our parents, for reading to us.
—Charles Bane and Sean Flory

Contents

Preface to the First Edition		ix
Preface to the New Edition		xi
Acknowledgments		xiii
Introduction		xv
Part I: Types of Novels		1
1	Novels of Comedy	2
2	Novels of Personal Writings	8
3	Novels of Life	11
4	Novels of Development	17
5	The Symbolic Novel	25
6	The Popular Novel	30
7	Novels of History	45
8	Novels of Realism	49
9	Novels of Region	56
10	Novels of Philosophy and Politics	61
11	Novels of Psychology	71
12	The Pure Novel: A Not-Yet-Realized Type	75
Part II: The Art of Fiction		81
13	Point of View	89
14	Story	98
15	Characters	101

16	Conflict	106
17	Time–Space	108
18	Theme	114
19	Plot	122
20	Structure	125
21	Style	137
22	Symbolism	153
23	Imagery	156
24	Unity	161
25	Innovative Techniques	165
26	Revision	178

Epilogue: Relationship between the Reader and Writer   183
Appendix: Critical Approaches   191
Selected Bibliography   195
Chronology: The Development of the Novel   211
Author and Title Index   245
Type and Technique Index   269
About the Authors   277

Preface to the First Edition

$\mathcal{A}$s writer, student, teacher, critic, and reader, I've often felt the need of a book such as *A Primer of the Novel*; forced to work without one for many years, I finally decided to put one together myself. I have done the job as much in the role of a novelist and reader as critic and teacher. Although most of the book is as objective as I could make it, personal opinions do flare up. And although I have drawn primarily upon existing knowledge and critical concepts, I have invented a few variations (especially on terms for types), and formulated several critical concepts, such as "the charged image." Because I think I have done work that will be useful to me, I imagine this book will have various uses for other fiction writers, teachers, students, critics, and general readers.

The book is organized so that it may be read from cover to cover, but I want to suggest to casual users some of its uses:

If you're interested only in reading a discussion of a particular technique—point of view, for instance—simply consult the table of contents under techniques, or consult the techniques index, which will tell you not only where to find the general discussion of point of view but also references to it throughout the book.

If you wish to read about a type—the historical novel, for instance—consult either the table of contents under types or the types index.

Following your own interests, you may wish to read sections out of order; for instance, you may begin with the essays in the "Close Analyses" section.

Suppose you're reading Dickens's *Bleak House* and you wonder what other novels were published in England or around the world in the same year or decade. Consult the chronology.

Or suppose you're reading *Bleak House* and you want to know more about Dickens's technique: consult the authors and titles index.

If you're a teacher, you may want to put together a course consisting of American novels of the thirties. See the chronology.

If you're in a creative writing workshop, you may wish to make use mainly of part 2, Techniques [renamed The Art of Fiction].

If you're studying short fiction, most of the material in this book applies as well to short stories and novellas (some novellas are discussed; for instance, Camus' *The Stranger*).

Here and there, critics are cited briefly. For fuller publication data, consult the selective bibliography of criticism of the novel (which also provides, by the way, an outline of critical approaches).

If you want to see how several technical concepts apply to a single work, read one of the essays in the "Close Analyses" section.

If you want to know the birth and death dates of an author and do not know the year of publication of any of his books, consult the index, where a "C" will indicate the page of the chronology on which that information is first given. Outside the chronology, publication dates for novels are given only in Part 1, Types (dates would have cluttered Part 2, Techniques, unnecessarily).

If you want to know the nationality of an author, consult the chronology. Nationalities are *usually* given also in Part 1, Types, *only* if the author is neither American nor English, on the assumption that American and English writers are better known to most English speaking readers; nationalities are much less relevant in Part 2, Techniques.

If what you seek is a history of the novel, this book will not directly serve your purpose; a kind of history emerges indirectly, especially from Part 1, Types, where I have *roughly* grouped types historically.

The organization of Parts 1 and 2 is not inevitable; I have dealt with types and techniques in an order that *feels* most effective.

I should stress again that I have conceived this primer not for a single kind of reader—not, for instance, solely for critics. As a fiction writer, I have one use for it; as a general reader another; as a teacher another; as a critic another; and I only wish that as a student I had had access to such a book. Scholars, critics, and teachers may disagree with some of my emphases and concepts and the use to which I put common knowledge; and some students in creative writing workshops may disagree with some of my pontifications about technique. But the fiction writer in me wants this book to be first of all suggestive, in the richest sense (to provoke thought by both agreement and disagreement), not just authoritative, in the driest objective sense.

—David Madden
Baton Rouge, Louisiana, 1978

Preface to the New Edition

*W*hen David Madden first published *A Primer of the Novel* twenty-five years ago, there were no books of its kind available. Since then, many authors and editors have produced works that attempt the same comprehensive coverage of the genre. However, these works tend to be either written solely for writers or solely for readers. More often than not, those written for readers tend to be aimed at advanced students or critics of the novel. Therefore, we felt the need to produce an updated edition that again would be aimed at a general readership including writers, teachers, and students who are just being introduced to the genre.

For this edition, we have left the organization of the book fairly untouched. However, we have grouped the various "types" into more comprehensive categories to help illustrate the historical development of various types of novels. Although all of the types present in the first edition are still represented, many have become more clearly defined. For instance, the Pornographic Novel of the first edition is now the Erotic Novel in order to show its development from the Victorian Era through the twentieth century. In addition, several types appear for the first time in this edition such as the Graphic Novel and the Novel of Magical Realism. As well as keeping all of the original examples from representative texts, we have tried whenever possible to add new examples of more recent works. Even if actual textual examples are not present, we have updated the list of novels within each type as well as bringing the chronology up to date.

The Art of Fiction section, formerly called "Techniques," has been basically preserved from the original. We feel that David Madden, a Pulitzer Prize–nominated novelist, knows far more about the craft of novel than we. At Mr. Madden's request, we have removed the section of close analyses, but have updated the comprehensive bibliography.

Our hope in this endeavor is to use more recent critical thought in order to make this edition as useful to a new generation of readers, writers, teachers, and students as the first edition was to its generation.

—Charles Bane and Sean M. Flory
Baton Rouge, Louisiana

Acknowledgments

J am grateful for invaluable editorial assistance that only Peggy Bach could have given. I want to thank Joyce Carol Oates for suggesting this project. Charlene Clark prepared an early version of the chronology. My wife, Robbie, offered many good suggestions in the early drafts, as did Larry Shaffer, Maureen Hewitt, and Martha Hall. I wish to thank the following publishers for allowing me to reprint material: Frank Magill; *Collier's Encyclopedia*; Scott-Foresman; Holt, Rinehart, and Winston; Southern Illinois University Press; and Crown.

—David Madden

We express our deepest gratitude to Paulette Guerin, Ilana Xinos, Scott Gage, and Scott Whiddon for reading passages, offering suggestions, and recommending novels during the many hours, days, weeks, and months we spent revising this book.

—Charles Bane and Sean Flory

Also, permission to use excerpts from the following works has been granted by the publishers: A. Camus, *The Stranger,* copyright © 1942 by Alfred A. Knopf; T. Capote, *Other Voices, Other Rooms,* copyright © 1948 by Random House, Inc.; J. Conrad, *Victory,* copyright © 1915, 1921 by Doubleday & Co., Inc., © 1915 by Joseph Conrad; W. Faulkner, *The Sound and the Fury,* copyright © 1929 by Random House, Inc.; F. Scott Fitzgerald, *The Great Gatsby,* copyright © 1925 by Charles Scribner's Sons, also by The Bodley Head; G. Garcia Marquez, *One Hundred Years of Solitude,* by Harper & Row; J. Heller, *Catch-22,* copyright © 1961 by Simon & Schuster; E. Hemingway, *The Sun Also Rises,* copyright © 1926 by Charles Scribner's Sons, and with the title, *Fiesta,* by Jonathan Cape, Ltd., with thanks to the executors of the Ernest Hemingway Estate; J. Joyce, *Portrait of the Artist as a Young Man,* copyright © 1916 by The Viking Press, Inc., and thanks also to The Society of Authors, representing the Estate of James Joyce; J. Joyce, *Ulysses,* copyright © 1934 by Random House, Inc.; D. H. Lawrence, *The Rainbow,* copyright © 1915 by The Viking Press, Inc.; thanks also to Laurence Pollinger, Ltd., and to the Estate of the late Frieda Lawrence Ravagli; C. McCullers, *The Heart Is a Lonely Hunter,* copyright © 1940 by Houghton Mifflin Co., © 1967 by Carson McCullers; S. Maugham, *Of Human Bondage,* copyright © 1915 by Doubleday & Co., Inc., thanks to A. P. Watt, Ltd. and to the Estate of the late W. Somerset Maugham; J. C. Oates, *With Shuddering Fall,* copyright © 1964 by Joyce Carol Oates, published by Vanguard Press, Inc.; M. Proust, *Remembrance of Things Past,* copyright © 1934 by Random House, Inc.; V. Woolf, *To the Lighthouse,* by Harcourt Brace Jovanovich, Inc., and by The Hogarth Press, Ltd.

—David Madden, Charles Bane, and Sean Flory

Introduction

The novel is the most difficult literary form to define. Most critics settle for a simple definition based on length. But many works called short stories, e.g., Joseph Conrad's "The Secret Sharer" and John Steinbeck's "The Pearl," are also called novellas, and many novellas, e.g., F. Scott Fitzgerald's *The Great Gatsby* and Albert Camus' *The Stranger*, are often called novels.

A controversy continues over whether to perpetuate the historical divorce between the early long fiction called *romance* (from the French *roman,* a term still used for the novel in most European countries) and the newer fiction called *novel* (from the Italian *novella*, or "little new thing"). Most literary scholars today agree that the term *novel* should be reserved for those works that present a realistic picture of life contemporary to the author and his readers; works that relate invented, more imaginary adventures, usually set in the past, with exotic locales, should be called *romances*.

One solution is to make the distinction as long as it is historically valid and drop it at that point in literary history (about the turn of the twentieth century) when the proliferation of types made a strict distinction arbitrary. It is clear, however, that a too careful or narrow and limiting definition would be unbecoming so venturesome a genre.

Despite rumors of the death of the novel, the debate continues as to whether ours is the age of fiction or nonfiction (see Norman Podhortez, "The Article as Art"). Traditionally, the distinction between fiction and nonfiction has been that each in its use of facts and other aspects of reality strives to present a different kind of truth. Although the boundaries between the two forms are becoming blurred, perhaps they differ less in subject matter than in the way they use style and technique to negotiate the relationship between writer and reader. The result is two different kinds of experience. In *The Nature of Narrative,*

Robert Scholes and Robert Kellogg argue that a greater interest in all narrative forms, fictional and nonfictional, should replace our exaggerated interest in the novel as we have known it for two centuries.

APPROACHES

"The House of fiction has . . . not one window," said Henry James, "but a million." There are many approaches to the house of fiction. Most readers experience no division between form and content, theme and subject, vision and raw material, technique and structure, style and expression. But there is a difference between simply reading a novel and studying the novel as a form. The novel may be studied in two general ways: in terms of types or techniques.

Since the days of Homer's epics, during both the oral and the written phases, literature has been considered an institution. Eventually, that institution produced scholars, then critics, dedicated to preserving traditions. Although the many critical approaches have always tended to impose rules or precepts upon literature, each kind of critical emphasis has been encouraged by fictions that stress one or more of its many possibilities.

The novel is new. The youngest of the major forms of literary expression, it is only about 200 years old. Its newness as a type of narrative derives from its departure from characteristics of the Greek *epic* poem (Homer, *The Odyssey,* c850 B.C.) and the prose-poem *romances* of the Middle Ages (*The Romance of the Rose,* c1235; 1280) and other ancient narratives in poetry and prose. But further back, oral narrative, which was mainly poetic, set patterns that evolved into the novel we read today. Like poetry and the drama, the early prose narratives, comic and heroic, were written mainly by and for the aristocracy.

The novelties of the novel have always attracted readers, but the historical development of the form is marked by the influence of other narrative forms (epic, drama, poetry, cinema) and other arts (painting, music, dance, architecture) and other kinds of knowledge (science, philosophy, psychology, history). The novel utilizes all characteristics of earlier oral and written forms of narrative and discourse: essay, character sketch, biography, autobiography, philosophical treatise, travel, folk tale, fable, fairy tale, anecdote, myth, legend, ballad, romance. The novel has also incorporated aspects of new forms such as the newspaper, the magazine, and advertising. These and other elements have been fused into types of narration.

Nearly every type and every technique came into use early in the history of the form; each can be traced to the present. For instance, the epistolary novel became popular with Samuel Richardson's *Pamela* (1740) and the protagonist's letter writing figures prominently in Saul Bellow's *Herzog* (1964). Various countries, east and west, have contributed types and techniques, from oral to written, from poetic to prose. The novel today is an amalgam of many kinds and a great variety of narrative elements. The author's originality arises from the way he or she transforms his or her universal material through traditional techniques; experimentation is a restructuring of tradition and convention.

EARLY NARRATIVES

The earliest types of narrative reveal a magical view of nature. There are many Greek allegories of fertility and death. Classical legends and myths out of the folk tradition formed the basis of early-recorded stories. Homer's narratives of heroic deeds, *The Iliad* and *The Odyssey,* were composed of poetic formulas. Through his epic poems the gods and heroes of ancient times were perpetuated in the living traditions of Greek civilization for centuries. In *The Long Journey* (1923–1924), Denmark's Nobel Prize winner Johannes V. Jensen wrote a cultural epic depicting the progress of man from the Ice Age to the twentieth century. Many modern novels have a mythic dimension, William Golding's *Lord of the Flies* (1954), for instance, is a fable about human nature. Some elements of the Homeric poems contributed to the comic epics of Henry Fielding, as in *Tom Jones* (1794). The anonymous *Beowulf* (c1000) is one of many legends that the English perpetuated in the Homeric tradition.

During the Middle Ages, many Scandinavian, German, and Frankish national epics that were dying out in the oral tradition were preserved in written literature. The term *saga* ("tell") is now used to describe large cycles, series novels, or trilogies that chronicle the experiences of a family from generation to generation against a larger historical or economic background. Most of the national epics transcribed in the eleventh and twelfth centuries were episodic.

The national novel depicts the history and development of a nation newly emerging into modern civilization or newly created, with an attempt to capture the spirit and articulate the purpose of the author's country. In these novels, there is something of the *Volksgeist* (national mind or genius) that created oral epics. While no concept in other countries quite parallels the American aspiration to produce the Great American Novel, many emerging nations have taken enthusiastically to the novel as though it were a new form, while many ancient, dormant civilizations, such as India and Japan, have begun to use the novel eagerly as a way of expressing new attitudes in the modern age.

ROMANCES

Romances, too, began with the Greeks. There were allegories (Greek:"to imply something else") of love, of grief, and pure romances. In the era of knighthood, romantic love and epic, heroic deeds produced the romance, first in verse, later in prose. These were tales about the adventures of a hero of chivalry. The literature about King Arthur and the Knights of the Round Table comprises several sophisticated prose works. Through allegory, many of the romances conveyed such ethical and personality concepts as: chastity, courtly love, courtesy, contemplation, equity, constrained abstinence, grace, holiness, honor, *fides*, genius, fame, fortune, largesse, error, idleness, love, jealousy, hatred, disdain, fear, despair, danger, *ira*, beauty, shame, peace, time, the transfiguration, vice, sloth, prayer, remembrance, penance, youth, physics, reason, pride, sacramentalism, pity, virtue, pleasure, tribulations, sleep, poverty, stoicism; and personifications of the Gods, the Devil, Eve, the Graces, the Seven Deadly Sins, Venus, Seven Wise Men, Saturn. These qualities may strike the modern reader as too obvious, but in subtle forms they pervade most of the early novels and in still subtler ways dominate works through Faulkner.

The pastoral romance is another manifestation of the romantic narrative. Langus (second to fifth century A.D.), a product of Greece's decadent period, wrote one of the first, *Daphnis and Chloe,* a predecessor of the modern novel. In 1621, John Barclay wrote *Argenis,* a pseudo-classical heroic allegory set in the Hellenistic era in Sicily. Written in Latin, it was a popular book for two centuries. Another romance, Madame de La Fayette's *The Princess of Cleves* (1678) anticipated the psychological novel and the roman a clef (novel based on well-known people). Some say it is among the first real novels according to the modern definition.

In the sixteenth and seventeenth centuries, when there emerged types of fiction with which comparisons could be made, the romance was considered a story whose setting was exotic, whose incidents were remote from ordinary life, and whose purpose was escape. A century later, the romance was thought of as an "extravagant fiction" full of "wild and wanton exaggeration; a picturesque falsehood."

Attitudes toward fiction expressed by scholars and critics have remained influenced by the classical or neo-classical tradition to the present day. Classical concepts of literature are based on a study of Greek and Roman works and regard art as a search for and expression of absolutes. Past customs and traditions—rather than the individual living in the present—are the source of authority for attitudes about literature. The classical mind judges literature by such characteristics as balance, unity, proportion, restraint, simplicity, grandeur, correctness, decorum, majesty and magnitude (as in the epic), and by the author's sincerity and seriousness. These and other characteristics assume readers who are trained in the classical tradition and who are receptive to them.

The traditional or classical forms are still with us in altered shapes. Felix Salten's *Bambi* (1923), which depicts animals in human terms in a pastoral allegory, was adapted in the next decade into one of Walt Disney's most famous animated feature cartoons. The Irish Renaissance or Celtic Twilight revived interest in the legendary romance, a good example of which is James Stephens' *Deidre* (1923). Many new forms are simply aspects of the old, exaggerated to achieve effects that better reflect our different world. For instance, out of two different emphases (social and psychological) upon the urge to realism come Honoré de Balzac's infatuation with objects and Alain Robbe-Grillet's terror of objects. The novel retains from its two main predecessors aspects of form and content: scope from the epic and imagination from the romance.

RISE OF THE NOVEL

The early romances were a product of the aristocracy. The middle-class modern realistic consciousness produced and read the novel; that the authors of this new form were supported not by the patronage of nobility but by publishers and readers was reflected in sales. Throughout much of its history, the novel has been regarded as a relatively inferior mode of expression. This attitude was partly influenced by the fact that so many women, often regarded as second-class citizens, wrote novels.

In *The Rise of the Novel* (specifically the English novel), Ian Watt discusses the forces that encouraged the growth of the form. Attitudes of individualism fostered by Puritanism encouraged a democratic spirit that, with the economic rise of the middle class, prevailed in many areas of human life, encouraging a literature that would describe individual experiences of real people. Secularization ameliorated the religious restrictions of Puritanism. So that even though religious and social attitudes forbade or disdained the reading of novels, too often written by women and read by girls to whom they were thought to be harmful, a growing worldliness excited interest in the lives of others as depicted in fiction.

Dualistic thinking in philosophy—analyzing the conflict between the individual ego and the external world—also prepared an intellectual atmosphere that would influence the writing and reception of the novel since the novel is uniquely suited to deal with the interaction between a character and his environment in empirical terms that appealed to the eighteenth-century mind. As a result, the philosophers of the Enlightenment generally worked with problems best illustrated in the novel.

Urbanization created new subject matter for the writer, and the novel was the form best suited to deal with it. Most of the readers of novels were concentrated in the cities, and they turned to the novel to describe to them their own private and public experiences and that part of which they were ignorant because of class distances. Urban women had more leisure to write and read novels.

With increased literacy and leisure and more efficient methods of printing, the middle-class reading public as a cultural phenomenon arose. These readers read more for pleasure than anything else and welcomed the ease with which novels could be consumed. Unlike earlier forms of literature, the novel is almost entirely a creature of print. (See Watt, *The Rise of the Novel.*)

And unlike poetry and drama, novels employ the gross materials of reality, just as the daily newspapers do. The expanding middle class wanted to know more about the wider world it was helping to create and in which it was rising in every sphere. The novel developed simultaneously with that other organ of middle-class information: the newspaper. From the beginning, the novel competed with other media in the dissemination of facts that described the way things are. Newspapers portrayed the public life; novelists imagined the private life behind the news item. Many novelists were formerly journalists; not until recent years has this sequence been reversed, in the creative reporting of American novelists Truman Capote, Norman Mailer, and Jean Stafford. The novel is a more private means of conveying the news, and it flourished in Japan just after the Second World War as that country experienced great changes in its public and private spheres.

The novel has traditionally half-denied its own existence by pretending to be what it is not: documentary, Daniel Defoe's *Journal of the Plague Year* (1722); diary and journal, Tobias Smollett's *The Expedition of Humphrey Clinker* (1771); letters, Samuel Richardson's two major novels *Pamela* (1740) and *Clarissa* (1748); travel account, Jonathan Swift's *Gulliver's Travels* (1726); treatise, William Godwin's *Caleb Williams, or Things as They Are* (1794). In the novel, these become mock or pseudo-forms. Still, the novel also satisfied a desire for transcendence of the ordinary. Daniel Defoe's *Robinson Crusoe* (1719), one of the first great English novels, depicted in very practical and realistic terms the everyday life of a man on a deserted island, thus fusing the commonplace and the exotic.

The prime purpose of the novel, as distinguished from other forms of narrative, is then to depict reality, even when the novel is confined to subjective worlds. In a figurative sense, of course, all narratives are, in the end, realistic, for in reflecting the *actual* ideals of the people who read them, even the French romances were realistic. Franz Kafka's special realism in *The Trial,* for instance, is a means to the end of revealing aspects of human experience just as abstract as the allegorical personifications of French romances, and the gothic novel more overtly used elements employed in Kafka, one of whose novels is set in a castle (*The Castle,* 1926).

Not only would some critics and novelists distinguish the novel from the romance (Nathaniel Hawthorne made that distinction for his own work, calling *The House of the Seven Gables* [1851] a romance—a form that allows a certain latitude), some would also make a distinction between the novel and forms such as prose satire like Swift's *Gulliver's Travels*. Graham Greene calls some of his fiction entertainments and other, more serious works novels.

A DEFINITION

The novel has always been a genre in constant flux. Today there are a great many more types than in the eighteenth century, and the techniques of fiction are put to so many uses that we need either to limit the term even more and create new categories or allow it to embrace every prose work that is fictional and is over a certain length. But since the novel, as it has come to be defined (as distinct from earlier long narrative forms like the poetic epic and the romance), usually brings the news about the life of real people in the ordinary world, we may settle provisionally for a median definition: a prose fiction narrative that is not only longer than either a short story or a short novel (novelette) but that usually subjects the reader to an experience in more detail and depicts a greater variety of characters who are involved in a plot constituted of a multiplicity of episodes, with greater scope in time and space, and that is concerned with real people in "a stable society" (Northrop Frye) in the real world but is distinguished from nonfiction in being the product of a more inventive imagination and in being expressed in language and through a structure that is usually more carefully controlled to create effects in the reader.

I

TYPES OF NOVELS

*S*ince no novel is a perfect example of a specific type, each novel cited as an example of one type will contain elements of several others. Thus, some novels are listed under as many as three or more type headings. Popular novels are also cited under various headings, and that broad type is itself discussed, along with several of its subtypes. Publication dates for each title are given each time it occurs. If the author is not well known, the author's nationality is given.

Characteristics of the types sometimes overlap, and none of these types is pure as each type includes aspects of others. Each type emphasizes an element of fiction that is common to other types. For instance, the philosophical novel reminds us that most good and great novels are to some extent philosophical. But we may also say that some types, such as the philosophical, depart further than others from the novel as it is generally conceived.

Among writers, general readers, reviewers, critics and scholars, and literary historians, there is little unanimity as to correct definitions of these types or even as to their usefulness. Some discussed here are not strict, formal types; at best those less-traditional terms share a quality that is characteristic of fiction itself, suggestibility. Discussion of all these types provides us with ways of talking about the nature and history of the novel, and of the short story and novella as well.

While some types emphasize technique, others emphasize subject matter. Some terms used for types are also used to describe techniques. For instance, the term "epistolary" refers both to a type of novel and to a technique that may be employed in a novel.

Novels of Comedy

THE COMIC NOVEL

$\mathcal{T}$he comic novel, written out of a comic vision of human behavior, provides pure delight through the use of incongruity and other devices and ends happily. As we laugh at the characters involved in extricating themselves from comic predicaments, we feel we are at least slightly superior to them; we feel scorn, and a little malice along with pure delight. When we recognize ourselves, to some extent, in these characters, we learn and gain insight, as in serious novels, but bypass one of the major experiences of the serious novel, empathy and compassion.

In the comic novel, as well as the closely related picaresque, the Spanish were very adept. There is Pedro Antonio de Alarcon's *The Three-Cornered Hat* (1874), a comedy of intrigue. But the English handled the type best, as in Kingsley Amis' *Lucky Jim* (1953). The anglophile Irish-American J. P. Donleavy's *The Ginger Man* (1955) is considered one of the first black comedies. R. K. Narayan, a South Indian, imitates the British manner in *The Guide* (1958), a comedy of misunderstanding about a dreaming rogue, Railway Raju, a tourist guide who becomes a bogus holy man. The American Gore Vidal created a black comic, almost farcical situation in *Myra Breckinridge* (1968), a story of a man who becomes a great movie love goddess.

Although "comedy" is a useful term for a type of drama, it becomes perhaps too broad when applied to the novel. Most novels contain comic elements or comic relief, but even within a category of novels that are usually considered to be predominately comic in nature, there is a wide variation ranging from the picaresque to the satire to broad farce. A good example of a predominantly comic epic is Henry Fielding's *The History of Tom Jones* (1749).

> Jones immediately interposing, a fierce contention arose, which soon proceeded to blows on both sides. And now Mrs. Waters (for we must confess she was in the same bed), being, I suppose, awakened from her sleep, and seeing two men fighting in her bedchamber, began to scream in the most violent manner, crying out Murder! Robbery! and more frequently Rape! which last, some, perhaps, may wonder she should mention, who do not consider that these words of exclamation are used by ladies in a fright, as fa, la, la, ra, da, etc., are in music, only as the vehicles of sound, and without any fixed ideas.

Francois Rabelais' *The Lives, Heroic Deeds and Sayings of Gargantua and Pantegruel, His Son* (1533–1567) is a burlesque of the older romance genre, a mockheroic chronicle of two giants.

> And so, I climbed up, the best way I could, and traveled a good two leagues over his tongue before entering his mouth . . .
>
> Going on from there, I made my way between the rocks, which were his teeth, and even climbed one of them, where I found the prettiest spot in the world, with fine large tennis-courts, handsome promenades, beautiful meadows, many vineyards, and an endless number of Italian summer-houses, scattered through delightful fields.

THE PICARESQUE NOVEL

If romances derive from myths, the picaresque novel derives much of its material from folklore. Myths are specialized, rarified distillations of legends out of folklore. On the other hand, folklore is composed of nonliterary tales, songs, sayings, fairy tales, ballads, proverbs, beast epics, jingles, incantations, and riddles that reveal the traditions, customs, and beliefs of a people. Paul Bunyan is a good example of a tall tale produced by the nonliterary folk culture. In a tale, the emphasis is on the story, with its interesting episodes, as in the picaresque, rather than on heroic character or noble ideals, as in the romance narrative. Although the brief folk tales are often about kings, events reduce them to the level of everyday human experience. In the picaresque novel, fancy—the source of imagination—is joined with reality to produce the cross-fertilized soil in which the realistic novel, with its emphasis on facts, was to grow.

In *The Hero with a Thousand Faces*, Joseph Campbell devises a basic pattern for most myths and legends, the "monomyth," in which the hero leaves his familiar home, wanders through strange regions of this world and the underworld, having adventures, and returns with some saving secret to bestow upon his people. There is a similar pattern in folk literature in the mock or pseudo-traveler's tale, which became a popular type of novel early in its history. If the narrator were the only person to have visited the remote place, the authenticity claimed for such a novel couldn't be verified. Bringing back the news of other places was a prelude to presenting the news about the society one lived in and the way its various classes lived. This interest in travel became one of the prime hallmarks of the picaresque. Typically, the picaresque involves many characters, episodes, and locales over a long time span. The usual picaresque tale is a first person narrative about a wandering *picaro* (rogue) whose many adventures on the road involve him with a variety of stereotypes on every social level and realistically and satirically reveal the mores of a society in a particular era. Contrasted with the rogue's criminal code, respectable people are often seen to be hypocrites. Satire of society usually is the result of the picaro's movements on all social levels.

Some writers use the mock journey device to create a cross-section of characters who represent, sometimes allegorically, aspects of human nature or of a society the author is satirizing. Irreverence for the traditional concept of the hero of myth, legends, and tales is one of the main elements of the picaresque throughout its history. Jonathan Swift's *Gulliver's Travels* (1726) satirizes in its very form the great mass of travel books popular in his time, a technique that John Barth later used in *The Sot-Weed Factor* (1960). A similar irreverence can be seen in the mock-heroic passages in Henry Fielding's *Tom Jones* (1749), Laurence Sterne's *The Life and Opinions of Tristram Shandy, Gent.* (1759–1767), and in James Joyce's *Ulysses* (1922) and *Finnegans Wake* (1939), in which the comparison between past and present becomes a critique of individual modern man's relative puniness.

Although the picaresque began in antiquity with works such as Petronius' *Satyricon* (1st century) and Lucius Apuleius' *The Golden Ass* (2nd century), it came to fruition in 16th-century Spain with the anonymous *La Vida de Lazarillo de Tormes* (c1554). Perhaps the greatest picaresque was Miguel de Cervantes' *Don Quixote* (Part I, 1605; Part II, 1615).

> At this point they caught sight of thirty or forty windmills which were standing on the plain there, and no sooner had Don Quixote laid eyes upon them than he turned to his squire and said, "Fortune is guiding our affairs better than we could have wished; for you see there before you, friend Sancho Panza, some thirty or more lawless giants with whom I mean to do battle. I shall deprive them of their lives, and with the spoils from this encounter we shall begin to enrich ourselves; for this is righteous warfare, and it is a great service to God to remove so accursed a breed from the face of the earth."
> "What giants?" said Sancho Panza.

Even more popular was Mateo Aleman's *La Vida y hechos del picaro Guzman de Alfarache* (*The Rogue*) (1599–1604). Another Spanish picaresque novel, the satirical, witty *La Vida del Buscon* (*Life of the Great Rascal*) (c1660), was written by Quevedo (Francisco Gomez de Quevedo Villegas). In England, Thomas Nashe wrote *The Unfortunate Traveller* (1594), a combination of realism and romance, and Daniel Defoe popularized the form with *Moll Flanders* (1722). The only great German narrative of the seventeenth century, H. J. C. Von Grimmelshausen's *Simplicissimus the Vagabond* (1669) is set during the Thirty Years War. A later Spanish example is Jose Maria de Pereda's *Pedro Sanchez* (1883).

In the twentieth century, the Spanish were still writing in a form they helped create; in a rather literary style, Ramon Perez de Ayala wrote *La Pata de la Raposa* (*The Fox's Paw*, 1924), about a rake, an adventurer who encounters many ladies of the world. Swedish writer Selma Lagerlof contributed *Gosta Berlings Saga* (1891). Mark Twain's *The Adventures of Huckleberry Finn* (1884), using the river as the means of travel and using the story of youthful innocence to make bitter satire, is perhaps the best-known example of the picaresque novel.

> I never felt easy till the raft was two mile below there and out in the middle of the Mississippi. . . . I was powerful glad to get away from the feuds, and so was Jim to get away from the swamp. We said there warn't no home like a raft, after all. Other places do seem so cramped up and smothery, but a raft don't. You feel mighty free and easy and comfortable on a raft.

The picaresque has remained one of the most popular types. Some examples of this early type put to serious modern use are William Faulkner's *As I Lay Dying* (1930), Louis Ferdinand Celine's somber *Journey to the End of the Night* (1932), Saul Bellow's *The Adventures of Augie March* (1953), Jack Kerouac's *On the Road* (1957), Gunter Grass's *The Tin Drum* (1959), Charles Bukowski's *Post Office* (1971), Douglas Adams' five-volume *Hitchhiker's Guide to the Galaxy* "trilogy" (1979–1992), Salman Rushdie's *Midnight's Children* (1980), Arthur Nersesian's *The Fuck-Up* (1991), and Irvine Welsh's *Trainspotting* (1993).

THE SATIRICAL NOVEL

The satirical novel ridicules humanity in order to correct its behavior. The targets of satire vary and may include humankind generally, a single person, a group, a social class, a nation, a system of thought, a movement in art, or an institution. The tone may vary from that of gentle amusement and delight to pessimistic and ferocious moral indignation, but the aim of satire is always the same: to expose, to diminish, or to destroy the target so that the reader gains insight into specific human excesses, follies, and vices, and can thus, perhaps, correct them. With ironic humor and passionate wit, the author expresses scorn, contempt, even malice, giving himself and his reader a vantage point of laughing or sneering superiority upon the target. Satire is always backed by a serious moral vision with which the author implies a greater scheme or vision of life at the same time as he or she destroys the one he despises, as Swift does in *Gulliver's Travels*. Basically conservative, the satirist would restore the original vitality of withering institutions. Voltaire's *Candide* (1759) is a classic example of the satirical novel.

> The terrified Candide stood weltering in blood and trembling with fear and confusion.
>
> "If this is the best of all possible worlds," he said to himself, "what can the rest be like? Had it only been a matter of flogging, I should not have questioned it, for I have had that before from the Bulgars. But when it comes to my dear Pangloss being hanged—the greatest of philosophers—I must know the reason why. And was it part of the scheme of things that my dear Anabaptist (the best of men!) should be drowned in sight of land? And Lady Cunegonde, that pearl amongst women! Was it really necessary for her to be disemboweled?"

Satire appears as early as the Italian Petronius' *Satyricon*. Of the many types of satire, here are a few: the Mexican J. J. Fernandez de Lizardi's *El Periquillo Sarniento* (*The Itching Parrot,* 1816–1830), a picaresque satire; the Chinese Shih Nai-an's *All Men are Brothers* (14th century), a picaresque romance; Alphonse Daudet's *Tartarin of Tarascon* (1872), a satirical romance about a braggart; Max Beerbohm's *Zuleika Dobson* (1911), a romantic satire; James Branch Cabell's *Cream of the Jest* (1917) and *Jurgen* (1919), satirical fantasies; Multatuli's *Max Havelaar* (1860); Pio Baroja's *Caesar or Nothing* (1919), a political satire; Guatemalan Miguel Angel Asturias' *El Senor Presidente* (1946), which uses folklore and grotesque elements; the Czech Jaroslav Hasek's *The Good Soldier Schweik* (1926); Anatole France's *The Gods Are Athirst* (1917); Philip Roth's *Portnoy's Complaint* (1969), a realistic satire; Joseph Heller's *Catch-22* (1961) and Kurt Vonnegut's *Slaughterhouse-Five* (1969) are important anti-war satires.

Some satires are simply humorous, often making satirical thrusts rather subtly, in the guise of the comic novel: Robert Smith Surtees' *Handley Cross* (1843), Mark Twain's *Huckleberry Finn* (1884), Ring Lardner's *You Know Me Al* (1916), Ellen Glasgow's *The Romantic Comedians* (1926), and Thomas Heggen's *Mister Roberts* (1946).

The social kind of satire, at which the English are most adept, embraces more novels than any other; the French, Russians, and Americans have also produced important social satires: Thomas Love Peacock's *Nightmare Abbey* (1818), Nikolai Gogol's *Dead Souls* (1842), William Makepeace Thackeray's *Vanity Fair* (1847–1848), Anthony Trollope's *Barchester Towers* (1857), H. G. Wells' *Tono-*

Bungay (1909), Saki's *The Unbearable Bassington* (1912), Norman Douglas's *South Wind* (1917), Sinclair Lewis' *Main Street* (1920) and *Babbitt* (1922), Evelyn Waugh's *Decline and Fall* (1928), Aldous Huxley's *Brave New World* (1932), Nathanael West's *Miss Lonelyhearts* (1933), John P. Marquand's *Wickford Point* (1939), Mary McCarthy's *The Groves of Academe* (1952), Randall Jarrell's *Pictures from an Institution* (1954), Hunter S. Thompson's *Fear and Loathing in Las Vegas* (1971), Tom Sharpe's *Wilt* (1976), David Lodge's *Small World* (1984), Tom Wolfe's *The Bonfire of the Vanities* (1987), Salman Rushdie's *The Satanic Verses* (1988), and Tom Perrotta's *Election* (1998).

An important subset of satire includes those works that deal directly with literary forms. In these works, authors write parodies of other authors' works in order to attack their aesthetic principles. Henry Fielding wrote a parody of Richardson's *Pamela* called *Shamela* (1741). Sometimes literary satires have a good deal of value in themselves, for instance, W. Somerset Maugham's *Cakes and Ale* (1930). A type more rare than literary travesty is the *burlesque* (Italian: "mockery") novel. A burlesque or caricature distorts a mere fault in a subject for amusement. This type includes two great classics that transcend the type, Cervantes' *Don Quixote,* a burlesque of medieval romances, and Francois Rabelais' *The Lives, Heroic Deeds and Sayings of Gargantua and Pantegruel, His Son* (1533–1567), a burlesque romance, a mock-heroic chronicle of two giants. Jane Austen's *Northanger Abbey* (1818) is a burlesque of Gothic novels. Vladimir Nabokov's *Pale Fire* (1962) parodies the conventions of literary-critical commentary. Many comic or satirical novels contain passages that parody, travesty, burlesque, or lampoon a specific target within the larger comic or satirical range, such as James Joyce's *Ulysses* (1922).

Novels of Personal Writings

THE EPISTOLARY NOVEL

The epistolary novel is a narrative composed of an exchange of letters. It is understandable that what is now considered a rather unusual type of narrative was an early form of the novel. The early novelist, especially in England, sought many ways of claiming authenticity. Nothing could seem more genuine than a collection of letters exchanged between two people or among members of a group. The illusion of reality, however, is defied by the technique itself; no matter how justified by circumstances, very few people write such long and so many letters, detailing the events of nearly every day. In the eighteenth century, both conversation and correspondence were an art, thus a favored form of first-person narration in the novel was the epistolary, best exemplified in one of the earliest English novels of consequence, Samuel Richardson's *Pamela* (1740). Pamela writes to her mother and father, and we get their replies.

> O that I had never left my little bed in the loft, to be thus exposed to temptations on one hand, or disgusts on the other! How happy was I awhile ago! How contrary now!—Pity and pray for Your afflicted Pamela.
>
> My Dearest Child,
>   Our Hearts bleed for your distress, and the temptations you are exposed to. You have our hourly prayers; and we would have you flee this evil great house and man, if you find he renews his attempts.

Other epistolary novels go beyond the family circle, for the novel was a reaching-out form in the early phases and letters were one such form of communicating. Smollett's *The Expedition of Humphrey Clinker* (1771) offers the letters of a variety of people, related through kinship or friendship. Pierre Choderlos de Laclos' *Les*

Liaisons Dangereuses (1782) consists mainly of letters between an unscrupulous pair of lovers who corrupt other young people.

Among modern writers, the Italian Guido Piovene is notable for his *Letters of a Novice* (1941). Mark Harris uses the form in *Wake Up, Stupid* (1959). In Saul Bellow's *Herzog* (1964), the narrator talks directly to the reader, often quoting letters he writes to famous people but never mails. James Patterson's *Sam's Letters to Jennifer* (2004), a woman's letters to her granddaughter, is a popular novel in this mode.

THE NOVEL IN JOURNAL FORM

In the journal, or diary, form of narration, the character usually speaks, as in the letter form, without the intervention of the author. But the diary is the opposite of the social form of communication, the letter, for the diary is private—a monologue, the character speaking directly to himself. Few actual diaries have been published, although two notable exceptions are the diary (1825) of Samuel Pepys, which reads like social letters to the world of London, and those of Anais Nin, which are considered superior to her surrealistic fiction.

The diary appears later than the epistolary in the history of the novel, related as it is to a later development in the attitude of the writer toward his characters—the stress is on private experience, and the character's own emotions are examined. Both Defoe's *Robinson Crusoe* (1719) and Goethe's *The Sorrows of Young Werther* (1774) are written partly in diary form, and Bram Stoker's *Dracula* (1897) combines letters with diary and journal entries. A modern example is Andre Gide's *Pastoral Symphony* (1919). Saul Bellow wrote *Dangling Man* (1944) and Jean-Paul Sartre wrote *Nausea* (1938) in this form.

> Monday, 29 January, 1932
>
> Something has happened to me, I can't doubt it any more. It came as an illness does, not like an ordinary certainty, not like anything evident. It came cunningly, little by little; I felt a little strange, a little put out, that's all. Once established it never moved, it stayed quiet, and I was able to persuade myself that nothing was the matter with me, that it was a false alarm. And now, it's blossoming.

Ostensibly, the journal is private, but sometimes a public or social use is foreseen, as in Daniel Keyes' *Flowers for Algernon* (1966) and Susan Daitch's *L.C.* (1986). Other examples include Gide's masterpiece, *Les Faux Monnyeurs* (*The Counterfeiters,* 1926) and Defoe's *A Journal of the Plague Year* (1722). Gide was himself keeper of one of the most readable journals any writer ever produced.

Kenneth Patchen, a poet, created a surrealistic prose journal, *The Journal of Albion Moonlight* (1941). Parts of journals augment novels that are primarily of some other type as when Joyce includes Stephen Dedalus' journal entries near the end of *Portrait of the Artist as a Young Man* (1916).

> April 26. Mother is putting my new secondhand clothes in order. She prays now, she says, that I may learn in my own life and away from home and friends what the heart is and what it feels. Amen. So be it. Welcome, O life! I go to encounter for the millionth time the reality of experience and to forge in the smithy of my soul the uncreated conscience of my race.

THE MEMOIR NOVEL

Although related to the journal form, the memoir novel differs in that it is a character's first-person account of a significant period in his life that is usually well in the past. More public than a journal, a memoir is usually as much about a writer's society at a given time as about the writer. "Memoir" is another term for the first-person narrative that has been in use since the beginning: Defoe's Moll Flanders tells the world about her worldly experiences, while Richardson's Pamela tells only her parents. The author must live up to the narrator's claim that his story is worth hearing. "I only am escaped to tell thee," Ishmael quotes from the book of Job at the end of Herman Melville's *Moby Dick* (1851). Huckleberry Finn and Holden Caulfield (in Salinger's *The Catcher in the Rye*) tell about the perils of trying to cope as a child in an adult's world. Holden says:

> If you really want to hear about it, the first thing you'll probably want to know is where I was born, and what my lousy childhood was like, and how my parents were occupied and all before they had me, and all that David Copperfield kind of crap, but I don't feel like going into it, if you want to know the truth. In the first place, my parents would have about two hemorrhages apiece if I told anything pretty personal about them. They're quite touchy about anything like that, especially my father. They're *nice* and all— I'm not saying that—but they're also touchy as hell. Besides, I'm not going to tell you my whole goddam autobiography or anything. I'll just tell you about this madman stuff that happened to me around last Christmas just before I got pretty run-down and had to come out here and take it easy.

Some novels are announced as memoirs: Walter De la Mare's *Memoirs of a Midget* (1921), Marguerite Yourcenar's *Hadrian's Memoirs* (1951), Umberto Eco's *The Name of the Rose* (1980), Jeanette Winterson's *Oranges Are Not the Only Fruit* (1985), Garrison Keillor's *Lake Wobegon Days* (1985), Jerry Stahl's *Permanent Midnight: A Memoir* (1995), and Arthur Golden's *Memoirs of a Geisha* (1997) are good examples of the type.

• *3* •

Novels of Life

THE AUTOBIOGRAPHICAL NOVEL

*A*utobiographical novels tell the entire life story of a character, and are based, unadmittedly in most instances, on the author's own life. They can be told in first or third person, and there is often a high degree of fictionalization of the material. The most famous example is Marcel Proust's *A la Recherche du Temps Perdu* (*Remembrance of Things Past*, 1913–1927), an interesting fabrication is his substitution of women characters for the men Proust loved.

> "Mademoiselle Albertine has gone!" How much farther does anguish pen-etrate in psychology than psychology itself. A moment ago, as I lay analysing my feelings, I had supposed that this separation without a final meeting was precisely what I wished, and, as I compared the mediocrity of the pleasures that Albertine afforded me with the richness of the desires which she pre-vented me from realising, had felt that I was being subtle, had concluded that I did not wish to see her again, that I no longer loved her. But now these words: "Mademoiselle Albertine has gone!" had expressed themselves in my heart in the form of an anguish so keen that I would not be able to endure it for any length of time. And so what I had supposed to mean noth-ing to me was the only thing in my whole life. How ignorant we are of our-selves. The first thing to be done was to make my anguish cease at once.

Look Homeward, Angel (1929) was the first of four massive novels recounting the life of Thomas Wolfe, who died at the age of 38. Henry Miller's works offer even more literal examples of the autobiographical novel, for he is named as the narrator of his novels *Tropic of Cancer* (1931) and *Tropic of Capricorn* (1939), which are more a series of actual memoirs than novels.

11

The autobiographical element can take several forms: Lawrence Sterne's *Sentimental Journey* (1768) is a novelized travel-autobiography; George Borrow's *Lavengro* (1851) and *The Romany Rye* (1857) are simulated autobiography; Swiss Gottfried Keller's *Der Grune Heinrich* (1854–1855) is an autobiographical romance; Chilean Eduardo Barrios' *Brother Ass* (1922) is a simulated autobiography; Japanese Dazai Osamu's (Shuji Tsushima) *No Longer Human* (1948) is a maudlin journal of a wild, suicidal buffoon, a travesty of autobiography; Canadian Malcolm Lowry's *Under the Volcano* (1947) is an allegorical, symbolic autobiographical novel that fails on the realistic level. A recent example is Ernest Gaines' *The Autobiography of Miss Jane Pittman* (1971). Other examples include Sylvia Plath's *The Bell Jar* (1963), Maya Angelou's *I Know Why the Caged Bird Sings* (1970), and Jeanette Winterson's *Oranges Are Not the Only Fruit* (1985).

THE PERSONAL HISTORY NOVEL

The personal history is a pseudo or simulated autobiography, as is Defoe's *The Fortunes and Misfortunes of the Famous Moll Flanders* (1722).

> My true name is so well known in the records or registers at Newgate, and in the Old Bailey, and there are some things of such consequence still depending there, relating to my particular conduct, that it is not to be expected I should set my name or the account of my family to this work; perhaps, after my death, it may be better known; at present it would not be proper, no, not though a general pardon should be issued, even without exceptions and reserve of persons or crimes.

Again, the author wants to assure his middle-class readers that he is offering reality, not an idle work of fancy. This claim is made with more intricate irony in Lawrence Sterne's *Tristram Shandy* (1760–1767). And there is an even more complex irony in John Barth's *Giles Goat-Boy* (1966), in which a character pretends to be the editor of a journal, memoir, or confession entrusted to him by the main character and narrator. With such novels, the pretense is sometimes that the work is published posthumously. Many of Charles Dickens's novels are written in this style.

THE CONFESSIONAL NOVEL

The confessional novel is narrated by a character moved by the compulsion to confess to a crime against humanity or society, as in Italian Italo Svevo's *La Coscienza di Zeno* (*Confessions of Zeno*, 1924), a comic, pseudo-autobiography, written in an economical style, as in Yukio Mishima's *Confessions of a Mask* (1958), about a homosexual, and as in Vladimir Nabokov's *Lolita* (1955).

> "Lolita, or the Confession of a White Widowed Male," such were the two titles under which the writer of the present note received the strange pages it preambulates. "Humbert Humbert," their author, had died in legal captivity, of coronary thrombosis, on November 16, 1952, a few days before his trial was scheduled to start.
>
> Lolita, light of my life, fire of my loins. My sin, my soul. Lolee-ta: the tip of the tongue taking a trip of three steps down the palate to tap, at three, on the teeth. Lo. Lee. Ta.
>
> She was Lo, plain Lo, in the morning, standing four feet ten in one sock. She was Lola in slacks. She was Dolly at school. She was Dolores on the dotted line. But in my arms she was always Lolita.

Actual confessions like St. Augustine's *Confessions* (397–401), Jean-Jacques Rousseau's *Confessions* (1784), and Thomas De Quincey's *Confessions of an English Opium Eater* (1822) inspired this fictional variant. Recently, a young Dutchman in *I, Jan Cramer* (1964) and a young American, Frank Conroy, in *Stop-time* (1967), wrote autobiographies with qualities of fiction. Bret Easton Ellis' *American Psycho* (1991) is the fictional confession of a serial killer. Chuck Barris' *Confessions of a Dangerous Mind* (2002) is the game show host's account of his life as an assassin for the United States government.

THE LYRICAL AUTOBIOGRAPHICAL NOVEL

Some poets have written autobiographical novels: e.e. cummings' *The Enormous Room* (1922), Kenneth Rexroth's *An Autobiographical Novel* (1966). This type differs from other novels that are written in highly poetic language, such as Emily Bronte's *Wuthering Heights* (1847), in that the lyrical autobiographical novel is an expression of the author's own feelings, as in a lyric poem. This can be either overt or projected through other characters. Lyrical qualities are usually joined with other elements, blending the inner private with the outer public world. The lyric novel is carefully compressed, impressionistic, and expresses a poetic vision of human experience. The following may be considered lyrical novels: Goethe's *The Sorrows of Young Werther* (1774); Djuna Barnes' *Nightwood* (1936); Friedrich Holderlin's *Hyperion, or The Hermit in Greece* (1797–1799); Novalis' *Heinrich von Ofterdingen* (1802); Rainer Maria Rilke's *The Notebooks of Malte Laurids Brigge* (1910); Andre Gide's *Les Nourritures Terrestres* (*Fruits of the Earth*, 1897), composed of loosely related images; Virginia Woolf's *The Waves* (1931); and William Goyen's *House of Breath* (1950).

Open the rusted iron gate and step across the stickerburrs blooming in the grass, go round past the rotted tire where the speckled canna used to live and turn towards the cisternwheel that does not turn. See the cistern, rusted and hollow and no water in it, and the wheel of the windmill wrecked and fallen and rats playing over the ruin. The wheel is like an enormous metal flower blighted by rust. Bend down to touch the fallen petals and, bending, hear the grinding groan of the wheel that begins to turn again in your brain of childhood, rasping the overtone of loneliness and moaning the undertone of wonder. Remember how it rose up on long legs out of the round, deep, lidded stock tub, and remember once when the lid was left off how the child of a Negro washwoman (recall her poking, head wrapped in a scrap of red bandanna, the steaming black iron pot full of Starnes and Ganchion clothes) climbed up and fell into the tub and was drowned and how the cows come to drink bellowed to find its corpse.

THE BIOGRAPHICAL NOVEL

The biographical novel is a type of historical novel in which the author deliberately and clearly claims to have fictionalized the life of a famous person, as in Dmitri Merejkowski's *The Romance of Leonardo da Vinci* (1902). Fact/fiction hybrids, combining elements of the historical novel, are often popular successes but seldom artistic achievements. The form began with such works as Xenophon's *Cyropaedia* (Fourth century B.C.). W. Somerset Maugham's *The Moon and Sixpence* (1919) offers genuine insight into the life of the French artist Paul Gauguin.

When so much has been written about Charles Strickland, it may seem unnecessary that I should write more. A painter's monument is his work. It is true I knew him more intimately than most: I met him first before ever he became a painter, and I saw him not infrequently during the difficult years he spent in Paris; but I do not suppose I should ever have set down my recollections if the hazards of the war had not taken me to Tahiti. There, as is notorious, he spent the last years of his life; and there I came across persons who were familiar with him. I find myself in a position to throw light on just that part of his tragic career which has remained most obscure. If they who believe in Strickland's greatness are right, the personal narratives of such as knew him in the flesh can hardly be superfluous. What would we not give for the reminiscences of someone who had been as intimately acquainted with El Greco as I was with Strickland?

Irving Stone is the author of many biographical novels such as *Lust for Life* (1934), the life of Van Gogh; *The Agony and the Ecstasy* (1961), on Michelangelo; and *The Passions of the Mind* (1971), on Freud.

Other examples of simulated biographies are John P. Marquand's *The Late George Apley* (1937), Carl Van Vechten's *Peter Whiffle* (1922), Steven Millhauser's *Edwin Mullhouse: The Life and Death of an American Writer, 1943–1954 by Jeffrey Cartwright* (1972), Thomas Kineally's *Schindler's List* (1982), Peter Ackroyd's *The Last Testament of Oscar Wilde* (1983), and Beryl Bainbridge's *The Birthday Boys* (1991).

THE ROMAN À CLEF

A novel loosely based on a famous person is called a *roman à clef*. This differs from the biographical novel in that the author has tried to conceal, but unsuccessfully, the identities of real people, usually famous, on whom he has based his characters. They are often written about political figures or scandals in order to satirize their subjects while avoiding libel charges. A well-known example is Ernest Hemingway's *The Sun Also Rises* (1926), his characters were quickly recognized by their real life counterparts, their friends, and their public.

> Robert Cohn was once middleweight boxing champion of Princeton. Do not think that I am very much impressed by that as a boxing title, but it meant a lot to Cohn. He cared nothing for boxing, in fact he disliked it, but he learned it painfully and thoroughly to counteract the feeling of inferiority and shyness he had felt on being treated as a Jew at Princeton. There was a certain inner comfort in knowing he could knock down anybody who was snooty to him, although, being very shy and a thoroughly nice boy, he never fought except in the gym. He was Spider Kelly's star pupil. Spider Kelly taught all his young gentlemen to box like featherweights, no matter whether they weighed one hundred and five or two hundred and five pounds. But it seemed to fit Cohn. He was really very fast. He was so good that Spider promptly overmatched him and got his nose permanently flattened. This increased Cohn's distaste for boxing, but it gave him a certain satisfaction of some strange sort, and it certainly improved his nose. In his last year at Princeton he read too much and took to wearing spectacles. I never met any one of his class who remembered him. They did not even remember that he was middleweight boxing champion.

Other examples include David Lodge's *Small World: An Academic Romance* (1984), a satire of academia; and Joe Klein's anonymously published *Primary Colors* (1996), an exposé of Bill Clinton's presidential campaign.

> "Glad you changed your mind. Jack's really excited you could do this."
> "What are we doing?" I asked. Howard had called and invited me to meet

Governor Jack Stanton, who might or might not be running for president. The governor was stopping in New York on his way to do some early, explanatory wandering through New Hampshire. The invitation came with an intriguing address—in Harlem, of all places. (There was no money in Harlem and this was the serious money-bagging stage of the campaign, especially for an obscure Southern governor.)

• 4 •

Novels of Development

BILDUNGSROMAN

$\mathscr{B}$eginning with Johann Wolfgang von Goethe's *The Sorrows of Young Werther* (1774) and *The Apprenticeship of Wilhelm Meister* (1795–1796), the *Bildungsroman* is originally a German type. This type shows the "formation" in relation to society of a young man or woman who is typical of his or her time and place. A modern example is Thomas Mann's *Der Zauberberg* (*The Magic Mountain*, 1924), in which a young man confined to a mountaintop tuberculosis sanitarium is schooled in philosophy, psychology, sex, etc., by the other inmates, most of whom are older men and women. The classic English example is Charles Dickens' *Great Expectations* (1860–1861).

> My father's family name being Pirrip, and my Christian name Philip, my infant tongue could make of both names nothing longer or more explicit than Pip. So, I called myself Pip, and came to be called Pip.
>
> I give Pirrip as my father's family name, on the authority of his tombstone and my sister—Mrs Joe Gargery, who married the blacksmith. As I never saw my father or my mother, and never saw any likeness of either of them (for their days were long before the days of photographs), my first fancies regarding what they were like, were unreasonably derived from their tombstones. The shape of the letters on my father's, gave me an odd idea that he was a square, stout, dark man, with curly black hair. From the character and turn of the inscription, "*Also Georgiana Wife of the Above,*" I drew a childish conclusion that my mother was freckled and sickly. To five little stone lozenges, each about a foot and a half long, which were arranged in a neat row beside their grave, and were sacred to the memory of five little brothers of mine—who gave up trying to get a living, exceedingly early in that universal struggle—I am indebted for a belief I religiously entertained

that they had all been born on their backs with their hands in their trousers-pockets, and had never taken them out in this state of existence.

The Germans also have a name for a type that is a variant of the *Bildungsroman*, the *Erziehungsroman* or novel of "upbringing" or initiation. Good examples are Charles Dickens' *David Copperfield* (1849–1850), Samuel Butler's *The Way of All Flesh* (1903), Doris Lessing's *The Children of Violence* series (1952–1969), Dorothy Allison's *Bastard Out of Carolina* (1992), and George Meredith's *The Ordeal of Richard Feverel* (1859).

> It was now, as Sir Austin had written it down, The Magnetic Age: the Age of violent attractions; when to hear mention of Love is dangerous, and see it, a communication of the disease. People at Raynham were put on their guard by the Baronet, and his reputation for wisdom was severely criticized in consequence of the injunctions he thought fit to issue through butler and house-keeper down to the lower household, for the preservation of his son from any visible symptom of the passion. A footmen and two housemaids are believed to have been dismissed on the report of Heavy Benson that they were in, or inclining to, the state; upon which an under-cook and a dairymaid voluntarily threw up their places, averring that "they did not want no young men, but to have their sex spied after by an old wretch like that," indicating the ponderous butler, "was a little too much for a Christian woman," and then they were ungenerous enough to glance at Benson's well-known marital calamity, hinting that some men met their deserts. So intolerable did Heavy Benson's espionage become, that Raynham would have grown de-populated of its womankind, had not Adrian interfered, who pointed out to the Baronet what a fearful arm his butler was wielding. Sir Austin acknowledged it despondently. "It only shows," said he, with a fine spirit of justice, "how all but impossible it is to legislate where there are women!"

This type differs from the novel of subjective adolescent perception that burgeoned in the 1940s and 1950s in America, such as Carson McCullers' *A Member of the Wedding* (1946), which emphasizes the psychological traumas of growing up rather than the whole scope of the protagonist's education.

KÜNSTLERROMAN

Closely related to the *Bildungsroman* is the *Künstlerroman*, a type of novel that shows the development of an artist. An early twentieth-century example is Samuel Butler's *The Way of All Flesh* (1903).

> It was after dinner, however, that he completed the conquest of his aunt. She then discovered that, like herself, he was passionately fond of music, and that,

too, of the highest class. He knew, and hummed or whistled to her all sorts of pieces out of the works of the great masters, which a boy of his age could hardly be expected to know, and it was evident that this was purely instinctive, inasmuch as music received no kind of encouragement at Roughborough. There was no boy in the school as fond of music as he was. He picked up his knowledge, he said, from the organist of St. Michael's Church, who used to practice sometimes on a weekday afternoon. Ernst had heard the organ booming away as he was passing outside the church and had sneaked inside and up into the organ loft. In the course of time the organist became accustomed to him as a familiar visitant, and the pair became friends.

It was this which decided Alethea that the boy was worth taking pains with. "He likes the best music," she thought, "and he hates Dr. Skinner. This is a very fair beginning." When she sent him away at night with a sovereign in his pocket (and he had only hoped to get five shillings) she felt as though she had had a good deal more than her money's worth for her money.

This type follows a new development in the novel itself and a new attitude of the bourgeoisie toward it: the novel as a work of art, the novelist himself as solely an artist, a concept that became contagious after Flaubert, who did not himself write a novel about the formation of an artist. The finest example is probably James Joyce's *Portrait of the Artist as a Young Man* (1916).

THE NOVEL OF CHARACTER

The novel of character has always been a major type. It shows the formation and operation of a character through interaction with other characters and with a stable society. The concept of "character" is basically optimistic: any person can willfully achieve good character and function usefully in society. A type practiced mainly by the English, the novel of character predominated in the Victorian era. Characters are regarded primarily in relation to their society, rather than as psychologically complex individuals or ideal types. Human nature is depicted as basically good and unchanging. The aim of such novels was generally to profit the reader by instruction and pleasure.

The eighteenth- and nineteenth-century concept of character assumes that external forces, and the individual's choices in response to them within a social framework, form and reveal qualities of character. Most of Charles Dickens' works are novels of character, although many are full of characters that are almost caricatures. Louisa May Alcott's *Little Women* (1868) and George Eliot's *The Mill on the Floss* (1860) are studies in character.

It may be surprising that Maggie, among whose many imperfections an excessive delight in admiration and acknowledged supremacy were not absent

now, any more than when she was instructing the gypsies with a view towards achieving a royal position among them, was not more elated on a day
when she had had the tribute of so many looks and smiles, together with
that satisfactory consciousness which had necessarily come from being
taken before Lucy's cheval-glass, and made to look at the full length of her
tall beauty, crowned by the night of her massy hair. Maggie had smiled at
herself then, and for the moment had forgotten everything in the sense of
her own beauty. If that state of mind could have lasted, her choice would
have been to have Stephen Guest at her feet, offering her a life filled with
all luxuries, with daily incense of adoration near and distant, arid with all
possibilities of culture at her command. But there were things in her
stronger than vanity—passion, and affection, and long deep memories of
early discipline and effort, of early claims on her love and pity; and the
stream of vanity was soon swept along and mingled imperceptibly with that
wider current which was at its highest force to-day, under the double ur-
gency of the events and inward impulses brought by the last week.

While the eighteenth century was a period of transition, the late nineteenth and
twentieth centuries have been periods of disintegration. Novels of character become less numerous as society becomes more heterogeneous. Novels of character are based on fixed assumptions about human nature, morality, the intellect,
and society; the serious undermining or destructions of these assumptions
makes these novels difficult to write. The more subjective novels of consciousness and of psychological analysis have replaced them. In these novels, events in
which characters come into conflict with each other within the social framework are replaced by conflicts within the character himself. In the twentieth
century human beings are seen mainly as victims. As external forces diminish
their humanity, they are driven to despair by doubts produced by introversion.

THE NOVEL OF MANNERS

Closely related to the novel of character is the novel of manners, which depicts
the way people within a clearly defined, small, and narrow culture relate to one
another. This type is best exemplified in Jane Austen's *Emma* (1815), *Persuasion*
(1818), and *Pride and Prejudice* (1813), a title that suggests aspects of conflicted
characters that must be worked out in a society of manners.

> "Your humility, Mr. Bingley," said Elizabeth, "must disarm reproof."
> "Nothing is more deceitful," said Darcy, "than the appearance of humil-
> ity. It is often only carelessness of opinion, and sometimes an indirect boast."
> "And which of the two do you call *my* little recent piece of modesty?"

"The indirect boast;—for you are really proud of your defects in writing, because you consider them as proceeding from a rapidity of thought and carelessness of execution, which if not estimable, you think at least highly interesting. The power of doing any thing with quickness is always much prized by the possessor, and often without any attention to the imperfection of the performance. When you told Mrs. Bennet this morning that if you ever resolved on quitting Netherfield you should be gone in five minutes, you meant it to be a sort of panegyric, of compliment to yourself—and yet what is there so very laudable in a precipitance which must leave very necessary business undone, and can be of no real advantage to yourself or any one else?"

Samuel Richardson's *Pamela* (1740) and *Clarissa* (1747–1748) are novels of manners in the epistolary mode. Others are Anthony Trollope's *Barchester Towers* (1857), William Dean Howells' *A Hazard of New Fortunes* (1890), Pierre Carlet de Chamblain de Marivaux's *Marianne* (1731–1741), and Henry James' social morality novel *The Spoils of Poynton* (1897). E. M. Forster's *A Room with a View* (1908), Edith Wharton's *The Age of Innocence* (1920), and John P. Marquand's *The Late George Apley* (1937) are some twentieth-century examples. If the concept of manners is widened, one can say that even Jack Kerouac's *On the Road* (1958) is a beatnik novel of manners. Many American southern fictions are novels of manners, including James Wilcox's *Modern Baptists* (1983).

THE SENTIMENTAL NOVEL

The sentimental novel (or novel of sensibility) depicts the behavior of resolutely moral, honorable, and somewhat humorless heroes and heroines whose compassionate and benevolent temperaments prompt them to weep at spectacles of sin and suffering. Merely to express feeling proves that one has breeding, virtue, and a kind soul. Such virtue is its own reward. These novels also demonstrate that villains can reform. A phenomenon of the late eighteenth century, these fictions appealed to the new middle classes, especially in England, and reflected their values. Again, in Richardson's *Pamela* (1740), a sentimental romance, the heroine's struggle to retain her virtue gains the reader's sympathy. Henry Mackenzie's *The Man of Feeling* (1771) and Oliver Goldsmith's *The Vicar of Wakefield* (1766) are two major novels of sentiment.

It were to be wished then that power, instead of contriving new laws to punish vice, instead of drawing hard the cords of society till a convulsion come to burst them, instead of cutting away wretches as useless before we have tried their utility, instead of converting correction into vengeance, it were to be wished that we tried the restrictive arts of government, and made law the protector but not the tyrant of the people. We should then find that creatures whose souls are held as dross only wanted the hand of a refiner; we should then find that wretches, now stuck up for long tortures lest luxury should feel a momentary pang, might, if properly treated, serve to sinew the state in times of danger; that as their faces are like ours, their hearts are so too; that few minds are so base as that perseverance cannot amend . . .

Sentimental romances are not confined to English literature. There are the Japanese Ibara Saikaku's *Five Women Who Loved Love* (c.1685), Madeleine de Scudery's *Artamene* (1646–1653), Madame de La Fayette's *The Princess of Cleves* (1678), Abbe Prevost's *Manon Lescaut* (1731), Goethe's *The Sorrows of Young Werther* (1774), Fanny Burney's *Cecilia* (1782)—a sentimental novel of manners—and John Esten Cooke's belated example, *The Virginia Comedians* (1854). Considered by some to be overly sentimental, Harriet Beecher Stowe's *Uncle Tom's Cabin, or Life Among the Lowly* (1852) was influential in the emancipation of American slaves.

Poor Cassy! when she recovered, turned her face to the wall, and wept and sobbed, like a child,—perhaps, mother, you can tell what she was thinking of! Perhaps you cannot,—but she felt as sure, in that hour, that God had had mercy on her, and that she should see her daughter,—as she did, months afterwards,—when—but we anticipate.

In the twentieth century, the amount of sentimentality in fiction has declined. Some authors deliberately play upon a reader's inclinations toward sentimentality; others deliberately avoid it and often treat it ironically or satirically. Today we find sentimentality in such popular novels, of varying quality, as Betty Smith's *A Tree Grows in Brooklyn* (1943), Kathleen Norris' *Mother* (1911), Faith Baldwin's *The Heart Remembers* (1941), and Harper Lee's *To Kill a Mockingbird* (1960), but there are strains of sentimentality even in the melodrama of John Steinbeck's *Of Mice and Men* (1937). Modern sentimental novels such as Erich Segal's *Love Story* (1970) and Robert James Waller's *The Bridges of Madison County* (1992) are often called tear-jerkers.

THE DIDACTIC NOVEL

Closely related to the novel of manners and of sentiment is the didactic (to teach) novel. The didactic novel manipulates narrative and exemplary characters who embody various virtues and vices to demonstrate explicitly a particular religious, moral, political, or philosophical doctrine. The context may be the circumstances of everyday life or allegory, fable, parable, even fantasy, and devices such as symbolism and personification may be utilized. Novels of character, manners, and sensibility were often didactic, but pure examples of this domestic type are rare, especially today.

Two major ways of actuating the didactic impulse are illustrative (through symbolism or allegory or personification, ancient devices) and representational (through imitation of reality); one is a clearly allegorical world, the other a world true to fact. A good example of the illustrative type of didacticism is John Bunyan's *Pilgrim's Progress* (1678) in which the protagonist, Christian, encounters characters personifying the qualities that give them their names (e.g., Mr. Worldly Wiseman). James Branch Cabell's *Jurgen* (1919) uses similar devices.

Exemplary characters function in representational novels, too, as in Richardson's *Clarissa*. "I thought the story might tend to promote the cause of religion and virtue," said Richardson. Clarissa is very real, and her world is full of realistic domestic detail. However, the quality of Clarissa's moral sensibility is exaggerated in this realistic setting. So, too, are the later male characters in Thomas Hughes' *Tom Brown's School Days* (1857) and in the novels of Horatio Alger: *Work and Win, Do and Dare, Try and Trust, Bound to Rise*, and *Up the Ladder* (1873). Illustrating the Puritan ethic of work and virtue, Alger's characters existed only to set a moral example for boys, as he suggests in his introduction.

> Harry Walton and Luke Harris were two country boys who had the same opportunities to achieve success. Harry Walton by his efforts succeeded, and Luke Harris's life was a failure. Read this story and you will see what qualities in the one brought about his success, and what in the other caused his downfall.

Harold Bell Wright, an ex-minister, performed the same function for adults in such novels as *The Winning of Barbara Worth* (1911).

Today, a strong element of didacticism is frowned upon, while a cruder form of moral assertion is considered sophisticated: that is, attacking evil or hypocrisy in social institutions, from the radical and proletarian novels of the 1910s to 1930s to such novels as Norman Mailer's *Why Are We in Vietnam?* (1967). The overall decline of overt didacticism in twentieth-century novels is a shift from earlier centuries when a writer like Anthony Trollope had to swear that "no girl has risen from the reading of my pages less modest than she was before" in order to combat charges that his novels corrupted young girls. Twentieth-century artists are more likely to agree with Oscar Wilde, who said, "There is no such thing as a moral or an immoral book. Books are well written or badly written."

THE ANTI-HERO NOVEL

The chaos and relativism of psychological introspection (see Novels of Psychology), combined with the breakdown of social, religious, cultural, and political institutions and absolutes, produced the anti-hero of existentialism. Heroes are possible only in a world of relatively stable concepts of character and patterns of behavior. An anti-hero is a character who lacks the traditional heroic attributes. His or her predicament is dramatized in cataclysmic world events and in instances of social injustice. In the anti-hero novel, there are no protagonists in conflict with antagonists, but characters dehumanized by psychological and cultural determinism, unjustly manipulated by external forces or pathetically acting as their own antagonists. Writers may depict these "fractured selves" through a fractured structure and a capricious style.

The anti-hero novel became popular with the rise of existential philosophy in France in the 1930s and '40s, based on the insights of Sartre and Camus (who rejected the term "existential" in favor of "absurd"). The existential philosophy rejects every type of orthodoxy, especially those based on absolutes; in this world of absurd freedom, human beings discover faith in others by virtue of a common condition—existence in a world without God or absolute meanings. The anti-hero results from a recognition by serious writers, themselves alienated from bourgeois society, that the heroic character is an anachronism. Unable to believe in heroes, these writers have made the anti-hero the dominant figure in serious twentieth-century literature.

Here are only a few examples of the existential, anti-hero novel: Dostoyevsky's *Notes From Underground* (1864), Jules Romains' *Death of a Nobody* (1911), Franz Kafka's *The Trial* (1925), Louis-Ferdinand Celine's *Journey to the End of the Night* (1932), Samuel Beckett's *Murphy* (1938), Jean-Paul Sartre's *Nausea* (1938), J. P. Donleavy's *The Ginger Man* (1955), Simone de Beauvoir's *The Mandarins* (1954), Iris Murdoch's *A Severed Head* (1961), Richard Farina's *Been Down So Long It Looks Like Up to Me* (1966), John Kennedy Toole's *A Confederacy of Dunces* (1980), Irvine Welsh's *Filth* (1998), and Albert Camus' *The Stranger* (1942).

> Then he tried to change the subject by asking me why I hadn't once addressed him as "Father," seeing that he was a priest. That irritated me still more, and I told him he wasn't my father; quite the contrary, he was on the others' side.
>
> "No, no, my son," he said, laying his hand on my shoulder. "I'm on *your* side, though you don't realize it—because your heart is hardened. But I shall pray for you."
>
> Then, I don't know how it was, but something seemed to break inside me, and I started yelling at the top of my voice. I hurled insults at him, I told him not to waste his rotten prayers on me; it was better to burn than to disappear. I'd taken him by the neckband of his cassock, and, in a sort of ecstasy of joy and rage, I poured out on him all the thoughts that had been simmering in my brain. He seemed so cocksure, you see. And yet none of his certainties was worth one strand of a woman's hair . . .

• 5 •

The Symbolic Novel

THE ALLEGORICAL NOVEL

*T*hough many types of novel employ various forms of symbolism, the allegorical novel operates almost entirely in a symbolic mode. In general, each character or event in an allegorical novel corresponds to a historical character, event, or concept that exists in the world outside of the text of the novel. The subjects of allegorical novels are varied, but allegorical novelists tend to focus on subjects like philosophy and religion in which abstract concepts are given concrete existence within the plot of the novel, or politics in which the symbolic mode of the narrative can allow novelists to express unpopular or revolutionary political views without incurring official displeasure. One example is John Bunyan's *Pilgrim's Progress* (1678), in which a young man named Christian is subjected to every typical test of faith and virtue by characters personifying the qualities that give them their names—Mr. Worldly Wiseman, Mr. Great-Heart, Lady Feigning—in such places as the City of Destruction, the Celestial City, the Slough of Despond, and Vanity Fair. These are called exemplary figures because they embody certain vices and virtues.

> Then I saw in my dream that when they were got out of the wilderness, they presently saw a town before them, and the name of that town is Vanity; and at the town there is a fair kept, called Vanity Fair; it is kept all the year long; it beareth the name of Vanity Fair, because the town where it is kept is lighter than vanity; and also because all that is there sold, or that cometh thither, is vanity. As is the saying of the wise, "all that cometh is vanity."

Later allegorical novels are less blunt in their identification of the symbolic meanings of their characters, as in Herman Melville's *Moby Dick* (1851).

He was intent on an audacious, immitigable, and supernatural revenge. . . . Here, then, was this gray-headed, ungodly old man, chasing with curses a Job's whale round the world, at the head of a crew, too, chiefly made up of mongrel renegades, and castaways, and cannibals—morally enfeebled also, by the incompetence of mere unaided virtue or rightmindedness in Starbuck, the invulnerable jollity of indifference and recklessness in Stubb, and the pervading mediocrity in Flask. Such a crew, so officered, seemed specially picked and packed by some infernal fatality to help him to his monomaniac revenge. How it was that they so aboundingly responded to the old man's ire—by what evil magic their souls were possessed, that at times his hate seemed almost theirs; the white Whale as much their insufferable foe as his; how all this came to be—what the White Whale was to them, or how to their unconscious understandings, also, in some dim, unsuspected way, he might have seemed the gliding great demon of the seas of life—all this to explain, would be to dive deeper than Ishmael can go. The subterranean miner that works in us all, how can one tell whither leads his shaft by the evershifting, muffled sound of his pick? Who does not feel the irresistible arm drag? What skiff in tow of a seventy-four can stand still? For one, I gave myself up to the abandonment of the time and the place; but while yet all a-rush to encounter the whale, could see naught in that brute but the deadliest ill.

Some examples of the genre include Friedrich de la Motte-Fouque's *Undine* (1811), Herman Melville's *Mardi* (1849), G. K. Chesterton's *The Man Who Was Thursday* (1908), Virginia Woolf's *Between the Acts* (1941), George Orwell's *Animal Farm* (1946), Walter Van Tilburg Clark's *The Track of the Cat* (1949), Par Fabian Lagerkvist's *Barabbas* (1950), Ernest Hemingway's *The Old Man and the Sea* (1952), Thomas Pynchon's *V.* (1963), Richard Adams's *Watership Down* (1972), Mario Vargas Llosa's *The War at the End of the World* (1984), and Art Spiegelman's *Maus* (1991).

THE RELIGIOUS NOVEL

Although most serious novels that deal at all with religion satirize it or treat it comically, especially novels about the clergy, many novels are directly about religion itself. These novels can range from didactic religious allegories like Bunyan's *Pilgrim's Progress* and William Faulkner's *A Fable* (1954) to novels about the clergy to novels about an individual's quest for salvation or spiritual enlightenment. An example of this latter type is Hermann Hesse's *Siddhartha* (1922).

But he, Siddhartha, where did he belong? Whose life would he share? Whose language would he speak?

At that moment, when the world around him melted away, when he stood alone like a star in the heavens, he was overwhelmed by a feeling of icy despair, but he was more firmly himself than ever. That was the last shudder of his awakening, the last pains of birth. Immediately he moved on again and began to walk quickly and impatiently, no longer homewards, no longer to his father, no longer looking backwards.

Other good examples include Graham Greene's *The Heart of the Matter* (1948); the Spanish Carmen Laforet's *Nada* (*Andrea*, 1945), about spiritual desolation; Benito Perez Galdos's *Dona Perfecta* (1876), a popular Spanish tragedy of religion in which modern ideas clash with bigotry and prejudice in a small Andalusian town; Franz Kafka's *The Castle* (1926); the French Catholic Françoise Mauriac's *Therese* (1927), about sin and guilt; William Gaddis's *The Recognitions* (1955), a modern divine comedy; and Eugene Vale's *The Thirteenth Apostle* (1959). Italian Antonio Fogazzaro's *The Saint* (1905), a trilogy, is a religious romance.

There are the popular religious chronicles or histories: Polish Henryk Sienkiewicz's *Quo Vadis* (1896); American Lew Wallace's *Ben Hur* (1880), a tale of Christ; Sholem Asch's *The Nazarene* (1939) and *The Apostle* (1943); Franz Werfel's *The Song of Bernadette* (1941); Lloyd C. Douglas' *The Robe* (1942); Robert Graves' *King Jesus* (1946); and Anthony Burgess's *The Kingdom of the Wicked* (1985). Tim Lahaye and Jerry B. Jenkins's popular *Left Behind* series (1995–2004) is a speculative chronicle of the apocalypse.

There are mystical works, such as French Remy de Gourmont's *A Night in the Luxembourg* (1906), Booth Tarkington's *The Magnificent Ambersons* (1929), T. F. Powys' *Mr. Weston's Good Wine* (1927), and the poetic mysticism of Hermann Broch's *The Death of Virgil* (1945).

THE ROMANTIC NOVEL

After these fable-like novels and the realistic novels of the eighteenth and early nineteenth centuries, the romantic novel was developed. Reviving elements of romance narratives—idealized heroes and heroines, exotic places of antiquity, the marvelous—and adding the bizarre and the grotesque, the romantic novel satisfied a relatively new type of sensibility that emerged with the romantic movement. The romantic, fascinated by the scope and complexity of life, attempts to project massive chunks of relatively unprocessed raw material, expressing everything through the self in a rich language. Goethe's phrase *sturm and drang* (storm and stress) describes romantics well.

Blake, Wordsworth, Coleridge, Byron, Shelley, and Keats, exemplified the romantic spirit in poetry, and most romantic novelists display strains of all six.

For instance, Sir Walter Scott's *The Heart of Midlothian* (1818) showed the so-cial concern of Shelley, who fought for liberal causes. However, more of the romantics focused on essentially private subjects. Sensitivity and subjectivity are major traits in the romantic temperament, combined with a seemingly para-doxical, aggressive theatricality, as seen in two psychological romances, Char-lotte Bronte's *Jane Eyre* (1847) and Alain-Fournier's *Le Grand Meaulnes* (*The Wanderer*, 1913). The romantic writer thinks of himself and thus of his usually autobiographical work as a unique product of personality and spontaneity. In asserting himself as a personality (as opposed to the earlier concept of charac-ter), the romantic as artist and as a protagonist alienates himself from middle class society. Goethe's *The Sorrows of Young Werther* (1774) is a famous example of this kind of romantic agony and melancholy, with suicide as the climax.

The romantics brought to the novel a wonder new to it. Before, most novelists put great stock in the probable, but the romantic was obsessed with the marvelous and with the natural world. Francois-Rene de Chateaubriand's *Atala* (1801) and *Rene* (1802) are philosophical romances set in an imagined "new world" where nature is supreme. The exotic is experienced in Lafcadio Hearn's *Chita: A Memory of Last Island* (1889), Joris-Karl Huysmans' *A Rebours* (*Against the Grain*, 1884), Donn Byrne's *Messer Marco Polo* (1921), and Frederic Prokosch's *Seven Who Fled* (1937). There are the adventure romances: Robert Montgomery Bird's *Nick of the Woods* (1837), Robert Louis Stevenson's *Kid-napped* (1886), Rudyard Kipling's *Captains Courageous* (1897) and *Kim* (1901), and H. Rider Haggard's *King Solomon's Mines* (1886), as well as impressionistic romances: Pierre Loti's (Julian Viaud's) *An Iceland Fisherman* (1886), Arthur Machen's *Hill of Dreams* (1907), and Emily Bronte's *Wuthering Heights* (1847).

> "Don't torture me till I am as mad as yourself," cried [Heathcliff], wrench-ing his head free, and grinding his teeth.
>
> The two, to a cool spectator, made a strange and fearful picture. Well might Catherine deem that heaven would be a land of exiles to her, unless with her mortal body she cast away her moral character also. Her present countenance had a wild vindictiveness in its white cheek, and a bloodless lip and scintillating eye; and she retained in her closed fingers a portion of the locks she had been grasping. As to her companion, while raising him-self with one hand, he had taken her arm with the other: and so inadequate was his stock of gentleness to the requirements of her condition, that on his letting go I saw four distinct impressions left blue in the colourless skin.
>
> "Are you possessed with a devil," he pursued savagely, "to talk in that manner to me when you are dying?"

During the Victorian era, the romantic novel went underground, although el-ements appeared in other types, especially in the adventure tale set in exotic places. A resurgence of romanticism, neo-romanticism, came when writers once again looked inward, inspired by the writings of Sigmund Freud and other psychologists. In poetry, it took the form of symbolism, inspired in part by the American gothic romanticist, Edgar Allan Poe.

The romantic temperament had a resurgence in Thomas Wolfe's four gargantuan novels; the last one, *The Web and the Rock* (1939), showed a Byronic self-awareness. Here is a quote from Wolfe's *Look Homeward, Angel* (1929) that shows that the romantic spirit lived on into the twentieth century.

> He cared nothing for the practical need of the world. He dared to say the strange and marvelous thing that had bloomed so darkly in him.
>
> "Laura," he said, hearing his low voice sound over the great plain of the moon, "let's always love each other as we do now. Let's never get married. I want you to wait for me and to love me forever. I am going all over the world. I shall go away for years at a time; I shall become famous, but I shall always come back to you. You shall live in a house away in the mountains, you shall wait for me, and keep yourself for me. Will you?" he said, asking for her life as calmly as for an hour of her time.
>
> "Yes, dear," said Laura in the moonlight. "I will wait for you forever."

Henry Miller is another ironic, Byronic novelist, as is Lawrence Durrell, whose *Alexandria Quartet* (1957–1960)—a series of strange, fascinating, interrelated novels that employ a lush style, psychological approaches to character as well as experimental techniques—helped revive the romantic novel once again.

· *6* ·

The Popular Novel

The classical writers considered one of the ends of art to be recreation. In popular fiction, that basic purpose has come to be called "escape." Popular novels are usually written out of commercial motives for a specialized or general mass readership for the purpose of entertainment. Sex (or romance) and violence, and an emphasis on stereotyped characters and plots written by an often-proven formula, are among the salient characteristics of the commercial or popular novel. While all "literature is the art of playing on the minds of others" (Valery), popular fiction exploits and manipulates familiar emotions and attitudes, accepted moral and social concepts, and strives to excite its readers without leaving them profoundly stimulated or disturbed. It is simple and easy to read. It is above all, as Stephen King, author of *Carrie* (1974), has said, "accessible."

Popular novels are dominated by their subjects, as the names of the types suggest: western, detective, science fiction, romance, historical, horror, and erotic. Inside these general types are specific types marketed towards a particular readership: war, sea, legal, religious, or exposé (e.g., celebrity, political, or sports).

A mid-nineteenth-century innovation, the dime novel, offered strongly but improbably and melodramatically plotted tales, featuring superhuman heroes based often on famous people, sometimes outlaws (Jesse James), and printed on pulp paper for mass distribution on newsstands.

The terms "commercial" or "popular" and "serious" run the risk, as labels do, of distorting. They are used here to describe, not to make judgments. Discussions of the novel have traditionally treated it as if it were solely a "serious" artistic form. The novels read by most people in a given culture at a given time have, supposedly, no relevance to the history and forms of the novel. But on the contrary, recent studies show that many popular types of novels have influenced serious novelists, especially *avant garde*, and the process works in the other direction as well. Popular novels often keep alive elements of serious works and are sometimes forerunners.

THE GOTHIC NOVEL

The gothic novel depicts the perverse, sometimes fantastic and terrible behavior of an introverted and decayed aristocracy at a time (usually the eighteenth and nineteenth centuries) when the old social order and political norms have been destroyed and is usually set in the ruins of castles built in the time of chivalry. The ambience is supernatural and the mode of behavior perverse. The romantic, said Victor Hugo, mingles the grotesque, once mainly the province of satire, with the sublime, as he did in his historical romance *The Hunchback of Notre Dame* (1831). The ugly, even the obscene, may be aspects of the divine in nature, while the supernatural may be an extension of the natural. The most famous classic examples of the gothic romance are Horace Walpole's *The Castle of Otranto* (1764), Mrs. Ann Radcliffe's *The Mysteries of Udolpho* (1794), Matthew Gregory Lewis' *The Monk* (1795), Charles Brockden Brown's *Wieland* (1798), and Irishman Charles Maturin's *Melmoth the Wanderer* (1820). Under the influence of romanticism, the gothic provided the basis for the Victorian and modern horror and science fiction novels such as Mary Shelley's *Frankenstein* (1817), Robert Louis Stevenson's *Dr. Jekyll and Mr. Hyde* (1886), and Bram Stoker's *Dracula* (1897).

The first great gothic romance was Charlotte Bronte's *Jane Eyre* (1847). With the publication of a modern gothic romance, *Rebecca* (1938), by Daphne du Maurier, a revival of the gothic type began; it is now extremely popular in America and Europe. It is interesting to compare *Jane Eyre* with *Rebecca*.

> No need to cower behind a gate-post, indeed!—to peep up at chamber lattices, fearing life was astir behind them! No need to listen for doors opening—to fancy steps on the pavement or the gravel-walk! The lawn, the grounds were trodden and waste: the portal yawned void. The front was, as I had once seen it in a dream, but a shell-like wall, very high and very fragile-looking, perforated with paneless windows: no roof, no battlements, no chimneys—all had crashed in.
>
> And there was the silence of death about it: the solitude of a lonesome wild. No wonder that letters addressed to people here had never received an answer: as well dispatch epistles to a vault in a church aisle. The grim blackness of the stones told by what fate the Hall had fallen—by conflagration: but how kindled? What story belonged to this disaster? . . .
>
> A cloud, hitherto unseen, came upon the moon, and hovered an instant like a dark hand before a face. The illusion went with it, and the lights in

the windows were extinguished. I looked upon a desolate shell, soulless at last, unhaunted, with no whisper of the past about its staring walls.

The house was a sepulchre, our fear and suffering lay buried in the ruins.

Some other modern examples of the genre include Henry James's *The Turn of the Screw* (1898), Shirley Jackson's *The Haunting of Hill House* (1959), Margaret Millar's *Beast in View* (1956), Ian McEwan's *The Cement Garden* (1978), and Mark Z. Danielewski's *House of Leaves* (2000).

SOUTHERN GOTHIC AND GROTESQUE NOVELS

The southern gothic novel (with its northern variants) is a rebirth of the spirit of the classic gothic novel. But the emphasis is less on descriptions of bizarre settings and weird actions than on Freudian perversions and psychoses grow- ing out of the traumatic changes in the South after the Civil War. Southern aristocrats going mad in decaying mansions in small towns certainly seemed both gothic and grotesque to northern and even to many southern readers.

The *grotesque* is a strong element in the gothic novel. But some distinction should be made. Both elements grew out of the American phase of romanti- cism. The grotesque deals with characters who are mentally and/or physically stunted or deformed, as in the stories and novels of Sherwood Anderson and Wright Morris. In the southern gothic novel, the style is usually ornate, echo- ing the lyricism of the romantics and the rhetorical flourishes of the early gothic writers; in the grotesque, the style is plain, as in a tale, for there is no in- dulgence in the romantic agony of being different for its own sake. The gothic character is often an aristocrat in decay, while the grotesque character is often a common person deformed by small town life or urban industrialism.

The typical southern gothic character is weak; afraid; impotent; trapped in a compulsive, self-destructive narcissism; and afflicted with a monstrous self love. Generally a neurotic, antagonistic, authoritarian family is a microcosm of the hostile environment beyond, as in Truman Capote's *Other Voices, Other Rooms* (1948).

Miss Wisteria stood so near he could smell the rancid wetness of her shriv- eled silk; her curls had uncoiled, the little crown had slipped awry, her yel- low sash was fading its color on the floor. "Little boy," she said, swerving her flashlight over the bent, broken walls where her midget image mingled with the shadows of things in flight. "Little boy," she said, the resignation of her voice intensifying its pathos. But he dared not show himself, for what she wanted he could not give: his love was in the earth, shattered and still, dried flowers where eyes should be, and moss upon the lips, his love was faraway feeding on the rain, lilies frothing from its ruin. Withdrawing, she went up the stairs, and Joel, who listened to her footfalls overhead as she in her need of him searched the jungle of rooms, felt for himself ferocious contempt: what was his terror compared with Miss Wisteria's? He owned a room, he had a bed. Any minute now he would run from here, go to them. But for Miss Wisteria, weeping because little boys must grow tall, there would always be this journey through dying rooms until some lonely day she found her hidden one, the smiler with the knife.

In most cases, the protagonist flees the nightmares of the real world into a dream world. Physically and mentally, he or she languishes in a claustrophobic, haunted room, insulated against outer nightmares by inner dreams. When the room is invaded, the self violated, he or she is forced to make journeys, sometimes pursued, into the "dark forests" of the real world, which proves to be full of distorting mirrors. Seeking but fearing love, unable to communicate with others, the protagonist finds only a grotesque reflection of his or her own disintegrating self. He or she flounders in a vicious circle. The tensions between social reality and private fantasy often erupt in violence.

Some examples of the southern gothic and grotesque are found in these novels: William Faulkner's *Sanctuary* (1931), Carson McCullers' *The Heart Is a Lonely Hunter* (1940) and *Reflections in a Golden Eye* (1941), Davis Grubb's *Night of the Hunter* (1953) Flannery O'Connor's *The Violent Bear It Away* (1960), James Dickey's *Deliverance* (1960), Barry Hannah's *Never Die* (1991), Dorothy Allison's *Bastard Out of Carolina* (1992), Lewis Nordan's *Wolf Whistle* (1993), and Cormac McCarthy's *Suttree* (1979).

Passing the creek mouth he raised one hand and waved slowly, the old blacks all flowered and bonneted coming about like a windtilted garden with their canes bobbing and their arms lifting hard and random into the air and their gaudy and barbaric costumes billowing with the movement. Beyond them the shape of the city rising wore a wrought, a jaded look, hammered out dark and smoking against a china sky. The grimy river littoral lay warped and shimmering in the heat and their was no sound in all this lonely summer forenoon.

Some of the same elements of the southern gothic are found in novels by writers of the north, including James Purdy's *Malcolm* (1959), John Hawkes's *The Lime Twig* (1961), and Joyce Carol Oates's *A Garden of Earthly Delights* (1967).

FANTASY, SCIENCE FICTION, AND HORROR NOVELS

Fantasy deals with incredible, magical, exotic, supernatural, monstrous characters and events and is often written in an ornamental, lyrical, or witty style. The genre probably originated with fairy tales and earlier poetic romances. Usually, our pleasure derives from the comparison of the totally created fantasy world, which has its own sophisticated and consistent reality, with our everyday world, but in many fantasies, incidents occur within the context of everyday reality. The most popular and successful fantasy is J. R. R. Tolkien's three-volume *The Lord of the Rings* (1954).

> *Thirdly and finally*, he said, *I wish to make an* ANNOUNCEMENT. He spoke this last word so loudly and suddenly that everyone sat up who still could. *I regret to announce that—though, as I said, eleventy-one years is far too short a time to spend among you—this is the END. I am going. I am leaving NOW.* GOOD-BYE!
>   He stepped down arid vanished. There was a blinding flash of light, and the guests all blinked. When they opened their eyes Bilbo was nowhere to be seen. One hundred and forty-four flabbergasted hobbits sat back speechless. Old Odo Proudfoot removed his feet from the table and stamped. Then there was a dead silence, until suddenly, after several deep breaths, every Baggins, Boffin, Took, Brandybuck, Grubb, Chubb, Burrows, Bolger, Bracegirdle, Brockhouse, Goodbody, Hornblower, and Proudfoot began to talk at once.

Some examples of fantasies are the Chinese Wu Ch'eng-en's *Monkey* (16th century); Norwegian Ludwig Holberg's fantastic *Journey of Niels Klim to the World Underground* (1741); John Ruskin's *The King of the Golden River* (1851); Lewis Carroll's *Alice in Wonderland* and *Through the Looking Glass* (1871); Oscar Wilde's *The Picture of Dorian Gray* (1891); W. H. Hudson's *Green Mansions* (1904); Kenneth Grahame's fantasy allegory *The Wind in the Willows* (1908); Franz Kafka's *The Trial* (1914), which objectifies universal guilt in terms of ordinary situations and relationships; David Garnett's *Lady into Fox* (1922); Robert E. Howard's *Conan the Barbarian* (1950); Andrew Sinclair's *Gog* (1967); Richard Adams's *Watership Down* (1972); J. G. Ballard's *The Unlimited Dream Company* (1979), and Guy Gavriel Kay's *The Fionavar Tapestry* (1985–1987).

Science fiction is to be distinguished from pure fantasy in that it uses present scientific achievements as a basis for imagining scientific discoveries in the future, usually enabling man to explore, colonize, settle, and govern other worlds in space. Science fiction is to the atomic age what the western was to the end of the Industrial Revolution. With their indulgence in the imagination as it takes flight into the historical past or the prophetic future from a basis in fact, both types are essentially romantic. Psychological analysis and supernatural speculation characterize some of these novels.

The range of this type is quite broad. Mary Shelley's *Frankenstein* (1816) is a gothic variant that anticipates science fiction. Some of the early classics extrapolate logically and, as it has turned out, prophetically from actual scientific knowledge to probable future developments: Jules Verne's *A Trip to the Moon* (1865) and H. G. Wells' *The War of the Worlds* (1898).

No one would have believed in the last years of the nineteenth century that this world was being watched keenly and closely by intelligences greater than man's and yet as mortal as his own; that as men busied themselves about their various concerns they were scrutinized and studied, perhaps almost as narrowly as a man with a microscope might scrutinize the transient creatures that swarm and multiply in a drop of water. With infinite complacency men went to and fro over this globe about their little affairs, serene in their assurance of their empire over matter. It is possible that the infusoria under the microscope do the same. No one gave a thought to the older worlds of space as sources of human danger, or thought of them only to dismiss the idea of life upon them as impossible or improbable. It is curious to recall some of the mental habits of those departed days. At most, terrestrial men fancied there might be other men upon Mars, perhaps inferior to themselves and ready to welcome a missionary enterprise. Yet across the gulf of space, minds that are to our minds as ours are to those of the beasts that perish, intellects vast and cool and unsympathetic, regarded this earth with envious eyes, and slowly and surely drew their plans against us. And early in the twentieth century came the great disillusionment.

Regarded until recently as a sub-literary genre, often lurid and overly spectacular, full of clichés in style, stereotyped characters and stock situations, the science fiction novel has, along with fantasy, recently achieved a kind of respectability, even in universities. The various types of science fiction can be used as bases for serious comment on the actual world. Social and political problems are implicit in science fiction. George Orwell's *1984* (1949) combines elements of proletarian fiction with dystopian futurism, and it may be termed more a prophetic than a science fiction novel of the usual sort. Aldous Huxley's *Brave New World* (1932) is a somber satire of utopias, while Anthony Burgess's *A Clockwork Orange* (1962) and Kurt Vonnegut's *Slaughterhouse-Five* (1970) and *Cat's Cradle* (1963) are black-humor satires.

> "I am thinking, young man, about the final sentence for *The Books of Bokonon*. The time for the final sentence has come."
> "Any luck?" He shrugged and handed me a piece of paper.
> This is what I read:
> If I were a younger man, I would write a history of human stupidity; and I would climb to the top of Mount McCabe and lie down on my back with my history for a pillow; and I would take from the ground some of the blue-white poison that makes statues of men; and I would make a statue of myself, lying on my back, grinning horribly, and thumbing my nose at You Know Who.

Other fine examples of the science fiction novel are: Karel Capek's *War with the Newts* (1937), C. S. Lewis' *Out of the Silent Planet* (1938), Ray Bradbury's

The Martian Chronicles (1950), Walter M. Miller Jr.'s *A Canticle for Leibowitz* (1959), Robert Heinlein's *Stranger in a Strange Land* (1961), Frank Herbert's *Dune* (1965), Walter Tevis's *The Man Who Fell to Earth* (1963), Ursula Le Guin's *The Left Hand of Darkness* (1969), Larry Niven's *Ringworld* (1970), Phillip K. Dick's *Flow My Tears, the Policeman Said* (1974), and William Gibson's *Neuromancer* (1984). Other important science fiction writers are Isaac Asimov, Robert Bloch, James Lish, Poul Anderson, August Derleth, H. P. Lovecraft, Frederick Pohl, G. Stanley Weinbaum, Theodore Sturgeon, Harlan Ellison, A. E. Van Vogt, Robert Silverberg, and Neal Stephenson.

One type of fantasy novel that is currently very popular is the occult or horror novel. These novels dramatize the workings of evil, or of good against human evil, through supernatural agencies. The undisputed master of the horror genre is Stephen King, who began his career with *Carrie* (1974).

> She paused on the lower step, looking at the flocks of people streaming toward the center of town. Animals. Let them burn, then. Let the streets be filled with the smell of their sacrifice. Let this place be called racca, ichabod, wormwood.
>
> *Flex.*
>
> And power transformers atop lightpoles bloomed into nacreous purple light, spitting catherine-wheel sparks. High-tension wires fell into the streets in pick-up-sticks tangles and some of them ran, and that was bad for them because now the whole street was littered with wires and the stink began, the burning began. People began to scream and back away and some touched the cables and went into jerky electrical dances. Some had already slumped into the street their robes and pajamas smoldering.
>
> Carrie turned back and looked fixedly at the church she had just left. The heavy door suddenly swung shut, as if in a hurricane wind.

Other major examples are William Blatty's *The Exorcist* (1971), Ira Levin's *Rosemary's Baby* (1967), Thomas Tryon's *The Other* (1971), Clive Barker's *Books of Blood* (1984), and Anne Rice's *Interview with the Vampire* (1993).

THE POP NOVEL

The same literary mind that rejects the popular fiction of the masses often resurrects it when the masses have buried it. The pop or camp novel is a recent phenomenon and demonstrates the effect on the novel of popular mass culture. Susan Sontag's essay "Notes on 'Camp'" in the *Partisan Review* in 1964 stimulated an interest in camp, which she defined as the product of an aesthetic sensibility that responds more to an artificial style than to content. The pop novel transforms everyday experience through "failed seriousness" and "the theatricalization of experience." It is anti-serious, comic, vulgar, and inclines towards Oscar Wilde's aesthetic principles. The pop novel is one aspect of the popular culture avant garde collusion. Some examples include L. J. Davis' *Cowboys Don't Cry* (1969), Robert Mayer's *Superfolk* (1977), and Donald Barthelme's *Snow White* (1967).

> "*Which prince?*" Snow White wondered brushing her teeth. "Which prince will come? Will it be Prince Andrey? Prince Igor? Prince Alf? Prince Alphonso? Prince Malcolm? Prince Donalbain? Prince Fernando? Prince Siegfried? Prince Philip? Prince Albert? Prince Paul? Prince Akihito? Prince Rainier? Prince Porus? Prince Myshkin? Prince Rupert? Prince Pericles? Prince Karl? Prince Clarence? Prince George? Prince Hal? Prince John? Prince Mamillius? Prince Florizel? Prince Kropotkin? Prince Humphrey? Prince Charlie? Prince Matchabelli? Prince Escalus? Prince Valiant? Prince Fortinbras?" Then Snow White pulled herself together. "Well it is terrific to be anticipating a prince—to be waiting and knowing that what you are waiting for is a prince, packed with grace—but it is still waiting, and waiting as a mode of existence is, as Brack has noted, a darksome mode. . . . I wonder if he will have the Hapsburg Lip?"

The pop novel, conceived in nostalgia and executed with satirical purpose, shows the extent to which a so-called inferior form of human expression can shape attitudes and predispose responses. Still, the pop novel has not caught on, any more than the ideological novel of the Thirties did; however, the pop novel did lay the groundwork for such genres as the postmodern novel and cyber fiction.

THE WESTERN NOVEL

The western novel is based on the history of the cowboy and his adventures in the "Old West." Typical features include cattle-rustlers, stage and train robbers, gunfights, and battles with Native Americans. Generally, there is a hero who is called upon to save the day and rides into the danger alone and either rides out alone or dies having fulfilled his destiny. Authentic or pseudo-authentic details about costume, setting, and firearms appeal to many readers. The first great western was Owen Wister's *The Virginian* (1902).

> It was now the Virginian's turn to bet, or leave the game, and he did not speak at once.
>   Therefore Trampas spoke. "Your bet, you son-of-a-."
>   The Virginian's pistol came out, and his hand lay on the table, holding it unaimed. And with a voice as gentle as ever, the voice that sounded almost

like a caress, but drawling a very little more than usual, so that there was almost a space between each word, he issued his orders to the man Trampas:—
    "When you call me that, *smile!*" And he looked at Trampas across the table.

One of the few novel types indigenous to America, the western was once a
major popular type, but has declined in recent years, though writers such as
Larry McMurtry (*Lonesome Dove*, 1987) and Cormac McCarthy (*The Border
Trilogy: All the Pretty Horses, The Crossing,* and *Cities of the Plain*, 1992–1998) are
helping to keep it alive. Other typical examples are Clarence E. Mulford's
Hopalong Cassidy (1910), Zane Grey's *Light of Western Stars* (1914), Emerson
Hough's *The Covered Wagon* (1922), Max Brand's *Destry Rides Again* (1930),
William MacLeod Raine's *Bucky Follows a Cold Trail* (1937), Luke Short's *Hard-
case* (1942), Ernest Haycox's *Alder Gulch* (1942), A. B. Guthrie's *The Big Sky*
(1947), Jack Schaefer's *Shane* (1949), and Louis L'Amour's *Radigan* (1958).

THE MYSTERY NOVEL

The mystery novel, a major popular genre, delineates the detection of clues and
the solution of a crime. Begun by the French, it was made famous and popular by American writer Edgar Allan Poe in his C. Auguste Dupin short-story
trilogy. After Poe's success, many British writers began to write detective novels, the most famous being Arthur Conan Doyle, whose Sherlock Holmes, a
detective who relied more on deduction than observation, first appeared in *A
Study in Scarlet* (1887).

> Like all other arts, the Science of Deduction and Analysis is one which can
> only be acquired by long and patient study. . . . Puerile as such an exercise
> may seem, it sharpens the faculties of observation, and teaches one where to
> look and what to look for. By a man's finger-nails, by his coat-sleeve, by his
> boots, by his trouser-knees, by the callosities of his forefinger and thumb, by
> his expression, by his shirt-cuffs—by each of these things a man's calling is
> plainly revealed. That all united should fail to enlighten the competent in-
> quirer in any case is almost inconceivable.

The popularity of the mystery novel continued to grow and reached its peak in
America between the major world wars. American mystery writers began to
vary the form and introduced sex and violence into it. The protagonist of these
new hard-boiled mystery novels was a "tough guy" who was sometimes a private eye, but more generally simply a victim of circumstance. The *pure* hard-
boiled novel depicts the down-and-out and the disinherited, who develop a rigid
attitude that enables them to maintain a granite-like dignity against hostile forces.

The traumatic wrench of the Depression caused a violent reaction in him. He is strategically placed to detect lies and hypocrisy in society's institutions. In his actions, he takes revenge upon the forces that shaped and ultimately destroy him. Even his attitudes seem acts of aggression.

Hard-boiled novels generally feature loose plot structures (some of Dashiell Hammett's and Raymond Chandler's best novels were forced combinations of scattered short stories) and are often written in a brutal first-person narrative. The aggressive, spare style owes much to Ernest Hemingway, who penned a single hard-boiled short story, "The Killers" (1927). Although generally considered to be written solely for entertainment, French critics gave credibility to the genre by pointing out that many hard-boiled novels such as Dashiell Hammett's *The Maltese Falcon* (1930), James M. Cain's *The Postman Always Rings Twice* (1934), and Horace McCoy's *They Shoot Horses, Don't They?* (1935) had serious, even existential implications and aesthetic qualities, a belief borne out by the fact that many "serious" novelists often write mystery novels as well. The French writer Georges Simenon (Georges Sim) writes a conventional detective series featuring inspector Maigret, but he also writes serious novels, such as *The Snow Was Black* (1950). Graham Greene is best knows for his novels *The Heart of the Matter* (1948) and *The End of the Affair* (1951), but he also wrote mystery thrillers—which he referred to as "entertainments," such as *This Gun for Hire* (1936) and *The Third Man* (1950). Raymond Chandler's *The Big Sleep* (1939) is in many ways the definitive serious mystery novel.

> Outside the bright gardens had a haunted look as though small wild eyes were watching me from behind the bushes, as though the sunshine itself had a mysterious something in its light. I got into my car and drove off down the hill.
>
> What did it matter where you lay once you were dead? In a dirty sump or in a marble tower on top of a high hill? You were dead, you were sleeping the big sleep, you were not bothered by things like that. Oil and water were the same as wind and air to you. You just slept the big sleep, not caring about the nastiness of how you died or where you fell. Me, I was part of the nastiness now. Far more a part of it than Rusty Regan was. But the old man didn't have to be. He could lie quiet in his canopied bed, with his bloodless hands folded on the sheet, waiting. His heart was a brief, uncertain murmur. His thoughts were as gray as ashes. And in a little while he too, like Rusty Regan, would be sleeping the big sleep.

In recent years, the mystery novel has begun to develop subgenres that focus on hard-boiled police detectives, such as Michael Connelly's Harry Bosch series (*The Black Echo*, 1992, *The Concrete Blonde*, 1994, and *A Darkness More Than Night*, 2001, etc.); lawyers, such as John Grisham's *A Time to Kill* (1989) and *The Firm* (1991); and scientific or medical mysteries, as in Robin Cook's *Vital Signs*

(1991). A hybrid genre has also developed in the western mystery with novels such as Tony Hillerman's *Dance Hall of the Dead* (1973) and *Skinwalkers* (1986), Susan Slater's *Pumpkin Seed Massacre* (1999) and *Thunderbird* (2002), and James D. Doss' *Shaman* Series (1994–).

Another subgenre of the mystery novel is the spy or espionage novel, which focuses less on the interior life of the protagonist and more on action and violence as the spy fights his way through impossibly exaggerated odds to defend the free world against maniacal villains bent on destroying it. The most famous spy novelist is Ian Fleming, whose James Bond first appeared in 1952's *Casino Royale*. The series has spawned many bestsellers and a successful movie franchise, including two films based on Fleming's *Thunderball* (1965).

> Bond got a foot against a lump of coral and, with this to give him impetus, flung himself forward. The man had no time to defend himself. Bond's spear caught him in the side and hurled him against the next man in line. Bond thrust and wrenched sickeningly. The man dropped his gun and bent double, clutching his side. Bond bored on into the mass of naked men now scattering in all directions, with their jet packs accelerated. Another man went down in front of him, clawing at his face. A chance thrust of Bond's hand had smashed the glass of his mask. He threshed his way up toward the surface, kicking Bond in the face as he went. A spear ripped into the rubber protecting Bond's stomach and Bond felt pain and wetness that might be blood or sea water. He dodged another flash of metal and a gun butt hit him hard on the head, but with most of its force spent against the cushion of water. It knocked him silly and he clung for a moment to a niggerhead to get his bearings while the black tide of his men swept past him and individual fights filled the water with black puffs of blood.

The mystery novel and its various subgenres show no signs of decline as new writers continue to spawn successful series. There is currently a trend among Scots-Irish writers, combining a strong literary tradition of dark humor and history with the elements of classic American hard-boiled fiction to produce some of the best mystery novels of the twentieth century. Some examples are Ian Rankin's *Knots and Crosses* (1987), Val McDermid's *A Place of Execution* (1999), John Connelly's *Every Dead Thing* (1999), Ken Bruen's *The Guards* (2001), K. T. McCaffrey's *End of the Line* (2003), Adrian McKinty's *Dead I Well May Be* (2003), and Cormac Millar's *An Irish Solution* (2004).

Other examples of traditional mystery novels include Wilkie Collins' *The Moonstone* (1868), Emile Gaboriau's *Monsieur Lecoq* (1869), Sir Arthur Conan Doyle's *The Hound of the Baskervilles* (1902), Mary Roberts Rinehart's *The Circular Staircase* (1908), G. K. Chesterton's *The Innocence of Father Brown* (1911), E. C. Bentley's *Trent's Last Case* (1913), S. S. Van Dine's *The Canary Murder Case* (1927),

Ellery Queen's *The Roman Hat Mystery* (1927), Agatha Christie's *Murder on the Orient Express* (1934), Georges Simenon's *The Patience of Maigret* (1940), Ed McBain's *Cop Hater* (1956), Robert Traver's *Anatomy of a Murder* (1958), Ross Macdonald's *The Underground Man* (1971), Ngaio Marsh's *Light Thickens* (1982), Sue Grafton's Kinsey Millhone Alphabet Series (1983–), Michael Innes' *Lament for a Maker* (1985), Dorothy L. Sayers's *Murder Must Advertise* (1986), Dick Francis's *The Edge* (1989), and James Lee Burke's *Heaven's Prisoners* (1990).

Other spy novels include Joseph Conrad's *The Secret Agent* (1907), Graham Greene's *The Ministry of Fear* (1943), W. Somerset Maugham's *Ashenden: Or, the British Agent* (1947), John Le Carre's *The Spy Who Came in from The Cold* (1963), Frederick Forsyth's *The Day of the Jackal* (1971), and Tom Clancy's *The Hunt for Red October* (1984).

Some classic hard-boiled novels are B. Traven's *The Treasure of Sierra Madre* (1927), W. R. Burnett's *Little Caesar* (1929), Dashiell Hammett's *Red Harvest* (1929), Carroll John Daly's *The Tag Murders* (1930), W. T. Ballard's "Bill Lenox" Stories (1933–1942), Hugh B. Cave's *Bottled in Blonde* (1934), Donald Wandrei's *Frost* (1934), Robert Leslie Bellem's *Blue Murder* (1938), D. L. Champion's *Footprints on a Brain* (1938), Mickey Spillane's *Kiss Me, Deadly* (1951), John D. MacDonald's *The Damned* (1952), Jim Thompson's *The Killer Inside Me* (1952), and Jay Dratler's *The Judas Kiss* (1955).

THE ROMANCE NOVEL

The romance novel, at present perhaps the major popular type, caters to assumptions its readers, mostly women, have about love. For the most part, romance novels focus on the relationship between two characters who are "meant to be together" but have been kept apart by circumstance. Almost all romance novels end happily, but not before the protagonists have surmounted many obstacles. One definitive best-selling romance novel is Erich Segal's *Love Story* (1970).

> I stood there at the bottom of the steps, afraid to ask how long she had been sitting, knowing only that I had wronged her terribly.
> "Jenny, I'm sorry—"
> "Stop!" She cut off my apology, then said very quietly, "Love means not ever having to say you're sorry."

Among other all-time best-selling love novels are E. M. Hull's *The Sheik* (1921), John O'Hara's *Butterfield 8* (1935), Elia Kazan's *The Arrangement* (1967), Jacqueline Susann's *Valley of the Dolls* (1966), Sidney Sheldon's *The Other Side of Midnight* (1973), Nora Roberts' *Search for Love* (1982), Jackie Collins' *Hollywood Wives*

(1983), Danielle Steele's *Season of Passion* (1989), and Janet Dailey's *Calder* series (1999–present).

THE EROTIC NOVEL

The erotic novel, which concentrates on the depiction of every conceivable sexual act, has a long tradition and is sometimes written by respected writers, as one way of breaking out (though within a constricted circle of readers until recently) of conventional modes of expression. In language, the erotic novel ranges from the wittiness of euphemism to naughty and bawdy to outright obscenity, and in intent from titillation to vicarious sexual gratification. Some of these novels have many qualities of works of art, for instance, Englishman John Cleland's *Fanny Hill, Memoirs of a Woman of Pleasure* (c1749); others have serious philosophical or social or psychological implications, such as the Marquis de Sade's massive *Justine* (1797). The Victorian period saw the publication of numerous anonymously written erotic novels, including *Raped on the Railway, My Secret Life*, and *The Shuttered Houses of Paris*. Published through illicit presses, many of these novels claimed to be the first-person accounts of wanton women, such as *Vicky, Pamela, Dorothea*, and *Miriam*.

As a type, the erotic novel began fading out as other popular types absorbed the frank sexuality and coarse language that was once the exclusive province of erotic fiction. But the erotic novel has recently resurfaced in such works as Anne Rice's (writing as A. N. Roquelaure) *Sleeping Beauty Trilogy* (1983–1985).

> Her face was perfect to him, and her embroidered gown had fallen deep into the crease between her legs so that he could see the shape of her sex beneath it.
> He drew out his sword, with which he had cut back all the vines outside, and gently slipping the blade between her breasts, let it rip easily through the old fabric.
> Her dress was laid open to the hem, and he folded it back and looked at her. Her nipples were a rosy pink as were her lips, and the hair between her legs was darkly yellow and curlier than the long straight hair of her head which covered her arms almost down to her hips on either side of her.

Other examples of more strictly erotic novels include Vina Delmar's *Bad Girl* (1928), Thorne Smith's *The Glorious Pool* (1934) and *Topper Takes a Trip* (1932), Tiffany Thayer's *Call Her Savage* (1931), Norman Lindsay's *The Cautious Amorist* (1932), Jack Woodford's *Four Eves* (1935), Donald Henderson Clark's *Millie's Daughter* (1939), Grace Metalious' *Peyton Place* (1956), and Terry Southern's *Candy* (1959).

THE GRAPHIC NOVEL

The graphic novel is a new development in literature and is similar to the Japanese *Manga*, which first appeared in Europe in the nineteenth century. *Manga*, which literally means "random pictures," greatly influenced the works of many twentieth-century surrealists including Max Ernst who invented the predecessor to the graphic novel, the collage novel. In collage novels, images are lifted from various other publications and linked together through theme to form a narrative. Important collage novels, all by Ernst, include *Les Malheurs des Immortels* (1922), *La Femme 100 Tetes* (1929), *Reve d'une Petite Fille . . .* (1930), and *Une Semaine de Bon* (1933–1934).

The term "graphic novel" was coined in 1964 by Richard Kyle in the November issue of the newsletter *CAPA-ALPHA*. Originally, the term referred to comic books that had been published in a higher quality format than traditional comic books. These long form stories were printed on high quality paper and bound rather than stapled. In 1978, artist Will Eisner popularized the term by using it on the cover of his *A Contract with God*. Although a graphic novel is often simply a high quality comic book whose story arc is too long for regular publication such as Frank Miller's *Batman: Year One* (1988), the term is most often used by creators and readers to differentiate "serious" artistic works from lighter works intended solely for entertainment. Examples include Joe Sacco's *Palestine* (1993), a historical first-person account of the plight of the Palestinian people; Neil Gaiman's *Sandman* (1993), a fantasy based graphic novel about the eternal forces that affect all, such as Death and Desire; Alan Moore and Eddie Campbell's *From Hell* (1995), a well-researched speculation about the identity of Jack the Ripper; Doug Murray and Michael Golden's *The 'Nam* (1986), another historical work that details the Vietnam War from the perspective of American soldiers; Max Allan Collins' *Road to Perdition* (1998), about a religiously convicted hit man for the Irish mob; Vince Locke and John Wagner's *A History of Violence* (2004), the tale of a mob hit man's attempt to walk the straight and narrow; and Art Spiegelman's *Maus: A Survivor's Tale* (1992), which recounts the struggle of Spiegelman's father to survive the Holocaust. In this groundbreaking work, Spiegelman portrays different groups of people as different species of animals: Jews are mice, Germans are cats, French are frogs, Poles are pigs, Americans are dogs, and so forth. This device was an ironic nod to Nazi propaganda images that depicted Jews as mice or rats.

When *Maus* won the Pulitzer Prize in 1992, it helped the graphic novel to gain an aura of respectability that comic books had never been able to attain. Most major book stores and public libraries now place graphic novels on the shelf with other works of literature. Spiegelman was one of the first novelists to tackle the September 11 attack on the World Trade Center with his graphic novel *In the Shadow of No Towers* (2004).

THE ADOLESCENT NOVEL

The term *adolescent novel* refers simply to novels written with an adolescent audience in mind. The adolescent novel encompasses all other major novel types—historical, horror, romance, memoir, etc.—with two major distinctions: the protagonists of adolescent novels are younger than the protagonists in "adult" fiction, and the vocabulary tends to be on a high school reading level. But many adolescent novels have crossed over and are enjoyed by many adult readers. A few examples are J. D. Salinger's *The Catcher in the Rye* (1951), William Golding's *Lord of the Flies* (1954), and most recently J. K. Rowling's highly successful *Harry Potter* series (1998–present), which follows the adventures of a young wizard throughout his education.

Novels of History

THE HISTORICAL NOVEL

*T*he historical novel projects its characters back into an era of the recent or distant past to achieve a serious illumination of, or an entertaining distraction from, the present. Serious historical novelists attempt to preserve a spirit of the past, striving for a sense of reality as authentic as that of contemporary novels. Some depict great moments of historical conflict to show characters enacting humankind's destiny. As in the movies, spectacle is a major element in historical fiction. With his *Waverley* novels (1814), Sir Walter Scott made the historical novel a world-famous genre, which he perfected with *Ivanhoe* (1819).

> "I marvel, worthy Cedric," said the Abbot, as their discourse proceeded, "that, great as your predilection is for your own manly language, you do not receive the Norman-French into your favour, so far at least as the mystery of wood-craft and hunting is concerned. Surely no tongue is so rich in the various phrases which the field-sports demand, or furnishes means to the experienced woodman so well to express his jovial art."
>
> "Good Father Aymer," said the Saxon, "be it known to you, I care not for those over-sea refinements, without which I can well enough take my pleasure in the woods. I can wind my horn, though I call not the blast either a *recheate* or a *morte*—I can cheer my dogs on the prey, and I can flay and quarter the animal when it is brought down, without using the new-fangled jargon of *curee, arbor, nombles*, and all the babble of the fabulous Sir Tristrem."
>
> "The French," said the Templar, raising his voice with the presumptuous and authoritative tone which he used upon all occasions, "is not only the natural language of the chase, but that of love and of war, in which ladies should be won and enemies defied."

Some examples of historical novels include Edward Bulwer-Lytton's *The Last Days of Pompeii* (1834), James Fenimore Cooper's *The Deerslayer* (1841), Alexandre Dumas' *The Count of Monte Cristo* (1844), Charles Kingsley's *Westward Ho!* (1855), Charles Reade's *The Cloister and the Hearth* (1861), Ouida's *Under Two Flags* (1867), Leo Tolstoy's *War and Peace* (1865–1869), Anthony Hope's *The Prisoner of Zenda* (1894), Booth Tarkington's *Monsieur Beaucaire* (1900), Mary Johnston's *To Have and To Hold* (1900), Winston Churchill's *The Crisis* (1901), Russian Stefan Zeromski's *Ashes* (1904), Joseph Hergesheimer's *Java Head* (1919) and *Three Black Pennies* (1917), Sigrid Undset's *Kristin Lavransdatter* (1920–22), Robert Graves' *I, Claudius* (1934), Stark Young's *So Red the Rose* (1934), Margaret Mitchell's *Gone with the Wind* (1936), Kenneth Roberts' *Northwest Passage* (1937), Riccardo Bacchelli's *The Mill on the Po* (1938–1940), Robert Penn Warren's *World Enough and Time* (1950), Brazilian Jorge Amado's *The Violent Land* (1954), Alfred Duggan's *Leopards and Lilies* (1954) and *The Cunning of the Dove* (1960), Mary Renault's (Mary Challans') *The Last of the Wine* (1956), T. H. White's *The Once and Future King* (1958), David Stacton's *A Dancer in Darkness* (1960), Cecelia Holland's *Rakóssy* (1966), George MacDonald Fraser's *Flashman* series (1969–present), Patrick O'Brian's *Master and Commander* series (1970–2004), E. L. Doctorow's *The Book of Daniel* (1971), George P. Garrett's *Death of the Fox: A Novel of Elizabeth and Ralegh*, William Golding's *Fire Down Below* (1989), Kazuo Ishiguro's *The Remains of the Day* (1989), Beryl Bainbridge's *The Birthday Boys* (1991), and David Madden's *Sharpshooter* (1996).

THE CHRONICLE NOVEL

A variation on the historical novel is the chronicle novel, which attempts a detailed panorama of a time and place with a multiplicity and great variety of representative characters, locales, and episodes that illustrate facets of the social and economic stratification. Victor Hugo's *Les Miserables* (1862) was one of the first great social chronicles.

> Jean Valjean, at that very moment, was a prey to a frightful uprising. All the gulfs were reopened within him. He also, like Paris, was shuddering on the threshold of a formidable and obscure revolution. A few hours had sufficed. His destiny and his conscience were suddenly covered with shadow. Of him also, as of Paris, we might say: the two principles are face to face. The angel of light and the angel of darkness are to wrestle on the bridge of the abyss. Which of the two shall hurl down the other? Which shall sweep him away?

In the 1920s and '30s a number of multi-volume novels appeared. These novels attempted to show how history determined the fate of families, groups, individuals, and nations. A species of realistic novel that stresses historical determinism more than the findings of social science, this type included Norwegian Olav Dunn's six-volume *The People of Juvik* (1918–1923), Ford Madox Ford's three volume *Parade's End* (1924–26), Roger Martin du Gard's eight-volume *Les Thibaults* (*The World of the Thibaults*) (1922–29), and John Dos Passos' *U.S.A.* (1937).

> U.S.A. is the slice of a continent. U.S.A. is a group of holding companies, some aggregations of trade unions, a set of laws bound in calf, a radio network, a chain of moving picture theatres, a column of stock-quotations rubbed out and written in by a Western Union boy on a blackboard, a public library full of old newspapers and dogeared historybooks with protests scrawled on the margins in pencil. U.S.A. is the world's greatest rivervalley fringed with mountains and hills, U.S.A. is a set of bigmouthed officials with too many bankaccounts. U.S.A. is a lot of men buried in their uniforms in Arlington Cemetery. U.S.A. is the letters at the end of an address when you are away from home. But mostly U.S.A. is the speech of the people.

Other social and historical chronicles are: Italian Ippolito Nievo's *The Castle of Fratta* (1867), Benito Perez Galdos' four-volume *Fortunate and Jacinta* (1886–1887), Thomas Mann's *Buddenbrooks* (1901), Mexican Mariano Azuela's *The Underdogs* (1915), Jules Romains' (Louis Farigoule's) ten-volume *Les Hommes de Bonne Volonte* (*Men of Good Will*, 1932–1946), James Clavell's *Shogun* (1975), Jean M. Auel's *The Clan of the Cave Bear* (1980), James Michener's *Texas* (1986), W. Michael and Kathleen O'Neal Gear's *People of the Wolf* (1990), and Charles Frazier's *Cold Mountain* (1997).

THE ANTIQUARIAN NOVEL

A very rare, but interesting, variation of the historical novel is the antiquarian novel, which either exploits or utilizes the diction and style of the period it is chronicling. When it is successful, this type offers a peculiar pleasure as with Thomas Pynchon's *Mason & Dixon* (1997).

> Snow-Balls have flown their Arcs, starr'd the Sides of Outbuildings, as of Cousins, carried Hats away into the brisk Wind of Delaware,—the Sleds are brought in and their Runners carefully dried and greased, shoes deposited in the back Hall, a stocking'd-foot Descent made upon the great Kitchen, in a purposeful Dither since Morning, punctuated by the ringing Lids of various Boilers and Stewing-Pots, fragrant with pie—Spices, peel'd Fruits, Suet, heated Sugar,—

John Fowles' *The French Lieutenant's Woman* (1969) is another example as is Giuseppe Tomasi di Lampedusa's *The Leopard* (1958), a historical family chronicle. Some say the series of novels by scientist C. P. Snow, *Strangers and Brothers* (1940), are antiquarian. John Seelye wrote a modern, unexpurgated version of Twain's novel in *The True Adventures of Huckleberry Finn* (1970), and Anthony Burgess' *A Dead Man in Deptford* (1993) and Michel Faber's *The Crimson Petal and the White* (2002) are recent examples.

· 8 ·

Novels of Realism

THE NOVEL OF REALISM

$\mathcal{A}$lthough realism is difficult to define, at its most basic level, it is an attempt to accurately represent a detailed account of the life of its characters. Literature is both general and particular; the realist emphasizes the particular to evoke the general. Endeavoring to avoid improbability, romanticism, and falsification, the realist novelist strives for plausibility, credibility, and, above all, verisimilitude. The realist novelist attempts to remain objective, avoiding a special philosophy about or a remedy for the problems she dramatizes.

Although realist novels attempt to remain objective, they are often subtly didactic in order to give an ethical, humanistic, and prophetic but not politically doctrinaire picture of the human condition. Andre Malraux's *La Condition Humaine* (*Man's Fate*, 1933) is a good example of that sort of realism.

> Ideas were not to be thought, but lived. Kyo had chosen action, in a grave and premeditated way, as others choose a military career, or the sea; he left his father, lived in Canton, in Tientsin, the life of day-laborers and coolies, in order to organize the syndicates. Ch'en—his uncle, taken as hostage at the capture of Swatow, and unable to pay his ransom, had been executed—had found himself without money, provided only with worthless diplomas, with his twenty-four years and with China before him. He was a truckdriver when the Northern routes were dangerous, then an assistant chemist, then nothing. Everything had pushed him into political activity; the hope of a different world, the possibility of eating, though wretchedly (he was naturally austere, perhaps through pride), the gratification of his hatreds, his mind, his character. This activity gave a meaning to his solitude.

The rise of socialism and Marxism led to Soviet realism, which reduces man to a collective creature, historically determined to act out his role in a mass revolution and the reconstruction of society. We see this type of realism in Boris Pilnyak's *The Naked Year* (1922) and in Mikhail Zoshchenko's *Restored Youth* (1933). Other examples include Gustav Freytag's *Debit and Credit* (1855), Edith Wharton's *The Age of Innocence* (1920), Ramon Sender's *The King and the Queen* (1948), Elio Vittorini's *The Red Carnation* (1948) and *In Sicily* (1949), Vasco Pratolini's *A Hero of Our Time* (1949), Nelson Algren's *The Man with the Golden Arm* (1949), Juan Goytisolo's *The Party's Over* (1962) and *Island of Women* (1962), John Irving's *The Cider House Rules* (1985), and Tom Wolfe's *A Man in Full* (1998).

THE NOVEL OF DOMESTIC REALISM

Domestic realism, mainly an English genre, gives a detailed picture of the everyday life of a family in a domestic setting. Examples of this type include Henry Fielding's *Amelia* (1761), Gerald Griffin's *The Collegians* (1828), George Eliot's *The Mill on the Floss* (1860) and *Silas Marner* (1861), E. M. Forster's *Howards End* (1910), and the Australian Christina Stead's *The Man Who Loved Children* (1940). William McFee's *Casuals of the Sea* (1916) offers a good example of the conventions of domestic realism.

> In a few days, after Minnie had brought a wheezy, ill-strapped dressbasket and a paper bag containing her Sunday hat, and taken up her quarters on a truckle bed which was hidden during the day under a yellow cover, she declared open war. In the first place, Minnie discovered with some surprise that the companionship of Mrs. Wilfley involved housework in all its branches, from washing dishes to cleaning hair-brushes with cloudy ammonia. Certainly the dishes were only breakfast dishes, and the latter task was begged from her as a favour, but the vertical furrow in the girl's forehead deepened for all that.

★ ★ ★

> Engrossed in his work of laying the breakfast-table the next morning, Hannibal did not hear the door leading to the Chief's room open; the roar of the coal pouring from the up-ended truck into the empty hold, the tramp of feet overhead, the soft slither of ropes and hissing of steam, overpowered all minor sounds. He turned and found a sharp-eyed lady looking him over.

Other non-English examples include Norwegian Jonas Lie's *The Family at Gillje* (1883) and *The Commander's Daughter* (1886), Prussian Theodor Fontane's *Effi*

Briest (1895), Mazo de la Roche's *Jalna* (1927), and Polish Isaac Bashevis Singer's *The Family Moskat* (1966).

THE NOVEL OF FORMAL REALISM

Another type is formal realism, or realistic formalism. A recent approach is propounded by French Alain Robbe-Grillet who argues that true realism depicts our relationships with the actual physical objects in our everyday environment. In ways that we intuitively sense and respond to, these objects are hostile or benevolent; they witness our gradual disintegration or even conspire with chance to destroy us. His best novels are *Jealousy* (1957) and *The Voyeur* (1955). To depict a man's feelings, one describes the objects around him.

> Along dark hallways lined with closed doors, up narrow stairways leading to failure after failure, he lost himself again among his specters. At one end of a filthy landing he knocked with his ring at a door with no knob which opened by itself. . . . The door swung open and a mistrustful face appeared in the opening—which was just wide enough for him to recognize the black and white tiles on the floor. . . . The large squares were of a uniform gray; the room he entered was not at all remarkable—except for an unmade bed with a red spread trailing on the floor. . . . There was no red bedspread, nor was there an unmade bed; no lambskin, no night table, no bed lamp; there was no blue pack of cigarettes, no flowered wallpaper, no painting on the wall. The room he had been directed to was only a kitchen where he put his suitcase flat on the big oval table in the middle. Then came the oil-cloth, the pattern on the oilcloth, the click of copper-plated clasp, etc.

The great tradition in the American novel has been realism of one sort or another. American realists often debunk society's established platitudes about life. Although Mark Twain told tales through the voice of a young boy, he gave a realistic, sometimes satirical, dark vision of small-town western America in *The Adventures of Huckleberry Finn* (1884). William Dean Howells showed that the dream of America's better opportunities in the city was false by illustrating disillusionment in urban settings in novels such as *The Rise of Silas Lapham* (1885) and *A Hazard of New Fortunes* (1890). Other examples of formal realism include Sherwood Anderson's *Poor White* (1920), F. Scott Fitzgerald's *The Great Gatsby* (1925), Ernest Hemingway's *The Sun Also Rises* (1926), and Willa Cather's *Death Comes for the Archbishop* (1927). Later formal realist novels include Bernard Malamud's ironic *The Natural* (1952) and Tom Wolfe's *The Bonfire of the Vanities* (1987).

Realism is as much a matter of style and technique as of purpose; the style is usually unadorned and the techniques are traditional and simple. The term "realistic," like the term "aesthetic," is too often used in an honorific sense. It should be applied descriptively.

THE NATURALISTIC NOVEL

The naturalistic novel is the logical development of the novel's original impulse to provide a realistic portrayal of the world. The naturalistic novel takes into account a scientific understanding of heredity and other biological factors, as well as investigating social conditions that determine the fate of individual characters. Naturalistic novelists are influenced by the philosophy of determinism, which is the "philosophical doctrine that every event, act, decision is the inevitable consequence" of physical, psychological, or environmental conditions and that human will in nature is ineffectual. "Naturalistic determinism" sees man as a "natural mechanism" and presents him with "clinical realism," making the naturalistic novel a branch of "social science."

The first great exponent and theorist of this type of novel was Emile Zola, whose main purpose was to delineate dramatically, but clinically, the effect of biology and environment upon his characters. Earlier novels stressed conflicts between characters produced by social institutions who are defeated by or victorious over other people and established forces. In Zola's naturalistic novels, the fall of a person is determined not so much by a flaw in character as by biological factors and economic conditions beyond his control. Prostitution defeats *Nana* (1880) and hard work wears out Gervaise in *L'Assomoir* (*The Dram Shop*, 1877).

Nana was left alone, her face turned upwards in the candlelight. It was a charnel-house, a mass of matter and blood, a shovelful of putrid flesh, thrown there on the cushion. The pustules had invaded the entire face, one touching the other; and, faded, sunk in, with the greyish aspect of mud, they already seemed like a mouldiness of the earth on that shapeless pulp, in which the features were no longer recognizable. One of the eyes, the left one, had completely disappeared amidst the eruption of the purulence; the other, half open, looked like a black and stained hole. The nose still continued to suppurate. A reddish crust starting from one of the cheeks, invaded the mouth, which it distorted in an abominable laugh; and on this horrible and grotesque mask of nothingness, the hair, that beautiful hair, retained its sun-like fire, fell in a stream of gold. Venus was decomposing. It seemed as if the virus gathered by her in the gutters, from the tolerated carrion that the ferment with which she had poisoned a people, had ascended to her face and rotted it.

The room was deserted. A strong breath of despair mounted from the Boulevard, and swelled the curtain.

The naturalists set out to compete with science as a source of information and truth, to popularize its findings, and by giving an extremely accurate picture, to persuade people to act. Because their novels portrayed the ugly, naturalists were often accused of mere sensationalism. But Zola argued that naturalists were "looking for the causes of social evil [by studying] the anatomy of classes and individuals to explain the derangements which are produced in society and in man." However, the purely naturalistic novel was short-lived as it came to be regarded as a kind of fad and the concept was regarded as a fallacy.

Maxim Gorki's *Mother* (1907) is a lyrical, visionary novel, but a good example also of Russian naturalism. Two English works are George Moore's *Esther Waters* (1894) and Arnold Bennett's *The Old Wives' Tale* (1908). V. Blasco-Ibanez is a kind of Spanish Zola, as seen in *Blood and Sand* (1908) and *The Four Horsemen of the Apocalypse* (1916). Giovanni Verga's *Mastro Don Gesnaldo* (1889) is an Italian example, and Camilo Jose Cela's *The Family of Pascual Duarte* (1942) is a Spanish one. A later naturalism is seen in Alberto Moravia's *Woman of Rome* (1947).

In America, especially, the contrast between the dream and the reality was shocking because the cities were filled with immigrants who fled the European nightmare. Stephen Crane's *Maggie: A Girl of the Streets* (1893) chronicles the life of an Irish immigrant family.

> Eventually they entered into a dark region where, from a careening building, a dozen gruesome doorways gave up loads of babies to the street and the gutter. A wind of early autumn raised yellow dust from cobbles and swirled it against an hundred windows. Long streamers of garments fluttered from fire-escapes. In all unhandy places there were buckets, brooms, rags and bottles. In the street infants played or fought with other infants or sat stupidly in the way of vehicles. Formidable women, with uncombed hair and disordered dress, gossiped while leaning on railings, or screamed in frantic quarrels. Withered persons, in curious postures of submission to something, sat smoking pipes in obscure corners. A thousand odors of cooking food came forth to the street. The building quivered and creaked from the weight of humanity stamping about in its bowels.
>
> A small ragged girl dragged a red, bawling infant along the crowded ways. He was hanging back, baby-like, bracing his wrinkled, bare legs.
>
> The little girl cried out: "Ah, Tommie, come ahn. Dere's Jimmie and fader. Don't be a-pullin' me back."
>
> She jerked the baby's arm impatiently. He fell on his face, roaring. With a second jerk she pulled him to his feet, and they went on. With the obstinacy of his order, he protested against being dragged in a chosen direction. He made heroic endeavors to keep on his legs, denounce his sister and consume a bit of orange peeling which he chewed between the times of his infantile orations.

Naturalism had a resurgence in the United States in the muck-raking journalistic novels of Upton Sinclair, whose *The Jungle* (1906) was instrumental in getting the Pure Food and Drug Act passed. Another naturalist was Frank Norris, who examines the railroad system in *The Octopus* (1901) and wheat production in *The Pit* (1903). Theodore Dreiser's *Sister Carrie* (1900) and *An American Tragedy* (1925) examine young women and men who moved to the city in hopes of finding a better life. Another good example of American naturalism is John O'Hara's *Appointment in Samarra* (1934). The novels of Joyce Carol Oates, especially *them* (1969), and James Dickey's *Deliverance* (1970) are seen as belonging to this tradition.

THE NOVEL OF MAGICAL REALISM

Magical realism is a term used to describe novels that blend elements of traditional realist novels with fantastic or magical plot elements. Often the laws of cause and effect seem not to apply to the events that occur in magical realist novels. What separates them from fantasy novels is that the characters in magical realist novels accept these magical elements and events as a part of reality. This type of novel often appears in repressive societies or in countries with authoritarian or totalitarian governments, which suggests that much of the fantastic material in magical realism represents a kind of political protest to intolerable conditions, as seen in Gunter Grass's *The Tin Drum* (1959).

> It is not so easy, lying here in this scrubbed hospital bed under a glass peephole with Bruno's eye in it, to give a picture of the smoke clouds that rose from Kashubian potato fires or of the slanting October rain. If I didn't have my drum, which, when handled adroitly and patiently, remembers all the incidentals that I need to get the essential down on paper, and if I didn't have the permission of the management to drum on it three or four hours a day, I'd be a poor bastard with nothing to say for my grandparents.
>
> In any case, my drum tells me this: That afternoon in the year 1899, while in South Africa Oom Kruger was brushing his bushy anti-British eyebrows, my mother Agnes, between Dirschau and Karthaus, not far from the Bissau brickworks, amid smoke, terrors, sighs, and saints' names, under four skirts of identical color, under the slanting rain and the smoke-filled eyes of two rural constables asking uninspired questions, was begotten by the short but stocky Joseph Koljaiczek.
>
> That very night my grandmother Anna Bronski changed her name; with the help of a priest who was generous with the sacraments, she had herself metamorphosed into Anna Koljaiczek and followed Joseph, if not into Egypt, at least to the provincial capital on the river Mottlau, where Joseph found work as a raftsman and temporary peace from the constabulary.

Some examples include Franz Kafka's *The Trial* (1937), Flann O'Brien's *At Swim-Two-Birds* (1951), Mikhail Bulgakov's *The Master and Margarita* (1967), Thomas Pynchon's *Gravity's Rainbow* (1973), Leslie Marmon Silko's *Ceremony* (1977), Toni Morrison's *Song of Solomon* (1977), Italo Calvino's *If on a Winter's Night a Traveler* (1979), Isabel Allende's *The House of the Spirits* (1982), Umberto Eco's *The Name of the Rose* (1983), Gabriel Garcia Marquez's *Love in the Time of Cholera* (1985), Salman Rushdie's *The Satanic Verses* (1988), and Don Delillo's *The Body Artist* (2001).

· 9 ·

Novels of Region

THE REGIONAL NOVEL

$\mathcal{R}$egionalism depicts faithfully the lifestyles, manners, customs, mores, dialects, and social organization of common people, mostly villagers and country folk, of a vanishing or vanished past. Regional novelists focus on a single region and its people, rather than a country as a whole, such as the New England villager, the southern black plantation laborer, the New Orleans Creole, or the California prospector. Regional novelists seem to take two opposing approaches: some exhibit a romanticized re-creation, others a realistic exposé of the past. Modern critical opinion on the value of regional writing is sharply divided. Some critics see it as a useful social and cultural art. Others claim that it confuses social and creative impulses and falsifies both. When studying regional novels, one might ask these questions: How does the region see itself? How do outsiders see the region? How does the regionalist writer see the region? How do people in the region view the works of these writers? How do readers *outside* the region view those writings?

Here, separated by region, are some salient examples of the regional novel in America. New England: Mary E. Wilkins Freeman's *A New England Nun* (1891), Sarah Orne Jewett's *A Country Doctor* (1884), and Elsie Singmaster's *A Boy at Gettysburg* (1913); the South: William Gilmore Simms' *Yamassee* (1835), George W. Cable's *The Grandissimes* (1880), Charles Egbert Craddock's *In the Clouds* (1887), Charles Waddell Chesnutt's *Conjure Woman* (1899), Thomas Wolfe's *Look Homeward, Angel* (1929), James Still's *River of Earth* (1940), William Faulkner's *The Hamlet* (1940), Eudora Welty's *Delta Wedding* (1946), Harriette Arnow's *Hunter's Horn* (1949), David Madden's *Cassandra Singing* (1969), and John Kennedy Toole's *A Confederacy of Dunces* (1980); the Midwest: Edward Eggleston's *A Hoosier School-*

master (1871), E. W. Howe's *The Story of a Country Town* (1883), Booth Tarkington's *The Gentleman from Indiana* (1899), Willa Cather's *O Pioneers!* (1913) and *My Antonia* (1918), Glenway Wescott's *The Grandmothers* (1927), Ross Lockridge Jr.'s *Raintree County* (1948), and Wright Morris' *The Home Place* (1948) and *The World in the Attic* (1949); the West: Helen Hunt Jackson's *Ramona* (1884), Owen Wister's *The Virginian* (1902), Walter Van Tilburg Clark's *The Ox-Bow Incident* (1940), and Wallace Stegner's *The Big Rock Candy Mountain* (1943).

Regionalism is not solely an American type. Other examples include Jose Maria de Pereda's *Sotileza* (1884), Boris Pilnyak's *The Naked Year* (1922), Sean O'Faolain's *A Nest of Gentle Folk* (1933), the Canadian Louis Hemon's *Maria Chapdelaine* (1916), the Argentinean Hugo Wast's (Gustavo Martinez Zuviria) *Black Valley* (1918), Mary Webb's *Precious Bane* (1924), the Argentinean Ricardo Guiraldes' *Don Segundo Sombra* (1926), the Venezuelan Romulo Gallegos' *Dona Barbara* (1929), and the Swiss Charles Ferdinand Ramuz's *When the Mountain Fell* (1935).

Often regional novelists narrow their focus to cover only a single small town. One excellent practitioner of this type is Sherwood Anderson, whose *Winesburg, Ohio* (1919) and *Poor White* (1920) influenced the style of many regional novelists. Other examples include Ruth Suckow's *The Folks* (1934), Sinclair Lewis' *Main Street* (1920) and *Babbitt* (1922), Edgar Lee Masters' *Kit O'Brien* (1927) and *Mitch Miller* (1920), Pio Baroja y Nessi's *The Restlessness of Shanti Andia* (1930), Kamala Markandaya's *Nectar in a Sieve* (1954), and Khushwant Singh's *Mano Majra* (*Train to Pakistan*, 1956).

NOVELS OF THE SOIL

Closely related to the regional novel is the novel of the soil, which depicts life in the country and humanity's struggle against nature in a rural setting. Behind the novels of the soil is the romanticism of William Wordsworth's "The Solitary Reaper," for readers are drawn to such novels less out of the desire to see life depicted realistically than to experience Jean-Jacques Rousseau's "noble savage" triumph over the forces of nature, as in O. E. Rolvaag's *Giants in the Earth* (1927).

> Bright, clear sky over a plain so wide that the rim of the heavens cut down on it around the entire horizon.... Bright, clear sky, to-day, to-morrow, and for all time to come.
> ... And Sun! And still more sun! It set the heavens afire every morning; it grew with the day to quivering golden light—then softened into all the shades of red and purple as evening fell.... Pure colour everywhere. A gust of wind, sweeping across the plain, threw into life waves of yellow and blue

and green. Now and then a dead black wave would race over the scene . . . a cloud's gliding shadow . . . now and then . . .

It was late afternoon. A small caravan was pushing its way through the tall grass. The track that it left behind was like the wake of a boat—except that instead of widening out astern it closed in again.

Other examples include Knut Hamsun's *Growth of the Soil* (1917), Ellen Glasgow's *Barren Ground* (1925), Pearl Buck's *The Good Earth* (1931), Erskine Caldwell's *Tobacco Road* (1932), John Steinbeck's *Of Mice and Men* (1937), and Norman MacLean's *A River Runs Through It* (1976).

THE LOCAL COLOR NOVEL

The local color novel is a type of regional novel that depicts rural or small town life in a distinctly remote or isolated area of a country. Rather than giving a balanced picture, the local color novel exploits the quaintness of the region depicted. The local colorist deliberately attempts to attract readers to the odd details of the distinctively different region he describes. Almost subordinate to their quirks, people become caricatures. Important local colorists include Nathaniel Hawthorne, Sarah Orne Jewett, Bret Harte, Kate Chopin, George W. Cable, Joel Chandler Harris, Hamlin Garland, and Mark Twain.

One subset of the local color novel that is not set in a rural area is the campus novel, about academia. Some campus novels are Vladimir Nabokov's *Pnin* (1957), Tom Sharpe's *Wilt* (1976), David Lodge's *Small World* (1984), and Edward Allen's *Mustang Sally* (1992).

THE NOVEL OF HERITAGE

The novel of heritage generally deals with some specific subset of the American population; a minority group, rather than a place, is the focus. The novel of heritage is a kind of off-shoot of the urban and the rural realistic novel. In novels of heritage, the author often attempts to understand himself in relation to his ethnic group, then to society at large, and his purpose is also to explain his people to themselves and to the general majority.

One important subgenre is the novel that deals with the American Jewish community. Examples include Michael Gold's *Jews Without Money* (1930), Saul Bellow's *Herzog* (1964), Philip Roth's *Portnoy's Complaint* (1967), Bernard Malamud's *The Tenants* (1971), and Edward Wallant's *The Human Season* (1973). Abraham Cahan's *The Rise of David Lavinsky* (1917) is an excellent example of the American Jewish heritage novel.

Sometimes, when I think of my past in a superficial, casual way, the meta-morphosis I have gone through strikes me as nothing short of a miracle. I was born and reared in the lowest depths of poverty and I arrived in America—in 1885—with four cents in my pocket. I am now worth more than two mil-lion dollars and recognized as one of the two or three leading men in the cloak-and-suit trade in the United States. And yet when I take a look at my inner identity it impresses me as being precisely the same as it was thirty or forty years ago. My present station, power, the amount of worldly happiness at my command, and the rest of it, seem to be devoid of significance.

Another important subset of the heritage novel is the African American novel. Some major African American novels are James Weldon Johnson's *The Autobi-ography of an Ex-Colored Man* (1912), Jean Toomer's *Cane* (1923), Zora Neale Hurston's *Their Eyes Were Watching God* (1937), Richard Wright's *Native Son* (1940), James Baldwin's *Go Tell It on the Mountain* (1953), LeRoi Jones' *The Sys-tem of Dante's Hell* (1965), Alice Walker's *The Color Purple* (1970), Toni Morri-son's *Beloved* (1987), and Ralph Ellison's *Invisible Man* (1952).

I am an invisible man. No, I am not a spook like those who haunted Edgar Allan Poe; nor am I one of your Hollywood-movie ectoplasms. I am a man of substance, of flesh and bone, fiber and liquids—and I might even be said to possess a mind. I am invisible, understand, simply because people refuse to see me. Like the bodiless heads you see sometimes in circus sideshows, it is as though I have been surrounded by mirrors of hard, distorting glass. When they approach me they see only my surroundings, themselves, or fig-ments of their imagination—indeed, everything and anything except me.

In the latter part of the twentieth century, other important subsets of the her-itage novel have developed, including Asian American Amy Tan's *The Joy Luck Club* (1989), Fae Myenne Ng's *Bone* (1993), and Maxine Hong Kingston's monumental *The Woman Warrior* (1975).

My American life has been such a disappointment.
"I got straight A's, Mama."
"Let me tell you a true story about a girl who saved her village."
I could not figure out what was my village. And it was important that I do something big and fine, or else my parents would sell me when we made our way back to China. In China there were solutions for what to do with little girls who ate up food and threw tantrums. You can't eat straight A's.
When one of my parents or the emigrant villagers said, "Feeding girls is feeding cowbirds," I would thrash on the floor and scream so hard I couldn't talk. I couldn't stop.
"What's the matter with her?"
"I don't know. Bad, I guess. You know how girls are. 'There's no profit in raising girls. Better to raise geese than girls.'"

"I would hit her if she were mine. But then there's no use wasting all that discipline on a girl. 'When you raise girls, you're raising children for strangers.'"

"Stop that crying!" my mother would yell. "I'm going to hit you if you don't stop. Bad girl! Stop!" I'm going to remember never to hit or to scold my children for crying, I thought, because then they will only cry more.

"I'm not a bad girl," I would scream. "I'm not a bad girl. I'm not a bad girl." I might as well have said, "I'm not a girl."

Native American: James Welch's *Winter in the Blood* (1973), Leslie Marmon Silko's *Almanac of the Dead* (1991), and N. Scott Momaday's Pulitzer Prize–winning *House Made of Dawn* (1968).

At dusk he met with the other hunters in the plain. San Juanito, too, had got an eagle, but it was an aged male and poor by comparison. They gathered around the old eagle and spoke to it, bidding it return with their good will and sorrow to the eagles of the crags. They fixed a prayer plume to its leg and let it go. He watched it back away and stoop, flaring its wings on the ground, glowering, full of fear and suspicion. Then it took leave of the ground and beat upward, clattering through the still shadows of the valley. . . . He felt the great weight of the bird which he held in the sack. The dusk was fading quickly into night, and the others could not see that his eyes were filled with tears.

And Latin American: Raymond Barrio's *The Plum, Plum Pickers* (1972), Rudolfo A. Anaya's *Bless Me, Ultima* (1972), Edmund Villasenor's *Macho!* (1973), Thomas Sanchez's *Rabbit Boss* (1973), Sandra Cisneros' *The House on Mango Street* (1984), and Richard Vasquez's *Chicano* (1970).

"God did not bring me back. I escaped. I am now a deserter from the Mexican Army. They'll be looking for me in the morning, to make an example of me."

Before his mother could begin wailing, Hector Sandoval took command. "All right. All of you listen. Neftali knows what we must do. He and I have talked it over before when we were alone working with the burros. We leave. Now. To go north. Quick. No talk. Pack our things. Neftali and I will go get the burros. We have six. We should be able to take everything and be a long way from here before another night."

Except for the boy, the others were stunned. "But, where . . . ?"

"To los Estados Unidos. Where there will no more of all that makes us suffer. Hurry now. You women wrap up everything and bring it out here. We can leave within an hour. Or the lieutenant might return for Neftali."

· *10* ·

Novels of Philosophy and Politics

THE PHILOSOPHICAL NOVEL

The philosophical novel demonstrates an intellectual proposition or a generally philosophical approach to life. Action is minimal and erudite dialogue among the characters is frequent as they search for enlightenment. Many philosophical novels devote much space to discourse that is closer to the imaginative essay than to fiction; for this reason the philosophical novel is often known as the *novel of ideas*. Oscar Wilde's *The Picture of Dorian Gray* (1891), inspired by J. K. Huysmans' *Against the Grain* (1884), analyzes the phenomena of the senses and the qualities of the aesthetic experience as often as it depicts or describes them. Some of the greatest philosophical novels were written by Thomas Mann, including *Doctor Faustus* (1947), *The Confessions of Felix Krull* (1954), and *The Magic Mountain* (1924).

> On the contrary, Naptha hastened to say. Disease was very human indeed. For to be man was to be ailing. Man was essentially ailing, his state of unhealthiness was what made him man. There were those who wanted to make him "healthy," to make him "go back to nature," when the truth was, he never had been "natural." All the propaganda carried on today by the prophets of nature, the experiments in re-generation, the uncooked food, fresh-air cures, sun-bathing, and so on, the whole Rousseauian paraphernalia, had as its goal nothing but the dehumanization, the animalizing of man. They talked of "humanity," of nobility—but it was the spirit alone that distinguished man, as a creature largely divorced from nature, largely opposed to her in feeling, from all other forms of organic life. In man's spirit, then, resided his true nobility and his merit—in his state of disease, as it were; in a word, the more ailing he was, by so much was he the man.

> The genius of disease was more human than the genius of health. . . . Had not the normal, since the time of man, lived on the achievements of the abnormal?

Other examples include Samuel Johnson's *Rasselas* (1759), Jean-Jacques Rousseau's *The New Heloïse* (1760), Goethe's *Elective Affinities* (1808), Honore de Balzac's *The Wild Ass's Skin* (1830), Herman Melville's *Pierre, or The Ambiguities* (1852), Joaquim Maria Machado de Assis' *Epitaph of a Small Winner* (1880), Joseph Henry Shorthouse's *John Inglesant* (1881), Walter Pater's *Marius the Epicurean* (1885), Thomas Hardy's *Jude the Obscure* (1894), George Gissing's *The Private Papers of Henry Ryecroft* (1903), Mikhail Artsybashev's *Sanin* (1907), Thornton Wilder's *The Bridge of San Luis Rey* (1927), Hermann Broch's *Die Schlafwandler* (*The Sleepwalkers,* 1930–1932), Jean-Paul Sartre's *La Nausee* (*Nausea,* 1938), Andre Gide's *Theseus* (1946), Robert Penn Warren's *World Enough and Time* (1950), Simone de Beauvoir's *Les Mandarins* (1954), Albert Camus' *The Plague* (1947) and *The Fall* (1956), Ayn Rand's *The Fountainhead* (1943) and *Atlas Shrugged* (1957), Iris Murdoch's *A Severed Head* (1961), Susan Sontag's *The Benefactor* (1963), Saul Bellow's *Herzog* (1964) and *Mr. Sammler's Planet* (1970), Herman Hesse's *Siddhartha* (1951) and *Steppenwolf* (1968), Walker Percy's *Love in the Ruins: The Adventures of a Bad Catholic at a Time Near the End of the World* (1971), John Fowles' *The Magus* (1965), Milan Kundera's *The Unbearable Lightness of Being* (1984), Cormac McCarthy's *Blood Meridian, or The Evening Redness in the West* (1985), and Umberto Eco's *Foucault's Pendulum* (1988).

A common criticism of philosophical novels is that they are limited because of the demand of their thematic content. The fact that characters must be intellectual and their action relatively obvious in illustrating abstract ideas can have the tendency to alienate the very readership that they are trying to reach. "The chief defect of the novel of ideas is that you must write about people who have ideas to express—which excludes all but about .01 percent of the human race," said Aldous Huxley.

THE POLITICAL NOVEL

The political novel may criticize a particular political system or situation, may advocate any number of political solutions, or may simply describe the politics of a given society. While the political novel may discuss philosophy, it differs from the philosophical novel in that its treatment is less abstract and focuses more on real world events, such as Anglo-Hungarian Arthur Koestler's *Darkness at Noon* (1941), about communist betrayals.

"You have heard the accusation and plead guilty."

Rubashov tried to look into his face. He could not, and had to shut his eyes again. He had had a biting answer on his tongue; instead he said, so quietly that the thin secretary had to stretch out her head to hear:

"I plead guilty to not having understood the fatal compulsion behind the policy of the Government, and to have therefore held oppositional views. I plead guilty to having followed sentimental impulses, and in so doing to have been led into contradiction with historical necessity. I have lent my ear to the laments of the sacrificed, and thus became deaf to the arguments which proved the necessity to sacrifice them. I plead guilty to having rated the question of guilt and innocence higher than that of utility and harmfulness. Finally, I plead guilty to having placed the idea of man above the idea of mankind . . ."

Other examples include Benito Perez Galdos' *Angel Guerra* (1890–1891), a political and religious tragedy; and Benjamin Disraeli's *Coningsby* (1844), Anthony Trollope's *Phineas Finn* (1869), and Alphonse Daudet's *Kings in Exile* (1879), all political romances. Examples of political realism are Ignazio Silone's *Fontamara* (1933) and *Bread and Wine* (1936); South Indian Raja Rao's mythical folk-epic, *Kanthapura* (1937), about the coming of Gandhi's struggle to a typical village; Mexican Agustin Yanez's *Al Filo del Aqua* (1947), another story of small town politics. Other examples are: Yugoslavian Ivo Andric's *The Bridge on the Drina* (1945), a part of a Bosnian trilogy; Gerald Green's *The Last Angry Man* (1957); Allen Drury's *Advise and Consent* (1959); Lagosian Cyprian Ekwensi's *People of the City* (1963), depicting facets of African urban life; South African Peter Abrahams's *A Night of Their Own* (1965); Nigerian Chinua Achebe's *A Man of the People* (1966) and Susan Daitch's *L.C.* (1986). Many novels describe politics without being dominated by the subject. Robert Penn Warren's *All the King's Men* (1946) transcends politics. The milieu depicted in many other novels exists as a consequence of political corruption, as in Norman Mailer's *Why Are We in Vietnam? A Novel* (1967).

"Politics in a work of literature," said Stendhal, "are like a pistolshot in the middle of a concert." (See Irving Howe, *Politics and the Novel*.)

THE THESIS NOVEL

The thesis novel is different from the philosophical or political novel in that it illustrates a rather simple proposition and advocates, at least by implication, a solution to a problem. For this reason, the thesis novel is often called a "problem" novel. The resources of the novel are used to elicit sympathy for an idea about people and institutions and disapproval of conditions that need changing.

Two early examples include Jonathan Swift's *Gulliver's Travels* (1726) and Jean-Jacques Rousseau's *Emile* (1762).

> Even if I considered that education was wise in its aims, how could I view without indignation those poor wretches subjected to an intolerable slavery and condemned like galley-slaves to endless toil?. . . . The age of harmless mirth is spent in tears, punishments, threats, and slavery. You torment the poor thing for his good; you fail to see that you are calling Death to snatch him from these gloomy surroundings.

★ ★ ★

> When our natural tendencies have not been interfered with by human prejudice and human institutions, the happiness alike of children and men consists in the enjoyment of their liberty.

Often thesis novels dramatize a specific social problem and report on it in journalistic detail. The various kinds of thesis novels deliberately set out either to inform and instruct readers to change their picture of man in society and in history or to shock them into corrective acts. These novels satisfy the ancient utilitarian criterion with a vengeance. Providing programs of action, they are useful to political and sociological movements and to individuals. Upton Sinclair's *The Jungle* (1906) is a good example of an American thesis novel.

> There were the men in the pickle-rooms, for instance, where old Antanas had gotten his death; scarce a one of these that had not some spot of horror on his person. Let a man so much as scrape his finger pushing a truck in the pickle-rooms, and he might have a sore that would put him out of the world; all the joints of his fingers might be eaten by the acid, one by one. Of the butchers and floorsmen, the beefboners and trimmers, and all those who used knives, you could scarcely find a person who had the use of his thumb; time and time again the base of it had been slashed, till it was a mere lump of flesh against which the man pressed the knife to hold it. The hands of these men would be criss-crossed with cuts, until you could no longer pretend to count them or to trace them. They would have no nails— they had worn them off pulling hides; their knuckles were swollen so that their fingers spread out like a fan. There were men who worked in the cooking-rooms, in the midst of steam and sickening odours, by artificial light; in these rooms the germs of tuberculosis might live for two years, but the supply was renewed every hour.

Other examples are Olive Schreiner's *The Story of an African Farm* (1883), Harold Frederic's *The Damnation of Theron Ware* (1896), Ivan Bunin's (Alexeiyevich) *The Village* (1910), Italian Corrado Alvaro's *Man Is Strong* (1938), Jose Lins do Rego's *Dead Fires* (1943), Lillian Smith's *Strange Fruit* (1944), Alan Paton's *Cry, the Beloved Country* (1948), John Hersey's *The Wall* (1950), and Ayi Kwei Armah's *The Beautiful Ones Are Not Yet Born* (1968).

The impulse that produces theses novels has resulted in the nonfiction novel. These nonfiction works use the actual facts of history combined with the devices of fiction to produce a strong personal narrative. They tend to offer more subjective insights than a simple historical account. One of the best examples remains Truman Capote's *In Cold Blood* (1966), a true account of a multiple murder and its consequences. Other examples include Hunter S. Thompson's *Fear and Loathing in Las Vegas* (1971), Carl Bernstein and Bob Woodward's *All the President's Men* (1974), Norman Mailer's *The Executioner's Song* (1979), Richard Preston's *The Hot Zone* (1989), Sebastian Junger's *The Perfect Storm* (1997), and Mark Bowden's *Black Hawk Down* (1999).

THE PROPAGANDA NOVEL

A subgenre within the thesis type is the propaganda or polemical novel, a type which is more blatantly rhetorical in the handling of its various elements than the strict thesis novel. The author selects characters and situations to preach a limited point of view, such as a political doctrine. Often its appeal can be only to the already converted, and thus its purpose may be defeated. Two of the most famous and artistically successful examples of this type are still two of the most widely read novels in the history of literature, Harriet Beecher Stowe's *Uncle Tom's Cabin* (1852) and George Orwell's *Animal Farm* (1946).

> Somehow it seemed as though the farm had grown richer without making the animals themselves any richer—except, of course, for the pigs and the dogs. Perhaps this was partly because there were so many pigs and so many dogs. It was not that these creatures did not work, after their fashion. There was, as Squealer was never tired of explaining, endless work in the supervision and organisation of the farm. Much of this work was of a kind that the other animals were too ignorant to understand. For example, Squealer told them that the pigs had to expend enormous labours every day upon mysterious things called "files," "reports," "minutes," and "memoranda." These were large sheets of paper which had to be closely covered with writing, and as soon as they were so covered, they were burnt in the furnace. This was of the highest importance for the welfare of the farm, Squealer said. But still, neither pigs nor dogs produced any food by their own labour; and there were very many of them, and their appetites were always good.
>
> As for the others, their life, so far as they knew, was as it had always been. They were generally hungry, they slept on straw, they drank from the pool, they laboured in the fields; in winter they were troubled by the cold, and in

summer by the flies. Sometimes the older ones among them racked their dim memories and tried to determine whether in the early days of the Rebellion, when Jones's expulsion was still recent, things had been better or worse than now. They could not remember.

Two other examples are Ecuadorian Jorge Icaza's *Huasipungo* (1934), about the enslavement of Indians, and African Bloke Modisane's *Blame Me on History* (1963), a traditional, historical panorama about apartheid.

THE NOVEL OF SOCIAL CRITICISM

The novel of social criticism portrays the effects of a society on its characters, and these portraits tend to be unflattering. E. W. Howe's *Story of a Country Town* (1883) exposes marital betrayal and loneliness in frontier town life. Portuguese Eca de Queiroz's *Os Maias* (1888) depicts in romantic, melodramatic fashion the decadence of upper classes in Lisbon. Two studies of the Russian aristocracy are Ivan Goncharov's *Oblomov* (1858) and Leo Tolstoy's *Anna Karenina* (1873–1877). Fedor Sologub's *The Petty Demon* (1907) is about a paranoid school teacher. James T. Farrell's trilogy *Studs Lonigan* (1932–1935) and Williard Motley's *Knock on Any Door* (1947) depict the way slums turn young men into criminals. Nigerian Alex La Guma's *A Walk in the Night* (1962) demonstrates the relation between criminality and communality, while Erskine Caldwell presents social melodrama in rural settings in *God's Little Acre* (1933) and *Tobacco Road* (1932).

> "I reckon old Jeeter had the best thing happen to him," Lov said. "He was killing himself worrying all the time about the raising of a crop. That was all he wanted in this life—growing cotton was better than anything else to him. There ain't many more like him left, I reckon. Most of the people now don't care about nothing except getting a job in a cotton mill somewhere. But can't all of them work in the mills, and they'll have to stay here like Jeeter until they get taken away too. There ain't no sense in them raising crops. They can't make no money at it, not even a living. If they do make some cotton, somebody comes along and cheats them out of it. It looks like the Lord don't care about crops being raised no more like He used to, or He would be more helpful to the poor. He could make the rich people lend out their money, and stop holding it up. I can't figure out how they got hold of all the money in the country, anyhow. Looks like it ought to be spread out among everybody."

Other examples are Edna Ferber's *So Big* (1924), Irwin Shaw's *The Young Lions* (1948), Japanese Shohei Ooka's *Fires on the Plain* (1951), Mac Hyman's *No Time for Sergeants* (1953), Jose Maria Gironella's *The Cypresses Believe in God* (1953), William Golding's *Lord of the Flies* (1954), and James Ngugi's *Chocolates for My Wife, Slices of My Life* (1961).

THE SOCIALIST NOVEL

The socialist novel, a species of political novel, illustrates the arguments of socialism and usually brings its characters and situations to the dawn of a socialistic era of reform. It is a thesis novel with socialism as the solution. Economics is seen as the source of consciousness in author and hero, and fiction is a weapon in the class struggle. Its end is to show "historical truth." (See Ellmann and Feidelson, *Modern Tradition*.) A good example is Jack London's *The Iron Heel* (1907).

> And through it all moved the Iron Heel, impassive and deliberate, shaking up the whole fabric of the social structure in its search for the comrades, combing out the Mercenaries, the labor castes, and all its secret services, punishing without mercy and without malice, suffering in silence all retaliations that were made upon it, and filling the gaps in its fighting line as fast as they appeared. And hand in hand with this, Ernest and the other leaders were hard at work reorganizing the forces of the Revolution.

Other examples are Edmondo de Amicis' *The Romance of a Schoolmaster* (1876), Isaac Kahn Friedman's *The Radical* (1907), Susan Glaspell's *The Visioning* (1911), Albert Maltz's *The Underground Stream* (1940), Howard Fast's *The Unvanquished* (1942), Ruth McKenney's *Jake Home* (1943), Joseph Freeman's *Never Call Retreat* (1943), Isidor Schneider's *The Judas Time* (1947), and Norman Mailer's *Barbary Shore* (1951).

THE PROLETARIAN OR PROTEST NOVEL

The proletarian or protest novel (a term rejected by most socialist novelists) was mainly an American phenomenon of the 1930s. These novels depict social and economic injustices, reflect a Marxist viewpoint, attempt to make the worker class-conscious, and often end with a violent uprising of the workers. Fiction is used as a weapon in the class war. Few Americans and, ironically, few workers read these novels. A typical example is Michael Gold's *Jews Without Money* (1930).

> And I worked. And my father and mother grew sadder and older. It went on for years. I don't want to remember it all; the years of my adolescence. Yet I was only one among a million others.

A man on an East Side soap-box, one night, proclaimed that out of the despair, melancholy and helpless rage of millions, a world movement had been born to abolish poverty.

I listened to him.

O workers' Revolution, you brought hope to me, a lonely suicidal boy. You are the true Messiah. You will destroy the East Side when you come, and build there a garden for the human spirit.

O Revolution, that forced me to think, to struggle and to live.

O great Beginning!

Other examples include Edward Dahlberg's *Bottom Dogs* (1930), Edwin Seaver's *The Company* (1930), Mary Heaton Vorse's *Strike!* (1930), Maxwell Bodenheim's *Run, Sheep, Run: A Novel* (1932), Catherine Brody's *Nobody Starves* (1932), Grace Lumpkin's *To Make My Bread* (1932), Jack Conroy's *The Disinherited* (1933), Arnold B. Armstrong's *Parched Earth* (1934), Robert Cantwell's *The Land of Plenty* (1934), Albert Halper's *The Foundry* (1934), Edward Newhouse's *You Can't Sleep Here* (1934), Daniel Fuchs' *Williamsburg Trilogy* (1934–37), Fielding Burke's (Olive Tilford Dargan) *A Stone Came Rolling* (1935), Tom Kromer's *Waiting for Nothing* (1935), Henry Roth's *Call It Sleep* (1934), Clara Weatherwax's *Marching! Marching!* (1935), James T. Farrell's *A World I Never Made* (1936), Josephine Johnson's *Jordanstown* (1937), Dalton Trumbo's *Johnny Got His Gun* (1939), Richard Wright's *Native Son* (1940), and Sembene Ousmane's *God's Bits of Wood* (1960). (See Madden, *Proletarian Writers*.)

THE UTOPIAN/DYSTOPIAN NOVEL

Using a combination of fantasy, philosophy, and prophecy, the Utopian novel depicts an ideal society. A novelist may intend this ideal society as a model for actual society, but usually the intention of the Utopian novel is to satirize actual abuses through a contrast between the ideal of the novel and the reality of society. One of the first was Thomas More's *Utopia* (1516), a proto-novel inspired by Plato's *Republic* that claimed to be a true account of the ideal society.

Under such a system, there's bound to be plenty of everything, and, as everything is divided equally among the entire population, there obviously can't be any poor people or beggars. Each town, you remember, sends three representatives to the annual Lietalk, or Parliament, at Aircastle. There they collect details of the year's production, and as soon as it's clear which products are plentiful in each area, and which are in short supply, they arrange for a series of transfers to equalize distribution. These transfers are one-way transactions, requiring nothing in return – but in practice the free gifts that

Town A makes to Town B are balanced by the free gifts that it receives from Town C. So the whole island is like one big household.

Francis Bacon conjured another Utopian vision in *The New Atlantis* (1627). Other Utopian novels include Edward Bellamy's *Looking Backward* (1888), William Morris' *News from Nowhere* (1890), H. G. Wells' *A Modern Utopia* (1905), James Hilton's *Lost Horizon* (1933), Herbert Read's *The Green Child* (1935), Austin Tappan Wright's *Islandia* (1942), and B. F. Skinner's *Walden Two* (1948).

Although these novels present the author's ideas about what the ideal society should be, most Utopian novels actually present Dystopias, societies whose inhabitants believe they are living in an ideal society but are actually being misled. A typical Dystopia tends to present a picture of what society could become if prevailing social practices continue unchecked. George Orwell's *1984* (1949) is prototypical of the Dystopia.

> The voice from the telescreen was still pouring forth its tale of prisoners and booty and slaughter, but the shouting outside had died down a little. The waiters were turning back to their work. One of them approached with the gin bottle. Winston, sitting in a blissful dream, paid no attention as his glass was filled up. He was not running or cheering any longer. He was back in the Ministry of Love, with everything forgiven, his soul white as snow. He was in the public dock, confessing everything, implicating everybody. He was walking down the white-tiled corridor, with the feeling of walking in sunlight, and an armed guard at his back. The long hoped-for bullet was entering his brain.
>
> He gazed up at the enormous face. Forty years it had taken him to learn what kind of smile was hidden beneath the dark mustache. O cruel, needless misunderstanding! O stubborn, self-willed exile from the loving breast! Two gin-scented tears trickled down the sides of his nose. But it was all right, everything was all right, the struggle was finished. He had won the victory over himself. He loved Big Brother.

Examples include Samuel Butler's *Erewhon* (1872), an anagram of "nowhere," Anatole France's *L'Ile des Pinguoins* (*Penguin Island*, 1908), Yevgeny Zamyatin's *We* (written 1920–1921), Aldous Huxley's *Brave New World* (1932), Ray Bradbury's *Fahrenheit 451* (1953), William Golding's *Lord of the Flies* (1954), Anthony Burgess' *A Clockwork Orange* (1962), Pierre Boulle's *Planet of the Apes* (1963), Kurt Vonnegut's *Cat's Cradle* (1963), Stephen King's *The Running Man* (1982), Margaret Atwood's *The Handmaid's Tale* (1985), Neal Stephenson's *Snowcrash* (1992), and Lois Lowry's *The Giver* (1994). Sometimes authors combine elements of both Utopias and Dystopias, as seen in Jonathan Swift's *Gulliver's Travels* (1726).

Ingratitude is among them a capital crime, as we read it to have been in some other countries; for they reason thus, that whoever makes ill returns to his benefactor, must needs be a common enemy to the rest of mankind, from whom he hath received no obligation, and therefore such a man is not fit to live.

★ ★ ★

After this preface he gave me a particular account of the Struldbruggs among them. He said they commonly acted like mortals, till about thirty years old, after which by degrees they grew melancholy and dejected, increasing in both till they came to fourscore. This he learned from their own confession, for otherwise there not being above two or three of that species born in an age, they were too few to form a general observation by. When they came to fourscore years, which is reckoned the extremity of living in this country, they had not only all the follies and infirmities of other old men, but many more which arose from the dreadful prospect of never dying. They were not only opinionative, peevish, covetous, morose, vain, talkative, but uncapable of friendship, and dead to all natural affection, which never descended below their grandchildren.

· // ·

Novels of Psychology

$\mathscr{I}$n contrast to those novels that deal with a character who is typical of his class and who develops in the external context of his social world, the psychological novel analyzes the subjective life of the individual. In these novels, the reader experiences a sense of how the mind and emotions function and the ways in which the characters experience consciousness of themselves; the senses are brought into full play, stimulated as much by memory as by present events. Psychological novels take the reader into the immediate mental processes of their characters, achieving a psychic intimacy. We are given impressions rather than realistic reconstructions of actual life.

In the twentieth century, the psychology of Sigmund Freud and Carl Jung; James Frazer's *Golden Bough* (1890), a study of primitive religion; and the experiments of the French Symbolist poets were especially influential on the psychological and mythical approach to fiction. Writers felt freed by insights into primitive thinking and the social psychology of myth; they saw a special imaginative validity in the form of mythical thought. Carl Jung's concept of the collective unconscious of the race appealed to critics and writers as a way of transcending everyday reality and cutting through traditions. Jung's concept of archetypes and their psychological function in our daily lives gave writers a new way of shaping characters and events. Psychoanalysis indicated that human beings perpetually relive the myths of their race. Modern novelists used Freud's theories as a modern mythology for their fiction that allowed them access to new imaginative types. Myth became modern humanity's memory, and works like Oswald Spengler's visionary interpretation of history, *The Decline of the West* (1918–1922) became possible. In *Freudianism and the Literary Mind* (1945), Frederick J. Hoffmann shows how Freud's concepts are illustrated in works that precede Freud and in many that follow him. Psychological fiction explicitly shows the force of the id, our basic drives, as revealed in dreams and in neuroses. We also see many examples in fiction of sublimation, an expression of censored sexual drives in expenditures of nonsexual psychic energy.

Despite the importance of Freud, Jung, and Frazer to twentieth-century literature, psychological investigation has never been far from the minds of novelists. The more theoretically informed explorations of twentieth-century psychological novels were anticipated by a number of psychological romances including Mikhail Yurievich Lermontov's *A Hero of Our Time* (1839).

> I learned not long ago that Pechorin had died on his way back from Persia. This news gladdened me very much, it gave me the right to publish these notes . . .

★ ★ ★

> While reading over these notes, I became convinced of the sincerity of this man who so mercilessly exhibited his own failings and vices. The history of a human soul, be it even the meanest soul, can hardly be less curious or less instructive than the history of an entire nation—especially when it is the result of self-observation on the part of a mature mind, and when it is written without the ambitious desire to provoke sympathy or amazement.

Other examples of psychological romances include Boccaccio's *L'Amorosa Fiametta* (1340–1345), Benjamin Constant's *Adolphe* (1815), Augustin Charles Sainte-Beuve's *Volupte* (1832), Emily Bronte's *Wuthering Heights* (1847), Nathaniel Hawthorne's *The Scarlet Letter* (1850), Eugene Fromentin's *Dominique* (1862), Gabriele D'Annunzio's *The Triumph of Death* (1894), Alain-Fournier's *The Wanderer* (1913), Joseph Conrad's *Victory* (1915), Liam O'Flaherty's *The Informer* (1926), Hermann Hesse's *Steppenwolf* (1927), William Faulkner's *Sanctuary* (1931), Jean Giono's *Song of the World* (1934), Graham Greene's *The Ministry of Fear* (1943), and Charles Jackson's *The Lost Weekend* (1944).

Developing from these largely symbolic works, came the urge to depict the mind as it actually works. In order to depict mental processes, authors developed various techniques. One method of showing the consciousness of the self was expressionism, a means of expressing outwardly in an exaggerated image or an action what the character feels inwardly. Often expressionism explores the consciousness by stimulating the senses. J. K. Huysmans' *Against the Grain* (1884) makes his character investigate natural sensations and then he creates artificial ones, as another way of knowing one's mind and body and the world outside them. Self-awareness causes awareness of the external reality, and the novelist tries to convey these experiences of consciousness in an epiphany or flow of moments. This type of novel is composed of a series of *gestalts* that become compressed into a single *gestalt* in the reader's own mind. Novelists who use this technique aim for an effect of vitalism that heightens readers' feelings for life. Some examples include Dostoyevsky's *The Brothers Karamazov* (1880), Norwegian Knut Hamsun's *Hunger* (1890), Stephen Crane's *The Red Badge of Courage* (1895), John Dos Passos' *Manhattan Transfer* (1925), Ernest Hemingway's *A Farewell to Arms* (1929), Thomas Wolfe's *Look Homeward, Angel* (1929) and *Of Time and the River* (1935), L. A. G. Strong's *The Garden* (1931), Albert Camus' *The Plague* (1947), and Carson McCullers' *The Heart Is a Lonely Hunter* (1941).

> The hot afternoon passed slowly and Mick still sat on the steps by herself. This fellow Motsart's music was in her mind again. It was funny, but Mister Singer reminded her of this music. She wished there was some place where she could go to hum it out loud. Some kind of music was too private to sing in a house cram full of people. It was funny, too, how lonesome a person could be in a crowded house. Mick tried to think of some good private place where she could go and be by herself and study about this music. But though she thought about this a long time she knew in the beginning that there was no good place.

Other techniques include the interior monologue and stream of consciousness. These attempt to transcribe all the impressions on the mind of the character whether the impressions are conscious or unconscious. First used in Edouard Dujardin's *We'll to the Woods No More* (1887), this technique became popular in the modernist movement and was employed in James Joyce's *Ulysses* (1922), Virginia Woolf's *Mrs. Dalloway* (1925), Conrad Aiken's *Blue Voyage* (1927), and William Faulkner's *The Sound and the Fury* (1929) and *As I Lay Dying* (1930).

In most cases, the goal of most psychological novels has been a realistic depiction of human subjectivity, no matter what technique is employed. Some other examples include Laurence Sterne's *The Life and Opinions of Tristram Shandy, Gent.* (1760–1767), Pierre Choderlos de Laelos' *Les Liaisons Dangereuses* (1782), Fyodor Dostoyevsky's *Crime and Punishment* (1866), *The Possessed* (1867), and *The Idiot* (1866–1869), Ivan Turgenev's *Fathers and Sons* (1862), Juan Valera's *Pepita Jimenez* (1874), Henry James' *The Ambassadors* (1903), Luigi Pirandello's *The Late Mattia Pascal* (1904), Marcel Proust's *Remembrance of Things Past* (1913–1927), Ford Madox Ford's *The Good Soldier* (1915), James Joyce's *Portrait of the Artist as a Young Man* (1916), Sidonie Gabrielle Colette's *Cheri* (1920), Grazia Deledda's *The Mother* (1920), Andre Gide's *The Counterfeiters* (1927), Francois Mauriac's *Therese* (1927), Julien Green's *The Dark Journey* (1929), Antoine de Saint-Exupery's *Night Flight* (1931), George Bernanos' *The Diary of a Country Priest* (1937), Elizabeth Bowen's *Death of the Heart* (1938), William Styron's *Lie Down in Darkness* (1951), Junichiro Tanizaki's *The Key* (1956), John Updike's *Rabbit, Run* (1960),

William Gaddis' *JR* (1975), Susan Daitch's *L.C.* (1986), Stephen King's *Gerald's Game* (1992), Daniel Clowes' *Ghost World* (1993), Nick Hornby's *High Fidelity* (1995), Chuck Palahniuk's *Fight Club* (1996), Maria Amparo Escandon's *Esperanza's Box of Saints: A Novel* (1999), and Virginia Woolf's *To the Lighthouse* (1927).

> No, she thought, putting together some of the pictures he had cut out—a refrigerator, a mowing machine, a gentleman in evening dress—children never forget. For this reason, it was so important what one said, and what one did, and it was a relief when they went to bed. For now she need not think about anybody. She could be herself, by herself. And that was what now she often felt the need of—to think; well, not even to think. To be silent; to be alone. All the being and the doing, expansive, glittering, vocal, evaporated; and one shrunk, with a sense of solemnity, to being oneself, a wedge-shaped core of darkness, something invisible to others.

The modern novel began with an interest in private, subjective experience. Marcel Proust and others made a new start. Novel reading itself is a private experience, intensified when one reads psychological analyses of private experience. The extreme expression of this impulse in fiction is an unconscious art that is closer to myth and magic, and is thus more public, than to realistic depictions of behavior. This art is irrational, emotional, spontaneous, and feeds on unfettered memory and imagination. And the form it takes resembles the processes of the mind itself.

· *12* ·

The Pure Novel

A Not-Yet-Realized Type

Two kinds of writers have written about two general types of artists. In *The Birth of Tragedy,* Nietzsche describes two kinds of "art-drives": "the Apollonian," which represents culture, civilization, classicism, reason, the artificial in art, but a kind of healing vision; and "the Dionysian," which represents anarchy, primitive instincts, unleashed psychic energy, nature, the senses, ecstasy, orgiastic outpourings, intoxication, narcosis, romanticism. Many writers try to achieve a synthesis of this dichotomy. The spectacle of the Dionysians has inspired the belief even among artists that the will to art is unnatural; certain Apollonians argue that art is more artifice than "real" experience.

Although some writers and critics see the imagination and nature in conflict, most argue an interaction; too much stress on the role of nature in artistic creation has caused periods of revolt against nature. The relation between imagination and thought reflects Nietzsche's dichotomy: art should produce doubt not certainty; it should draw no conclusions; some even argue that it should not transmit ideas. Keats proposed a "negative capability." There has been a perpetual argument over the importance of style as opposed to subject, and whether style should be simple or magnificent; the Apollonian insists that the style should be appropriate to the subject; thought and expression should be harmonious with each other. Vorticism was a classical revival in poetry by T. E. Hulme in 1914 that affected attitudes about fiction.

The two kinds of artists argue about rules, laws, precepts, principles, the Apollonian insisting that rules set limitations which free the artist and that classical works are the source of these rules; the Dionysian rebels against all rules as unnatural inhibitors of freedom and decries the slavish limitation of the classics. Romantics follow nature, not rules. Georges de Scudery argues for rules: "The works of the spirit are too significant to be left to chance; and I had rather be accused of having failed consciously, than of having succeeded without knowing what I was about." Discipline more than inspiration produces great art. The Apollonian knows that, as novelist Sean O'Faolain says, "the art of writing is rewriting." He or she knows that all art is by its nature artificial, that what seems to be natural today will appear artificial in the future; a work of art is an artifice by definition. But the Dionysian declares that any kind of artifice destroys the illusion of reality, whether it is internal or external. To the romantic, formal excellence is no criterion for art. In opposition to the classic demand for balance, he may strive for deliberate imbalance. The classicist would strive for purgation of all impure feelings and thoughts; the romantic immerses himself in such elements and absorbs them into his being. To the classicist, excellence of expression is sublime; but the romantic reaches back and forth across the spectrum from the sublime to the ridiculous. He strives not to arrange aesthetic pleasure for a spectator, but rather to engage a reader so fully as a co-creator that he experiences aesthetic joy rather than repose.

The desire to create a pure novel is a classical or Apollonian impulse. The pure novel strives to create a world as constricted as a lyrical poem. Flaubert aspired to write a novel with no people in it. A product of the art-for-art's-sake sensibility, the pure novel depends as little as possible on any carry-over into the real world; it tries to contain every aspect of the experience within the work itself: "The pure novel (and in art, as in everything else, purity is the only thing I care about)," says Gide's writer-hero in *Les Faux Monnayeurs* (*The Counterfeiters*, 1925). The French popular novelist, Georges Simenon, whom Gide admired, said, "I would like to carve my novel in a piece of wood." Simenon continues:

> The "pure" novel will do only what the novel can do. I mean that it doesn't have to do any teaching or any work of journalism. In a pure novel you wouldn't take sixty pages to describe the South or Arizona. . . . Just the drama, with only what is absolutely part of this drama. What I think about novels today is almost a translation of "the rules of tragedy into the novel."

Simenon believes that the novel, like tragedy, should be short enough to enable a reader to absorb it in one sitting. It should be, one might add, as brief as a movie and as unified in its effects and impressions as a poem.

The novels of James M. Cain suggest that the novel should raise and answer its own necessary questions and depend as little as possible upon anything beyond the bounds of its own immediacy. All fictive elements should effect one clean, simple thrust, as do the first twenty-three pages of *The Postman Always Rings Twice,* Cain's nearest realization of the "pure" novel.

> Then I saw her. She had been out back, in the kitchen, but she came in to gather up my dishes. Except for the shape, she really wasn't any raving

beauty, but she had a sulky look to her, and her lips stuck out in a way that made me want to mash them in for her . . .

I took her in my arms and mashed my mouth up against hers. . . . "Bite me! Bite me!"

I bit her. I sunk my teeth into her lips so deep I could feel the blood spurt into my mouth. It was running down her neck when I carried her upstairs.

★ ★ ★

I was in my room when he drove off, and I turned around to dive down in the kitchen. But she was already there, standing in the door.

I went over and looked at her mouth. It was the first chance I had had to see how it was. The swelling was all gone, but you could still see the tooth marks, little blue creases on both lips. I touched them with my fingers. They were soft and damp. I kissed them, but not hard. They were little soft kisses. I had never thought about them before. She stayed until the Greek came back, about an hour. We didn't do anything. We just lay on the bed.

Like a piece of music, a "pure" novel should be an experience that has rhythm, tempo, style, movement, pattern, motif; it is generated by time or pace, following (to use a term from drama) a "spine."

While the novelist, by the very nature of his medium, cannot entirely avoid making moral and social value judgments, writers in one tradition have tried since Flaubert, Valery, and Verlaine to make the novel or the poem as "pure" a work of art as a statue. For instance, in Rodin's sculpture we find subject and treatment; but form and space provide the most exciting aspects of the experience. Stephen quotes Aquinas in Joyce's *Portrait of the Artist as a Young Man*: "That is beautiful the apprehension of which pleases." Necessary to aesthetic stasis are "wholeness, harmony, and radiance." Is it possible for a novel to possess any of these qualities to the extent that the plastic arts—and also those forms devoid of apparent subject matter, music and architecture—do? Stephen argues that "art necessarily divides itself into three forms, progressing from one to the next"—the lyrical, the epical, and the dramatic, "the form wherein [the artist] presents his image in immediate relation to others." It is to this last, and finest, form that the "pure" novel belongs. "Pure" means to the novel what "nonobjective" means to painting. To paraphrase Archibald MacLeish, a pure novel should not *mean* but *be*. The serious reader returns to Cain's *The Postman* not for its meaning, or even for its characters, but to experience *again* an aesthetic emotion. He regards thought and content as seriously as he would if he were looking at a loaded gun on a table.

The artistic novelist sometimes tries to achieve parallels or analogies with other arts. "All art," said Walter Pater, "aspires to the condition of music." Artistic success often proves to be in areas common to all or most arts anyway; what is called musical structure in certain novels is really a property of literature it-self, simply used more deliberately. "What I should like to do is something like the art of fugue writing," said Gide's author/character in *Les Faux Monnayeurs*. "And I can't see why what was possible in music should be impossible in lit-erature . . ." Painting, drama, and poetry also have provided forms that en-hanced the artistic novel.

The poetic novel is mainly a use of language and imagery as concentrated as poetry: Lautreamont's (Isidore Lucien Ducasse) *Maldoror* (1868–1869). Many novelists have wanted most of all to be poets (Thomas Hardy, Thomas Wolfe). While few poets have wanted to be novelists, several poets have written good novels: e.e. cummings' *The Enormous Room* (1922), an autobiographical work, Conrad Aiken's *The Great Circle* (1933), William Carlos Williams' *White Mule* (1937), Lawrence Ferlinghetti's *Her* (1960). Tennessee Williams—primarily a playwright—has written many short stories but only two novels, *The Roman Spring of Mrs. Stone* (1950) and *Moise and the World of Reason* (1975). Some nov-elists have written works with the care and precision of the best modern po-etry: Virginia Woolf, *The Waves* (1931). And Flaubert saw affinities between his classical sort of fiction artist and the scientist; the novel should become as ob-jective and precise as science.

Ever since the English poet Swinburne defiantly and proudly asserted the importance of "art for art's sake," there has been a misunderstanding about this phrase even though few writers ever repeated it approvingly. The popular image became that of the artist in his garret or ivory tower. Swin-burne was mainly arguing against the prevailing insistence that literature convey a moral; Baudelaire called this moral imperative "the heresy of di-dacticism." Both Dionysian and Apollonian writers have taken this attitude about art: that it is something that has a value in itself. For the classicist, art is an objective artifact, impersonal, held in stasis; for the romantic, it is the product of individual, personal, subjective, spontaneous expression of one's inner being.

Few novelists have thought of themselves as aesthetes. Oscar Wilde did, and he has expressed the art-for-art's-sake philosophy best: "Art never expresses anything but itself." "The only beautiful things are the things that do not con-cern us." "Life imitates Art far more than Art imitates Life." "Lying, the telling of beautiful untrue things, is the proper aim of Art."

Art-for-art's-sake, the image of the aesthete writing from an ivory tower (or a grimy garret), disdainful of any audience but himself, and possibly his friends, expresses a hostility to conscious art as it if were a threat to life itself. But if life is superior, why read at all? Some writers have considered "style as absolute"; they are not far from primitive conceptions of creation or from the Christian "in the beginning was the Word." Many people feel that a work of fiction must justify its existence by being something more than a pleasure achieved through hard work by both creator and perceiver; it must perform some utilitarian function, from bearing ideas about the "real" world to providing escape from it. Reacting against this demand, some writers have tried to achieve pure poetry, pure fiction, with as few extensions beyond itself as possible—a self-contained experience, like nonobjective painting. But unlike geometrical shapes and colors, words are not pure abstractions.

A little more acceptable is the conviction that art transforms the world into a greater reality. Poems, says poet Marianne Moore, are "imaginary gardens with real toads in them." Gatsby—Fitzgerald's creation—is larger than all his real-life models put together; he transcends mortality and will live forever in Fitzgerald's work of art, *The Great Gatsby* (1925); so will Huck Finn; and not just characters, but places: Joyce's Dublin, Dickens' London, Faulkner's Mississippi; and moments such as Don Quixote attacking the windmills, Gatsby's reunion with Daisy, Meursault confronting the Arab, Jake Barnes fishing at Burgette, Heathcliff at Cathy's deathbed. Human beings' ability to make things makes them human; their ability to transform things makes their potential for transcendence palpable.

From this attitude evolved a kind of "aesthetic mysticism," the notion of art as an aristocratic mystery. (See Ellmann and Feidelson, *Modern Tradition*.) Flaubert said to despondent Guy de Maupassant, "Sacrifice everything to Art." Some call this attitude, at its worst, snobbery; the writer writes for him- or herself and/or perhaps for a small knowing group who are better than the average reader, the vulgar public; serious writing versus commercial writing; and the snob takes pleasure in being one of the elite. The classical writers pictured the ideal, or proposed at least a reaching for it, and they created a love of the ideal itself as art embodied it; the romantic yearned to achieve an ideal state of consciousness and express it in all its frenzy. Perfection, though perhaps unattainable, was the end of learning, and the purpose of literature, said the classicist, is to show perfection of character. Out of this attitude was bound to come the concept of the autonomy of art, of purity, of the nondidactic, and of the notion of the permanence of art and the aesthetic principles that produced it and of the true and the good portrayed in it; a work's likelihood to have permanence was a sign of greatness. Though they longed for some sort of spiritual transcendence, the romantics were just as concerned with the imperfect and the transient.

Around the turn of the century, for both Apollonian and Dionysian, art became a modern absolute. Aesthetic quality came to have a moral dimension after all, for we judge artistic fiction good if its authors or characters revere the aesthetic experience and if the book is aesthetically fine. For art transforms life and such a transformation is a moral act improving life. It is art that establishes certain values. Art is an ethical experience, perhaps even a religious experience; certainly, some writers seem to have been prophets. "To be hopeful in an artistic sense," said Conrad, "it is not necessary to think that the world is good."

II

THE ART OF FICTION

*H*enry James said that we must grant the writer his *donnee,* that is, the basic materials he starts with and the technical approach he takes. We may quarrel only with the way he handles the elements he has chosen. James implies, rightly, that any form, any content is admissible to the house of fiction, within its million windows. Few critics seriously disagree. Critics only seem—to each other as well as to their readers—to be prescriptive in their theories. There are conventional techniques (once experimental, now assimilated into the tradition of the novel) and there are experimental or special techniques. The two often intermingle in today's novels, as in Thomas Pynchon's *Gravity's Rainbow,* John Barth's *Giles Goat-Boy,* David Madden's *Bijou,* and David Foster Wallace's *Infinite Jest.* Eclecticism, a fusion of diverse techniques, less than tradition or experimentalism, characterizes fiction today.

A study of techniques entails a study of all the other arts, for techniques and terms from one are often appropriated by others. The novel is so lacking in terms of its own origination that, more than any other art form, it draws heavily on others for devices to create and words to describe its own processes. And because, more than any other form, all life is its province, some assert that the novel cannot, in fact, be an art, except in isolated instances—for instance, a short novel such as *The Great Gatsby.* The novel, they maintain, is some other kind of experience, not inferior to art forms, simply different. But let us continue to speak of the novel as an art form.

A technique is any method a writer uses, consciously or unconsciously, to stimulate a response in his reader. In the broadest sense, technique is the combination of methods a writer uses to present his raw material. "Literature," said the French symbolist poet Paul Valery, "is the art of playing on the minds of others." On that assumption, Wayne C. Booth wrote one of the great works of fiction theory, *The Rhetoric of Fiction*. The rhetoric of fiction is a congeries of techniques that enable the writer to persuade his reader to accept the world he is creating and to respond to it in the way he wishes, with the purpose of achieving maximum effects on all levels of the experience.

The term *style* is sometimes used to include technique. One hears of a particular writer's style in this sense more often than his technique. Style differs somewhat from technique in that style, the arrangement of words for specific effects, is the medium through which techniques are employed. Style is one aspect of the larger realm of technique. But if style is taken to mean the author's handling of words, and technique to mean his handling of all facets of the work, then style is included in the concept of technique.

Novelist-critic Mark Schorer said in "Technique as Discovery," perhaps the single most influential essay in modern criticism: "When we speak of technique, then, we speak of nearly everything. For technique . . . is the only means" the writer "has of discovering, exploring, developing his subject, of conveying its meaning, and, finally, of evaluating it." Dostoyevsky recognized his own limitations in that respect: "Yes, that was and ever is my greatest torment—I never can control my material. . . . I have allowed myself to be transported by poetic enthusiasm." Philip Rahv ("Fiction and the Criticism of Fiction") expresses a point of view in opposition to Schorer's and to all New Critics. Dostoyevsky's greatness, he says, lies not in his style but in his scenes, in the kind of life-experiences that revitalized narrative fiction in the early realistic phases of the development of the novel. What matters, he says, is realistic detail more than aesthetic form, which is too often discussed in terms of poetry, thus impeding our understanding of the nature of fiction. What is most important in Proust is sensibility, not a learned technique. There is too much emphasis on interpretation, on locating symbols, which some seem to think demonstrates excellence in a work, says Rahv; the life forces in a novel, which encourage contrary reactions, are neglected because aesthetic elements lend themselves more readily to critical analysis.

It is true that discussions of technique predicate, to some extent at least, the viability of aesthetic constants, values, rules, and norms out of great traditions, and of criteria in relation, as Booth says, to author, reader, and the work itself. But that point did come when *someone* devised a few concepts, deriving them in part from the Classical tradition that nurtured him: "I am, in reality, the founder of a new province of writing," said Henry Fielding, "so I am at liberty to make what laws I please therein." Some of the criteria that have evolved are appropriateness, consistency, simplicity (or complexity, depending on other factors), subtlety, whether to *tell* in narrative summaries or to *show* in dramatic scenes, and the importance of avoiding anachronisms. There are many ways to see techniques at work in a novel. One might begin by reading the author himself as he discusses the germination and development of his own work. (See *Novelists on the Novel,* Allott, ed.)

As a demigod creating a world, the writer must exert *control* over all the elements of his creation. To most writers, this control means being critically conscious at some crucial stage in the process of composing the novel. "Interest in the technicalities of his art can alone prevent the mind dulling, the imagination losing power," said Graham Greene ("Fiction," *The Spectator*). Other writers regard control as dishonest, unnatural; in their own way, they are being true to fact, that is, to life as it is lived. The other kind of writer is being true to art, an artificer in his own right, not an unconscious mirror or an ape of god.

Some writers mistake the notion of control for lack of freedom. For them freedom is, or ought to be, the natural state of humanity; therefore, to write out of this freedom is to depict people as they are, deep down, or should be once again—natural people, feeling what comes naturally. Such writers must pretend that they are not using mechanical symbols, such as words, as the essence of their creation, and that they are free of the influence of everything they have ever read that works differently from their own writing. The conscious artist, on the other hand, does not deny influences, nor even that imitation contributes to his formation (Faulkner admitted the influence of Conrad and Thomas Wolfe). The artist is in control because he knows what he creates, and he creates deliberately. He or she does not mistake self-discipline for externally imposed discipline, or self-control for external control. Freedom lies in being able to control whatever creation one chooses to become engaged in. "Be always faithful to the conception of a limit," said T. E. Hulme.

The writer takes no risks when he thinks of himself as totally free. And it is only in taking risks within a context of self-imposed control that one sees all the possibilities of one's material and avoids missing opportunities for creating effects that reveal the deepest essence of one's subject. Such a writer shares with the reader his pleasure in skillfully executing his mastery. In willfully choosing not to be in control, a writer becomes a slave to chance, sometimes with very interesting results, it must be admitted; and the controlled artist may sometimes end in controlling only a robot. But generally when we examine a good novel, we find that what is good in it is the result of control.

Technique enables a writer to discover possibilities in his raw material that would otherwise remain submerged in it. Raw material is the subject matter the writer processes through imagination, conception, and technique into a story. "By raw material," says Wright Morris, "I mean that comparatively crude ore that has not yet been processed by the imagination—what we refer to as life, or as experience, in contrast to art. By technique I mean the way the artist smelts this material down for human consumption. . . . Technique and raw material are dramatized at the moment that the shaping imagination is aware of itself" (*The Territory Ahead*). Specific techniques may be most naturally appropriate for transforming a particular kind of raw material. In *The Field of Vision*, Morris used a multiple point of view technique to transform the fragments of his raw material.

The raw materials of a work are drawn from nature and society; the author must be true to nature and to life in his or her society even as he or she reconceives and re-creates it in his or her imagination, which is a recombining agent that makes a new perspective or vision occur (Melville and, recently, Gabriel Garcia Marquez). Even when it must operate within the strictest externally or internally imposed limitations, what holds a reader is the author's imagination and his techniques for conceptualizing those elements he expects will make us feel his imagination at work. "The materials have to take the place of God," said Sherwood Anderson.

It is not enough to be in control of the elements of one's creation; one must also achieve a *conception* about the entire body of raw material out of which one creates. Content with random effects and sensations and bizarre images, the spontaneous writer never strives for a conception. While it is true that "there is nothing in the intellect that is not first in the senses" (Aristotle), it is also true that "feeling does not make poetry" (Flaubert). Conception is a willed act of intelligence wedded to imagination.

The opposite of a conception is a *notion,* the kind of clever premise that comes often and easily to the inventive mind. A notion can usually be formulated in the question: "What would happen if . . . ?" A notion is a launching pad. Most stories begin with a notion; many never transcend notion into the realm of conception.

A genuine conception offers the reader a different kind of experience. An intuitive fusion of emotion and idea produces a conception. A conception is a total, gestalt-like grasp of the story that enables the author to control the development of the situation, the characters, theme, plot, style, and technique so that in the end they cohere, as in a single charged image. A concept orders, interprets, and gives form to the raw material of the story and infuses it with vision and meaning. Notion-mongering freezes the imagination and many opportunities are missed; a conception frees it to explore all possibilities. This fusion of raw material, imagination, and conception is best seen today in the nineteen novels of Wright Morris. His concept of the hero and the witness is at work not only in his own novel, *The Field of Vision,* but also in *Don Quixote, Moby Dick, Lord Jim, The Great Gatsby, All the King's Men, The Heart Is a Lonely Hunter, A Separate Peace,* and *One Flew Over the Cuckoo's Nest.* In the conceptualizing process, intuition remains important, as expressed by F. Scott Fitzgerald: "All good writing is swimming under water and holding your breath."

The kind and degree of distance between the writer and his raw material and between the reader and the experience the novel offers determine a great deal. There are several kinds of distance: perceptual, conceptual, psychic, aesthetic, authorial, tonal, time and space, social, moral, and emotional. A novel may suffer if the distance is too near, or too far.

The author's attitude determines the distance he has from his material. A writer's attitude toward his raw material or his subject is revealed in the *tone* of his narrative voice. "Everything is in the tone," said Sherwood Anderson, whose own was generally that of the old-fashioned teller of tales. The pervasive tone of a work can be tragic, comic, ironic, skeptical, pessimistic, compassionate, sentimental, and so on. The author's distance in relation to his story affects his tone. It is important that the tone be appropriate to the kind of experience a writer is trying to create. Compare the satirical with the lyrical attitude: the one is relatively cold, far, and formal, the other warm, near, and intimate. A writer can hardly create a tragedy if she is too close to her characters; intimacy may produce pathos, or even bathos, instead of tragedy. Distance is greater in the comic than in the serious novel.

Aesthetic (or psychic) distance is a theatrical term that refers to the degree of objectivity audience and writers have toward the characters and the action. Paradoxically, by being removed, we are able to experience more intensely, but without losing our ability to see the action in some larger perspective. Some writers want to destroy this distance and immerse the reader, while some want to widen it even further with alienation effects to achieve didactic aims. Aesthetic distance (a tautology since "aesthetic" originally meant distance) is achieved through the techniques of art as perceived, intellectually and emotionally, by the reader.

Flaubert argued that the master writer, as a pure creative force, must, like the architect and the composer, achieve an impersonal relation to his or her creation. "The less one feels a thing, the more likely one is to express it as it really is." Joyce put this attitude of detachment into an epigram: "The artist, like the God of creation, remains within or behind or beyond or above his handiwork, invisible, refined out of existence, indifferent, paring his fingernails." The writer's field of consciousness may be narrow, constricted (Joyce's *Portrait of the Artist as a Young Man*) or extensive (Joyce's *Ulysses*), promoting subjectivity or objectivity; the degree will produce different kinds of work. In the 1830s, the French Parnassians Victor Hugo, Alfred de Vigny, Alphonse de Lamartine, Theophile Gautier insisted on an objectivity that would produce poetry as impersonal as sculpture; the English Parnassians Algernon Swinburne and Edmund Gosse of the 1870s kept this attitude in force, and it affected some fiction writers.

Every writer is stretched on a rack, some on the rack of their own subjectivity, others on a rack especially designed by them to produce a transcendent agony. The subjectivity rack produces the inspiration fallacy or the conviction that the writer is able to plug into the Muses' Switchboard and receive inspiration from a divine power source. Such writers often seem obsessed with what Plato called "poetic madness." Although Wordsworth spoke of "emotion recollected in tranquility," the Romantics made frequent use of the Muses' Switchboard. On the me-rack, writers, especially young writers, sacrifice themselves to the two-headed god subjectivity/self-expression. The hysterical discovery of the obvious fallacy follows from the conviction that the axis of the universe is the author's own navel. And on a broader plane, me-rack writings produce the fallacy of expressive form, the conviction that if the writer's feelings are sufficiently intense their reflection in the work will be a true expression of those feelings. Readers often distort a novel or poem by insisting that such and such is the poet's real intention. Writers themselves sometimes work out of mistaken intentions. The compulsion to re-port on actual events results in the it-really-happened fallacy. There is an even greater suffocation of imagination in the it-really-happened-to-*me* fallacy.

The writer who places great value on intuition or inspiration as opposed to the rational working out of a novel belongs to a category that includes many fine novelists (Thomas Wolfe, Henry Miller, and Louis-Ferdinand Celine). Certainly most novelists write their first drafts spontaneously, in response to in-tuition. Many finished novels include bursts of lyricism, stretches of seemingly spontaneous writing, and the effect is dramatic immediacy, which creates and sustains the illusion of reality: the author, or the character, is really, right now, feeling this way. "The sudden gut joy of beer when the visions of great words in rhythmic order all in one giant archangel book go roaring thru my brains" (Jack Kerouac, *The Subterraneans*). But the writer who is primarily lyrical or subjective places great value on spontaneity as a sign of sincerity, as opposed to fabrication or calculation; he refuses to alter the product of that spontaneous process. In a few cases, that process produces some fine, though limited, writ-ers. The reader's interest, however, is less aesthetic than biographical: she wants to see what Jack Kerouac or Thomas Wolfe is really like, through exposure to the uninhibited action of naked consciousness. Or the reader simply enjoys the sensation of seeing a sensitive person's emotions reacting to life's erratic events.

The notion of spontaneous creation as a virtue and a value is restricted almost entirely to certain modern types of painting, dance, sculpture, poetry, and fiction. Few people want to live in a spontaneously built house or sit on a spontaneous chair or fly in a spontaneous airplane. But they like to feel that there is some area of human experience where spontaneity is possible and vi-able. Writers and readers sometimes make a cult of spontaneity and attempt to carry it over into a lifestyle; they often make the discovery that life is where it works best, and give up writing and reading altogether. Ken Kesey stopped writing after his second novel *Sometimes a Great Notion* (1964). The charge is often made that this sort of creation is self-indulgent, a form of daydreaming, a charge few young writers seldom make, however, engaged as they are in that sort of writing. For the uninitiated reader, the result of self-indulgence is obscurity and irrelevance. The author of free writing claims an unearned relevance to the lives of others; in the '60s, nothing was considered more relevant than freedom of expression itself, regardless of content or excellence. But other writers claim that the best moments of literature are the product of self-imposed discipline in solving problems posed by a combination of externally and self-imposed limitations; the result is freedom of a different sort.

Lack of control often produces ambiguity. Ambiguity occurs in a novel when an element (statement, action, or symbol, for instance) lends itself to more than one interpretation. Ambiguity is the result of unresolved conflicts between one possibility and another, as in the endings of *A High Wind in Jamaica* by Richard Hughes and *Lord of the Flies* by William Golding. Sometimes a style may be characterized as frequently ambiguous—unintentionally, if the writer is unaware of what he is doing and lacks control; deliberately, if he wants the reader to explore possibilities and experience the tensions among them, causing a deeper involvement in the story and thus a more lucid revelation perhaps at the end (Faulkner's *Light in August*). Unintentional ambiguity results in obscurity; it is often the result of confusion in the author's mind as to the meaning of his ideas or of inability to express his ideas clearly. Uncontrolled ambiguity promotes a kind of subjectivity in the reader by encouraging him to merge with the author (usually subjectively involved himself) and the characters (usually self-reflective).

Sometimes the writer lacks distance on his material because the subject itself overwhelms him. When the artist or the hack is so bemused by the timeliness, the controversy, the strangeness, the importance, the subjective relevance of his raw material that he neglects the mysterious dictates of art, he is in the act of writing a *subject-dominated* novel (Madden, *Poetic Image in Six Genres*). The writer is so overwhelmed by his subject, which may be an idea or a thesis, or something more spectacular, such as sex, war, or dope, that he is blind to the problems of craft that must be solved if the novel is to be a work of the imagination, a work of art. Overwhelmed by his vision of a reform or his awareness of his reader's given interest in his subject, he neglects the art of handling that subject in novelistic terms. The naturalists fostered the notion that the writer's function is to reproduce "a slice of life." The imitation fallacy assumes that art and life are synonymous.

The process is, however, marvelously reciprocal, for life imitates art quite frequently, and sometimes quite terrifyingly. The writer who is a creator does not praise her work because it is "just like life," but because it heightens our awareness of ordinary life; she does not claim that the events in her novel "really happened," but that they "really happened in my imagination." In Ralph Ellison's *Invisible Man,* one of the most successful novels about African Americans in the North and the South, outrage has been refined into art. Ezra Pound said, "Literature is news that stays news." Sensational subject matter is not enough.

With or without the effects of aesthetic distance, every novel provides a perspective on life, and some achieve a larger dimension by creating some context of myth, religion, philosophy, history (Scott's *Heart of Midlothian*), science, mysticism, or social significance (the naturalists). *Allusion* is one device that enables the writer to evoke an added dimension. An allusion is a reference to a person, event, or aspect of culture that a writer assumes most of his readers will recognize. A literary allusion may evoke a familiar line from a poem, or a character from a novel or play. Some of the effects in the novels of Cocteau and Joyce, Camus' *The Fall*, Walker Percy's *The Moviegoer*, depend upon such allusions. "No, I am not a spook like those who haunted Edgar Allan Poe," says the narrator of Ralph Ellison's *Invisible Man*. Fiction casts a spell most intensely when the reader feels that the illusion which fiction seeks to create and the larger dimensions that emanate from it come from a master faculty or dominant psychic state, which we sense, for instance, in Faulkner, but not in Truman Capote. Most successful works of the imagination, however, do succeed at least in giving us a sense of mystery, wonder, exhilaration, and in satisfying the curiosity they stimulate in the reader. And the kind, quality, and degree of all these elements are determined by varieties of distance.

Let us look at some of the techniques writers have at their command. Techniques are used, of course, in combinations; thus a novel cited to illustrate one technique may serve just as well for others. No novel embodies all techniques to the same degree or in the same way; some are emphasized more in one novel than in another; not every novel utilizes them all.

A study of technique has the same general usefulness for the reader as for the writer—it provides a guide to understanding what makes a novel express what it does. Each reader, each writer, must make his or her own use of these techniques, in his or her own way. Most of the techniques discussed apply to other forms of writing, and in different ways to other art media. And most of the techniques apply just as well to a study of the short story—both for readers and writers—as they do to a study of the novel. Some of the concepts discussed here—conflict, characterization, theme—are elements of fiction rather than techniques, but they are best examined in the process of talking about techniques.

It must be reiterated that the effects of techniques being described here operate at best unconsciously upon the reader, though the more receptive (because perhaps better trained) reader will be aware of some of these effects as he reads. Not all good novels strive for, or create, these effects, but they are at work to some degree in all fiction.

· 13 ·

Point of View

$\mathcal{T}$he reader responds to the voice of a creator, surrenders herself to an authority. Where does that authority, the author, stand in relation to her work? The writer uses many techniques that are artificial, but her purpose is to create an illusion of reality. The writer must make technical choices. And the technique that most directly affects the choice and use of all others is *point of view*. Everything in a novel is told through a certain point of view from which the writer decides to tell the story.

There are three major types of point of view: omniscient, first person, and third person/central intelligence. The omniscient narrator is godlike; the narrator sees, hears, feels, knows all; she moves anywhere she wishes, in time and space, giving us objective views of her characters' actions, or subjective views of their thoughts. The omniscient narrator tells us her story in the third person. Tolstoy's *Anna Karenina*:

> Happy families are all alike; every unhappy family is unhappy in its own way.
> Everything was in confusion in the Oblonsky household. The wife had discovered that the husband was carrying on an affair with their former French governess, and she had announced to her husband that she could not go on living in the same house with him. This situation had now lasted three days, and not only the husband and wife, but also all the members of their family and household, were painfully conscious of it. Every person in the house felt that there was no sense in their living together, and that people who met by chance in any inn had more in common with one another than they, the members of the Oblonsky family and household. The wife did not leave her own room; the husband had not been home for three days. The children ran wild all over the house; the English governess quarreled with the housekeeper, and wrote to a friend asking her to look out for a

new position for her; the chef had walked out the day before just at din-
nertime; the servants' cook and the coachman had given notice.

Other examples of novels using the omniscient point of view are: Henry Fielding's *Tom Jones*; Laurence Sterne's *Tristram Shandy*; William Thackeray's *Vanity
Fair*; Anthony Trollope's *Barchester Towers*; Nikolai Gogol's *Dead Souls*; Honore
de Balzac's *Pere Goriot*; Charles Dickens' *A Tale of Two Cities*; George Eliot's *Mill
on the Floss*; George Meredith's *The Ordeal of Richard Feverel*; Ivan Turgenev's
Fathers and Sons; Sherwood Anderson's *Poor White*; E. M. Forster's *Howards End*;
John O'Hara's *Appointment in Samarra*; and Allen Wier's *Tehano*.

In the first-person point of view, the author surrenders part of his control
over the elements of the story by allowing one of the characters to tell it. We
experience only what that character sees, hears, feels, knows, while the author
works in the background. The character-narrator combines his own subjective
thoughts and feelings with his role as omniscient storyteller. Hemingway's *The
Sun Also Rises*:

> "Don't be sentimental."
> "You make me ill."
> We kissed good night and Brett shivered. "I'd better go," she said. "Good
> night, darling."
> "You don't have to go."
> "Yes."
> We kissed again on the stairs and as I called for the cordon the concierge
> muttered something behind her door. I went back upstairs and from the
> open window watched Brett walking up the street to the big limousine
> drawn up to the curb under the arclight. She got in and it started off. I
> turned around. On the table was an empty glass and a glass half-full of
> brandy and soda. I took them both out to the kitchen and poured the half-
> full glass down the sink. I turned off the gas in the dining-room, kicked off
> my slippers sitting on the bed, and got into bed. This was Brett, that I had
> felt like crying about. Then I thought of her walking up the street and step-
> ping into the car, as I had last seen her, and of course in a little while I felt
> like hell again. It is awfully easy to be hard-boiled about everything in the
> daytime, but at night it is another thing.

Other examples of first-person point of view are: F. Scott Fitzgerald's *The Great
Gatsby*; Ford Madox Ford's *The Good Soldier*; Daniel Defoe's *Moll Flanders*;
Mark Twain's *Huckleberry Finn*; and W. Somerset Maugham's *The Razor's Edge*
(in which Maugham is not only the narrator but a character, under his own
name, as well). As a means of controlling (and thus releasing) the tremendous
romantic-demonic energy of Heathcliff and Cathy, Emily Bronte uses two
other characters as first-person narrators. A male voice, Mr. Lockwood's, frames

the story, most of which Nellie Dean tells. Bronte moves from Lockwood's to Nellie's voice in this passage from *Wuthering Heights*:

> She returned presently, bringing a smoking basin, and a basket of work; and, having placed the former on the hob, drew in her seat, evidently pleased to find me so companionable.
>
> Before I came to live here, she commenced—waiting no further invitation to her story—I was almost always at Wuthering Heights . . .

The third-person/central intelligence point of view is a combination of omniscient and first person; this point-of-view technique allows the reader to experience everything from inside a single character, but the story is told in the third person; all the elements are filtered through a single character (the central intelligence), revealing his personality. James Joyce's *Portrait of the Artist as a Young Man*:

> It was not thought nor vision though he knew vaguely that her figure was passing homeward through the city. Vaguely first and then more sharply he smelt her body. A conscious unrest seethed in his blood. Yes, it was her body he smelt: a wild and languid smell: the tepid limbs over which his music had flowed desirously and secret soft linen upon which her flesh distilled odour and a dew.

Other examples of third person/central intelligence include Henry James' *The Ambassadors*, John Cheever's *Falconer*, Truman Capote's *Other Voices, Other Rooms*, Graham Greene's *The Heart of the Matter* (with a few shifts to other characters for contrast), and Frederick Buechner's *A Long Day's Dying*.

In both the first-person and third-person/central intelligence points of view, the author works outward from inside the character; it is through that character's perspective that the elements of the story are worked out.

In many novels, several point of view techniques are used in combination: Charles Dickens' *Bleak House*, William Faulkner's *The Sound and the Fury*, Wright Morris' *The Huge Season* and *Cause for Wonder*.

Because it most directly affects the choice and use of all other elements, point of view is the most important technique. In the creative process, a writer may ask himself: Is this the best point of view for the story I want to tell? Does the choice itself mean something or is it arbitrary? What are the consequences of this choice, affecting character creation, character relationships, what the reader sees and feels, the style, and so on? What is the psychological effect of telling this story in the third person as opposed to letting a character tell it in his own voice? What are other possible points of view and their effects? The student of fiction may ask similar questions about the finished work.

The major fallacy from which all other fallacies spring is the point of view fallacy. If the writer uses poor judgment in his choice of the point of view through which the elements of his story are presented or if he mishandles the one he chooses, he sets up a chain reaction that demolishes most of his carefully prepared intentions and effects. The reader may commit a similar fallacy if he fails to identify and follow the workings and implications of the author's point of view technique.

The writer who is in control of his material strives to make the point of view consistent. He takes care not to attribute to a character things he could not know, think, or feel; nor does he attribute an unlikely vocabulary to his character (unless deliberately, for a special effect, as in Faulkner's *As I Lay Dying*). He avoids jumping from one character's mind to another's without careful transition or without re-orienting the reader. The writer does not allow the reader to become confused as to whose evaluation of events he is getting. Whatever type of narrator the writer chooses—whether active agent in the story or mere passive observer, the reader must feel that the point of view through which the story is filtered is the inevitable one.

Each type of point of view allows the writer its own particular freedoms and imposes its own particular limitations. Unless he intrudes in his own voice to make a pact with his reader that he is going to limit his vision, the omniscient narrator is obligated to tell all because he sees and knows all and can go anywhere. But he can so ingratiate himself with his reader that he is not reproached for withholding information or failing to render a scene which the reader knows he can render. The classic authors spoke directly to the reader. "Our doctrine is," said Trollope, "that the author and reader should move along together in full confidence with each other." The omniscient narrator may provide us with privileged information, though it can never be total. "It is hardly necessary that I should here give to the public any lengthened biography of Mr. Harding, up to the period of commencement of this tale" (Anthony Trollope, *Barchester Towers*).

The third-person/central intelligence method provides us with inside views; the stream of consciousness technique provides the deepest view of the character's thoughts and feelings; the roving, omniscient narrator strives for balance between interior and exterior views of his characters.

The omniscient author intrudes to make explicit authorial comments, analyses, and judgments and manipulates the reader intellectually and emotionally, *telling* him in generalized commentaries instead of *showing* him in dramatic scenes, or the author may intrude his judgments with relative subtlety or even deviousness. The history of the novel reveals a pattern of emphasis on either telling (Tolstoy's *Anna Karenina*) or showing (Hemingway's *The Sun Also Rises*), on rendering experiences in terms of scenes or on telling in passages of summary. The emphasis today is on dramatic narration, conveying a sense of events happening now, not told as having happened in the past. Wayne C. Booth would like to see more novels using a combination of scene and summary.

A distinction is also made between *story* and *plot*. A story is what happens; that is the conventional, rather mechanical notion of plot, also. But Ronald Crane argues that plot "is the particular temporal synthesis of the elements of action, character, and thought that constitute the matter of" the "writer's invention. . . . There are, thus, plots of action, plots of character, and plots of thought." Crane advocates "the more specific kind of criticism of a work that takes the form of the plot as its starting point and then inquires how far and in what way its peculiar power is maximized by the writer's invention and development of episodes . . . his handling of diction and imagery, and his decisions as to the order, method, scale, and point of view of his representation" ("The Concept of Plot").

Authorial intrusion can provide relief from dramatic pacing, and perform many other functions, such as enabling the author to cover a great deal of important but nondramatic territory through generalization enlivened with the author's distinctive first-person voice. Until recently, modern writers, critics, readers generally objected to the commentary approach because it shattered the illusion that real people are involved in a real event; unity also is shattered because a reader must re-orient himself each time a shift is made from dramatization to commentary. Wayne C. Booth argues that the narrating voices of Thackeray and Fielding, for example, must be taken as creations of the authors, just as Becky Sharp and Tom Jones are creations. A distinction must be made between the writer and her literary projection of herself; her voice is this second self. It is not the real-life voice of Faulkner that the reader listens to; unconsciously, sometimes deliberately, the writer creates a persona, a mask, or second self, which determines the level or depth of the relationship between narrator and reader. This voice provides the reader with perspectives on the story. There are varying degrees of intimacy between reader and narrator, between the author and her second self, and between the second self and her characters.

This implied author comes through in her technical choices, such as point of view and style, if not in commentaries; the reader who experiences the richer context of the actual and the implied authors, and the tensions between them and himself, develops a deeper interest in the novel. The reader himself becomes a different "mock reader" with each novel (even each novel by the same author) he reads. We pretend to be someone else in response to the author's assumptions about her ideal reader.

Traditionally, either the first person (a character as narrator) or the omniscient (the author as narrator) was used. In a way, the first-person narrator has as much mobility and freedom and as much license to comment on the action as the omniscient narrator. The omniscient point of view was most appropriate and effective in times when the author might pretend to know all, to be the creator of the world he described, as Dickens could. Today's writers, feeling that to pretend to know all is an impertinence, specialize in select areas, and use the mind of a single character through which to reveal this select area of experience to the reader. Thus, the first-person and third-person/central intelligence points of view are favored today. William Gaddis in *The Recognitions* is one of the few contemporary writers who can move from the mind of one character to another and also give an omniscient, panoramic view of all history and the contemporary scene as well.

The first-person narrator may be a witness or a participant in the story he tells. He soliloquizes to a clearly identified or implied or ambiguous audience, which is usually physically present. "Really, *mon cher compatriote,* I am grateful to you for your curiosity. However, there is nothing extraordinary about my story" (Albert Camus, *The Fall*). Or he writes his story, for readers generally: "So I'm in the death house, now, writing the last of this, so Father McConnell can look it over. . . . If they get me, he's to take it and see if he can find somebody to print it" (James M. Cain, *The Postman Always Rings Twice*).

James Joyce borrowed the interior monologue (daydream, reverie) technique from Edouard Dujardin (*We'll to the Woods No More*, 1887), then modified and perfected it in *Ulysses*.

> I'm going to have a splendid time. Now why is the stair carpet turned up at the corner here? A grey patch on the line of upward red, on the red strip looping up from step to step. Second storey; the door on the left. *Office*. I only hope he hasn't gone; no chance of running him to earth if he has. Oh well, in that case, I'd go for a stroll down the boulevard. No time to lose; in! The outer office. Where is Lucien Chavainne? The huge room ringed with chairs. There he is, leaning over the table; overcoat and hat on; he's arranging some papers with one of the clerks; seems in a hurry. Over there the library of blue files, rows of knotted tapes. I pause on the threshold. A great time I shall have telling him all about it! Chavainne looks up; he sees me. Hullo! . . .
>
> Mr Bloom entered and sat in the vacant place. He pulled the door to after him and slammed it tight till it shut tight. He passed an arm through the armstrap and looked seriously from the open carriage window at the lowered blinds of the avenue. One dragged aside: an old woman peeping. Nose whiteflattened against the pane. Thanking her stars she was passed over. Extraordinary the interest they take in a corpse. Glad to see us go we give them such trouble coming. Job seems to suit them. Huggermugger in corners. Slop about in slipperslappers for fear he'd wake. Then getting it ready. Laying it out. Molly and Mrs Fleming making the bed. Pull it more to your

side. Our windingsheet. Never know who will touch you dead. Wash and
shampoo. I believe they clip the nails and the hair. Keep a bit in an enve-
lope. Grow all the same after. Unclean job.

The history of art is full of such instances; the innovator is obscure, while the
man who best uses the discovery becomes famous. Another early practitioner
was Dorothy Richardson (*Pilgrimage*).

There is a difference between the stream of consciousness technique and
the interior monologue. The term stream of consciousness was coined by
William James to describe a psychological phenomenon. (For the distinction,
see Humphrey's *Stream of Consciousness in the Modern Novel*.) Pure instances of
the stream of consciousness technique are few; Joyce's *Ulysses* is classic, particularly the Molly Bloom soliloquy at the end.

> . . . a quarter after what an unearthly hour I suppose they're just getting up
> in China now combing out their pigtails for the day well soon have the
> nuns ring the angelus they've nobody coming in to spoil their sleep except
> an odd priest or two for his night office the alarm-clock next door at cock-
> shout clattering the brains out of itself let me see if I can doze off 1 2 3 4
> 5 what kind of flowers are those they invented like the stars the wallpaper
> in Lombard street was much nicer the apron he gave me was like that some-
> thing only I only wore it twice better lower this lamp and try again . . .

Stream of consciousness and interior monologue techniques are ways of getting
at the character's subconscious; in a way, the reader feels that the writer is trying to tell him the news about the way the mind works (just as Defoe told in
authentic detail the way a plague spreads). Another device for opening up the
unconscious through free association (in this instance, the author's) is automatic
writing, a random stream of words that come directly from the writer's own
subconscious. Some of Gertrude Stein's writings seem to have been affected by
her experiments in automatic writing. There are few instances of novels produced solely by automatic writing, though some may have started that way.

Each type of narration imposes limitations upon the writer, but he can
sometimes turn those limitations to his advantage. For instance, the first-person narrative is limited to those things the character has witnessed himself or
that have been reported to him; he cannot get into the minds of other characters as the omniscient (god-like, all-knowing) narrator can. But his narration is
dramatically immediate (as all quoted speech is) and thus has great authority:
"And I only am escaped to tell thee," says Ishmael (quoting Job) in *Moby Dick*.

The author himself is most absent in the first-person narration, in which
he impersonates one of his own characters, ventriloquizing his voice. The author may exit in other ways. Influenced by Henry James (*The Ambassadors*) and

Flaubert (*Madame Bovary*), to some degree, a great many writers have favored the third-person/central intelligence or center of consciousness method. In the language of his second self, the author paraphrases the narration from the mind of a main character; we see only what the character sees. To use James' phrase, the character is a reflection, not a straight teller of incident. The advantage of consistency of point of view is that we experience everything through the character's own mind and emotions with greater intimacy and intensity. But this method is dramatically weak because we cannot see the character himself in action; he is often a creative witness to an action involving characters more dramatic than himself; he remains physically passive and almost invisible. In *The Great Gatsby,* Nick Carraway is such a character:

> I wanted no more riotous excursions with privileged glimpses into the human heart. Only Gatsby, the man who gives his name to this book, was exempt from my reaction—Gatsby, who represented everything for which I have an unaffected scorn. If personality is an unbroken series of successful gestures, then there was something gorgeous about him, some heightened sensitivity to the promises of life.

"As to making known my own opinion about the characters I produce," said Flaubert, "no, no, a thousand times no!" The author must efface himself, he must be invisible and his voice must be neutral, silent, impartial, impersonal, disinterested; as much as is humanly possible, he must not take sides with one character against another and he must refuse to respond to and express attitudes about every passing controversy or social issue. "It is one of my principles that one must not write oneself into one's work," said Flaubert. "The artist must be in his work as God is in creation, invisible yet all-powerful; we must sense him everywhere but never see him." This camera-eye objectivity can never be total, of course. And the authorial silence may result in a dialogue with the reader, based on the reader's ongoing interrogation of the author's quietly implied attitudes.

The nature of fiction is to feign, to dissemble, to create a figment. Still critics have always fought over the question of whether the writer should give himself free reign or impose restrictions. Involved with this question is the problem of sincerity as a criterion of excellence; again, some critics declare that the writer's personal sincerity does not matter; the work is what it is and the critic's criteria must determine only how good it is. Wayne C. Booth, in his major contribution to criticism, *The Rhetoric of Fiction,* raises the old question again. He feels that the modern overuse of the first person and the central intelligence method creates a fallacious, even immoral, ambiguity. A famous short story example is Ring Lardner's "Haircut." Too often the author's tone is misleading and the relationship between the character's perceptions and an implied reality is so heavily ironic that the reader can never know what the author's own true feelings are, and thus the reader is left without a frame of reference within which to evaluate the character's behavior. Other critics argue that in leaving moral issues unresolved, modern writers are being true to the spiritual, intellectual, and moral temper of our times, which is relativistic, situational, and, unlike that of the early novelists, nonabsolute. Booth objects mainly to the degree of lack of control over the reader's moral responses, for surely the writer herself is not as undecided as her novel seems to be.

In novels in which several points of view are separately, and still objectively, presented, the problem of unreliability (if it is indeed a problem) is improved or worsened to the extent that the writer is committed to a relativistic view. Aldous Huxley asks, Why not let there be more than one or two implied novelists in a single novel? (See *Point Counter Point*.) While there are few examples of this multiplicity of authorial second selves, there are many novels in which objective and subjective points of view are presented along a continuum, with frequent shifts. A matrix of points of view is used in the works of Wright Morris, especially in *The Field of Vision*. He shuttles back and forth among five different characters, at least five times each, rendering their points of view in third person. The end of one character's vision impinges upon the beginning of the next, as in this example. McKee's point of view ends: " 'Well, here we are, Lois.' he said, opened the door, then just stood there, a smile on his face, waiting for what he knew she would say." Lois's point of view begins: " 'If anything should happen to that boy—' she said, and saw his mouth pucker, like a hen's bottom." Other examples of novels that use a matrix of points of view are: Virginia Woolf's *To The Lighthouse* (quite similar to *The Field of Vision*), Faulkner's *The Sound and the Fury* (three very different first-person narratives, ending with the author's omniscient point of view), Djuna Barnes' *Nightwood*, Carson McCullers' *The Heart Is a Lonely Hunter*, Shelby Foote's *Shiloh*, and William March's *Company K* (a short novel that uses 113 points of view). (See Percy Lubbock, *The Craft of Fiction*; Norman Friedman, "Point of View in Fiction"; Wayne C. Booth, "Distance and Point-of-View"; Scholes and Kellogg, *The Nature of Narrative*; Moffett and McElheny, *Points of View*; Wallace Hildick, *Thirteen Types of Narrative*).

• *14* •

Story

$\mathcal{W}$hat is it that is being structured, controlled, and formed through the point-of-view technique? A story or plot of some kind, or a process (usually psychological). The traditional writer has a compulsion to tell a story in response to the universal plea, "Tell me a story." There is a primitive urge to respond to that craving, and the writer becomes conscious of his craft to tell a story well or many stories in many different ways. Isaac Singer (*The Slave*) is a recent writer for whom story telling is a compulsion. "The eagerness of a listener quickens the tongue of a narrator" (Bronte, *Jane Eyre*). Recently, the emphasis has been on a conscious desire to bring order to chaos. This impulse is natural in a time when the more technological progress we achieve the less social cohesion we experience. But from the start, the telling of stories has been a form of play, and the impulse to play has struggled continually with the compulsion to use the story for more "serious" purposes.

Stories first became stylized and serious with *myths,* which are based on events far out of reach of memory, the original inspiration having been exaggerated out of all realistic context. The *tale* bears some resemblance to possibility. Myths are inspired partly by a religious impulse to embody in human action supernatural forces. Tales and legends answer to a desire to express the hope that humans can become more than themselves physically, in their struggle against nature and other humans in brute encounters. Modern novelists have tried to give their novels mythic and epic dimensions in various ways: by parallel, for satirical purposes (Joyce's *Ulysses*), by sheer size or scope (Tolstoy's epic *War and Peace*), and by mythic patterns (Lockridge's *Raintree County*).

Many stories of the ancient past were tales. Americans and Russians returned the world to that stage because they re-enacted before the eyes of the world stages through which Europe had already passed. Tales remained the nar-

rative form of ancient civilizations such as India, China, Japan, until they became forcibly westernized. In America, the tall-tale came into being, inspired
by the mysteries of a new life in a new land. These were mixed with elements
from the tales of kings and heroes of the old countries to form the tall-tales
about Mike Fink, the personal tall-tales of Davy Crockett. The tale of Beowulf
kept the community together with a code; the tall-tale's absurd, bitter humor,
often black and irreverent, sustained the frontiersman living in isolation from
communities.

The novel is the story of humanity in a way that history isn't; it is an
affirmation of the everyday human experience in a way that the romance tale
isn't. The novel tells the story of that which would seem to have no story. For
a story was originally conceived as being the narrative of an extraordinary
event as in myths, legends, tales. But there is nothing extraordinary about
Pamela or Moll Flanders or Tom Jones, except that their creators managed to
interest us in them quite as much as listeners of old were absorbed in the legendary exploits of Beowulf.

The art of narrative has been part imitative, part inventive or fabricative
from the beginning—in the oral tradition on up through the poetic to the dramatic to the prosaic and the cinematic. This is the way it happened to Beowulf,
as retold by me, says the *scop*, even as he vows to tell it the way it was told to him.

Narrative is not a special characteristic of the novel; all other fictive and
factual forms, and even the dance and fine arts, employ narrative. But the novel
handles narrative in its own way and each word used to delineate that narrative
must, because of the high signative nature of words, with their several denotative and many connotative meanings, evaluate the narrative. The novel's words
evaluate in a way that, compared with poetic narrative, is, apparently, straight-
forward. Poetic devices tend more obviously to embellish the narrative poem.

Some writers of fiction have managed to break out of the purely narrative thrust of words. There is something too nearly inevitable and fatalistic,
maybe masochistic about stark narrative. "Story is the spoiled child of art," said
Henry James. Writer and reader reach for a more human dimension in those
techniques that allow for something more. "What I should like to do is to
write a book about nothing," said Flaubert, "a book which would have hardly
any subject. . . . That is why there are neither good nor bad subjects . . . from
the point of view of pure art, there are none at all, style being itself alone an
absolute way of looking at things." So stories aren't the only subjects of novels. "His childhood and youth alone is enough to provide a born novelist with
an immense amount of literary nourishment," said Francois Mauriac.

There has always been debate about the subjects of narrative. The classical
attitude is that some subjects are unworthy of treatment; there are important
and there are trivial subjects, and the work is judged accordingly. But again, as

James argued, "We must grant the artist his subject, his idea, his donnee; our criticism is applied only to what he makes of it." There has been a debate as to whether the events in a narrative should be credible, possible, probable, or whether the incredible should also be treated. The romance treats the incredible occasionally, but the province of the novel is indeed the credible, sometimes made marvelous. The novelist strives for verisimilitude—a sense of reality, not necessarily an exact imitation of it.

• 15 •

Characters

*A*ccording to Novalis, the German romantic, "Character is destiny." It is upon characters that most stories concentrate. In fact, many novels take their titles from their main characters, as in *Moll Flanders, Madame Bovary, Don Quixote, Gargantua, Tom Jones, Tristram Shandy, Young Werther, Sister Carrie, Studs Lonigan, Eugenie Grandet, Lord Jim, Huckleberry Finn, Augie March, Anna Karenina, Oliver Twist, The Great Gatsby,* and others too numerous to list. But in a good story it is not what happens *to* a character or what he *does* that matters. Most important is what he *feels* and *thinks,* the effect upon him of what happens to him or of what he does or thinks; and more important is the ultimate meaning or implication of his problem. A character is revealed in action. "Character is action." Fitzgerald hung that statement on the wall in the room where he wrote. In a good novel action and character are so interrelated that the character is action—neither means much without the other.

Action need not be only physical—it may be psychological as well. Thus, we need to understand what motivates a character. The success of most stories depends upon the degree to which we are able to achieve *empathy* (put ourselves in his place) with the character. If we empathize with a character who is having a hard time, the effect may be pathos. We feel what he feels because for the moment we are the character for whom we have empathy.

First the writer, then the reader may ask: Is the main character well-developed; does he grow; does he experience some change in his circumstances, his attitude; do his personality and his actions affect others? Are any of the characters not fully enough explored? Are relationships among them clear? If the answers to these questions are not clear, then characterization has failed. As Hugo von Hofmannsthal said, "Characters without action are lame, action without characters blind."

101

Characterization is the creation of imaginary people through descriptions of physical appearance, actions, speech, thoughts, or what other characters say or think about them. The early heroes were exemplars, who taught by example. They personified such traits as are found in allegories like dignity, nobility, honor, and patience. The traditional concept of character saw conflict mainly in terms of two different kinds of characters opposing each other: protagonist (hero) and antagonist (villain). Today all characters are guilty, no one is entirely innocent, so individuals are seldom one way or another, although recently the concept of the Establishment or the system has become so strong that anyone who represents the Establishment is a villain who victimizes the often passive main character. Conflict is dissolved into ways of coping with Systems managed by tainted people. But most often the main character is his own antagonist. He is caught up in a conflict of ideas or a conflict within his own psychological make-up. Hermann Hesse's *Steppenwolf*:

> There was once a man, Harry, called the Steppenwolf. He went on two legs, wore clothes and was a human being, but nevertheless he was in reality a wolf of the Steppes. He had learnt a good deal of all that people of a good intelligence can, and was a fairly clever fellow. What he had not learnt, however, was this: to find contentment in himself and his own life. . . . It might . . . be possible that in his childhood he was a little wild and disobedient and disorderly, and that those who brought him up had declared a war of extinction against the beast in him . . .

W. J. Harvey in his essay "Character and the Context of Things" points out that serious fiction tells us more about characters than we ever know of real people or want known about ourselves, and this function of literature makes some people uncomfortable—they turn to escape fiction. Fiction gives us both intrinsic and contextual knowledge of people. Generally, the realistic novel has dealt with typical characters who must seem natural to the reader; naturalness is a criterion of quality in such works. Characters and their backgrounds must be particularized, individualized while remaining typical.

E. M. Forster thought in terms of flat and round characters. The flat characters are there to help round out the more fully developed ones. The flat isn't the same as the stock or the stereotyped character, which often destroys verisimilitude. Everything about them has been shaped in previous novels, good and bad. A stereotype is a character or situation that has been overused in life or in fiction. The stereotype is cut to a pattern or conforms to a formula that seldom varies. The shootout between the sheriff and the outlaw in front of a Western saloon is a stereotypical situation involving stereotyped characters. A stereotypical character is like a cliché expression. The serious writer generally strives to create real, complex people, not literary stereotypes. Of course, in modern fiction, the alienated, super-sensitive character is a cliché, but the best writers present him in a new light. Stock characters populate the popular novels in stereotyped situations. A stock character is always in stock, available immediately to any writer on demand; the good writer resists the temptation to take one out of stock; she tries to invent her own or re-imagine or resurrect stereotypes. The popular writer earns his royalties by satisfying his mass readers' desire for the same characters and situations, depicted through a set formula.

"Character types" is a different term. These may be found in any novel; the question of stereotypes comes up when the types are handled unimaginatively. Dickens was a master at handling a gallery of character types, and some of his combinations are with us today. *Bleak House*:

> The old gentleman is rusty to look at, but is reputed to have made good thrift out of aristocratic marriage settlements and aristocratic wills, and to be very rich. He is surrounded by a mysterious halo of family confidences; of which he is known to be the silent depository. There are noble mausoleums rooted for centuries in retired glades of parks, among the growing timber and the fern, which perhaps hold fewer noble secrets than walk abroad among men shut up in the breast of Mr. Tulkinghorn. He is of what is called the old school—a phrase generally meaning any school that seems never to have been young—and wears knee-breeches tied with ribbons, and gaiters or stockings. One peculiarity of his black clothes, and of his black stockings, be they silk or worsted, is, that they never shine. Mute, close, irresponsive to any glancing light, his dress is like himself. He never converses, when not professionally consulted. He is found sometimes, speechless but quite at home, at corners of dinnertables in great country houses, and near doors of drawingrooms, concerning which the fashionable intelligence is eloquent; where everybody knows him, and where half the Peerage stops to say "How do you do, Mr. Tulkinghorn?" he receives these salutations with gravity, and buries them along with the rest of his knowledge.

Ficelle is James' term for the confidante whose questions, as in a play, draw out the first-person/narrator or one whose own knowledge of events is limited; the omniscient author has less need of such a character. A *pawn* is a character whose only purpose is functionary. A *protatic* character is brought in only once for a specific use and then dropped. The *card* is an eccentric character who doesn't change; oddly enough he may be remembered more vividly than the hero—Dr. Pangloss more than Candide. A *fragrant* character is one whose influence is pervasively felt even though he may seldom appear directly. Gran'-paw McDaniel dominates, unseen, in David Madden's *Cassandra Singing*:

> Then Momma turned to Lone. "Son, you just don't know what that old man's done to us *all* without even comin' near us. All those years Coot tried

to make a farm to please his daddy, and then that hateful thing just went in the house when he saw who it was comin' up the path."

"Well, you needn't git on that," said Coot.

"You," she said, turning on Coot, "ain't never done a single thing in all your life without it somehow aimed to please your daddy. And knowin' how the old man hates the very sight of you."

"It's not Gran'paw's fault, Momma!" Lone wanted to keep Gran'paw separate from Coot and Momma, and even from Cassie.

"You don't know a thing about him—never even seen him."

"We used to dream up stuff about him all the time," said Cassie. "Want to hear my best song about him?"

"Least he stays up on Black Mountain," said Lone. "Where he don't bother and he ain't bothered." Lone knew that Gran'paw lived in a cove at the foot of Big Black Mountain, but he always thought of him as standing on the top—highest point in Kentucky—five thousand feet above Harmon.

Some modern novelists like to deal in archetypes. These are types of human roles that have always existed and are described by Jung as Mother, Father, Son, Daughter, Priest, Mentor, Authority Figure. By making his reader feel the presence, subtly at best, of archetypes, the writer gives his characters stature-by-association and expands the dimensions of his work. (See Northrop Frye, "The Archetypes of Literature.") D. H. Lawrence tried to present his characters in generalized somewhat archetypal terms but with other qualities. "You musn't look in my novel for the old stable ego of the character. There is another *ego*, according to whose action the individual is unrecognizable, and passes through, as it were, allotropic states."

The creation of character does not depend upon the writer's having a good memory of fascinating people he has known. "If I spoiled the portrait of old La Perouse," says Gide, "it was because I clung too closely to reality." Jean-Paul Sartre has argued that characters should be totally free of any of society's preconceived schemes of order, even if the author accepts those schemes. The novels in which they thrive should seem to be natural objects, not planned artifices; the reader is just as free.

There is less emphasis today on the creation of characters who interact with each other out of something known as character. Personality, a relatively superficial quantity, is more often the focus. The novel attempts more now to render states of being, attitudes. Readers often wish they could know more fully the people who have these states of being. The novel becomes a graph of the author's, and at best the reader's, own state of being. As writers came more and more to feel that character was a protean phenomenon and that there was no such thing as human nature and that people behave irrationally as often as not, they began to de-emphasize the dramatization of *motive* and examine psychological processes instead. Jean-Paul Sartre's *Nausea*:

The thing which was waiting was on the alert, it has pounced on me, it flows through me, I am filled with it. It's nothing: I am the Thing. Existence, liberated, detached, floods over me. I exist.

I exist. It's sweet, so sweet, so slow. And light: you'd think it floated all by itself. It stirs. It brushes by me, melts and vanishes.

Gently, gently. There is bubbling water in my mouth. I swallow. It slides down my throat, it caresses me—and now it comes up again into my mouth. Forever I shall have a little pool of whitish water in my mouth— lying now—grazing my tongue. And this pool is still me. And the tongue. And the throat is me.

Characters lost individual characteristics as the anti-hero came into vogue; our interest was directed not so much to the formation of character as to the deformation by environment of anonymous creatures with little will or volition, moving about in a vaguely defined world. Franz Kafka's K in *The Trial* is less real and less fully delineated than his predicament. Often in such novels the main character is the only character at all well defined; others merely reflect some facet of the main character, who very gradually takes shape in the reader's mind. We gain insight into other characters indirectly.

Early readers turned to the novel to learn why people behave as they do, and to experience the behavior of people different from themselves. Today's reader knows far too much about psychology and sociology to depend as much on the novel. The novel must present human behavior from radically new perspectives, by ordering in various combinations the chaos of sensory perception, for instance. Thus, motivations are not given or dramatized so much as symbolically embodied or suggested or abstractly objectified, through such techniques as impressionism and expressionism; juxtaposition and montage of character and narrative fragments replace the sequential rendering of character in action.

But the prevalent attitude, even today, is that characters should be well-articulated, in terms of their idiosyncrasies and eccentricities. The reader is interested to know and to experience that character's motivations for choosing— or refusing to choose. A character makes choices and thus so must his creator, and the reader's interest lies in following the consequences of those choices.

· *16* ·

Conflict

*I*n one form or another, conflict energizes every work of fiction. Traditionally, the conflict is between two people. But if a conflict is seen as a struggle between two opposed forces, it may take many forms: a character may have an external conflict with another character, a group, or with society or nature in general. Willard Motley's *Knock on Any Door*:

> Nick walked into the courtroom. His head was up, his shoulders back, his chin in, his long lashes drawn halfway down over his eyes. The crowd gawked. He enjoyed their staring eyes, their mouths held open a little, their silence and attention. He swaggered toward his chair at the counsel table. The news photographers started taking pictures of him. He grinned broadly.
> I didn't know I was such a big shot!

Or he may have an internal conflict within himself between two opposed attitudes. Graham Greene's *The Heart of the Matter*:

> But human beings were condemned to consequences. The responsibility as well as the guilt was his—he was not a Bagster: he knew what he was about. He had sworn to preserve Louise's happiness, and now he had accepted another and contradictory responsibility. He felt tired by all the lies he would sometime have to tell: he felt the wounds of those victims who had not yet bled.

Identification of the conflict helps the reader to comprehend everything else in a story. Minor conflicts may enhance the major conflict. As *complications* accumulate, these conflicts, usually in a story that has a *beginning* (introduction of the problem), *middle* (development of the problem through complications), and an *end* (*denouement*) or climax, will further sustain interest through suspense:

106

what happens next, will the hero survive, how will it all end? The climax of a story comes at that point when the complications of the *plot* are most fully developed and a resolution of the problem is in sight. Each episode or scene may have its own climax. When a story depends heavily upon suspense for its effects, the climax is especially intense. Some stories reach a quiet, subtle, almost submerged climax. Conflict, *tension,* and suspense are sometimes confused as being very much the same. They are not, though they do enhance each other.

Suspense for its own sake has come to be regarded as a cheap device for holding a reader, and is dependent upon a mechanical plot line. Suspense, allied with raw curiosity, is the province of popular fiction. Some writers deliberately destroy suspense to force the reader to pay attention to other values in the novel, such as the quality of experience for its own sake, rendered in a complex way, from which suspense would only distract the reader. Nevertheless, the psychological satisfaction of suspense has not been fully explored by critics or writers, while most readers go on hungering for it. It is still used as an attention-getter in serious works that deliberately omit other major elements, such as dramatic event or character development, as in, for instance, some of the French novels of the fifties and sixties.

Some readers are often less interested in the present moment, which the artist tries to arrest and present as fully as possible, than in plunging ahead into the future—to arrive at the denouement or resolution often is his goal, and the satisfaction of having all his anticipations consummated in the end is very great. As he brings the development of one episode to an end, a writer may introduce an element that anticipates an episode to come. The writer may satisfy that anticipation immediately or he may deliberately frustrate it for an even more interesting effect. The reader then expects that a certain event or development will occur. Indications or suggestions of what is to come are often called *foreshadowing* or *plants.* But in many recent novels a dramatic resolution may precede the opening of the novel, and subtler, more complex resolutions, ideological or aesthetic, may be striven for in the work, as in the novels of Wright Morris (*The Deep Sleep*, for instance). Just as the reader enjoys deviations from the main line of developments, some writers delight in departing altogether from conventional expectations; and there are those readers who feel that the richer experiences are those that these deviations produce. But such novels are dependent upon the prior existence of conventional novels from which writer and reader collaborate in departing.

• *17* •

Time-Space

*C*haracter relationships and conflicts occur in a time scheme and in a space pattern. The type of point of view used will determine the kinds of time and space patterns that emerge. Novelists pay little attention to the ancient quarrel in drama over the three unities (action, place, and time), but those three major elements are interwoven in different ways in fiction, and point of view is the dynamic medium in which a different unity is achieved; the mind of the narrator discovers relationships among all facets of those three elements. Each novel has its own spatial and temporal pattern or principle of organization; the possible varieties are infinite. Edwin Muir points out that in the dramatic novel time flies; we have a sense of time running out to the end. In the novel of character, time moves slowly; characters seem beyond time and change, deathless. (See Muir, *The Structure of the Novel*.)

In some of the finest modern novels, the characters achieve a deeper sense of self through their conscious involvement with time and space, as do Quentin in Faulkner's *Absalom, Absalom!* and *The Sound and the Fury*, Jack Burden in Robert Penn Warren's *All the King's Men*, Darley and Pursewarden in Lawrence Durrell's *The Alexandria Quartet*, and Gerard in Jorge Semprun's *The Long Voyage*. In a note to the second novel in *Alexandria Quartet*, Durrell describes his intention:

> A four-decker novel whose form is based on the relativity proposition.
>
> Three sides of space and one of time constitute the soup-mix recipe of a continuum. The four novels follow this pattern.
>
> The three first parts, however, are to be deployed spatially . . . and are not linked in a serial form. They interlap, interweave, in a purely spatial relation. Time is stayed. The fourth part alone will represent time and be a true sequel.
>
> The subject-object relation is so important to relativity that I have tried to turn the novel through both subjective and objective modes.

108

"A story," said E. M. Forster, "is a narrative of events arranged in a time sequence." Time may be seen as a mechanical factor: how much time does it take the reader to finish a book, and what kind of time is it: intermittent or continuous?

In most novels, the tense is past. But A. A. Mendilow observes that the reader always translates past tense into present. The author's technique can facilitate this process to promote the illusion of immediacy (*Time and the Novel*). Very few novels can justify the use of the historical present. An example of effective use is Walker Percy's *The Moviegoer.*

> *Panic in the Streets* with Richard Widmark is playing on Tchoupitoulas Street. The movie was filmed in New Orleans. Richard Widmark is a public health inspector who learns that a culture of cholera bacilli has gotten loose in the city. Kate watches, lips parted and dry. She understands my moviegoing but in her own antic fashion. There is a scene which shows the very neighborhood of the theater. Kate gives me a look—it is understood that we do not speak during the movie.
>
> Afterwards in the street, she looks around the neighborhood. "Yes, it is certified now."
>
> She refers to a phenomenon of moviegoing which I have called certification.

Dialogue always happens in the dramatic present. A source of pleasure to the reader is the tension between the immediacy of dialogue and the past tense of narration. Denis Diderot's *Rameau's Nephew* is told almost entirely in dialogue, and Ivy Compton-Burnett's novels are unusually full of dialogues.

What is the chronological time scope of the novel, and how does the writer handle transitions? Sequential time governs *War and Peace* and most other traditional novels.

Another mechanical use of time, though it may be handled subtly, is the movie device of *flashbacks.* Such time-shifts are most effective if the very fact of their occurrence contributes to the revelation of character and theme, as in the Benjy section of Faulkner's *The Sound and the Fury.* Bergson, among other philosophers, has influenced writers such as Joyce and Proust in their handling of time. Psychological time governs Virginia Woolf's *To the Lighthouse;* a middle section called "Time Passes" provides contrast. Past and present interact like a fugue in Wright Morris' *The Field of Vision.* Everything that happens during a bullfight in the present reminds each of the characters of events in the past. "Don't it take you back, Boyd?" asks McKee. Joyce's *Ulysses* takes place in Dublin in a single day (Bloomsday, Doomsday) but that day contains within it all Western time. Time rhythms—a day, a week, a moment that embodies a lifetime, a year, an hour, a decade, a day—are set up and the reader responds to these rhythms, perhaps more than to shifts from place to place. Responding to four different kinds of consciousness, types of narrators, the reader responds to four different kinds of time in Faulkner's *The Sound and the Fury.*

The old-fashioned way of conveying a sense of the time-space milieu of the characters was to present a block of description. Thomas Hardy's *Return of the Native:*

> A Saturday afternoon in November was approaching the time of twilight and the vast tract of unenclosed wild known as Egdon Heath embrowned itself moment by moment. Overhead the hollow stretch of whitish cloud shutting out the sky was as a tent which had the whole heath for its floor.
>
> The heaven being spread with this pallid screen and the earth with the darkest vegetation, their meeting-line at the horizon was clearly marked. In such contrast the heath wore the appearance of an instalment of night which had taken up its place before its astronomical hour was come: darkness had to a great extent arrived hereon, while day stood distinct in the sky.

Time and place are simple matters in Cain's *The Postman Always Rings Twice*; the time is the mid-1930s; the place is Los Angeles; and there's not much more to it. Modern techniques present time and place as filtered through the perceptions of characters, as in *Cassandra Singing* by David Madden.

> The backfiring of a motorcycle as it roared over the loose planks of the swinging bridge opened Lone's eyes. Through melting frost on the windowpane, he looked down the hollow and saw Boyd jounce off the bridge onto the highway in front of an overloaded coal truck.
>
> From the kitchen came the ringing clatter of a stove lid. Looking up past the catalpa tree, Lone watched Coot, followed by the snaking line of hounds, trudge up the ridge behind the barn, shotgun riding his shoulder.

Eudora Welty once said, "Feelings are bound up in place." This sense of place is a major part of the fictive experience as represented in *Howards End* by E. M. Forster.

> Howards End,
> Tuesday.
> Dearest Meg,
>   It isn't going to be what we expected. It is old and little, and altogether delightful—red brick. We can scarcely pack in as it is, and the dear knows what will happen when Paul (younger son) arrives tomorrow. . . . Why did we settle that their house would be all gables and wiggles, and their garden all gamboge-coloured paths?

In Gabriel Marquez's *One Hundred Years of Solitude* place becomes a philosophical problem of space and time.

Melquiades had not put events in the order of man's conventional time, but had concentrated a century of daily episodes in such a way that they coexisted in one instant . . . impatient to know his own origin, Aureliano skipped ahead. Then the wind began, warm, incipient, full of voices from the past, the murmurs of ancient geraniums, sighs of disenchantment that preceded the most tenacious nostalgia . . . he found the instant of his own conception among the scorpions and the yellow butterflies in a sunset bathroom where a mechanic satisfied his lust on a woman who was giving herself out of rebellion. He was so absorbed that he did not feel the second surge of wind either as its cyclonic strength tore the doors and windows off their hinges, pulled off the roof of the east wing, and uprooted the foundations . . . he began to decipher the instant that he was living, deciphering it as he lived it, prophesying himself in the act of deciphering the last page of the parchments, as if he were looking into a speaking mirror. Then he skipped again to anticipate the predictions and ascertain the date and circumstances of his death. Before reaching the final line, however, he had already understood that he would never leave that room . . .

To shift time or place, the writer risks disorienting his readers. Sometimes, for a particular effect, he deliberately disorients. He may delay telling where we are, letting us become gradually aware.

The *setting* of a story is the time and place in which the events occur. The time may mean the historical period or the season or time of day in which a story is set. The place may be geographic or psychological. An author may make time or place indeterminable. Settings can express something about a character metaphorically. Impressionistic or expressionistic description of setting can be one way of revealing character or a general climate of feeling, an atmosphere: In *Orlando,* Virginia Woolf depicts the story of Orlando over 500 years, during which we encounter various cultures and Orlando changes from a man to a woman. She evokes a sense of the Victorian era in her description of weather: "Damp swells the wood, furs the kettle, rusts the iron, rots the stone. So gradual is the process . . . and the whole thing drops to pieces in our hands, that we suspect even that the disease is at work." Setting can be significant because of the sense of history (Robert Penn Warren's *All the King's Men* and Faulkner's *Absalom, Absalom!*) or utter lack of it (Samuel Beckett's *The Unnamable* and Camus' *The Stranger*). The reader likes to be oriented securely in time and space, but disorientation can be another valid kind of experience. Sometimes the time scheme is jumbled to allow for juxtapositions of scenes and descriptions not otherwise possible, as in John Hawkes' *The Cannibal.*

More than in earlier kinds of narrative, people in novels live and die in particular places at particular times. Character and personality are shaped by environment; the novelist must therefore describe or evoke the landscape, the cityscape, in detail, humanize it.

To test the degree to which setting affects all other elements in a novel, the reader might ask: Could the story be shifted, without serious effect, to another locale? In a fine novel, the answer is usually no. The writer re-imagines real places so that, in fictive terms at least, the Brontes created, through consistency and passion of vision, the English moors; Thomas Hardy created the English small town; Faulkner created Mississippi; Balzac, Paris; Sinclair Lewis, the midwestern small town; Willa Cather and Wright Morris, rural Nebraska; William Styron and Ellen Glasgow, Virginia; Twain, Missouri; Robert Penn Warren, Kentucky; Steinbeck, small town California; Farrell and Algren, the slums of Chicago.

Setting is usually a matrix of place, time, and social context. Place may be suggested by characters, by common speech, dress, ornamentation, manners, taboos, religion, or by the researched details of a period in the past. Setting may have the force of destiny, as in naturalistic novels. Setting becomes a narrative element when description of the setting is involved with the depiction of physical, emotional, and mental action. Or setting may be mere backdrop, like a picture postcard, as in local color novels, with their manipulation of clichés.

Out of a sense of obligation to describe a setting exhaustively, writers often spend too much time setting the scene or they do it clumsily. Other writers try to avoid describing the setting in a lump. They try to avoid excess or mere decoration, or overemphasizing setting when it isn't really important; that can be distracting or misleading. However, setting usually is important. There are subtle ways of describing setting, as in dialogue, with the use of the curious questioner. With restraint, with a selective use of detail, the best novelists interweave setting and character in action.

Atmosphere is the mood or climate of a story. Sometimes writers feel that mood or atmosphere is enough to sustain a story, but atmosphere is more meaningful when it envelops characters who have problems. An author establishes atmosphere by the objects he selects to describe, by how he describes them, and by the setting in which he places them. The term atmosphere embraces setting and mood. We feel the author's tone of voice, or attitude, toward his material and his readers. Mood is an emotional ambience of sadness, gloom, decay, pessimism, gaiety.

Tone expresses an attitude that creates degrees of distance. "In order to acquire the correct tone I occasionally read a few pages of the Code Civil," said Stendhal of the writing of *The Charterhouse of Parma*. The pervasive tone may be tragic, comic, ironic, skeptical, pessimistic, compassionate, sentimental. A variety of these is possible within a single novel that has great scope and many shifts in time and place. Atmosphere is a rather vague term and a difficult quality in a novel to assess, but it is very important that we catch it and determine its manifestations. "Her sudden appearance seemed to throw a trance across the garden: a butterfly, poised on a dahlia stem, ceased winking wings, and the rasping of bumblebees droned into nothing" (Truman Capote, *Other Voices, Other Rooms*).

Style, more than anything else, conveys the writer's tone; he or she creates an atmosphere of tragedy, comedy, satire, melodrama, cynicism, optimism, or an elegiac mood. These three terms—tone, atmosphere, and mood—are similar but not quite the same. Tone suggests a voice, and the novelist's voice speaks more intimately to the reader than his devices for creating atmosphere and mood. Atmosphere suggests an emphasis on place, and mood an emphasis on character states. "I am an invisible man. No, I am not a spook like those that haunted Edgar Allan Poe. . . . What did I do to be so blue? Bear with me" (Ralph Ellison, *Invisible Man*).

When two or more elements pull the reader simultaneously in different directions, the reader feels a *tension* that sustains emotional involvement in the story. The author may set up a tension between literal and metaphorical meaning, between characters, between techniques themselves. Tension derives partly from the interaction of tone, feeling, and mood that make up atmosphere. The reader's excitement comes partly from becoming involved in the development of the relationship between himself and the author, between the author and his material, and among certain elements dynamically interactive in the material itself—relationships between characters or between a character and society; but also the tension between the author's language and his subject matter. Tension is the simultaneous existence of literal and metaphorical meaning organized in a novel, as in Carson McCullers' *The Heart Is a Lonely Hunter* and Conrad's *Victory*.

· 18 ·

Theme

$\mathcal{A}$n overview of some of the major thematic concerns is just as useful as a survey of types, or genres and subjects, and techniques. The theme is the story's main idea or its underlying meaning. Sometimes *theme* is used to designate subject matter, but not in this book. Characters and events express theme, but techniques, style, and form may also be expressive of theme.

"It is certain," said Novalis, "that my conviction gains infinitely the moment another soul will believe it." Part of the novelistic impulse is to persuade the reader to believe the illustrative or metaphysical truth of his work. The old term for this thought content was theme, replaced today by the search for meaning, and ultimately truth, about the characters and their predicament and ultimately about life. We try to discern the moral reference, purpose, attitude, or vision of the parts and the totality of the novel. A system of moral relationships is set up among the author, the fictive world he creates, and the reader. The traditional concept of moral or message was that it be positive, as the Bible is. Leslie Fiedler declares that the moral obligation of today's novels is to be negative, to say "No in thunder," to wake people up to the true nature of life in our time.

Truth, like realism, is too often used as an honorific term as it relates to literature. Literature can be nonfactual and still convey a kind of truth that facts cannot convey: truths about the way men behave, think, feel, perceive. Aesthetic truths are self-proven, that is, it is *true* that readers experience aesthetic pleasure re-reading *The Great Gatsby* for the twentieth time. Science deals in different kinds of truth, based on observable or demonstrable facts. There are intrinsic or implicit and extrinsic or explicit truths. Fiction mainly "proves" the former; at best, these kinds fuse.

How clear should the "truth" or "theme" be? Some novelists deliberately cause mystification for a special effect (Conrad's *Lord Jim* and the novels of

114

Thomas Pynchon, Joseph Heller, and Faulkner); in lesser writers it may cover certain shortcomings. Others create mystery as an end in itself. Beyond that there is willful obscurity, often on the premise that in trying to cope with obscurity, a diligent reader happens onto multiple and profound meanings not otherwise possible (Djuna Barnes' *Nightwood* and some of the works of Joyce, Faulkner, and John Hawkes). Just as the writer experiences pleasure in making obscurities clear, he also enjoys providing the reader with occasions for doing that on his own. While most people enjoy solving a mystery or puzzle, readers often resent the feeling that the author has simply not bothered to make essential matters clear, or has sacrificed clarity for some other, lesser value. But each of these negatives may be used positively.

Related to meaning, theme, and truth is the question of *universality.* "The whole secret of fiction," said Thomas Hardy, "lies in the adjustment of things unusual to things eternal and universal." Universality is a very abstract notion, but it quickens to life as soon as a reader feels it in a novel. Universality begins with the individual. Thus, there is a quality of solitariness about it—the reader reading alone. We speak of universal meaning, predicaments, characters, feelings. There are private and universal dimensions to values; the novelist makes us feel simultaneously at both poles. Universal, also, is used as an honorific term. But what writer *can't* be universal?

There is in the teaching of literature today perhaps too much emphasis on *theme-mongering,* that is, a search for complexities of meaning, with symbols as clues. Theme is sometimes called a moral, even worse, a message. Obviously, every novel has a theme, but if it is a good novel, its theme is inseparable from its form and content, although it may be discussed apart. Some novels are obviously theme-dominated, but excessive theme-mongering can detract from other elements. Too often, form and technique are neglected, and the student is left with a course in philosophy. Although theme and content more often dictate form than the reverse, it is form and technique that enable the reader to experience meaning in the author's handling of the elements of fiction: character, scene, description, narrative.

In the romance narrative, the aim was illusion that revealed reality; in the novel, the aim is reality that reveals illusion. The grand theme of the novel—and most other arts—is the conflict between appearance and reality, often resulting in illusions and disillusions. And no wonder, since the essential medium and aim of fiction is illusion itself; thus, the novel's central subject and theme is its own nature. This conflict is reflected in the history of the novel itself, a conflict between an approach through reason as against an approach basically through the irrational, described in Nietzsche's concept of the Apollonian and the Dionysian attitude.

There are those writers who believe in the autonomy of a work of art—that it has no direct dependence upon a context outside itself—and those who see the work as part of the life process. But no matter what basic approach to form, all writers have dealt with similar themes. What follows is a representative sampling of those themes.

A theme (*a* because most novels are composed of more than one) that dominates the works of Henry James and Wright Morris is the relationship between life and literature, life and art, fact and fiction. Which influences which and how; is it a reciprocal process?

One facet of the life and literature theme is the concept of the artist as con man and the con man as artist, developed in Thomas Mann's *The Confessions of Felix Krull* and in David Madden's *Pleasure-Dome*. *Pilgrim's Progress* demonstrates the forces of good and evil in an allegorical, objective way; *The Brothers Karamazov* in more subjective ways, delving into the nature of good and evil. Graham Greene (*The Power and the Glory*) and Francois Mauriac (*Viper's Tangle*) show the relationships between man and God, and the conflict between faith and doubt. Most writers deal in some way with the conflict between man's spiritual aspirations and his compulsions toward obsession with material things. On a more imaginative but perhaps less serious level, the supernatural has been one way of dealing with spiritual problems, as in James' *The Turn of the Screw* and Charles Williams' *All Hallows Eve*.

Agnostic writers have raised doubts about man's religious quests, certainly about the effect of Christianity upon the individual, victimizing him if he refuses to or cannot conform, as in Hawthorne's *The Scarlet Letter*. Atheist writers, such as Sartre, have argued the death of God. The hypocrisy of those who force Christianity upon the community is demonstrated in a great many novels, two of which are Samuel Butler's *The Way of All Flesh* and Sinclair Lewis' *Elmer Gantry*.

The conflict between orthodoxy and freedom in various spheres of human activity is dramatized in a majority of novels, with most writers advocating freedom. A few are conservative; for instance, James Gould Cozzens, in *The Just and the Unjust*, a realistic story of small town lawyers, written in a flat, matter-of-fact, though sometimes ornate style, rather intellectual in tone. And a few are anarchical: Jack Kerouac in *On the Road*. Stendhal's *The Red and the Black* is one of the first great psychological and realistic depictions of the rise of a young man in nineteenth-century France. Julien's fall is tragic because he has a good mind that is directed only toward detecting the hypocrisies in a society so he can take advantage of them. Meursault in Camus' *The Stranger* is aware of shams almost as a second nature and doesn't even want to rise in society. The individual in conflict with society often has a compulsion to confess, as in Camus' *The Fall* and Dostoyevsky's *Crime and Punishment*.

The failure of society to satisfy the deepest needs of the individual is seen in the way national aspirations collapse; thus, in American fiction, one of the dominant themes is the conflict between American dreams and American nightmares, the promise and the reality, as in Fitzgerald's *The Great Gatsby* and Faulkner's *Absalom, Absalom!* (See Madden, *American Dreams, American Nightmares.*)

The failure of national ideals stems from the modern source of the ideals themselves, faith in science and technology to enable a nation to rise to less material levels. But the negative effect of technology on individuals and groups is the theme of many novels, as in Frank Norris's *The Octopus.* Cultural and social isolation is a prevalent theme, as in McCullers' *The Heart Is a Lonely Hunter.* Usually, the protagonist of a modern novel is a victim of society; he almost never wins, as in Saul Bellow's *The Victim.*

Some writers conceive of human experience in materialistic terms; others depict the negative results of a culture's emphasis on material things, to the neglect of spiritual values, as in John O'Hara's *Appointment in Samarra.* Characters belong to and are victims of mass society, whose values many writers abhor—understandably, since their medium, fiction, is itself a nonmaterialistic venture. The theme of dehumanization by mass technology dominates much modern literature, as in Harriette Arnow's *The Dollmaker.* Some novels depict the conflict between the individual and society as in James T. Farrell, *The Studs Lonigan Trilogy;* others depict the group against society as in Emile Zola's *Germinal.*

The modern concept of alienation is one of the major themes of fiction. Technology turns the individual into a member of the mass, and social institutions do not provide him with the means of coping with neither his environment nor his inner conflicts. He becomes alienated from society, because society pretends that nothing is wrong, that its tenets are sound even in the face of obvious contradictions.

Even so, some writers believe that though humans are originally estranged from nature and our human institutions are corrupt, the only alternative to suicide is to become engaged in the affairs of men, to be committed to something. This is possible in wartime, as in Andre Malraux's *Man's Fate* and *Man's Hope,* but difficult in peace, as in Camus' *The Plague.* To many writers, a falseness permeates life, and people must seek some kind of authenticity as in Sartre's *Nausea.*

Another modern theme is the conflict between determinism and choice: Theodore Dreiser's *An American Tragedy* and Joyce Carol Oates' *them.* And there is the conflict between man and nature, individually and in groups: Rolvaag's *Giants in the Earth* and Knut Hamsun's *Growth of the Soil.* Conrad and others have shown that the primitive still exists in modern man; his environment has changed more rapidly than his inner nature as an animal: *Victory* by Conrad and *Lord of the Flies* by William Golding. Nature is depicted as a struggle, as mechanical force, as organism. Some writers present thought as a natural rather than simply a human event: Nathalie Sarraute, *Tropisms.*

The novel deals with the author's present era, but often tries to recapture a sense of the past. Men "stand like giants immersed in time," said Proust. Jung's concepts of the collective unconscious have inspired writers to explore our primitive origins. Inhibited by modern social concepts, man suppresses his unconscious; many writers urge a liberation of the unconscious and a response to the blood: Lawrence in *Women in Love* and *The Rainbow*. Some writers examine the role of instincts in our lives, and depict efforts to break through social restraints as in Nikos Kazantzakis' *Zorba the Greek*. An examination of man's dream life is one way to discover man's inner nature, for his outer relationships are corrupt and unfulfilling, as in Anais Nin's *A Spy in the House of Love*.

Human beings seek reconciliation within themselves and with others as a social animal, and modern novels attempt to relate their characters to a larger scheme than history. Some novels present a mythic pattern as a way of giving a dimension and some significance to modern life, as in Joyce's *Ulysses*, Gide's *Theseus*, Faulkner's *The Bear*, Fitzgerald's *The Great Gatsby*. Other writers return to folk elements and origins and show their continuing relevance and effects as in Chinua Achebe's *Things Fall Apart* and Amos Tutuola's *The Palm Wine Drinkard*.

Aware that in the nature of things, he must die, no matter what the outcome of his struggles within himself and in society, modern man experiences dread and anxiety. Mutability haunts many novels; characters, realizing they have no stake in eternity, attempt to live fully in the moment, as in Oscar Wilde's *The Picture of Dorian Gray* and J. K. Huysmans' *Against Nature*.

Related to various perspectives on the reality versus illusion theme, the search for identity is perhaps the most important modern theme. Though society may force the individual to conform, as it fails to nourish him even physically, man turns inward; some writers deal with the theme of self-realization through self-consciousness. Psychological maladjustment within oneself and in relation to others is a frequent result, as in J. P. Donleavy's *The Ginger Man*. This maladjustment may be expressed in various forms of aggression—especially in this age of national aggressions: Thomas McGuane's *Ninety-Two in the Shade*.

The theme of the divided self has fascinated many writers; if society is divided against itself, and individuals are alienated from it, and groups are in conflict with it, some characters find an inner conflict between one aspect and another of their natures. The doppelganger (double) is a fascinating theme for many writers. Most often this divided self is perverse, as in Dostoyevsky's *The Brothers Karamazov*. Some characters deliberately set out to understand their divided natures, and one method is deliberate perversity or the cultivation of inconsistency as a way of making a breakthrough into self-revelation. The gratuitous act of Gide's characters is double-edged; it enables the character to see himself in sharp relief and it is a deliberate act of alienation from society, so that he is forced to examine himself as an individual.

Sometimes this concentration upon oneself is depicted as an escape into oneself from the conflicts of society, as in J. D. Salinger's *The Catcher in the Rye.* Other characters go into a spiritual and physical exile, leaving their own society to move more easily within a foreign one in which they feel less involved and can therefore examine and cultivate their inner lives. Usually, these are artists. Thus, the formation of the artist is another theme more modern than others; it is not found among the early novels. In Joyce's *Portrait of the Artist as a Young Man,* we see his estrangement from the very society he depicts.

The artist's own failure to communicate with an indifferent bourgeois audience causes him to examine characters who are unable to communicate with each other on all levels of society. This problem is particularly acute for adolescents, who are neither children nor adults: Carson McCullers' A *Member of the Wedding.* The spiritual isolation of individuals is a larger variant of the failure to communicate: William Gaddis's *The Recognitions.*

Nor can people relate physically in a society that frowns upon sexual contact, and the psychotic effect of sexual mores on people is a major theme: Ludwig Lewisohn's *The Case of Mr. Crump.* As soon as the novel begins to deal with sex, individuality becomes more clearly defined; love can be handled in general terms, but not sexuality.

Thus estranged from society and from each other, some men come to see all life and its values as relative. Writers have always sensed this relativity, questioning values, abstractions, and notions, but today it has become a way of looking directly at *any* claim. In the novel today, attempts at moral choices are beset with ambiguity; the moral quest almost always fails; relativism triumphs. The claim is made either that it is the quest itself that matters most or that the quest is intrinsically destructive, futile.

If everything is relative, all life is basically absurd: Camus is consequently optimistic (*The Stranger*) and Kafka is pessimistic (*The Trial*). Existentialism is a philosophy that attempts to put some order into this shattering concept, as in the novels of Sartre (*Nausea*) and Simone de Beauvior (*The Mandarins*). The major question becomes—a la Sartre—one of *Being and Nothingness,* not one or the other, but the simultaneity of the two, and the tensions between.

The ancients declared: *Carpe diem* (seize the day). Saul Bellow, in his novella *Seize the Day,* uses the term ironically, showing that modern man is incapable of acting on that philosophical attitude. The result is black humor, victim psychology, and the only salvation seems to lie in man's capacity for compassion and imagination, as we see in the works of Wright Morris and in William Gaddis's *The Recognitions.*

Just as there exist polarities of artists (classic and romantic, makers and dreamers, Apollonian and Dionysian), there are polarities in visions of life, as conducive to order and as intractable. There are attitudes basically of intellect or of feeling, objective and subjective, public and private. And just as there are writers, critics, and readers who take either single or pluralistic approaches to literature, there are writers whose visions of life may be seen along a spectrum from narrow to pluralistic. The author's vision of man in the world, against a background of nothingness or of the divine, determines everything in his novel; technique helps him not only to focus but to discover what his vision is. When a writer achieves a vision of the "real" world that is sufficiently coherent, we begin to speak, for example, of "the world" of Conrad's novels or of Mann's, which is relatively not much more comprehensive than that world we individually speak of as ours, but which is charged more electrically with feeling, meaning, and power of perception, and perhaps of order.

The author's general vision may be mainly tragic or mainly comic, or, in rare instances, balanced, as in Charles Dickens' *Bleak House*, George Meredith's *The Ordeal of Richard Feverel*, and Faulkner's *Light in August*. The skeptical vision is usually productive of little, and paradoxical for two reasons: the true skeptic scorns any communication at all, and the partial skeptic, because he does speak, often makes his readers believers to some degree. The consistently cynical vision is even rarer, for cynicism stifles imagination. Pessimism is a dynamic combination of skepticism and cynicism that cannot finally make up its mind. Nihilism is pessimism that *has* made up its mind, and there's an end to creation. The great writers achieve two things that transcend the raw materials of their own time: a universality of theme and a vision that is made unique by the author's imagination and technique (Dostoevsky's *The Brothers Karamazov*, Conrad's *Nostromo*, Thomas Mann's *The Magic Mountain*, Faulkner's *The Sound and the Fury*).

Allen Tate defines the *communication fallacy* as "the use of poetry to communicate ideas and feelings which should properly be conveyed by non-poetic discourse" (Beckson and Ganz, *A Reader's Guide to Literary Terms*). This is sometimes called the propaganda, thesis, didactic, or moral fallacy: the notion that the writer must communicate a moral or lesson, or an attitude about social evils. Most of the proletarian novels of the thirties are as dead as the headlines that inspired them; the works of the "tough guy" writers of that era are, on the other hand, still very much alive (Hammett, Chandler, Cain, McCoy, Traven). "For messages," said James M. Cain, "I use Western Union." Writers should not enlist or allow themselves to be conscripted as "celestial bellhops." Archibald MacLeish said, "A poem should not mean/ But be," and then turned around and committed the communication fallacy himself during WWII.

A work of the imagination is first an experience, meaning and emotion fused in the instant of communication. The writer knows, or discovers, how that act is performed. Wimsatt and Beardsley, in *The Verbal Icon*, talk about the *affective fallacy* as "a confusion between the poem and its results (what it *is* and what it *does*)." Too many writers today seem distracted by what they want their work to *do* thematically, and neglect what it *is*. Other writers strive to bring an imagined world into being, to make the word flesh.

Eventually, discussion of any element of fiction reveals some aspect of theme; theme should emerge from the reader's emotional and intellectual experience in reading the story. An over-preoccupation with the theme of individual novels will reveal very little about the nature of fiction. Joyce Cary said, "A novel should be an experience and convey an emotional truth rather than arguments." (See Ellmann and Feidelson, *Modern Tradition.*)

· *19* ·

Plot

$\mathcal{P}$lot, as defined by Aristotle, is the arrangement of narrative events to demonstrate the development of an action involving characters. R. S. Crane argues a slightly more sophisticated approach: plot is the simultaneous ordering of all the elements, not just characters in action, in such a way as to produce a unified effect. A description of the plot sometimes traces the development of the story's meaning simultaneously with its storyline, for plot is an action that illustrates a basic idea.

In commercial fiction, plot means the skeleton of the story. For that very reason, some writers, horrified by the predictability of the movement of a plot, have abandoned plot altogether, either to achieve organic form or random effects. Even George Eliot referred to "the vulgar coercion of conventional plot." And later, Ivy Compton-Burnett said, "As regards plots, I find real life no help at all. Real life seems to have no plots. And as I think a plot desirable and almost necessary, I have this extra grudge against life." Elizabeth Bowen is more robust: "There must be combustion. Plot depends for its movement on internal combustion."

It has been said that there are only a few basic plots—the rest is variation and incidental inventiveness and imaginative enrichment. What appears to be plagiarism is often only the nature of fiction manifesting itself; "borrowing" and "imitation" are more apt words, frequently. What makes the difference is each individual writer's ability to invent and to imagine rich variations on the many kinds of plots.

Traditionally, a complete story has a beginning, middle, and end, each with perhaps three phases of development within itself. The main line of action is generated by some specific circumstance or act. We then become involved in the complications, or the entanglement or the tying of the knot. We follow "a rising action," a line of events more positive than negative. As the plot unfolds, the reader becomes aware of an enveloping action: the social background or the milieu in which events have preceded the action of the narrative and will continue once it ends. Walter O'Grady has suggested that many novels move from interior events to exterior incidents as changes occur, and the shifts create a rhythm that the reader enjoys ("On Plot"). The reader also delights in discovering how one event causes another, following cause-and-effect patterns throughout the novel, and in seeing the consequence in the plot of a character's choices. The plot reaches a turning point or a pivotal event, causing a reversal of fortune or situation for a character. There is a "falling action" toward a final solution. Then comes a crisis, climax, or catastrophe, followed by the denouement, resolution, or the unraveling of the complications, the untying of the knot. Character and plot developments should be so arranged as to make the ending seem inevitable.

There is satisfaction in a *resolution* or clarification at the end; the resolution follows the climax of the action. The mind dwells upon the bringing together of all loose ends, in the calm after the climax. Toward the end, the character may experience a discovery of the truth. This is sometimes called a moment of revelation or recognition, in which perhaps he understands himself and his relation with others. Elizabeth in Jane Austen's *Pride and Prejudice* finally recognizes faults based on prejudice. Jack Burden, the narrator of Robert Penn Warren's *All the King's Men,* realizes at the end that

> if you could not accept the past and its burden there was no future, for without one there cannot be the other, and if you could accept the past you might hope for the future, for only out of the past can you make the future . . . and soon now we shall go out of the house and go into the convulsion of the world, out of history into history and the awful responsibility of time.

The writer tries to avoid anti-climaxes, sudden jolts in tone or attitude after the climax, or an ending that simply fades out (though the latter, done deliberately, may have a good effect, thus giving the term anticlimax a less negative connotation).

A plot may embrace a *subplot* or a double or multiple plot. A subplot or underplot is a story developed along with the main plot, enhancing it, but not strictly meshed with it, as with Levin's story in Tolstoy's *Anna Karenina.* Some novelists are frowned upon for concocting too many subplots—Dickens and George Eliot—in some instances, for they can distract from the main experience, all the more so if ineptly handled. The subplots in Dickens contribute to the sense of scope and richness; in the novels of Thomas Wolfe (*Look Homeward, Angel*), the subplots are justified because the basic premise is the very notion of the infinite richness of living in a world of many different kinds of people. Dickens designs most of his subplots so that they eventually mesh, as in *Bleak House;* Wolfe and others do not necessarily do that. Some current writers deliberately cultivate the subplot for special effects, to get at areas of experience not otherwise renderable. Camilo Jose Cela's *The Hive* describes many lives in Madrid. When subplots are part of an integrated vision of life, they cease, in the ordinary, in the negative sense, to be subplots.

A *double plot* is not the same thing as a subplot. In a double plot, the two may have almost equal value and are pursued simultaneously, as in Faulkner's *The Wild Palms* and Joyce's *Ulysses* (Stephen's and Bloom's narratives). A *multiple plot* is another thing: a deliberate presentation of three or more stories alternately, with varying degrees of final coherence (John Dos Passos' *U.S.A.*, Irwin Shaw's *The Young Lions*). Readers delight in such plot variety. A story-within-a-story is not, strictly speaking, the same as subplot. A famous example is the Grand Inquisitor's story in *The Brothers Karamazov*, which, transcribed in the first person by Ivan and interrupting the stream of the main story, illuminates the overall plot of the book. A later example is Jack's story of Cass Mastern in Warren's *All the King's Men*.

As the plot develops, the writer may use various devices to hold reader interest and enhance the main elements. He may foreshadow what is to come, as Anna Karenina's suicide at the end is foreshadowed by the accidental death of a man at the railroad station early in the novel. Dickens often stimulates the reader to anticipate that something will happen, then satisfies or frustrates, or manipulates that anticipation; he sometimes delays it, or reverses it with a surprise.

A writer may present a key moment, an incident endowed with meaning for everything presented so far, as when Meursault shoots the Arab at the exact center of Camus' *The Stranger*. Accidents and *coincidences* are frowned upon in serious fiction, but they can be presented in such a way as to suggest a vision of life. In Wright Morris' *Ceremony in Lone Tree*, events cause McKee to conclude that "in more cases than he cared to remember what was described as an accident was the most important event of a man's life . . . the accident made sense." And in Morris' *One Day*: "It is one of Cowie's notions that meaningful events are accidents." One of the major experiences for the reader (more than for the characters) is the perception of patterns of coincidences in William Gaddis's *The Recognitions* and Joyce's *Ulysses*.

Later writers depart in various ways from basic plot formulas, realizing that life does not develop or resolve in patterned ways. One writer imitates the natural chaos of actual life, adding one episode and detail to another (William Gaddis's *JR*). Another writer imposes an aesthetic pattern, the product of his own unique mind and intelligence, producing a sensation of beauty for the reader in the form itself, while leaving the lives of the characters perhaps still in flux (Joyce, *Ulysses*).

• 20 •

Structure

$\mathcal{T}$he arrangement or organization or structure of the elements of a novel determines its power, force, charm, and excellence. Structure and plot are rather mechanical concepts, but they are not quite the same. A writer structures a plot, and there is usually variety in the way he does so. Some episodes are long, some short, some detailed, some general. (See O'Grady, "On Plot.") E. M. Forster sees a difference between the structure of a story and a plot: story is "a narrative of events arranged in their time-sequence"; plot is a narrative also, but with the "emphasis falling on causality."

The structure of a novel reflects the way an author's mind works, his vision of life, and the world around him. Structure is also partially dictated by the type of story being told, the theme, characters, and plot concept. The structure of a narratively intricate novel (D. H. Lawrence's *The Rainbow*) will differ greatly from that of a novel that renders psychological processes (Virginia Woolf, *To the Lighthouse*). Even novels that pretend to imitate chaos have structure, derived from the repetition of certain elements, ideas, sensations, types of characters (Julio Cortazar, *Hopscotch*). No novel, told in words that signify, no matter how hard a writer tries to make them meaningless, can contain chaos—it's a contradiction. A novel by virtue of its existence is a denial of chaos. Sometimes chaos can be felt best when presented in a highly controlled and artificial manner (Jerzy Kosinski, *Steps*). Randomness is not the same as chaos; a novel can give an impression of randomness by being spontaneous (William Burroughs's *Nova Express* or Steve Katz's *The Exaggerations of Peter Prince*). The structure of a historical or a chronicle novel is dictated by type. Sometimes a realistic sequence of events in a character's life dictates the structure (Dicken's *David Copperfield* and Harriette Arnow's *The Dollmaker*). Some novels are composed of vignettes or episodes isolated in time and space, featuring characters

125

whose relationship to each other is apparent more to the reader than to themselves (Virginia Woolf's *The Waves*).

Most novels are divided into chapters. Philip Stevick in "Fictional Chapters and Open Ends" observes that because chapters must end, they give the novel a quality of discontinuity, even though the reader knows that the novel will continue; this tension of contradiction is exciting to a reader, and some writers play off the starts-and-stops conventions for special effects. In *Tristram Shandy*, Laurence Sterne parodies the use of chapters. Philip Wylie uses sudden one-line chapters for shock effect: "I played bridge." Kurt Vonnegut in *Cat's Cradle*, Joan Didion in *Play It As It Lays*, and Evan S. Connell in *Mrs. Bridge* make frequent use of chapters less than three pages long. Because of the gestalt-making tendency of readers, there is a need, especially in a long novel, to limit and control the span of concentration.

The writer must control the sequence of events, and of other elements; it is important to determine what comes when and what is to be stressed in sequence. Beginnings and endings are especially troublesome. A good novel begins where it has to. Ford Madox Ford often wondered whether he should have a dramatic or a reflective opening: "Openings are therefore of necessity always affairs of compromise." Most writers try to get the novel's patterns started in the opening passages. "Beginnings are always troublesome," George Eliot observed. "Conclusions are the weak point of most authors, but some of the fault lies in the very nature of conclusion, which is at best a negation." Chekhov said, "At the end of a novel . . . I must artfully concentrate for the reader an impression of the entire work." Virginia Woolf achieves that effect with the last line of *To the Lighthouse*: "It was done; it was finished. Yes, she thought, laying down her brush in extreme fatigue. I have had my vision."

A plot may be broken down into scenes, which are to be distinguished slightly from episodes. A scene usually has dialogue, and is a term taken for that reason from the theater, while an episode may be pure narrative, as in Samuel Butler's *The Way of All Flesh* (which has very few dialogue scenes). Some critics make an analogy between a scene in fiction and an image in a poem. The reader enjoys moving from scene to generalization, or *panorama,* as Percy Lubbock calls an authorial overview of a stretch of time or of a character's general state of mind, followed by scenes of varying length (see Lubbock, *The Craft of Fiction*). Some novels are episodic in structure: *Tom Jones, Huckleberry Finn,* Saul Bellow's *Adventures of Augie March,* and Celine's *Journey to the End of the Night*.

Emphasis and stress are achieved through the scenic or the panoramic picture method. The scenic method may be either objective (like a play or a movie), relying heavily on dialogue, or there may be some rendering of the thoughts of the characters. In any case, the scenic method is the most immediate. The *panorama* is an omniscient view at some distance, giving a general picture through narrative summary (Lubbock, *Craft of Fiction*). W. Somerset Maugham's *Of Human Bondage:*

> For the next three months Philip worked on subjects which were new to him. The unwieldy crowd which had entered the Medical School nearly two years before had thinned out: some had left the hospital, finding the examinations more difficult to pass than they expected, some had been taken away by parents who had not foreseen the expense of life in London, and some had drifted away to other callings. One youth whom Philip knew had devised an ingenious plan to make money; he had bought things at sales and pawned them . . . the young man had gone out to bear the White Man's Burden overseas. The imagination of another, a lad who had never before been in a town at all, fell to the glamour of music-halls and bar parlours; he spent his time among racingmen, tipsters, and trainers, and now was become a book-maker's clerk. . . . A third, with a gift for singing and mimicry, who had achieved success at the smoking concerts of the Medical School by his imitation of notorious comedians, had abandoned the hospital for the chorus of a musical comedy. Still another, and he interested Philip because his uncouth manner and interjectional speech did not suggest that he was capable of any deep emotion, had felt himself stifle among the houses of London. He grew haggard in shut-in spaces, and the soul he knew not he possessed struggled like a sparrow held in the hand, with little frightened gasps and a quick palpitation of the heart: he yearned for the broad skies and the open, desolate places among which his childhood had been spent; and he walked off one day, without a word to anybody, between one lecture and another; and the next thing his friends heard was that he had thrown up medicine and was working on a farm.

If the writer is to create an illusion of reality, he must handle these two narrative techniques—scenic and panoramic—in skillful combinations, as do Henry James, Thomas Mann, George Eliot, Jane Austen, and Tolstoy.

The problem of which elements to stress comes up in the matter of *digressions*. Readers today are tolerant of episodic structure but especially impatient with digressions, such as Melville's long dissertations on the cetology of the whale in *Moby Dick,* Hugo's on politics in *Les Miserables,* Faulkner's story of the three-legged race horse in *A Fable,* the numerous digressions in *Don Quixote,* and Fielding's own digressions as the author in *Tom Jones.*

Usually, the episodic plot is the least effective. One feels that scenes or episodes are linked without enough regard for necessity or probability, as in many epics and romances. However, some fine novels deliberately violate this general rule: the surrealistic novel, such as William Burroughs' *Naked Lunch,* the sexually nightmarish but realistic *Steps* by Jerzy Kosinski, the philosophical *Hopscotch* by Julio Cortazar, William March's realistic war story *Company K,*

Joaquim Machado de Assis' *Epitaph of a Small Winner,* and Cesare Pavese's *The Moon and the Bonfires,* a personal, poetic, allusive book rendering the past in memory in terse five-page chapters. One might say that the units of these novels are almost epigrammatic rather than episodic.

A *situation* is not the same as a scene or an episode, although it is partly presented in the form of a scene. A situation is a general predicament the character is in. In *Great Expectations,* Pip's efforts to help Magwitch the convict escape is only one of the situations in which he becomes involved. Just as there are stock characters, there are stock situations, and, again, whether that is bad depends on how well they are handled. But even in the best novels, when the girl goes home to mother after a fight with her husband, we wince, not only because we have experienced that before, but we've had it too often, and the situation doesn't admit many variations. We will endure it once again only with the implicit promise of something more inventive coming up.

Frame is another structural concept. It is as mechanical as a frame around a window, though the best novels use it as a device along the way. Time frame: Dreiser's *An American Tragedy* opens and closes with the same scene, described in almost the same words, to emphasize the passing of time and the absence from the scene of Clyde Griffiths. Space frame: William Styron's *Lie Down in Darkness* begins and ends with a train crossing the Virginia landscape and ends when it arrives in Port Warwick; the novel's events are presented in flashback between these space images. Narrative frame: events on a single day, the 4th of July 1892, frame a series of flashbacks that make up the body of Ross Lockridge's *Raintree County.* Character frame: the story Rosa Coldfield tells Quentin Compson in Faulkner's *Absalom, Absalom!* is important mainly in its effect on the listener. The effect is the same as with a frame around a painting: to set off, define its best features, enhance its coloration and size.

The *pace* of a novel refers not only to the handling of action in measured doses, but to the rate of movement of all the novel's parts, and it is set by the nature of the other elements. An author may accelerate pace by using abrupt transitions or short bits of dialogue; the pace may be slowed by using narrative description. The author's regulation of pace affects the reader's responses to all the other elements in a story. Pace may contribute to the sense of inevitability we feel about the way the story turns out; pace may excite psychological tension and sustain narrative tension.

One technique that most writers consider vital but that may slow down the pace of a narrative is *exposition.* "It is the function of the exposition to introduce the reader into an unfamiliar world," says Meir Sternberg (in her essay "What Is Exposition?" in Halperin's *The Theory of the Novel*), "by providing him with the general and specific background information indispensable to the understanding of what happens in it. . . . This expositional information the author is obliged to communicate to the reader in one way or another." Most offer exposition in the beginning, some delay it, some concentrate it all in one place, some distribute it piecemeal throughout; sometimes, it is incidental, rather than crucial. "But the location and the form of exposition are always worth inquiring into because they are usually indicative of and often integral to the structure and compositional principles of the work as a whole."

Pace and exposition, in very different ways, are time problems for the writer, and the way he solves the problem of exposition will affect pace. James M. Cain is a master of pace in the tough school of the '30s but his best novel, *The Postman Always Rings Twice,* is not action-packed. However, the pace of the novel persuades the reader to believe that in thirty pages, Frank has met Cora and their passion for each other is so powerful they have decided to kill Cora's husband, Nick. (Compare with the pace of Camus' *The Stranger,* a philosophical novel modeled after *Postman;* compare also with another "existential" tough-guy novel, Horace McCoy's *They Shoot Horses, Don't They?*) The pace of Gide's short, simple, lucidly written novel *The Immortalist* is very slow; it is a meditative book. The pace of *All the King's Men* is varied, with alternating sections of action and meditation, and that is part of the reader's experience.

> So I had it after all the months. For nothing is lost, nothing is ever lost. There is always the clue, the canceled check, the smear of lipstick, the footprint in the canna bed, the condom on the park path, the twitch in the old wound, the baby shoes dipped in bronze, the taint in the blood stream. And all times are one time, and all those dead in the past never lived before our definition gives them life, and out of the shadow their eyes implore us.
>
> That is what all of us historical researchers believe.
> And we love truth.
>
> Chapter Six
> It was late March in 1937 when I went to see Miss Littlepaugh in the foul, fox-smelling lair in Memphis, and came to the end of my researches. I had been on the job almost seven months. But other things had happened during that period besides my researches. Tom Stark, a sophomore, had made quarterback on the mythical All Southern Eleven and had celebrated by wrapping an expensive yellow sport job around a culvert on one of the numerous speedways which bore his father's name.

No matter how much action a novel offers, if the pace is wrong, the novel fails. Other masters of pace are Graham Greene (*The Heart of the Matter*) and Ivan Turgenev (*Fathers and Sons*).

For some novels, a better term might be *rhythm.* E. M. Forster speaks of rhythm as opposed to pattern, as in Forster's own novel, *A Room with a View.* What is being moved are the author's commentaries and the flow of blood through a living organism. The term *tempo* applies to the variable speed of the rhythm.

To facilitate pace, rhythm, and tempo, *transitions* must be handled effectively. A transition is the point in a story when we move from one time, place, position, or idea to another. A transitional device is any method a writer uses to accomplish a transition. Transitions are often difficult to make because the writer must re-orient the reader and make a new start. Transitional devices enable the writer to make shifts in time and place without disturbing the reader's concentration. In some instances a subtle transition is most effective; in others an abrupt or jolting change may work best. Faulkner's complex methods—reorganization of time and shifts in space—require that he handle transitions effectively, as in the bewildering Benjy section of *The Sound and The Fury*.

> "They haven't started yet," Caddy said.
> *They getting ready to start, T.P. said.*

The shift in dialogue in quotation marks to dialogue in italics suggests a transition from one time to another. The similarity in what Caddy and T. P. say also signals a time shift. T. P.'s scene ends: "'Git on the box and see is they started.'" Faulkner then shifts back to Caddy's scene with: "'They haven't started because the band hasn't come yet,' Caddy said." Of course, most transitions are very simple. "I did not see Brett again until the night of the 24th of June. 'Did you hear from Cohn?'" (Hemingway's *The Sun Also Rises*). Some transitions are very carefully controlled. In *A Death in the Family*, James Agee moves at the end of chapter 2, from the mother's point of view to that of the father at the start of chapter 3:

> She was never to realize his intention of holding the warmth in for her; for that had sometime since departed from the bed.
>
> Chapter 3
> He imagined that by about now she would about be getting back and finding the bed. He smiled to think of her finding it.

Just as the reader delights in experiencing smooth or clever transitions, she also delights in unexpected *reversals* (this is the opposite of the operation of suspense, for here the reader knows what is happening and thus thinks he knows what will happen). When the reader is led to expect or anticipate a certain development and the reverse occurs, the surprise may delight him; if the reversal is contrived or forced, he may be resentful. A reversal may also deepen a reader's understanding of what he has experienced so far. A master of reversal is Henry James, as in *The Wings of the Dove* when Densher's and Kate's elaborate scheme against Milly misfires.

"Her memory's your love. You *want* no other."

He heard her out in stillness, watching her face, but not moving. Then he only said: "I'll marry you, mind you, in an hour."

"As we were."

"As we were."

But she turned to the door, and her headshake was now the end. "We shall never be again as we were!"

Even when the narration is filtered through the mind of a character, mental processes need to be enhanced by the interplay of objects. T. S. Eliot, in describing metaphysical poetry, gave us a useful term: *objective correlative.* The writer of fiction may describe an object or an action in such a way that we feel it correlates to a subjective experience of one of the characters. Much of Hemingway functions that way, as in the fishing scene at Burgette in *The Sun Also Rises.* Another term for this device is the poetic or the charged image.

A related technique of heightening mental experiences is the use of *contrasts,* a device used in all point-of-view strategies, but differently for each. For instance, the omniscient narrator may use a contrast of character types: Elizabeth's prejudice against Darcy's pride in Jane Austen's *Pride and Prejudice.* The first-person narrator uses contrast to make us feel the reality of the narrator as more than a voice: The unnamed female narrator of Daphne du Maurier's *Rebecca,* contrasted with Mrs. Danvers. The central intelligence point of view implies the contrast of illusion and reality: the reader perceives that the boy in Henry Roth's *Call It Sleep* understands very little of what he experiences.

The expressionistic device is an exaggeration of the use of contrasts and objective correlatives. *Expressionism,* a technique once used in avant-garde painting (Munch) and theater (Eugene O'Neill's *The Emperor Jones*), now thoroughly assimilated, even in Broadway musicals, is a deliberate distortion of the real to suggest an intense subjective reality. The device is used intermittently in some novels, as in Dickens' *Bleak House.* Tulkinghorn lies murdered under a dome where a Roman is depicted pointing his finger.

For many years, the persistent Roman has been pointing with no particular meaning from that ceiling. It is not likely that he has any new meaning in him to-night. Once pointing, always pointing—like any Roman, or even Briton, with a single idea. There he is, no doubt, in his impossible attitude, pointing, unavailingly, all night long. Moonlight, darkness, dawn, sunrise, day. There he is still, eagerly pointing, and no one minds him.

But, a little after the coming of the day, come people to clean the rooms. And either the Roman has some new meaning in him, not expressed before, or the foremost of them goes wild; for, looking up at his outstretched hand, and looking down at what is below it, that person shrieks and flies.

★ ★ ★

He is pointing at a table, with a bottle (nearly full of wine) and a glass upon it, and two candles that were blown out suddenly, soon after being lighted. He is pointing at an empty chair, and at a stain upon the ground before it that might be almost covered with a hand. These objects lie directly within his range. . . . It happens surely, that every one who comes into the darkened room and looks at these things, looks up at the Roman, and that he is invested in all eyes with mystery and awe, as if he were a paralyzed dumb witness.

So, it shall happen surely, through many years to come, that ghostly stories shall be told of the stain upon the floor, so easy to be covered, so hard to be got out; and that the Roman, pointing from the ceiling, shall point, so long as dust and damp and spiders spare him, with far greater significance than he ever had in Mr. Tulkinghorn's time, and with a deadly meaning. For, Mr. Tulkinghorn's time is over for evermore; and the Roman pointed at the murderous hand uplifted against his life, and pointed helplessly at him, from night to morning, lying face downward on the floor, shot through the heart.

But very few novels use an expressionistic technique throughout. Words cannot function expressionistically in a work as long as a novel; the effect of exaggeration cannot be sustained that long. Another example is Faulkner's *Absalom, Absalom!*

. . . and opposite Quentin, Miss Coldfield in the eternal black which she had worn for forty-three years now, whether for sister, father, or not husband none knew, sitting so bolt upright in the straight hard chair that was so tall for her that her legs hung straight and rigid as if she had iron shinbones and ankles, clear of the floor with that air of impotent and static rage like children's feet, and talking in that grim haggard amazed voice until at last listening would renege and hearing-sense self-confound and the long-dead object of her impotent yet indomitable frustration appear, as though by outraged recapitulation evoked, quiet inattentive and harmless, out of the biding and dreamy and victorious dust.

Expressionistic devices might also be called *kinetic* because they act directly upon the senses, to shock, startle a reader into a breakthrough of some sort. Ideally, the reader has a physical sensation. One such kinetic technique is the *collage*, based on a principle somewhat like the montage. The author composes a sequence, using pieces of this and that, jamming them together in seeming chaos. William Burroughs has written an entire novel in this manner, throwing the pieces into the air and typing them as he picks them up at random

(*Naked Lunch*). Another novelist offers the reader a packet of loose pages which he may assemble any way he wishes. The pastiche novel, made up of pieces of other novels, is rare. Another possibility is the found-objects novel, made up of descriptions of events encountered accidentally from the moment one begins to the moment one ends the novel.

These and similar techniques are used by avant-garde theater groups (the Open Theater), composers (John Cage), and painters (Andy Warhol). Although few novels make exclusive use of any one, or a combination of these devices, a number of novels make incidental use of them for various effects, such as to shatter the illusion of reality; to thrust the reader suddenly into shifting realms of sensory experience, to ridicule traditional forms, or to satirize institutions by satirizing first of all the forms of literature as an institution. The *dadaist* and *surrealist* movements initiated many of these techniques in the 1920s. (See Wallace Fowlie, *Age of Surrealism,* and back issues of *transition.*)

Quite different from kinetic devices, although some effects intermingle, are *impressionistic devices* (another term borrowed from painting). Here the emphasis is upon realistic psychological processes as opposed to simulated, brutal physical processes. The writer gives us a series of interrelated impressions to create a sense of an experience, as in art, Monet, Cezanne, Renoir, Degas; in music, Debussy's *La Mer;* and in the novel, Virginia Woolf's *To the Lighthouse* and very differently, Jack Kerouac's *The Subterraneans.*

> So some random light directing them with its pale footfall upon stair and mat, from some uncovered star, or wandering ship, or the Lighthouse even, the little airs mounted the staircase and nosed round bedroom doors. But here surely, they must cease. Whatever else may perish and disappear, what lies here is steadfast. Here one might say to those sliding lights, those fumbling airs that breathe and bend over the bed itself, here you can neither touch nor destroy. Upon which, wearily, ghostily, as if they had featherlight fingers and the light persistency of feathers, they would look, once, on the shut eyes, and the loosely clasping fingers, and fold their garments wearily and disappear. And so, nosing, rubbing, they went to the window on the staircase, to the servants' bed rooms, to the boxes in the attics; descending, blanched the apples on the dining-room table, fumbled the petals of roses, tried the picture on the easel, brushed the mat and blew a little sand along the floor. At length, desisting, all ceased together, gathered together, all sighed together; all together gave off an aimless gust of lamentation to which some door in the kitchen replied; swung wide; admitted nothing; and slammed to. (*To the Lighthouse*)

> . . . the cold winter rainy nights when Charles would be crossing the campus saying something witty, the great epics almost here sounding phantom

like and uninteresting if at all believable but the true position and bigburn importance of not only Charles but a good dozen others in the light rack of my brain, so Mardou seen in this light, is a little brown body in a gray sheet bed in the slums of Telegraph Hill, huge future in the history of the night yes but only one among many, the asexuality of the WORK—also the sudden gut joy of beer when the visions of great words in rhythmic order all in one giant archangel book go roaring thru my brain, so I lie in the dark also seeing also hearing the jargon the future worlds—damaje-eleout-ekeke-dhkdk-dldoud, ——d, ekeoeu-hdhdkehgyt—better not a more than which strangely he doth mdodudltkdip—baseeaatra—for example because of mechanical needs of gyping, of the flow of river sounds, words, hark, leading to the future and attesting to the madness, hollowness, ring and roar of my mind which blessed or unblessed is where trees sing—in a funny wind—well-being believes he'll go to heaven— (*The Subterraneans*)

A special effect can be created when two elements are set side by side, or juxtaposed. Some *juxtapositions* are accidental; others are deliberate. Sometimes a writer may juxtapose two images that have no special impact separately but that spark an idea or an emotion when set side by side. The two words, images, or events may be so deliberately and carefully chosen that they spark a third element that exists only in the reader's mind.

In *Portrait of the Artist as a Young Man*, Joyce allows Stephen to hold forth eloquently on the subject of beauty in art.

—This hypothesis, Stephen began.
A long dray laden with old iron came round the corner of Sir Patrick Dun's hospital covering the end of Stephen's speech with the harsh roar of jangled and rattling metal . . .
—This hypothesis, Stephen repeated, is . . . that, though the same object may not seem beautiful to all people, all people who admire a beautiful object find in it certain relations which satisfy and coincide with the stages themselves of all aesthetic apprehension.

By juxtaposing to Stephen's philosophical flights a description of a "dray laden with old iron," Joyce does not himself directly say, rather, he implies, that the ordinary realities of this world clash with aesthetic theorizing; but he also implies in the very use and effect of the technique of juxtaposition that in a novel all such contraries are reconciled, for both elements are part of the reader's aesthetic experience of that passage and of his apprehension of how it contributes to the unity of the novel.

In the movies this technique is called *montage*. Sergei Eisenstein, the Russian director, describes montage in this way: "Two pieces of film of any kind, placed together, inevitably combine into a new concept, a new quality, arising out of that juxtaposition." (*Film Forum*) Juxtaposition or montage is a technique that involves the reader as a collaborator in the creative process so that he sees and feels much more.

Montage is used in novels, sometimes for expressionistic, sometimes impressionistic or psychological effects. When two or more different images are juxtaposed, the effect is an image, insight, intuitive experience greater than the sum of the parts. The movie *Hiroshima, Mon Amour* is full of such images: as the French woman gazes at her sleeping Japanese lover, memory images of her dead German lover flash rapidly, breaking up the living image before her. *Impingement* is another term in fiction for this device. Impingement is also a stylistic technique—one word or phrase impinges kinetically upon another, giving style an immediacy, an active, dynamic quality.

The term *flashback* is appropriated from the movies, also. Until recently a flashback was signaled by the screen's going blurry, but today many movies shift back and forth from present to past (sometimes forward to the future, and the movie catches up eventually) with very little warning. And this kinetic way of experiencing the flux of time is part of the whole experience. In fiction, the same thing has happened, especially in *The Cannibal* by John Hawkes. Compared with the smooth use in movies, flashbacks are handled obviously and crudely even in some good fiction; but Conrad in *Lord Jim* and Faulkner in *Sanctuary* have used this device in complex and profound ways, so that one experiences, in the technique itself, the vision of the work.

Flashbacks and montage, the more subtly they are used, cause deliberate discontinuity in the plot sequence to achieve effects that would not be possible with continuity. This technique is based on sound psychological insights into the way the mind, emotions, perceptions, work. Discontinuity in technique is often an expression of the same quality in the lives of the characters, or it may be a more direct expression of the author's vision of life, which may differ from that of his characters.

A major characteristic of the language of poetry is *compression* or *condensation*; the same technique is often used effectively in the structure of a novel, as in, for instance, the panoramic passages described earlier. To some extent, of course, all works of fiction are compressions of the endless ramifications of real life, but a conscious use of this technique as a principle of structure has special results.

Focus and *emphasis* control the reader's responses so that his experience will be more concentrated, intense. To achieve emphasis, as distinguished from focus, a writer may select only those details that isolate a specific moment.

Most structures are logically put together, but the structure of some recent novels, especially French, are alogical; they follow a logic that is peculiar to themselves and ostensibly can't be repeated for other novels. The sense they make, the structure that results, may not be visible there in the work; it may occur only in the mind of the perceiver, the reader, and the main character may be engaged in the same task, as in Robbe-Grillet's *The Voyeur,* Nathalie Sarraute's *Tropisms*, and Claude Mauriac's *The Marquise Went Out at Five.* No novel is ever totally plotless, for we read on to the end to be able to look back on some kind of wholeness.

Action need not be narrative, or physical. Even style can in itself be action if what it describes is a developing attitude or state of mind. Psychological movement is the mind constantly reacting, so there is a feeling of mental movement forward toward a solution or realization. Words and phrases and perceptions interact, impinge upon each other, juxtapose violently, as in the novels of James, Virginia Woolf, Fitzgerald, Faulkner, Hemingway, and Wright Morris. Overt action is often too superficial and can be just as boring as inert description presented for its own sake. The proportion of action is sometimes an index to a novel's achievement. The balance of action with other major elements is another positive factor.

The depiction of action requires a great deal of special skill; some writers seem incapable, artistically or temperamentally, of presenting action credibly; some don't intend to (Henry James, for instance). Action is *too* active an ingredient in popular fiction; one thinks of westerns, crime stories, adventure tales of sea and air. But even a war story could be relatively actionless and still grip a reader. (See Edwin Muir, *The Structure of the Novel.*)

· *21* ·

Style

$\mathcal{A}$s the novel matured, approached art, its medium—language—became more self-conscious, controlled, *made*. Style, narrowly speaking, is the author's use of language. Style is choice of words (diction) and syntax (arrangement of words in a sentence) and the handling of sentence and paragraph units by varying patterns to achieve a specific effect. "The sentence is a single cry," said Herbert Read. "It is a unit of expression, and its various qualities—length, rhythm, and structure—are determined by a right sense of this unity." About paragraphs, Read said: "As the thought takes shape in the mind, it takes a shape. . . . There is about good writing a visual actuality. It exactly reproduces what we should metaphorically call the contour of our thought. . . . The paragraph is the perception of this contour or shape" (*English Prose Style*). Katherine Mansfield says, "In 'Miss Brill' I chose not only the length of every sentence, but even the sound of every sentence. I chose the rise and fall of every paragraph to fit her, and to fit her on that day, at that very moment."

Despite its importance, style is one of the least discussed aspects of technique because descriptions of its effect are difficult. The term style should not be confused with the more general term technique, which is all the methods the writer uses to produce the whole literary creation. The term may be used as a general synonym of excellence—some have it, some don't. Or as a term of classification: a satirical, a lyrical, a witty, an objective style. When an analysis of a writer's style is carried far enough, it ends in the man himself—Hemingway, for instance.

The total of the qualities that characterize an individual writer's style (some of which may be too subtle ever to be detected) constitutes his literary personality and reflects his personal or psychological one. Style is, then, the man. If the man beguiles himself with his style, he ends up with a mannered style, as Hemingway did. Many of the secrets of style are matters of tone, of the perfect recognition of the writer's relation to the reader in view of what he wants to say and the congruence of his feelings with the reader's.

Style is texture of writing: verbal detail, imagery, connotations and sounds of words, their order in sentences, the lengths of sentences and of paragraphs. Together, style and point of view are the major technical considerations in analyzing fiction. Variations on the author's basic style are somewhat determined by the point of view an author decides to employ. One aspect of style is the use of rhetorical devices (proven ways of stimulating the desired emotion, attitude, or idea in the reader) and figurative language (the use of metaphors and similes, for instance). "Metaphorical language," says Mark Schorer in "Fiction and the 'Analogical Matrix,'" "gives any style its special quality," "expresses, defines, evaluates theme," can be "the basis of structure," as "overthought" or "underthought," "reveals to us the character of any imaginative work." Our responses to a story are controlled by language artfully arranged to achieve carefully prepared effects.

To detect ways in which the writer tries to affect her reader, analyze her style. The words a writer chooses to express feelings, thoughts, and action will tell you a great deal about her relationship with her raw material and the way she wants her readers to respond to it. What are the dictates of style in a particular novel? Is the style appropriate to the subject matter and to the point of view the author uses?

Few writers really arrive at a distinctive style of their own. It is easier to recognize most writers by their handling of other techniques. The essential differences between great writers remain mysterious and cannot be discussed, but one may be more receptive to that essence if one learns to recognize distinguishing characteristics. It is distinctive style wedded to technique or craft that distinguishes most great novelists from each other. "There is no branch of criticism in which learning as well as good sense," said Henry Fielding, "is more required than to the forming an accurate judgment of style." And Flaubert (whose *Madame Bovary* has taught many modern novelists to write) said: "One never tires of anything that is well written. Style is life! Indeed it is the lifeblood of thought! . . . I shall try to show why aesthetic criticism has remained so far behind historical and scientific criticism: *it had no foundation.* The knowledge everyone lacked was *analysis of style,* the understanding of how a phrase is constructed and articulated." "I would sooner die like a dog than hurry my sentence by so much as a second before it is ripe. . . . A phrase is an adventure." He strove for the "*mot juste*" (the right word). Zola said, "A well-made phrase is a good action," giving good style an almost moral quality.

Generally, we may speak of simple, complex, and mid-styles. Economy, objectivity, and indirection or underwriting characterize the *simple style.* It is concrete, clear, exact, vivid, brief, in combinations that are fresh. War-weary Frederick Henry in Hemingway's *A Farewell to Arms* offers a credo for under-writing: "There were many words you could not stand to hear and finally only the names of places had dignity. . . . Abstract words such as glory, honor, courage, or hallow were obscene beside the concrete names of villages, the numbers of roads, the names of rivers . . . and the dates." A fine example of un-derwriting is the fishing scene at Burgette in the middle of *The Sun Also Rises*. Gertrude Stein's simple style influenced Sherwood Anderson's. The dog "did not die with a real sickness. She just got older and more blind and coughed and then more quiet, and then slowly one bright summer's day, she died" (*The Good Anna*). Stein's simplicity was consciously and deliberately artificial and literary, and finally complex. With a kind of folk simplicity in storytelling and in narrative line itself, Anderson made a breakthrough in style: "Wing Biddle-baum talked with his hands. . . . The story of Wing Biddlebaum is a story of hands." Anderson once said: "Any clearness I have in my own life is due to my feeling for words." Both Stein and Anderson influenced Hemingway's style. *A Farewell to Arms* opens with a muted portentous lyricism:

> In the late summer of that year we lived in a house in a village that looked across the river and the plain to the mountains. In the bed of the river there were pebbles and boulders, dry and white in the sun, and the water was clear and swiftly moving and blue in the channels. Troops went by the house and down the road and the dust they raised powdered the leaves of the trees. The trunks of the trees too were dusty and the leaves fell early that year and we saw the troops marching along the road and the dust rising and leaves, stirred by the breeze, falling and the soldiers marching and afterward the road bare and white except for the leaves.

John O'Hara exerts sophisticated control over the simple style in *An Appoint-ment in Samarra*. James T. Farrell in the *Studs Lonigan* trilogy uses a tough, func-tional, simple style to serve his ideas about life in city slums. Graham Greene in *Brighton Rock* fuses purpose, technique, and style.

The complex style is elaborate, rhapsodic, lyrical, subjective, sometimes overwritten, especially in the misuse of hyperbole (exaggeration, or rhetoric in excess of the occasion). Henry James in *The Wings of the Dove* shows himself a master of the complex baroque style:

> The two ladies who, in advance of the Swiss season, had been warned that their design was unconsidered, that the passes would not be clear, nor the air mild, nor the inns open—the two ladies who, characteristically had braved a good deal of possibly interested remonstrance were finding them-selves, as their adventure turned out, wonderfully sustained.

The complex style is at work in the arch, sophisticated, snobbish tone of Mary McCarthy's *The Groves of Academe*. Frederick Buechner's modification of the Jamesian style in *A Long Day's Dying* is intricate and sensitive. Personal anguish in the struggle between response to the subject and inability to capture or express one's feelings about the actual thing in words produces the desperately reaching-out style of James Agee in *A Death in the Family*. There is an expressionistic complexity in the style of Faulkner's *Absalom, Absalom!*, a rhapsodic excess in Thomas Wolfe's *Look Homeward, Angel*, an exploitation of the bizarre in Djuna Barnes' intricate, baroque, highly metaphorical *Nightwood*, symbolic expressionism in the style of D. H. Lawrence's *The Rainbow*, a tangle of puns and comic repetition gives complexity to Joseph Heller's style in *Catch-22*, and Herbert Read's style in *The Green Child* alternates between the philosophical and the weirdly lyrical.

The *mid-style* consists of combinations of the simple and the complex. It is conservative, traditional, characterized by wit and satire, and allows more objectivity—the freedom but also the occasional dullness of neutrality. Jane Austen's traditional style is at dead center in *Emma*.

> Happily it was not necessary to speak. There was only Harriet, who seemed not in spirits herself, fagged, and very willing to be silent; and Emma felt the tears running down her cheeks almost all the way home without being at any trouble to check them, extraordinary as they were.

The southern writer Carson McCullers is lyrical in her use of the mid-style in *The Heart Is a Lonely Hunter*, speaking of Singer the mute:

> And then sometimes when he was alone and his thoughts were with his friend his hands would begin to shape the words before he knew about it. Then when he realized he was like a man caught talking aloud to himself. It was almost as though he had done some moral wrong. The shame and sorrow mixed together and he doubled his hands and put them behind him. But they would not let him rest.

There is a midwestern laconic quality in Wright Morris' lyrical, impressionistic, nostalgic opening of *The Works of Love*.

> In the dry places, men begin to dream. Where the rivers run sand, there is something in man that begins to flow. West of the 98th Meridian—where it sometimes rains and it sometimes doesn't—towns, like weeds, spring up when it rains, dry up when it stops. But in a dry climate, the husk of the plant remains. The stranger might find, as if preserved in amber, something of the green life that was once lived there, and the ghosts of men who have gone on to a better place.

There is a more controlled tone of nostalgia in the opening of Morris' *Ceremony in Lone Tree:* "Come to the window. The one at the rear of the Lone Tree hotel. The view is to the west." Even in setting a scene Morris' style moves. Other novels written in a mid-style are Flaubert's *Madame Bovary*, Dreiser's *An American Tragedy*, Sinclair Lewis' *Babbitt*, James Gould Cozzens' *The Just and the Unjust*, Willa Cather's *Song of the Lark*, and Steinbeck's *The Grapes of Wrath*.

Some novels employ a combination of styles. Melville's *Moby Dick* is a strange mixture of styles and techniques within the first-person point of view. In *Bleak House*, Dickens employs the effective strategy of alternating chapters of narration by a good woman with his own omniscient, present-tense, roving-eye view, modulating the style from chapter to chapter, as he shifts point of view. In *Howards End*, E. M. Forster speaks often in his own voice, but modulates objective narration ironically with the thoughts of his characters. In *Portrait of the Artist as a Young Man*, Joyce's style is lyrical but controlled, becoming more and more complex as Stephen matures. Joyce's *Ulysses* uses many literary styles, conventional and experimental, serving a complex form and a profound theme.

The style of most fiction is a careful amalgam of words that denote and words that connote. Some writers use denotative (explicit) words more than others, such as James T. Farrell, James M. Cain, and Erskine Caldwell.

> Lov opened the sack, selected a large turnip, wiping it clean with his hands, and took three big bites one after the other. The Lester women stood in the yard and on the porch looking at Lov eat. Ellie May came from behind the chinaberry tree and sat down not far from Lov on a pine stump. Ada and the old grandmother were on the porch watching the turnip in Lov's hand become smaller and smaller with each bite. (Erskine Caldwell, *Tobacco Road*)

Some writers use connotative (suggestive) words, and thus move closer to poetry, such as Virginia Woolf, Jean Cocteau, J. P. Donleavy, Malcolm Lowry, Gabriel Miro, Vladimir Nabokov.

> Their visits to that islet remained engraved in the memory of that summer with entwinements that no longer could be untangled. They saw themselves standing there, embraced, clothed only in mobile leafy shadows, and watching the red rowboat with its mobile inlay of reflected ripples carry them off, waving, waving their handkerchiefs; and that mystery of mixed sequences was enhanced by such things as the boat's floating back to them while it still receded, the oars crippled by refractions, the sunflecks now rippling the other way like the strobe effect of spokes counterwheeling as the pageant rolls by. (Vladimir Nabokov, *Ada*)

In fiction, language more often connotes than it denotes. The writer tries to evoke something that is not literally denoted in the lines on the page. We experience then what the words evoke. Sometimes the specific limitations of the point of view the author has chosen prevent him from literally stating, force him to evoke explanations, for instance, and the reader then perceives them. "I want to use a minimum of words for a maximum effect," says Wright Morris. "Underwriting seems to be a species of underwater swimming. Is the pool empty? That is how it often looks." Hemingway said, "If a writer of prose knows enough about what he is writing about he may omit things that he knows and the reader, if the writer is writing truly enough, will have a feeling of those things as strongly as though the writer had stated them. The dignity of movement of an iceberg is due to only one-eighth of it being above water."

Zola felt style could be abused if wedded to excess emotion: "We are in fact rotten with lyricism; we believe, quite wrongly, that the grand style is the product of some sublime terror always on the verge of pitching over into frenzy; the grand style is achieved through logic and clarity." When a writer goes too far in his descriptive passages, becoming too lyrical, he ends up with a "purple patch" that calls attention to itself. "Under the pavements trembling like a pulse, under the buildings trembling like a cry, under the waste of time, under the hoof of the beast above the broken bones of cities, there will be something growing like a flower, something bursting from the earth again, forever deathless, faithful, coming into life again like April" (Thomas Wolfe, *You Can't Go Home Again*). Over-written prose is often devoted to descriptions of the sky, of settings, or of the hero waking up in the morning or walking down the street. The realist despises "fine writing," which writers such as Walter Pater, J. K. Huysmans, Ronald Firbank, and Oscar Wilde strive for. The following is from J. K. Huysmans' *Against Nature*.

> With a withdrawn, solemn, almost august expression on her face, she begins the lascivious dance which is to rouse the aged Herod's dormant senses; her breasts rise and fall, the nipples hardening at the touch of her whirling necklaces; the strings of diamonds glitter against her moist flesh; her bracelets, her belts, her rings all spit out fiery sparks; and across her triumphal robe, sewn with pearls, patterned with silver, spangled with gold, the jewelled cuirass, of which every chain is a precious stone, seems to be ablaze with little snakes of fire, swarming over the mat flesh, over the tea-rose skin, like gorgeous insects with dazzling shards, mottled with carmine, spotted with pale yellow, speckled with steel blue, striped with peacock green.

The high style often ends up being affected. Overuse of exotic phrases, archaic words, or juiced-up mannerisms can over-ornament a style. Some writers strive, unfortunately, for a literary tone.

Another threat is *abstract language*. The first eighty pages of *Salt* by Herbert Gold (he is often a good writer) consist almost solely of two kinds of general, abstract statements: "He ate, he slept, he worked, he juggled, and the identical days filed by." "'You love me?' He guessed that he did. He pitied her, cherished her, admired her, and was bored by her. He did not want to be bothered." Very little is immediate or dramatized in those eighty pages. The style is often scintillating, but almost always the experience is abstract. Too little happens in the immediate present. Too many passive verbs render one's style sluggish or inert. Judiciously used, abstract style has its function, but often a writer dupes himself into thinking a high-sounding abstraction contains more emotion and power than it possibly can. Ezra Pound said to the Imagist poets, "Go in fear of abstractions."

By becoming too chummy with the reader, the writer may commit the *cute-tone fallacy*, characteristic at one end of the literary spectrum of many popular magazine stories and at the other of "little" or underground magazine pieces.

"That man has no soul," said Oscar Wilde, "who can read of the death of Little Nell without laughing." Wilde was revolted by the *fallacy of sentimentality*: "The suspension of the activities of the intelligence, of the powers of ethical and intellectual judgment . . . emotion unimpeded by thought." (Beckson and Ganz, *A Reader's Guide to Literary Terms*). "Sentimentality is sentiment in excess of the occasion" (John Crowe Ransom). Today, the use of the *pathetic fallacy* is associated with sentimentality. Ruskin defined it as "the attribution of human characteristics to inanimate objects" (a device akin to personification). "Trees looked down scornfully upon Jeb." Trying too hard for pathos, or sublimity, the writer stumbles into bathos. A similar overreaching is displayed in the *unintentional hyperbole fallacy*, which can be described as rhetoric in excess of the subject or occasion. This fallacy often stands in for imagination when the writer must describe extreme emotions, such as mental anguish, or extreme action, such as physical violence.

Certain qualities contribute to the power of either the complex or the simple style. Deliberate *repetition* enhances the effect of a particular phrase and contributes to a sense of unity. Joseph Heller's *Catch-22* is a good example of effect by repetition.

> "Cut," said a doctor.
> "You cut," said another.
> "No cuts," said Yossarian with a thick, unwieldy tongue.
> "Now look who's butting in," complained one of the doctors. "Another country heard from. Are we going to operate or aren't we?"
> "He doesn't need an operation," complained the other. "It's a small wound. All we have to do is stop the bleeding, clean it out and put a few stitches in."
> "But I've never had a chance to operate before. Which one is the scalpel? Is this one the scalpel?"
> "No the other one is the scalpel. Well, go ahead and cut already if you're going to. Make the incision."

"Like this?"

"Not there, you dope!"

"No incisions," Yossarian said, perceiving through the lifting fog of insensibility that two strangers were ready to begin cutting him.

The reader settles down in his or her response to *texture* in structure and language. Reading Hemingway, the reader feels a tight, though not complex texture, while in reading James, the reader feels a woven texture. The writer's style gives a work a surface texture and his or her voice a resonance. This texture acts upon the mind of the reader almost sensually. The reader feels the loose texture of Carson McCullers in *The Heart Is a Lonely Hunter*, the rough of Norman Mailer in *The Naked and the Dead* and James Jones in *From Here to Eternity*, the smooth of E. M. Forster in *A Passage to India*, and the ragged of Dreiser in *An American Tragedy*. Texture affects a reader's attitude toward what he is reading, disposes him well or ill toward the writer, according to the reader's own temperament.

The reader also responds to prose-rhythm, which differs generally with the two styles, and specifically with every writer. The cadence of good prose differs from ordinary prose when the writer has a feeling for the rhythms of language beyond the sense.

Fictionists have less latitude for inventiveness in language than poets. Since words are the medium for describing characters and telling stories, the illusion is broken if words call attention to themselves. Still, a few writers manage to create a highly volatile style and still sustain the illusion of a heightened reality. One way of giving a new power to language is in the creation of *portmanteau words*. Used by Lewis Carroll and Charles Dickens, portmanteau words were a vogue in the '20s, beginning with the surrealists and perfected by Joyce. James Joyce created a new dream language for *Finnegans Wake,* made up mainly of puns and portmanteau words, and mongrel words from many languages. "And look at here! This cars weeseed. Pretty mites, my sweetthings, was they poor—loves abandoned by wholawidey world? Neighboulotts for newtown. The Eblanamagna you behazyheld loomening up out of the dumblynass. But the still sama sitta. I've lapped so long." He suggested that the language is indeed protean, governed only by appropriateness, the terms of which are implicit in the choices the writer makes about raw material and techniques. In such words themselves we see the principle of juxtaposition or montage at work. The writer's inventive use of words is encouraging a linguistic study of literature. Faulkner, Joyce, and other writers even make up new words. Sometimes new words are coined after a character: Snopes, Babbitt, Scrooge.

A *cliché* is an expression that once had the force of originality and freshness but has become trite and stale through overuse. Some writers (and some readers) do not object as strongly as others to clichés, but a writer tries to be as original as he or she can without calling too much attention to his style.

Some writers deliberately use clichés to give an aura of everyday reality to the world they are creating. Other writers prepare a special context for a cliché that resurrects its original vitality with a new meaning or emotional power. Clichés are sometimes used deliberately. Wright Morris resurrects and transforms the buried cliché frequently in his nineteen novels. In *Man and Boy,* Warren Ormsby, an ordinary man, muses upon the fate of his son, missing in action and remembers a Christmas they never shared: "How did one grasp something like that? . . . Oh, it was one thing to be dead, but what was the word for describing what it was to have been not quite alive? Well, he knew. The words for that were *nipped in the bud.* During a war one heard them everywhere."

Colloquial language in the author's own narrating voice, along with ungrammatical elements, dialect, slang, profanity, even archaisms, can achieve special effects: "Folks this here is the story of the Loop Garoo Kid . . . Men called him brother only to cop his coin" (Ishmael Reed, *Yellow Back Radio Broke-Down*).

A writer's style not only reflects the way his or her mind works, on conscious and unconscious levels, but the way the mind as an organ works. The mind is naturally involved in processes of condensation, concision, concentration of the miscellaneous data taken in by the senses. There are contrary forces at work in every part of the psyche (ego, superego, id, libido). The writer deliberately stimulates these forces, pits one against the other as he or she creates. As this conflict is dramatized implicitly and overtly in the narrative, the style of language in which it is expressed will convey to the reader a sense of the tensions between meaning and expression. Style is a dynamic process that imitates the psyche's own processes. The best style exploits this relationship to the full. Although the writer often speaks directly, he is seldom euphemistic—less today than ever. An early novel by John Lyly, *Euphues, the Anatomy of Wit* (1579), introduced that stylistic concept, but it has almost disappeared from realistic fiction.

For writers such as Flaubert, James, and Joyce, style becomes a kind of absolute. Zola said, "For the writer, genius is not to be found only in the feeling, in the *a priori* idea, but is also in the form and style." Stendhal also testifies: "Often I ponder a quarter of an hour whether to place an adjective before or after its noun." Maupassant is even more exact: "Whatever you want to say, there is only one word to express it, one verb to set it in motion and only one adjective to describe it." Conrad carries this attitude to a higher altitude. "A work that aspires, however humbly, to the condition of art should carry its justification in every line." And Pound gives it an absolute tone: "Literature is language charged with meaning. Great literature is simply language charged with meaning to the utmost degree."

Dialogue is a major element in fiction. Stylistically, it is more a problem of imitation, relatively, than the straight prose passages. It differs in that it is always in the present, and thus dramatic, while most narration is in the past tense. "I can only reach my dramatic effect," said Flaubert, "by the interplay of dialogue and contrast of character." The novelist may learn from the playwright, the movie scriptwriter, and the dramatic monologue in poetry. Striving for the illusion of immediacy, many writers today overuse dialogue. "Only the significant passages of their talk should be recorded," said Edith Wharton, "in high relief against the narrative." Some writers, such as Ivy Compton-Burnett in *A God and His Gifts* and Henry Green in *Loving* are well-known for their deliberate, effective overuse of dialogue. If they are to seem real and alive, characters must speak, but a skillful writer can make passages of description also express character.

A skillful writer employs various techniques to make his lifelike dialogue serve more than one function: convey basic information, reiterate motifs, keep the narrative going, suggest descriptions of other characters who are present or absent from the scene. While most writers do not use nonstandard English in the straight narrative passages, it can be used effectively in dialogue and thus provide some relief and contrast to the general style. "'Yes, Pip, dear boy, I've made a gentleman on you! It's me wot has done it!' . . . The abhorrence in which I held the man, the dread I had of him, the repugnance with which I shrank from him, could not have been exceeded, if he had been some terrible beast" (Dickens, *Great Expectations*). What may seem obvious or obtrusive elsewhere may seem quite natural coming from the mouth of a character. When he attributes an idea or an observation to a character in dialogue, the author is not held responsible. Ernest Hemingway is a master in the many uses of dialogue, as in *The Sun Also Rises*:

> We climbed down. It was clouding over again. In the park it was dark under the trees.
> "Do you still love me, Jake?"
> "Yes," I said.
> "Because I'm a goner," Brett said.
> "How?"
> "I'm a goner. I'm mad about the Romero boy. I'm in love with him, I think."
> "I wouldn't be if I were you."
> "I can't help it. I'm a goner. It's tearing me all up inside."
> "Don't do it."
> "I can't help it. I've never been able to help anything."
> "You ought to stop it."
> "How can I stop it? I can't stop things. Feel that?"
> Her hand was trembling.
> "I'm like that all through."
> "You oughtn't to do it."
> "I can't help it. I'm a goner, now, anyway. Don't you see the difference?"
> "No."

"I've got to do something. I've got to do something I really want to do. I've lost my self-respect."

"You don't have to do that."

"Oh, darling, don't be difficult. What do you think it's meant to have that damned Jew about, and Mike the way he's acted?"

"Sure."

"I can't just stay tight all the time."

"No."

"Oh, darling, please stay by me. Please stay by me and see me through this."

"Sure."

"I don't say it's right. It is right though for me. God knows, I've never felt such a bitch."

"What do you want me to do?"

"Come on," Brett said. "Let's go and find him."

In dialogue the writer attempts to be true to the way people *really* talk; he or she may be much more careful, more unique, in narrative descriptive passages, although too great a contrast may jar.

Although some writers today still rely heavily on *description* (C. P. Snow, James Gould Cozzens, Harriette Arnow, Herbert Gold, John Fowles), descriptive passages are not in themselves as important in today's fiction as in the works of Hardy, Dickens, Tolstoy, or Wolfe. Modern writers have tried to make description active and expressive of character, especially in the central intelligence and first-person points of view, as does Wright Morris' poetically conceived and stylistically compressed *In Orbit*.

This boy comes riding with his arms high and wide, his head dipped low, his ass light in the saddle, as if about to be shot into orbit from a forked sling.

★ ★ ★

That's the picture: there are those who can take it in at a glance. . . . But perhaps the important detail escapes you. He is in motion. Now you see him, now you don't. If you pin him down in time he is lost in space. Somewhere between where he is from and where he is going he wheels in an unpredictable orbit. He is as free, and as captive, as the wind in his face. In the crown of his helmet are the shoes of a dancer with one heel missing, one strap broken. Such things come naturally to knaves, dancers, lovers and twists of the wind. This cool spring morning the rain-scoured light gleams on his helmet, like a saucer in orbit, where the supernatural is just naturally a part of his life.

Descriptions of nature, said Chekhov, and other background features, should be very brief.

Writers differ a great deal in their use of *detail*. The principle of selectivity is employed by most of the best writers; however, some good ones use the additive method (James Farrell, Joyce Carol Oates). But, generally, excessive details and character and background description are detrimental in today's fiction. "However detailed . . . description is," said Ivy Compton-Burnett, "I am sure that everyone forms his own conceptions, that are different from everyone else's, including the author's."

Description is always determined by the point of view. The third-person omniscient author describes objectively, directly, for the reader's benefit. Classic novelists tended to offer chunks of description, inert blocks, that were passive: "The room is surrounded by sticky buffets holding carafes which are dirty and chipped, round mats with a metallic sheen, piles of plates of thick blue-bordered porcelain, manufactured at Tournai" (Balzac, *Père Goriot*). An active style can make a passive passage of description move. (See the selection from *The Great Gatsby* quoted below; notice how quickly events are thrust forward in that passage.) The writer need not delay the reader while he passively describes a setting or character or events. One thing can be made, through style, to happen right after another.

The third-person/central intelligence point of view shows us only what the main character sees and how he responds, reveals the world filtered through his subjectivity, thus reveals his character and personality: "Scobie looked at the next stretcher load and looked away again. A small girl—she couldn't have been more than six—lay on it. She was deeply and unhealthily asleep; her fair hair was tangled and wet with sweat; her open mouth was dry and cracked, and she shuddered regularly and spasmodically. 'It's terrible,' Scobie said" (Graham Greene, *The Heart of the Matter*).

The first-person narrator combines the subjective act of self-discovery with the desire to show the reader objectively what he or she has seen; the narrator is both omniscient storyteller and subject of his story:

> A breeze blew through the room, blew curtains in at one end and out the other like pale flags, twisting them up toward the frosted wedding-cake of the ceiling, and then rippled over the winecolored rug, making a shadow on it as wind does on the sea. The only completely stationary object in the room was an enormous couch on which two young women were buoyed up as though upon an anchored balloon. (Nick speaking, in Fitzgerald's *The Great Gatsby*)

The style is active and the characters move within the setting Fitzgerald describes.

Description is colored by the mood and tone of the narrator of whatever type: melancholic, elegiac, ironic, tragic, sardonic, rhapsodic, or lyrical. It is also affected by the physical point of view: time of day, season, range or scope (close or far away: size), and the senses that are affected. Any description must be consistent with the context of a specific scene and, beyond that, the entire story thus far.

Descriptions convey sensory impressions through imagery. Abstract descriptions, using general words, don't describe but merely offer information or exposition dully. If it's effective, description doesn't report, it re-creates. Conventional descriptions of characters and scenes are often abstract and inert. Figurative descriptions employ figures of speech like similes ("The red sun was pasted in the sky like a wafer," Stephen Crane's *The Red Badge of Courage*) and metaphors ("The sun was a lordly lamp," Thomas Wolfe's *Look Homeward, Angel*). Concrete descriptions do not stop the action to describe a still-life. They create an active sense of movement; they appeal to the senses. They have a freshness of diction, avoiding overuse of adjectives.

The realistic writer chooses his details to create the illusion of actuality; other writers try to evoke a sense of life (verisimilitude) rather than render it fully and literally. The impressionistic writer evokes a sense of a complete and actual world through careful *selection* of details, with some use of symbolism, as does James Agee in *A Death in the Family*.

> On the rough wet grass of the back yard my father and mother have spread quilts. . . . All my people are larger bodies than mine, quiet, with voices gentle and meaningless like the voices of sleeping birds. One is an artist, he is living at home. One is a musician, she is living at home. One is my mother who is good to me. One is my father who is good to me. By some chance, here they are, all on this earth; and who shall ever tell the sorrow of being on this earth, lying, on quilts, on the grass, in a summer evening, among the sounds of the night. . . . After a little I am taken in and put to bed. Sleep, soft, smiling, draws me unto her: and those receive me, who quietly treat me, as one familiar and well-beloved in that home: but will not, oh, will not, not now, not ever: but will not ever tell me who I am.

Just as the technique of selection enables the writer to suggest a sense of fullness, the stylistic technique of *suggestion* enables him to evoke something more than the words in a sentence or paragraph literally state: "In her eyes she seemed to be afraid of him. Her face was full of little lines he had never seen before; they were as small as the lines in her mended best teacup" (James Agee, *A Death in the Family*). Some writers such as Henry James sometimes rely too much on suggestion; some writers are often not suggestive enough (James T. Farrell, John Steinbeck, Erskine Caldwell).

Some of the methods of suggesting or evoking qualities are the use of color or sense imagery: "I tried to fascinate his attention with roadside treasures (an old soggy firecracker whose faded colored stripes were run together, half a ping pong ball containing rainwater) but he took no notice of anything . . ." (Stephen Millhauser, *Edwin Mullhouse*). "Colors, scents and sounds correspond," said Baudelaire.

In *The Great Gatsby,* Fitzgerald selects details carefully, rather than piling one on top of another. Omitting unnecessary details, he strives for emphasis. He strikes a dominant note, creates a dominant impression, subordinates minor details. Rather than cluster descriptions of a character (Daisy) or place (The Valley of Ashes), he breaks them up, presenting single details a bit at a time, placing them strategically. He creates a pattern of description throughout the novel (interiors and exteriors). He works indirectly, letting one character, for instance, describe another in dialogue, thus raising the reader's expectations, as no direct description could: "Her voice is full of money," Gatsby says of Daisy. Fitzgerald orders and arranges, coordinates a succession of details along a narrative thread. Description and narrative are at best inseparable. The distinction is that description emphasizes the image and narrative the action: they are two different kinds of beads on a string.

Other features of point of view and of style are wit, irony, and paradox (important elements of modern poetry as well), seen at work most effectively in the works of Ford Madox Ford, E. M. Forster, and G. K. Chesterton. These rhetorical devices lend intellectual vitality and meaning to a novel, but must be justified by the general context. The meaning of *wit* has changed through literary history; today, it is revealed in clever, mocking observations: in Richard Farina's *Been Down So Long It Looks Like Up to Me,* Stanley Elkin's *The Dick Gibson Show,* Kurt Vonnegut's *Breakfast of Champions.* "It's all very well to say smoking in the lobby only, but have you seen the lobby lately?" (Wilfred Sheed, *Max Jamison).* Some writers are especially well-known for their wit: Ronald Firbank, James Branch Cabell, John Updike, Mary McCarthy, Vladimir Nabokov, Kingsley Amis, Muriel Spark, Honor Tracy, Evelyn Waugh. Sarcasm is almost never used by the author himself, although he may betray a sardonic tone: "Nately's death almost killed the Chaplain" (Joseph Heller, *Catch-22).*

Irony exists when there is a discrepancy between the appearance and the reality of a situation or when the reverse or opposite of what a reader expects happens. Verbal irony occurs when a writer deliberately says the opposite of what he means. Often, a reader sees the irony in a situation while the characters do not. Verbal irony is the use of statements by the author that are contradicted by actual events: "At first he had not understood the four people at all. They talked and they talked—and as the months went on they talked more and more. He became so used to their lips that he understood each word they said" (Carson McCullers, *The Heart Is a Lonely Hunter).* The irony is that Mr. Singer doesn't really understand any of the four people, and they are all convinced that he above all does. The novel is based on a paradoxical theme (the need for privacy and the fear of it) expressed in a series of ironic relationships. Irony is one of the chief sources of pleasure for readers of complex stories. Using subtle stylistic techniques, Ford Madox Ford gives readers one of the great first-person ironic narrators in *The Good Soldier.*

Paradox and irony characterize the view of life presented in much of modern fiction. These attitudes sometimes promote objectivity, as against the sentimental indulgence of William Saroyan in *The Human Comedy.* A *paradox* is a seemingly contradictory statement with an underlying truth factor that reconciles the contradiction. For G. K. Chesterton, paradox is a mark of style, as in *The Man Who Was Thursday:* "Chaos is dull"; "It is always the humble man who talks too much." And for Wright Morris: "What is it that strikes you about a vacant house? . . . It's forever occupied" (*The Home Place*). Today, in a time when most serious fiction is packed with irony, irony-hunting, like symbol-hunting, is a literary sport. The ironic experience is rather serious and limiting, while the paradoxical impulse encourages the imagination to play.

The term "symbolism" is often used for elements that aren't really symbolic or which might, for fiction, better be designated by other terms such as *motif,* counterpoint, parallel, analogues, correspondences, associations. "Comparisons consume me like flies," said Flaubert. Those comparisons must come together in patterns. In a famous essay, Mark Schorer discusses the "matrix of analogy" in *Persuasion, Wuthering Heights,* and *Middlemarch.* He traces the "dominant metaphorical" qualities of these novels, which other critics might call symbolic patterns. Motifs should not be confused with symbols. In *The Great Gatsby* noses (Jordan's, the butler's, etc.) are not used symbolically; they are motifs. Eyes, on the other hand, are used symbolically, so often in so many variations that they also become motifs, patterned throughout.

A *motif* is an element that is repeated, usually with variation, throughout a story. A motif may be a recurring subject, idea, or theme. The use of motif controls character, story, and theme in Aldous Huxley's *Point Counter Point.* Parallels are a type of motif. Motifs should not be confused with symbols, although symbols may be part of a pattern of motifs. Motifs and leitmotifs (terms from music) are aids to emphasis and focus. For example, all through *Gatsby* runs the motif of cars, to emphasize and focus the death car near the end. ("Motive" is sometimes used in this sense.) Some writers employ motif very consciously and consider it one of the major techniques of the art (Joyce, Faulkner, D. H. Lawrence, Proust), while other writers seem to leave such enhancements entirely up to chance (James M. Cain, John O'Hara, Nelson Algren). Motifs aid the process of anticipation. The knife-scissors motif in *To the Lighthouse* leads us to anticipate an event or insight related to or caused by some sharp object.

A *parallel* is an element that moves alongside another element. The two mutually enhance each other's effect, sometimes through contrast or comparison. A parallel is something like a motif in a pattern. It is sometimes mistaken for a symbol. In both Ernest Hemingway's *The Sun Also Rises* and Wright Morris' *The Field of Vision* aspects of the bullfight are related to aspects of character relationships. Some of those aspects are symbolic, some are motifs, but some are merely parallels that give unity to the novel.

Repetition is a device that intensifies the reader's response by enabling him to remember important elements as the story moves ahead. An element is introduced, then repeated, with variations in a pattern, throughout the story. Repetition is a major unifying device.

A final word on style. In "Fiction and the 'Analogical Matrix,'" Mark Schorer says, "Style is conception. It is style, and style primarily that first conceives, then expresses, and finally tests subject matter and theme." The forging of a style is a difficult and lifelong task. Words cannot easily be forced into flesh.

· 22 ·

Symbolism

$\mathcal{S}$ymbolism is the technique of representing one thing by means of another through resemblance or association. An object, image, event, or character may symbolize an idea or theme in a novel. The use of symbolism enables the writer to show relationships among people, nature, society, the intellect, and the spirit. Symbols may be incidental or a story may be unified by a symbolic design. Symbols, like charged images, help to focus ideas and feelings so that the story's impact is stronger and deeper.

The influence of the French Symbolists is still at work in world literature. Most symbolist poets were interested in the way words could signify or evoke subtle sensory experiences. They tried to achieve for poetry the condition of music. Because most novels must create an illusion of reality, the writer's use of symbolist techniques must be very subtle. The purely symbolic imagination is rather rare in fiction, but some writers are much more symbolic than others, Jean Cocteau, Thomas Mann, and William Faulkner more than John Dos Passos, James T. Farrell, and John Steinbeck.

One major kind of unity is achieved by symbolic design. In *The Rainbow* D. H. Lawrence develops a pattern consisting of the rainbow and the cathedral, sexuality and the rhythms of rural life.

> The arc bended and strengthened itself till it arched indomitable, making great architecture of light and colour and the space of heaven, its pedestals luminous in the corruption of new houses on the low hill, its arch the top of heaven.
>
> And the rainbow stood on the earth. She knew that the sordid people who crept hard-scaled and separate on the face of the world's corruption were living still, that the rainbow was arched in their blood and would quiver to life in their spirit, that they would cast off their horny covering of

153

disintegration, that new, clean, naked bodies would issue to a new generation, to a new growth, rising to the light and the wind and the clean rain of
heaven. She saw in the rainbow the earth's new architecture, the old, brittle
corruption of houses and factories swept away, the world built up in a living fabric of Truth, fitting to the over-arching heaven.

In Michel Tournier's *The Ogre,* Tiffauges, the ogre, lives in a "universe of signs
and symbols," of symbolic and mythic patterns, and the reader shares his perceptions of them. "For his vocation was not only to decipher essences but also
to exalt them, to bring their qualities to the point of incandescence. He was
going to give this country a Tiffaugian interpretation, and at the same time
raise it to a higher power, never yet attained." Tiffauges perceives both benign
and malign inversions of conventional signs and symbols. A symbolic design relates a blind elk, a blue horse, a bicycle to his own function as a person who
carries other persons, experiencing euphoria. "Yes, it was a sort of euphoria
that enfolded me from head to foot when I took Jeannot's inanimate body in
my arms . . . a total joy of all my being." Conrad rendered many of his stories
against a symbolic landscape or seascape (*Victory*). The landscape in Mann's *The
Magic Mountain* is obviously symbolic. A very obvious symbol is the letter A in
Hawthorne's *The Scarlet Letter.* In Proust's *Remembrance of Things Past,* the magic
lantern is a symbol of memory and imagination.

> My bedroom became the fixed point on which my melancholy and anx-
> ious thoughts were centered. Some one had had the happy idea of giving
> me, to distract me on evenings when I seemed abnormally wretched, a
> magic lantern, which used to be set on top of my lamp while we waited for
> dinner-time to come: in the manner of the master-builders and glass-
> painters of gothic days it substituted for the opaqueness of my walls an im-
> palpable iridescence, supernatural phenomena of many colours, in which
> legends were depicted, as on a shifting and transitory window.

Ezra Pound advised poets that the natural object is the most effective symbol (a
wound is a "red badge of courage" in Stephen Crane's novel) as opposed to the
rhetorical, the contrived, or the literary symbol that overpopulates Thomas
Mann's *The Magic Mountain,* for instance. The habit of symbol-hunting in modern classrooms and in criticism, encouraged, of course, by the over-infatuation
among writers with symbols, has led to the impression that symbolism has
harmed the novel. As James M. Cain (who made a shark stand for the terror in
all beauty) has said, "Who can't make up symbols?" And most readers might ask,
"And who wants to hunt them down once writers do make them up?" This attitude detracts from the vital importance of a subtle use of symbols and symbolic patterns in works produced by genuine symbolic imaginations: John

Barth's *The Floating Opera*, Joyce's *Ulysses*, Camus' *The Plague*, William Styron's *Lie Down in Darkness*, and Kobo Abe's The *Woman in the Dunes*. In Fitzgerald's *The Great Gatsby*, the Valley of Ashes and the eyes of T. J. Eckleburg symbolize decay of the American vision of a garden of Eden, and Daisy and the green light at the end of her dock symbolize the idealistic American's vision of the American dream.

> This is the valley of ashes—a fantastic farm where ashes grow like wheat into ridges and hills and grotesque gardens.... Above the gray land and the spasms of bleak dust which drift endlessly over it, you perceive, after a moment, the eyes of Doctor T. J. Eckleburg ... their retinas one yard high. They look out of no face, but, instead, from a pair of enormous yellow spectacles ... his eyes, dimmed a little by many paintless days under sun and rain, brood on over the solemn dumping ground.

★ ★ ★

> And as I sat there brooding on the old, unknown world, I thought of Gatsby's wonder when he first picked out the green light at the end of Daisy's dock. He had come a long way to this blue lawn, and his dream must have seemed so close that he could hardly fail to grasp it. He did not know that it was already behind him, somewhere back in that vast obscurity beyond the city, where the dark fields of the republic rolled on under the night.
>
> Gatsby believed in the green light, the orgiastic future that year by year recedes before us. It eluded us then, but that's no matter—tomorrow we will run faster, stretch out our arms farther.... And one fine morning—
>
> So we beat on, boats against the current, borne back ceaselessly into the past.

· 23 ·

Imagery

$\mathcal{I}$n the beginning was the word, and the word was the author, and the word was with the author, if one may, respectfully, paraphrase St. John. The philosopher Ernst Cassirer says that all thinking, all knowledge began with language itself, and language started as poetry, the compressing of the many into the one (all the aspects of a tiger into the word *tiger*). "Word magic is everywhere accompanied by picture magic," he said. "Wisdom speaks first in images," said Yeats. Figurative language is language expanded beyond its usual literal meaning to achieve intensity and vividness. A figurative expression usually contains a stated or implied comparison to express a relationship between things essentially unlike. *Metaphors* and *similes* are two common types of figures of speech. The metaphor "John is a lion" is an implied comparison which is more immediate and dramatic than "John has some of the characteristics of a lion." "John is like a lion" is a simile, a stated comparison. The word *like* specifies that a similarity exists between John and a lion. "As if" and "as though" are other signals that a simile is being introduced in a sentence.

Writers of fiction use similes more often than metaphors because metaphors tend to try a reader's patience. "John is a lion" may make some readers reply, "No, he isn't." A reader is more likely to accept the simile "John is like a lion." Metaphors and similes may be implied rather than overtly stated. They are most effective when the reader feels that they are appropriate to the context of the story, that they seem to be part of a pattern, rather than created for a passing occasion.

Imagery is the collection of descriptive details in a literary work that appeals to the senses. An author uses an image to arouse emotion in the reader and to help create the predominant mood of the story. The writer attempts to embody in vivid images all abstractions and generalizations about character and meaning; to stimulate the reader's senses; to arouse his emotions; to stimulate his imagination.

"An image," said Pound, is "that which presents an intellectual and emotional complex in an instant of time." Yasunari Kawabata is known for his startling images. In *Snow Country* the hero on the train sees a girl's face reflected in the window as the mountain landscape flows by outside: "Shimamura had the illusion that the evening landscape was actually passing over the face, and the flow did not stop. . . . It was a distant cold light. As it sent its small ray through the pupil of the girl's eye, as the eye and the light were superimposed one on the other, the eye became a weirdly beautiful bit of phosphorescence on the sea of evening mountains." Novels are made up of many other kinds of images: auditory, sensory, intellectual.

When Ezra Pound defines literature as "language charged with meaning," the word "meaning" may be taken as a fusion of emotion and idea in the imagination. The controlling or dominant image, the image-nucleus in a work that is organically unified, has the potency of a poetic image, discharging its power gradually, as the story moves from part to part. After the reader has fully experienced the story, fully perceived it in a picture, that focal image continues to discharge its power. The symbolic image of the green light at the end of Daisy's dock in *The Great Gatsby* becomes a condensation and abstraction of many other images in that novel. The developing elements in a novel become integrated finally, Croce tells us, in an image, and "what is known as an image is always a tissue of images." Yeats said, "I seek not a book but an image."

The concept of the charged image is a way of talking about coherence and synthesis in a work of art. The important elements of a story are condensed and compressed into this charged image. It can evoke all the other elements—theme, character, setting, conflict, style, and so on. The image is highly charged with emotion and meaning. Some examples are Don Quixote and Sancho Panza on the road approaching the windmills, Huckleberry Finn and Jim on the raft on the Mississippi River between adventures, the green light passage from *Gatsby* quoted earlier, Mick Kelly, Jake Blount, Doctor Copeland, and Biff Brannon sitting around Mr. Singer in his kitchen in Carson McCullers' *The Heart Is a Lonely Hunter.* In Yves Berger's *The Garden,* the charged image is the symbolic polarity of the garden of the imagination surrounded by the world of actuality.

On Virginia's shoulders I stroke the wheels of the wagons, the runaway mules, the fur of the guzzling bears. I listen to an earthquake which quiets down, subsides. ". . . Words, nothing but words and when you have said them, when you have wallowed in them, on them, when you have made yourself drunk with words, then you open your eyes, they fall on me who am waiting, waiting for you, a real Virginia, of flesh and blood—"

This charged image from early and late (a separation of 500 years) in Virginia Woolf's fantasy *Orlando* captures the concept of timelessness and of the simultaneity of all time.

> Flinging himself from his horse, he made, in his rage, as if he would breast the flood. Standing knee deep in water he hurled at the faithless woman all the insults that have ever been the lot of her sex. Faithless, mutable, fickle, he called her; devil, adulteress, deceiver; and the whirling waters took his words, and tossed at his feet a broken pot and a little straw.

★ ★ ★

> But descending in the lift again—so insidious is the repetition of any scene—she was again sunk far beneath the present moment; and thought when the lift bumped on the ground, that she heard a pot broken against a river bank.

The charged image in Camus' *The Stranger* comes at the exact center of the novel.

> Then everything began to reel before my eyes, a fiery gust came from the sea, while the sky cracked in two, from end to end, and a great sheet of flame poured down through the rift. Every nerve in my body was a steel spring, and my grip closed on the revolver. The trigger gave, and the smooth underbelly of the butt jogged my palm. And so, with that crisp, whipcrack sound, it all began . . .

The novelist, no less than the poet, is the maker of images. In a novel, the images are less concentrated, and are dispersed among discursive passages. Conrad said, "My task which I am trying to achieve is, by the power of the written word to make you hear, to make you feel—It is, before all, to make you see. That—and no more, and it is everything."

The *epiphany* is a special kind of image that creates a moment of illumination more for the character perhaps than the reader. James Joyce perfected the epiphany: "A sudden spiritual manifestation, whether in the vulgarity of speech or of gesture or in a memorable phase of the mind itself . . . the most delicate and evanescent of moments" (*Stephen Hero*). We experience this perfect moment in many novels, including Joyce's *Portrait of the Artist as a Young Man*.

> A girl stood before him in midstream, alone and still, gazing out to sea. She seemed like one whom magic had changed into the likeness of a strange and beautiful seabird. Her long slender bare legs were delicate as a crane's and pure save where an emerald trail of seaweed has fashioned itself as a sign upon the flesh . . .

She was alone and still, gazing out to sea; and when she felt his presence and the worship of his eyes her eyes turned to him in quiet sufferance of his gaze without shame or wantonness . . .

Her image has passed into his soul for ever and no word had broken the holy silence of his ecstasy. Her eyes had called him and his soul had leaped at the call. To live, to err, to fall, to triumph, to recreate life out of life! A wild angel had appeared to him, the angel of mortal youth and beauty, an envoy from the fair courts of life, to throw open before him in an instant of ecstasy the gates of all the ways of error and glory. On and on and on and on!

There are very similar epiphanies involving the idealized woman in *The Great Gatsby*; *Look Homeward, Angel; Raintree County*; *The Rainbow*; and Bloom experiences an anti-epiphany in Joyce's *Ulysses* when he gazes at Gertie.

Motifs, symbols, parallels, images, epiphanies culminate, into a pattern or contrasting sets of patterns that contribute to organic unity, as in Ford Madox Ford's *The Good Soldier*, Albert Camus' *The Stranger*, Ralph Ellison's *Invisible Man*.

Patterns emphasize the relationships among all the characters and elements in a novel. In the best novels, we don't want merely to find out what happens; we enjoy accumulatively apprehending some order over the content, and through that order an emotion and some insight into its meaning. We respond to design, to incremental, converging patterns, whether they are narrative or mainly expressive of character.

Pattern or *design* is the repetition through complications of the central incident or idea. As we sense the pattern or design of the story we feel that it is moving forward at the same time that the main line of interest is being sustained. Pattern has to do with the organized relationships between the various elements or aspects of the story. Through a careful concern with these elements, form evolves and we have a sense of unity when we have finished the story. Each part functions in its relationship to the whole. The story's form enables us to keep before us as the story moves a comprehension of the whole. The effectiveness of a pattern is in the way the reader follows it to its completion.

Some may argue that such patterns are mere embroidery, and may be described modestly as amplification with various gradations and modulations, employing contrast as a device. Perhaps in its simplest form this process may be thus mechanically described; but in most of the finest novels, handling of designs and patterns unifies the work and thus transmits its power. A major principle at work in achieving this end is the technique of *selectivity*.

"Life being all inclusion and confusion, and art being all discrimination and selection . . . life persistently blunders and deviates . . . life . . . is capable . . . of nothing but splendid waste," said Henry James. Robert Louis Stevenson said, more succinctly, that the writer must "suppress much and omit more." A good example of a work that would have benefited from selection is Alexander

Solzhenitsyn's *The Gulag Archipelago*. A novel in which selection is intelligently employed is Turgenev's *Fathers and Sons*.

The technique of selectivity enables the writer to choose scenes that reveal something, rather than just scenes that would occur in life. Artistry, not life, is the final criterion for what the writer leaves in his story. Out of all the possibilities in a situation, he attempts to choose, select, those details that tell the most, that suggest the whole scene, and perhaps give "clues to character, situation, and theme." Since a writer cannot tell all, he or she must select what will be most effective; and sometimes he or she does not *tell* at all—he or she merely suggests, and the reader proceeds from there. The importance of selectivity applies not only to scenes and dialogue but to the writer's choice of details as well. He strives to create, imagine details that reveal. Such repeated details not only give a sense of unity to the story but evoke aspects of character and mood.

An irritating type of misplaced emphasis is the tedious reproduction of *trivia,* or the *lighting a cigarette fallacy.* The hero's most trivial action is described as though stars were altered in their courses. The reader regards that kind of cause and effect as purely literary. The writer must also take care not to commit the *claims fallacy.* "McPheeters was the funniest man in the world." The reader expects the writer to demonstrate proof of that claim.

· *24* ·

Unity

*T*he repetition of motifs, situations, character relationships contributes to the effect of *unity.* The reader is pleased to sense that some kind of harmony of the elements of a novel is slowly being achieved. To make the reader aware of this harmony, the writer may use devices of dissonance, as in music, by contrast; the four parts of Faulkner's *The Sound and the Fury* with their very different narrative voices rasp against each other.

In all novels, some principle of integration is at work, striving for structural, thematic, symbolic, spatial, temporal unity, the effect of which is an intense, and, most important for many novelists, lasting experience for the reader. They cause, sometimes, a metamorphosis or transformation. Every novel is an act of metamorphosis or transformation, but the deliberate effect of some novels is to make the reader experience more intensely the process of transformation.

The total effect of the devices that contribute to unity is to create a sense at the end of *simultaneity* and *inevitability.* When all the elements in a story are coordinated and controlled by techniques, the effect is a sense of simultaneity, a feeling at any given moment that all the elements interact in our minds and emotions. The reader holds all the elements in the consciousness at once, as in a *gestalt.* If the reader has this sense of simultaneity throughout the story, he or she feels at the end a sense of inevitability. Everything has happened as it has because it has to. "Before everything," said Ford Madox Ford, "a story must convey a sense of inevitability."

Form and unity work against chaos in the reader's responses; the reader doesn't like to feel that the elements of a novel are there gratuitously or accidentally.

Many recent novels strive for something different from unity. We may experience in some so-called plotless novels the ongoing stages of a process that flows and shifts, with moments of verisimilitude and a general feeling of anti-form, anti-structure. Process is a more apt term for these novels than plot (the novels of Nathalie Sarraute, Claude Simon, and Alain Robbe-Grillet are defined by a carefully created context). Context may suggest a rather mechanical building up; ambience is created by a more impressionistic technique as in Virginia Woolf's novels.

Structure as used today is not quite the same thing as form. The one is relatively mechanical, the other organic; the one is apt more for aesthetic works, the other for traditional novels. "Form follows function," said Susanne K. Langer. If the function of the novel is to tell a story, the structure will be sequential, architectural, and when the roof goes on, and smoke goes out the chimney, the reader has had a very different kind of experience from one involving form. If the novel's function is to stimulate in the reader the same perceptions the character experiences, with a sense of wholeness at the end that is denied the character, then the form will seem to follow the gestalt-making mental process, the convolutions of emotions rather than the mechanics of episodes, while simultaneously growing, through various techniques, toward an organic whole. The reader apprehends this process of growth and beholds it at the end, recognizes that it has been prefigured every moment along the way. Stephen Dedalus in James Joyce's *Portrait of the Artist as a Young Man* invokes Aquinas: "Three things are needed for beauty, wholeness, harmony, and radiance." Form and structure generate energy, life, emotion, and they shape meaning. But form is a mysterious phenomenon when it is achieved by a master, structure less so. Still, talk about form alerts the reader to its manifestations; one must develop a facility for responding to the evolution of form; it does not come easily for many of those readers who find the structural approach more readily apprehendable. "Form alone *takes,* and holds and preserves substance," said Henry James.

The fundamental opposition between the Apollonian and the Dionysian mentality takes another shape in the formalist-mimetic conflict. In criticism and in fictional practice there is a dualism of word and idea, expression and thought, manner and matter, form and content or substance, treatment and subject, language or style and content, theme and form. Paralleling questions about form is a less trenchant question: are some subjects more suitable to fiction than others?

There are various general notions of form that spring from subject matter itself: imitative or mimetic form (the writer imitates things, people, events just as they are found in reality), expressive form (intense feeling produces its own natural form), and spatial form (metaphorical use of space as a basis for form). The most artistic novels of the twentieth century (Faulkner's *The Sound and the Fury,* for instance) exhibit "organic form" (Samuel Coleridge's term) which is "innate" in content, as in nature—the idea and the form of a snake are one. "Cut a good story anywhere," said Chekhov, "and it will bleed." The organic analogy asserts that art follows processes similar to those in nature. "A novel is a living thing," said James, "all one and continuous, like every other organism." The organic concept requires the detachment of an architect or a musician. "The less one feels a thing," said Flaubert, "the more likely one is to express it as it really is." A kind of dynamism arises from the deliberate cultivation of the tensions between content and form. The conflict here with the notion of expressive form is obvious.

The organic formalists are inclined to use musical analogies (fugue, symphonic) when discussing form, and James used the metaphor "architectonics" when discussing structure. The formalist approach harks back to classical principles of symmetry and proportion, and to strict concepts of genre, such as Joyce's Stephen sets forth in "lyric, epic, and dramatic." But a principle that applies to all these approaches is dynamics, for any approach to form will work in its own way if it has its own special means of presenting its elements dynamically.

The novel is a protean form—it can take any shape, even, as James observed, "great fluid puddings." The traditional concept of the aesthetic experience is that, though it shimmers with many vibrations, it should come to an end, it should close. Recent novelists have rejected conventional structure, but have also reacted against the notion of aesthetic harmony. The aesthetic experience is a series of explosions that go on and on, they suggest. The novel can be a launching pad for endless reiterations of the novel's basic elements, as we see in Julio Cortazar's *Hopscotch*. Thomas Pynchon's *Gravity's Rainbow* is another such "open-ended" work.

Whether the writer works best with structure or in creating closed or open forms, he acts out her will to *make*, his compulsion to create order out of fragmentation and chaos. Some novels are much more ordered than life itself, and some seem to be much less. The nature of the elements of the novel defeat any nihilistic attempt to copy disorder. The imitative fallacy operates here: an imitation of boredom can be very fascinating, and thus it ceases to be boredom and becomes fiction. Chaos on paper is order impersonating chaos.

One also ought to ask whether the novel can ever tell the truth as science seems to. The novel must necessarily distort in order to clarify. Its paradoxes of form and function are the source of its triumphs and its failures. Some readers mistake the obvious triumphs for the only possibilities, and some writers mistake the failures for the only route to possibilities. For instance, words are the medium, but most of the best writers make readers forget that and create an illusion of reality as the reader on his or her part willingly suspends disbelief in the transaction. However, some superb writers, recognizing that words are the medium, devote all their energies to pursuing all the ramifications of language—lesser writers go the same way to failure.

A novel's structure may be described in many ways. For instance, there is the Marxian triad concept: thesis, anti-thesis, and synthesis results in form. In an epic novel, the term *amalgam* of various components or *epic synthesis* is used. More critics than novelists cling consciously to one or another structural approach. What is needed among critics, and also among novelists and their readers, is a pluralistic overview or eclectic approach to matters of technique. Few will disagree that the novel's subject matter is the entire province of human experience, but controversy about technique continues. Few writers work out of multiple possibilities.

· 25 ·

Innovative Techniques

$\mathcal{T}$o some degree every fiction, even the simplest, defies definite interpretation, and that is especially true of innovative fictions. They are so far outside recognizable contexts that they cannot be judged good or poor—they simply *are*. Avant-garde stories seem immune to literary analysis. No literary criteria can be applied to the question, "Are the writers in control of their materials?" Some critics labor to explain and describe what innovative fiction strives to achieve, but there is an inherent contradiction in trying to explain a story that was originally conceived to defy analysis. All we can expect to do here, then, is suggest a few ways of approaching and perhaps getting into stories by avant-garde, experimental, or innovative writers.

Generally, the novel has been the most conservative of art forms. It lends itself to greater variety in subject matter, but fewer possibilities in form. " 'The novel, of all literary genres, is the freest, the most lawless,' held forth Edouard. . . . Is it for that very reason, for fear of that very liberty (the artists who are always sighing after liberty are often the most bewildered when they get it), that the novel has always clung to reality with such timidity?'" (Gide, *The Counterfeiters*). Gide's novel itself was a narrative innovation, but within this genre few distinct innovations have made a lasting and pervasive impression.

The most influential avant-garde movements in the novel were affected by the French Symbolist poets who reacted against the rationalism of the Victorian Age and the old-fashioned romanticism of earlier eras. They turned art to the complex operation of the senses. They explored the unconscious and the dream world as a major area of human experience not adequately depicted in art. Because conventional concepts of human experience and beauty were related mainly to bourgeois ethics and religion, these poets explored experiences not previously touched upon. They were drawn to the world of the poor, the criminal,

165

the forbidden, to the abnormal. These poets described states of being that verged on the illegal, that posed a threat to conventional society. They used irrational means to explore the irrational and the subconscious. Relativism reigned. Words and their associations were examined in numerous combinations, in what might be called the explosion of poetic license. Self-expression became, as never before, an end in itself. They introduced symbolism to the literary world, although, of course, it had been used less consciously in such works as Melville's *Moby Dick* (see the chapter on the Whiteness of the Whale). Proust, Joyce, Woolf, and James were directly affected by the symbolists.

The surrealists decided the symbolists had not gone far enough. They focused upon the life of the subconscious and dreams as manifestations of mankind's true nature. Andre Breton's *Nadja* was the first, perhaps best, of the surreal romances.

> When the dessert is served, Nadja begins looking around her. She is certain that an underground tunnel passes under our feet, starting at the Palais de Justice (she shows me which part of the building, slightly to the right of the white flight of steps) and circling the Hotel Henry IV. She is disturbed by the thought of what has already occurred in this square and will occur here in the future. Where only two or three couples are at this moment fading into the darkness, she seems to see a crowd. "And the dead, the dead!" The drunkard lugubriously continues cracking jokes. Nadja's eyes now sweep over the surrounding houses. "Do you see that window up there? It's black, like all the rest. Look hard. In a minute it will light up. It will be red." The minute passes. The window lights up. There are, as a matter of fact, red curtains . . . I confess that this place frightens me, as it is beginning to frighten Nadja too. "How terrible! Can you see what's going on in the trees? The blue and the wind, the blue wind. I've seen that blue wind pass through these same trees only once before. It was there, from a window in the Hotel Henry IV, and my friend, the second man I told you about, was about to leave. And there was a voice saying: 'You're going to die, you're going to die.' I didn't want to die, but I felt so dizzy . . ."

Anais Nin, in such novels as *House of Incest*, is one of the few writers who remained committed to the surrealistic vision. (Compare style and technique with Barnes' *Nightwood*.)

> Men recognized her always: the same effulgent face, the same rust voice. And she and I, we recognized each other; I her face and she my legend.
>   Around my pulse she put a flat steel bracelet and my pulse beat as she willed, losing its human cadence, thumping like a savage in orgiastic frenzy. The lamentations of flutes, the double chant of wind through our slender bones, the cracking of our bones distantly remembered when on beds of down the worship we inspired turned to lust.

As we walked along, rockets burst from the street lamps; we swallowed the asphalt road with a jungle roar and the houses with their closed eyes and geranium eyelashes; swallowed the telegraph poles trembling with messages; swallowed stray cats, trees, hills, hedges, Sabina's labyrinthian smile on the keyhole. The door moaning, opening. Her smile closed. A nightingale disleafing melliferous honey-suckle. Honey-suckled. Fluted fingers. The house opened its green gate mouth and swallowed us. The bed was floating.

The poems and novels of the surrealists were ways of exploding the barriers between the conscious and the unconscious life. There was a great emphasis on spontaneity, such as automatic writing, championed by Gertrude Stein. Free-association writing was prevalent in the movement (Joyce's *Ulysses,* passages in Virginia Woolf's novels). In free-association, these writers discovered relationships among objects and events that rational means cannot uncover. The process stimulated remembrance of things forgotten, and there was an associational progression in their works. Images that stylized reality filled their novels. Some writers employ surrealistic passages, without producing a sustained surreal vision: Nathanael West in *The Dream Life of Balso Snell*, John Hawkes in *The Cannibal*, Djuna Barnes in *Nightwood*, Susan Sontag in *The Benefactor*, Kenneth Patchen in *The Journal of Albion Moonlight*, Henry Miller in *Tropic of Capricorn*, and William Burroughs in *Naked Lunch*.

white flash . . . mangled insect screams . . .
I woke up with the taste of metal in my mouth back from the dead
trailing the colorless death smell
afterbirth of a withered grey monkey
phantom twinges of amputation. . .
"Taxi boys waiting for a pickup," Eduardo said and died of an overdose
in Madrid. . .
Powder trains burn back through pink convolutions of tumescent flesh . . .
set off flash bulbs of orgasm . . . pin-point photos of arrested motion . . . smooth
brown side twisted to light a cigarette . . .
He stood there in a 1920 straw hat somebody gave him . . .
soft medicant words falling like dead birds in the dark street. . . .
"No . . . No more . . . No mas . . ."

Surrealists banded together—painters, playwrights, poets, movie makers, novelists—and published their own works in their own magazines, issuing manifestoes: "The writer expresses. He does not communicate," declared Eugene Jolas in *transition* magazine in 1929.

If most of the symbolists were too disciplined for the surrealists, for the Dadaists the surrealists weren't revolutionary enough. While the symbolists were eminently unpolitical, although they were sometimes moralists and social critics (especially Baudelaire), many of the surrealists and Dadaists became communists or socialists, working for a new order (which ironically, would certainly reject their art). The Dadaists were anti-aesthetic as well as anti-rational, but they were at the same time anarchists and revolutionaries, deliberately causing confusions in every aspect of their activities. They set out to destroy all art forms and show through their own methods the madness of all human existence. Nothing was sacred; nothing was absolute; no patterns in life, society, or art were valid. They juxtaposed images that had no logical relation whatsoever. Louis Aragon's *Anicet* is the best of the few novels the Dadaist movement spawned.

The surrealists and the Dadaists together were truly avant-garde in seeking the frontiers of human (and perhaps animal) sensual experience and in testing conventional aesthetic notions. The result, once the shock wore off, was that their techniques and attitudes were absorbed by less militant writers, and with great self-control and artistic discipline, those writers were able to make use of the discoveries and new emphases of the surrealists and the Dadaists. The movements themselves did not produce a single poem, novel, or play of lasting value. While some of the paintings are fascinating, especially those of surrealists Dali, Max Ernst, Chirico, Paul Klee, Miro, Magritte, Chagall, Yves Tanguy, and a few others, most of the work looks old-fashioned, outmoded. The French Symbolist poets have fared far better; the works of Mallarme, Corbiere, Valery, Nerval, Baudelaire, Verlaine, Rimbaud are, of course, still vital, exciting, and relevant as art, and their effects continue to be felt. These lines from "Golden Verses" by Nerval anticipate the anti-novelists, especially Robbe-Grillet:

> . . . life bursts from all things
> "Everything's sentient!" and works on you.

> Beware! from the blind wall one watches you:
> even matter has a logos all its own . . .
> Pure spirit grows beneath the surface of stones.

The experimental novel uses new forms and techniques (symbolism, impressionism, expressionism, surrealism, Dadaism, automatic writing) to express new insights and attitudes. Many of the works of the avant-garde are as ephemeral as thesis-ridden or subject-dominated novels because their claim to the reader's attention is that they are new and unique and depart from or revolt against the conventional novel. But when experimental or avant-garde techniques have become accepted and are used frequently, sometimes even in so-called popular fiction, the particular innovative work ceases to be exciting and becomes a curiosity in the history of literature. Most surrealistic novels are almost as unreadable as most popular novels of the twenties and proletarian novels of the thirties. Their achievements have been skillfully absorbed into the mainstream of literature. That is as it should be, for the very nature of an experiment is that it prepares for something more important and lasting than itself.

Most writers experiment constantly, but in private. The so-called experimental writer offers his experiments to a limited public that finds the mere act of experimenting intrinsically important and meaningful. But often, the meaning is exterior to the work; it is valued as an act of rebellion against an established literature that has withered or ceased to interest the experimental writer and his audience.

The experimental writer knows and writes for his audience—unconsciously perhaps—as obviously as the best-seller writer. In fact, avant-garde art of every kind has always had a great deal in common with folk and popular art; it came into being *with* the mass media. Innovative writing often derives as much from pop as from high-culture models. The avant-garde writer often uses popular fiction elements as his material and distorts them to his purposes, to explode conventional forms and to outrage the bourgeoisie. (Camus patterned *The Stranger* on Cain's *The Postman Always Rings Twice*). Both popular and experimental writers emphasize pure experience over meanings.

The audience for experimental writing is limited, perhaps because it is difficult to see the value of form divorced from logical meaning. There is a predisposition to be confused—why make a part of an experience the whole? With the increasing sophistication of the mass media and its audience, avant-garde may be in danger of becoming totally absorbed, for few techniques are shocking in a culture that has few norms to which the majority conforms.

The major innovations of the deliberately avant-garde or experimental writer are: stream of consciousness (Dujardin and Joyce); collage (William Burroughs' *Nova Express*); surrealism (Breton, Cocteau); Dadaism (Louis Aragon, *Anicet*); black humor (Bruce Jay Friedman, Donald Barthelme, Kurt Vonnegut Jr.); montage (Lautreamont, Patchen); new uses of language (Gertrude Stein, Joyce).

Avant-garde and experimental novelists try new things with form and language, seldom with theme and content (Joyce, Stein, Cortazar). This observation suggests that the basic effect of the novel, like most art forms, is aesthetic. But too often experimentalists simply take a device or technique used by many novelists, as one among many techniques, and exaggerate it. This technique is used by Joseph Heller in *Catch-22*, by Gertrude Stein in *Three Lives*, Gunter Grass in *The Tin Drum*, Curzio Malaparte in *The Skin*, and also by Dickens, somewhat less comically, in *Bleak House*.

One delayed consequence of the Dadaist movement, joined with existentialism and the concept of the absurd, is the black humor movement, which is also political in nature, as was the Dadaist movement. The black humorists of today are not as philosophically grounded in the absurd and in existentialism as were the writers who inspired black humor. Black humor often deliberately employs low comedy kinds of humor to express the senselessness and futility of life in the electronic age; a style composed of disjointed syntax and barren clichés expresses man's inability to communicate. Life is an absurd, black, terrifying farce. The black or absurd humorist attempts to exorcize every vestige of sentimental allegiance to decayed institutions and paralyzing attitudes and values. Here are a few examples: J. P. Donleavy's *The Ginger Man*; Terry Southern's *The Magic Christian*; Kurt Vonnegut's *Mother Night*; James Purdy's *Cabot Wright Begins*; John Barth's *The Sot-Weed Factor*; Joseph Heller's *Catch-22*; and Bruce Jay Friedman's *A Mother's Kisses*.

Black humor is a source of power to writer and reader, appealing strongly to somewhat impotent people who feel incapable of coping with the forces that victimize man in our computerized age. The cruel laughter is directed mainly at those who create the horrible conditions in our world, but includes the passive victims as well. The hero is liberated by his black vision to little more than endless gallows humor. The idea of a solution is painfully laughable. Like most destructive visions, this one thrives on an inverted sentimentality. Some readers' hatred of literature makes them warm to a literature of hatred.

The anti-novel uses techniques devised to frustrate the reader's expectations about fiction, derived from reading traditional novels. The responsive reader is then open to new kinds of fictive experience. By violating traditional concepts of the novel, the author attempts to set it free, to delineate new states of consciousness. Today, the terms "anti-novel," "anovel," "aliterature," "*noveau roman*" (the new novel), "ante-novel" or "thingism," "realistic formalism," "objectivism," or "phenomenalism" describe the work mainly of the French: Robbe-Grillet (*Jealousy*), Natalie Sarraute, Samuel Beckett (an Irishman who writes in French), Michel Butor (*The Modification*), Claude Mauriac (*The Marquise Went Out at Five*). Bernard Pingaud has said of the antinovel: "What the new novelists describe or relate is what takes place before the novel in the classic sense has begun, previous to any characters or story." Calling for a new realism, Robbe-Grillet asserts that "the discovery of reality will continue only if we abandon outworn forms." The novel "does not express . . . it explores itself" (*For a New Novel*). Mainly, these writers want to throw out conventional notions of story and characterization and focus upon the phenomenal world of objects and natural events (Natalie Sarraute, *Tropisms*) and through them evoke the inner life of anti-heroes.

Just as naturalism depicted the hero as victim, the psychological experimental novel usually presents a character whose distinguishing characteristic is self-pity. The self-pitying or self-contemptuous hero in search of himself often results in a book in search of its form, as in Julio Cortazar's *Hopscotch*. Some of the experimental novels exhibit an alogical structure (a logic peculiar to the specific work) employing a plastic language, multiple vision, an image in process of taking shape, kaleidoscopic progression. (See Richard Ellmann and Charles Feidelson, The *Modern Tradition*.) With Samuel Beckett, the focus is mainly on language; it, and what it describes, is reduced to the bare essentials, style without substance, as in the *Unnamable,* in which the narrator clings to life by the frail strands of rhetoric.

> Where now? Who now? When now? Unquestioning. I, say I. Unbelieving. Questions, hypotheses, call them that. Keep going, going on, call that going, call that on. Can it be that one day, off it goes on, that one day I simply stayed in, in where, instead of going out, in the old way, out to spend day and night as far away as possible, it wasn't far. Perhaps that is how it began. You think you are simply resting, the better to act when the time comes, or for no reason, and you soon find yourself powerless ever to do anything again. No matter how it happened. It, say it, now knowing what. Perhaps I simply assented at least to an old thing. But I did nothing. I seem to speak, it is not I, about me, it is not about me. These few general remarks to begin with. What am I to do, what shall I do, what should I do, in my situation, how proceed? By aporia pure and simple? Or by affirmations and negations invalidated as uttered, or sooner or later? Generally speaking . . .

Some of these writers (Robbe-Grillet, Susan Sontag, Marguerite Duras) have turned to film as a way of capturing *the thing itself,* evoking sterility, deja vu, ennui, and the nostalgia of despair.

Here are some arguments defending avant-garde fiction's effects. Experimental writers reject traditional techniques because those techniques fail to depict facets of our contemporary experience. Glibly, sympathetic commentators continue to cite conditions that by now have become clichés: Bureaucracy and technology have dehumanized civilized man, overwhelming social dislocations have fragmented individual identity, even group identity has proven inadequate, scientific and psychological models for living have failed, and life since the end of World War II has become boring, insipid, banal, dull, and conformist.

Racial, social, and economic inequality, the threat of the bomb, insane wars, terrorism, ecological breakdown, and political treachery inspire in many innovative fictionists a pessimistic view of man as a degraded creature. They argue that as mankind experiences rapid social and psychological changes, fiction should simultaneously reflect and contribute to the process of change. But traditional fiction has failed to do that, they charge, because the possibilities of its forms have been exhausted. Experimental writers often point out that while other art media reflect a changing world, fiction remains the most "conservative art of midcentury," the "most self-imitative," the most predictable and formulaic. Fictionists are inspired by innovations in other media more than by those in their own: abstract expressionist painting, free-form sculpture, method acting, modern dance, the improvisations of jazz, the music of chance.

In the opening paragraphs of *The Death of the Novel* (a novella), Ronald Sukenick expresses the view of many fictionists.

> Fiction constitutes a way of looking at the world. Therefore I will begin by considering how the world looks in what I think we may now begin to call the contemporary post-realistic novel. Realistic fiction presupposed chronological time as the medium of a plotted narrative, an irreducible individual psyche as the subject of its characterization, and, above all, the ultimate, concrete reality of things as the object and rationale of its description. In the world of post-realism, however, all of these absolutes have become absolutely problematic.
>
> The contemporary writer—the writer who is acutely in touch with the life of which he is part—is forced to start from scratch: Reality doesn't exist, time doesn't exist, personality doesn't exist. God was the omniscient author, but he died; now no one knows the plot, and since our reality lacks the sanction of a creator, there's no guarantee as to the authenticity of the received version. Time is reduced to presence, the content of a series of discontinuous moments. Time is no longer purposive, and so there is no destiny, only chance. Reality is, simply, our experience, and objectivity is, of course, an illusion. Personality, after passing through a phase of awkward self-consciousness has become, quite minimally a mere locus for our experience. In view of these annihilations, it should be no surprise that literature, also, does not exist—how could it? There is only reading and writing, which are things we do, like eating and making love, to pass the time, ways of maintaining a considered boredom in face of the abyss. Not to mention a series of overwhelming social dislocations.

Therefore, Sukenick ends his novel *Out*:

> this way this way this way this way this way this way this
> way out this
> way out
> 0

In "Title," a short story, John Barth's writer-narrator recognizes the fictionist's special problem: "I believe literature's not likely ever to manage abstractions successfully, like sculpture for example. . . . Well, because wood and iron have a native appeal and first-order reality, whereas words are artificial to begin with, invented specifically to represent" something else. In the short story "The Birds," Ronald Sukenick's writer-narrator, like Barth's, wants to do what sculpture, theater, even music are doing, what prose fiction hasn't done, isn't doing, won't, perhaps can't do: "Destroy this as you read it. It is printed in a soluble ink which you can lick off the page sentence by sentence. The ink has various flavors depending on the parts of speech to make this easier to understand and swallow." The conditions of his medium allow him only to pretend to offer the reader such an experience.

Innovative writers are trying to add their own contributions to those of other art media in the effort to break out of traditional forms. In several introductions to collections of avant-garde writing, commentators offer the following characteristics of the new fiction: It makes use of aspects of past innovations; of the symbolist, Dada, surrealist, impressionistic, expressionistic, imagist movements in various media. It reflects elements of bohemian, beatnik, hippie, and other subcultures. Its techniques are those of the con man and the magician. It has an aggressively comic spirit that revels in nonsense as an end in itself, that employs elements of satire, parody, burlesque, lampoon, invective, and black humor. Not afraid to take uncalculated risks, this new fiction strives to be vital, exuberant, and audacious.

Innovative writers attempt, their defenders tell us, to experience phenomena purely, innocently: The naked "I" sees with a naked eye. They use techniques that "fracture" the "purely personal flow of perception," producing a "non-narrative succession of fragmented impressions" and "revelatory moments." The focus is "on the experiencing mind" of the author (and/or character) and the reader. It is no wonder that much avant-garde writing has an air of being under the influence of mysterious, mythic forces. It is incantatory, visionary, and prophetic. To achieve those effects, each experimental writer reaches for a unique style, using techniques that "shatter syntax" to recycle, revive, or resurrect what such writers consider to be a used-up or dead language. They labor to forge a pure language, free of empty rhetoric.

Innovative writers attempt, we are told, a "calculated demolition of the conventions" of fiction to break down "the applicability of traditional categories both of judgment and description," categories such as "perceptiveness, good taste, intelligence, the ability to create credible characters, the satisfactory resolution of themes." They are against chronological structure and plot. Refusing to create illusions of real life, they are attracted to bizarre subject matter and depict "implausible people doing incredible things." They are against such messages and themes as "the discovery of love, the loss of innocence, reconciliation to the fact of death, the renunciation of self-interest, the recognition of evil" (Stevick, *Anti-Story*).

Anti-Story (1971) is an anthology of fiction that reveals what is happening in the experimental realm. Philip Stevick, the editor and a fine critic, provides us with some very suggestive titles and subtitles of sections: The new fiction is "against mimesis" (imitation of life); it is "fiction about fiction," he says. It is against reality, preferring to explore the uses of fantasy. It is against depicting events, asserting instead the primacy of the author's creative voice. Against "subject," it is "fiction in search of something to be about." It is against "the middle range of experience," reaching for "new forms of extremity." It is against intellectual "analysis," trying to make us experience "the phenomenal world" directly. It is against "meaning," exploring instead "forms of the absurd." It is against "scale," insisting that a novel can be as short as one paragraph.

Commentators on innovative fiction argue that willful obscurity may enable the imagination to explore possibilities and to push into far-out realms where transformations may occur. In the innovative approach, they point out, there is an infinite range of structural possibilities. Many innovative works reach beyond the limitations of the normal printed page. Each page becomes a visual unit; the reader encounters the fiction first through the naked eye, words are mixed with photos and other page-exploding graphics, causing impingement of words upon images. Each fiction extends the possibilities of life and art.

Innovative fiction breaks up the surface appearances of everyday life and remains unresolved on levels of action, theme, and character. Refusing to impose order upon disorder, innovators force their readers to ride the wild horses of chaos. To force us to experience the relativity of all things, they distort chronology, thwart continuity. They offer us experiences in disintegration, for their fictions do not progressively cohere; they self-destruct, line by line. Unlike traditional stories, the commentators warn, innovative fictions offer not patterns to live by, but freedom from patterns. Everything in the fiction is pure invention; and what we experience is the imagination at play. The fiction does not reflect the real world. It is its own world, and we must accept it as an alternative world. Each fiction is atypical, idiosyncratic, an act of pure creation. The world the author creates exists nowhere beyond the page; it exists only in a language continuum. It does not report on already made and finished things and events; it is in itself a new thing, a new event. Each fiction is about the process of its own creation. A world created by imagination and intuition, it is an aesthetic object, a "self-contained, artificial universe."

Andre Gide's personal credo may stand for the innovative fictionist: "My function is to disturb." Innovative writers and critics assume or claim that the new fiction, using "techniques that perpetually astonish," has certain effects on the reader (even those that sound negative are, in these writers' frame of reference, positive). Innovative fiction does violence to the reader. It startles, provokes, disorients, disturbs, frightens, alienates the reader. Its impact is almost physical; it rapes the reader's senses and sensibility. It violates his preconceptions and expectations about life and art; it shatters ethical and spiritual certainties. Inviting the reader's subjective responses, it "foments radically unusual states of mind." It can inspire the reader's own experimentations in perception and behavior that may change his life. Ronald Sukenick has said in an interview that innovative "fiction is one of the ways we have of creating ourselves." For the reader, experimental fictions offer "experiences to respond to, not problems to figure out." We should "improvise our art as we improvise our lives. No hysterical impositions of meaning."

And here are some arguments attacking avant-garde fiction's effects. Readers who resist innovative writing cite many of the characteristics described so far as reasons for their rejection of it. The majority's most powerful resistance to these experiments is neglect or indifference. But some readers react with overt hostility, charging that innovative writers are arrogantly subjective, willfully perverse, self-indulgent, self-conscious and, in their leftist views, self-righteous. They produce claustrophobic, irrational, deranged, and paranoid works that reek of futility. They write out of destructive, anti-social impulses. Dark, decadent, amoral, subversive, anarchistic, offensively violent, often pornographic, and blasphemous, their abstract, abstruse, arbitrary, ambiguous, bizarre, obscure works lack form, unity, coherence, and control. Because these writers assume too much of the, reader their fictions are to some readers too complex, difficult, exasperating, depressing. To others they are simply too cute, shallow, and boring, and they are often in bad taste. The anti-heroes of these unrealistic concoctions fail to achieve insights, to learn from their experiences. Innovative works, these readers insist, are of only passing interest or relevance; and some are fraudulent put-ons.

These unsympathetic readers further argue that a major limitation of avant-garde writing lies in its very nature: Because the innovative writer can choose only to be free, his freedom is a self-contradiction. On the other hand, the eclectic writer is much freer to choose; he can skillfully use both traditional and innovative techniques. The innovative writer often simply exaggerates a single device or technique that most writers use as one among many in the creative process. The anti-story's basic problem, the unsympathetic reader insists, lies in its negative impulse: It thrives by virtue of being what something else is not, and thus narrows rather than expands possibilities. And the world of the novel—of all genres—has been an expansive one.

Critics point out this limitation in the works of avante-garde writers themselves: Samuel Beckett has not gone far beyond *Watt*; Joseph Heller wrote only two novels, *Catch-22* and *Something Happened*, in fifteen years; John Barth's *Giles Goat-Boy* contains little new and anticipates all consequent Barth; Jean Genet's *Our Lady of the Flowers* contains all Genet's possibilities. The so-called freedom of the avant-garde is a contradiction.

Since their visions differ radically from the majority view, innovative writers often feel they are outlaws in society; as outsiders, they pride themselves on the labels their critics paste on them; they turn every hostile objection into a possible description of their experimental intent; thus when a critic shows how an innovative work violates the rules of traditional fiction, he succeeds only in describing the work's achievement.

Hostile critics charge that innovative writers make pretentious, sometimes hysterical claims to originality in vision and technique, seemingly ignorant of a fact of literary history, that innovation always runs parallel to tradition, that the one never does or should replace the other. In the stream of literature, turbulence comes and goes; the sediment remains. Scholars are fond of citing one of the very earliest novels, Laurence Sterne's *The Life and Opinions of Tristram Shandy, Gent.* (1760), which contains numerous innovative devices, techniques, and ways of rendering human perception. "The machinery of my work is a species by itself," says Sterne, through Shandy. "Two contrary motions are introduced into it, and reconciled, which were thought to be at variance with each other. In a word, my work is digressive, and it is progressive, too, and at the same time." Many graphic devices, such as blank or black pages, and drawings or signs and symbols, were introduced in *Tristram Shandy.* A recent young French novelist offered a novel in a box; readers were invited to reassemble the loose pages any way they wished—few readers did. Steve Katz in *The Exaggerations of Peter Prince* (1968), an odd-sized book, employs photographs, rejected or revised pages of the novel, different sizes and styles of print, drawings, blank spaces, marginalia, as though Sterne had never lived. You can blow up the same monument only once, these scholars observe, and Sterne lit the first fuse.

Experimental writing may prove less difficult if one keeps the foregoing pro and con observations in mind, and if one realizes that every novel offers the reader hints about the ways it should be read. The reader of a story always goes through a creative process that parallels that of the writer, a fact that is especially clear in experimental fictions. All art is in a primary sense about itself—every story is about the process of storytelling, about the relationship between the writer and the reader. That is more obvious in experimental than in traditional novels. The reader should let each fiction happen to him the first time he reads it. Many innovators remind us that "in the beginning was the word . . . and the word was made flesh." They try to expose us to the pure, bracing potency of the word. The best way to get into innovative fiction's sometimes murky waters, then, is to plunge from the highest diving board.

Several of the following sources provided concepts for this section: Joe David Bellamy (ed.), *The New Fiction: Interviews with Innovative American Writers* (Barthelme, Barth, Sukenick, Oates); Madeline Gins, "Brief Autobiography of a Nonexistent," in David Madden (ed.), *Creative Choices*; Beverly Gross and Richard Giannone (eds.), *The Shapes of Fiction*; Rust Hills (ed.), *Writer's Choice*;

Frederick Karl and Leo Hamalian (eds.), *The Naked i*; Jerome Klinkowitz (ed.), *Innovative Fiction*; Richard Kostelanetz (ed.), *Twelve from the Sixties* and *Breakthrough Fictions*; Richard Seaver and Terry Southern (eds.), *Writers in Revolt*; Philip Stevick (ed.), *Anti-Story*; and Ronald Sukenick, *The Death of the Novel*, "The New Tradition" in *Partisan Review 39* (1972), 580–588, and interview in *The Falcon* Numbers 2/3 (Spring 1971), 5–25.

· 26 ·

Revision

$\mathscr{A}$ study of a writer's techniques through an examination of the various versions of a work from notes through conception and revision to final product develops student receptivity to the effects of those techniques (what they do to the reader and *how* they do it) and enables the student to understand the nature and appreciate the effects of the various forms: not only fiction, but also poetry, plays, films, imaginative nonfiction. What the student learns from studying revisions of a particular work enables him or her to apply what he or she has learned to any other work in the genre. The emphasis is not on studying the specific work for its own sake—although that occurs—but on studying the form in which the work is written.

Here is what some writers have said about the importance of rewriting: "The art of writing is re-writing" (Sean O'Faolain), "The best reason for putting something down on paper is that one may then change it" (Bernard de Voto), "Rewrite—the effort always brings some profit, whatever this may be. Those who do not succeed fail because they are lazy" (Albert Camus), "It is in order to shine sooner that authors refuse to rewrite. Despicable. Begin again" (Camus), "It is not every day that the world arranges itself into a poem" (Wallace Stevens, poet).

Joseph Conrad's wife locked him into his study, as she did every morning. When she released him for lunch, she asked, "Joseph, what did you do this morning?" "I put in a comma," he replied. After lunch, she locked him in again. When she released him for dinner, she asked, "And what did you accomplish this afternoon, Joseph?" And he replied, "I took the comma out." This is a very serious illustration of the importance of style, and of revision, in the creative process.

Writers rewrite for many reasons and make many kinds of revisions. One kind of stylistic revision is the attempt to move from telling the reader how a

178

character feels to implying. Suppose that in telling a reader how a character feels, the writer has given the reader three statements in logical order. "John gazed out the window. Because he felt disgusted with the whole world. He pulled the shade." The task in revision is to cut out one of those three statements and to reword the remaining two so that they imply how the character feels. "Restless, John went to the window and gazed out at the city. Smog hazed his vision. He pulled the shade." The experience of "disgust" is not described on the page; it is evoked in the reader through a phantom circuit of the imagination. The best style is one that requires the reader's active, imaginative, intellectual, emotional collaboration.

Compare two versions of a key scene in Wright Morris' *Man and Boy*, expanded from the short story "The Ram in the Thicket." Most of Morris' revisions are omissions; he removes (or slightly rewrites) phrases or lines that too obviously *tell* the reader. His aim is to evoke, to suggest, to reveal. A major stylistic technique is his deliberate use of clichés. The following are from Wright Morris' "The Ram in the Thicket" (*Wright Morris: A Reader*, 594–595) as revised for the novel, *Man and Boy* (pages 26–29). The revised version is underlined.

1. <u>The basement toilet had been put in to accommodate the help,</u>
   The basement toilet had been put in to accommodate the help,
2. <u>who had to use something, and Mother wouldn't have them on her</u>
   who had to use something, and Mother would not have them on her
3. <u>Oriental rug. But until the day he dropped some money on the</u>
   oriental rug. Until the day he dropped some money out of his
4. <u>floor, and had to strike a match, inside, to look for it, Mr. Ormsby</u>
   pants, and had to strike a match to look for it, he
5. <u>hadn't noticed just what kind of a stool it was. Mother had picked it</u>
   had never noticed what kind of a stool it was. Mother had picked it
6. <u>up, as she had told him, second-hand. There was no use, as she had</u>
   up secondhand—she had never told him where—because she couldn't
7. <u>pointed out, why she should buy anything new or fancy for a place</u>
   see buying something new for a place
8. <u>that was meant to be in the dark. He hadn't pushed the matter and</u>
   always in the dark.
9. <u>she hadn't offered more than that. What he saw was very old.</u>
   It was very old,
10. <u>with a chain pull, and operated on a principle that was very</u>
    with a chain pull, and operated on a principle that
11. <u>effective, but invariably produced quite a splash. The boy had</u>
    invariably produced quite a splash.

12. <u>named it the Ormsby Falls. That described it pretty well, it was</u>
13. <u>constructed on that principle, and in spite of the splash they both</u>
But in spite of that, he
14. <u>preferred it to the</u>
preferred it to the one at the store and very much more than the
15. <u>one upstairs. This was a hard thing to explain, as the seat was</u>
one upstairs. This was rather hard to explain since the seat was
16. <u>pretty cold over the winter:</u>
pretty cold in the winter and the water sometimes nearly froze.
17. <u>but it was private, like no other room in the house.</u>
But it was private like no other room in the house.
18. Considering that the house was as good as empty, that was a strange
19. thing to say, but it was the only way to say how he felt. If he
20. went for a walk like the boy, Mother would miss him, somebody
21. would see him, and he wouldn't feel right about it anyhow. All
22. he wanted was a dark quiet place and the feeling that for five
23. minutes, just five minutes, nobody would be looking for him.
24. Who would ever believe five minutes like that were so hard to
25. come by? The closest he had ever been to the boy—after he had
26. <u>The first time the boy had turned up missing, he had been there.</u>
given him the gun—was the morning he had found him here on the
stool.
27. <u>It was that time when the boy had said—when his father nearly</u>
It was then that the boy had said,
28. <u>stepped on him—"Et tu, Brutus," and sat there blowing through his</u>
et tu, Brutus, and they had both laughed so hard
29. <u>nose. Laughing so hard Mr. Ormsby thought he might be sick,</u>
they had to hold their sides. The boy had put his head in a basket
30. <u>Like everything the boy said</u>
of wash so Mother wouldn't hear. Like everything the boy said
31. <u>there had been two or three ways to take it, and there in the dark</u>
there were two or three ways to take it, and in the dark Mr. Ormsby
32. <u>Mr. Ormsby couldn't see his face. He had just stood there, not</u>
could not see his face.
33. <u>knowing what to say. Then the boy stopped laughing and said:</u>
When he stopped laughing the boy said,
34. <u>"You think we ought to make one flush do, Pop?" and Mr. Ormsby</u>
Well, Pop, I suppose one flush ought to do, but Mr. Ormsby
35. <u>had had to brace himself on the door. To be called Pop had made him</u>
had not been able to say anything. To be called Pop made him
36. <u>so weak he couldn't speak, his legs felt hollow, and when he</u>
so weak that he had to sit right down on the stool, just like he was

37. <u>got himself back to the stairs he had to sit down.</u>
    and support his head in his hands.
38. <u>Just as he had never had a name for the boy, the boy had never</u>
    Just as he had never had a name for the boy, the boy had never
39. <u>had a name for him—one, that is, that Mother would permit him to use.</u>
    had a name for him—none, that is, that Mother would permit him to
    use.
40. <u>And of all the names she couldn't stand, Pop was the worst.</u>
    Of all the names Mother couldn't stand, Pop was the worst,
41. <u>Mr. Ormsby didn't like it either, he thought it just a vulgar</u>
    and he agreed with her, it was
42. <u>common name, a comic name used by smart alecks to flatter old men.</u>
    common, and used by strangers to intimidate old men.
43. <u>He agreed with her, completely—until he heard the word in the</u>
    He agreed with her, completely—until he heard the word in the
44. <u>boy's mouth.</u>
    boy's mouth. It was only natural that the boy would use it if
45. <u>It was hard to believe a common word</u>
    he ever had the chance—but he never dreamed that any word,
46. <u>like that could mean what it did.</u>
    especially *that* word, could mean what it did. It made him weak,
47. he had to sit down and pretend he was going about his business,
48. and what a blessing it was that the place was dark.
49. <u>Nothing more had been said, ever, but it remained their most</u>
    Nothing more was said, ever, but it remained their most
50. <u>important conversation—so important that they were both afraid</u>
    important conversation—so important that they were both afraid
51. <u>to improve on it.</u>
    to try and improve on it.

Here are a few suggestions for the study of revisions: Compare the two published versions of F. Scott Fitzgerald's *Tender Is the Night*. Compare *A Happy Death* by Camus with the related novel *The Stranger* (also consult his notebooks). Compare *Stephen Hero* with the later *A Portrait of the Artist as a Young Man* by James Joyce. Compare William Faulkner's *Flags in the Dust* with the shorter, revised *Sartoris*. Compare the two published versions of John Fowles' *The Magus*. Read John Steinbeck's *Journal of a Novel: The East of Eden Letters*. Read the notebooks, diaries, letters of Fitzgerald, Conrad, James, Mansfield, Woolf, Thomas Wolfe, Maugham, Anais Nin, James Joyce, Gide, Dostoyevsky, D. H. Lawrence, and Flaubert.

Some understanding of the ways the imagination works in the revision process may illuminate the nature of fiction. The role of the imagination is today seriously, perhaps perilously, neglected when the creative process is discussed. "Write about what you know" is the most misused piece of advice ever pontificated upon young writers. "What you know" can be a rich world created out of one's imagination—rather than simply what it's like to grow up in a middle-class suburb. "By refusing to write about anything which is not thoroughly familiar," says Saul Bellow, author of the imaginative novel *Henderson the Rain King,* "the American writer confesses the powerlessness of the imagination and accepts its relegation to an inferior place." Imagination is perhaps more important than experience and inspiration. Many writers do not want to give a faithful report on real life incidents; they want to transform them in their imaginations so that the story itself becomes an event—not just a report referring to something else. A child prefers to be told a story that is made up rather than to listen to one being read. He or she wants to experience *the process itself* as the imagination invents.

It is while looking closely, imaginatively at every word (every comma) in the revision process that the imagination may suddenly soar, and see larger possibilities. As the writer first imagines characters and their story, the source of creative energy is usually inspiration. In the imagination, in the revision stage (the re-seeing stage) of the creative process, characters and their story are re-shaped many times, in many possible ways. When the *reshaping imagination* is at work, the source of creative energy is almost always the techniques of writing themselves. We do not often discuss the third way the imagination works. It is of absolute importance. One may call it the technical imagination. Often, the writer is inspired to see the characters and their stories in the imagination, but cannot see how the story can be told. He must wait for a *technical inspiration.* Or he must willfully imagine a technique for telling that story. Some writers get just as great a thrill discovering the right technique to solve problems in a story's first draft as they do from the initial inspiration. Inspiration dies very quickly, but technique opens up many possibilities. Unconsciously in the first draft and consciously in the revision stage, the *stylistic imagination* is at work. Imagination does not work simply on the larger elements of plot and characters, and in the realm of technique; it works line by line in style.

See John Kuehl, *Creative Writing and Rewriting*; Thomas McCormack, *Afterwords: Novelists on Their Novels*; William E. Buckler, *Novels in the Making*; John Braine, *Writing a Novel*; and Wallace Hildick, *Word for Word* and *Writing with Care.*

Epilogue

Relationship between the Reader and Writer

$\mathcal{I}$s the novel a criticism of life? Most serious novels give a grim, skeptical, or cynical view of life, full of doubt; some offer no conclusions or solutions. It might be argued that such novels lie, for they give only half of reality. Is an optimistic view unreal? Is only a grim view real? Keats spoke of "negative capability," and Fitzgerald said that "the test of a first rate intelligence is the ability to hold two opposed ideas in the mind at the same time and retain the ability to function." Few writers or readers pass that test.

The novelist as activist must take one point of view or another. The novelist as moralist sees only what his morals allow him to see. Many of the problems of the relationship between the writer and his audience have been attributed to the decline of a consensus of moral vision, making it difficult for either the writer or the reader to form moral judgments about characters and events depicted in novels; relativism has caused a distaste for terms such as "good" and "bad"; but the fact remains that current fiction is highly moral and hence somewhat hypocritical. The radical novelist who would destroy conventions often fails to realize how conservative he is, for he is usually criticizing the imperfect manifestations of those conventions. The new morality of revolutionary victors is the same old morality with a new, sometimes monstrously fervent, resolve to abide by it.

Moral concerns have been replaced by something called "relevance." To some a novel is relevant if it can be used as a kind of guide or handbook or how-to-cope manual in the solving of life's "real" problems. This approach moves away from the novel. Another concept of relevance moves more deeply into the novel than some think it necessary to plunge. This approach argues that literature becomes relevant when equal attention is given to the reader's experience as is now generally given to the "text." Relevance occurs when the reader, avoiding an overemphasis on analysis, makes a total emotional and intellectual response to the work.

Another approach is to see the novelist's role as a special one: to attempt to show the world simply as it is, without distorting it to favor one approach or another. Human feeling could go into creation for its own sake, rather than to promote one morality over another. The phrase "art for art's sake" distorts a reality that has never really had a chance to flourish. "Art for humanity's sake" is more accurate. Let the novel deal with everything under the sun, but let its transcendent quality be its achievement as an aesthetic object to be enjoyed finally for its own sake, as is the sun itself.

Indirectly, the study of the novel is a study of the relationship between author and reader, a measuring of the distance between them, and an analysis of the way that distance is handled. But this relationship has not been directly studied nearly enough (see Booth, *Rhetoric of Fiction*). The relationship begins with the writer in his compulsion to tell a story, but it has become increasingly complex. James said that the author makes "his reader much as he makes his characters." Wright Morris has said much the same thing (*About Fiction*). Thus, related to the question of distance is the question of the artist's relationship to his readers within the present human condition. Is the writing a direct result of the writer's participation in the great social issues of his or her time—is the writer a product of his time primarily, or is he or she the aesthetic writer who is primarily trying to create a work of art that is timeless, even though the theme may be relevant to the problems of his time? Such attitudes affect every aspect of the novel. "Gentle Reader," the conventional way of addressing the reader in the early history of the novel, has become a sardonic salutation. The reader was once approached as an equal, to instruct and delight. Now the reader is often considered an inferior, who is to be shocked into recognizing his inferiority. The techniques for managing these two contrasting relationships are very different; rather, the techniques may remain basically the same, but the handling, the use of them has changed.

From the inception of printing, there have been many reading publics or "fiction publics." Between the writer and the reader, there has always been what Booth calls a secret contract, collaboration, collusion, communion which determines the degree of literary involvement or engagement that is achieved. The writer must understand his audience if he is to induce it to use its imagination; some writers have always respected the demands of and made concessions to the audience, while others have catered to its prejudices and assumptions.

Nevertheless, each writer has, consciously or not, an ideal reader, sometimes a reflection of himself. In the past, he was the general public, made up of different types; the author often made direct appeals to his ideal reader's prejudices and predilections. It is on such relationships that fame is based. Authors and certain works become popular, and audiences crave the popular. Some writers appeal to the general fiction public because of their urbanity (John P. Marquand), others because of their pseudo-primitiveness (James Jones in *From Here to Eternity,* for instance). A smaller group delights in being part of an elite—the more powerfully inbred this group becomes, the more inclined they are toward decadence, as in the symbolist movement.

The most mysterious area in this reader–author relationship is *taste.* Education in the forms and techniques of literature is one thing; the tenacity of taste is another. Taste is a personal preference or liking for something, often influenced by mysterious emotional factors. Tastes and critical judgments may clash. For instance, a reader may have a taste for a certain type of fiction that his critical faculties tell him is inferior. Of all the forces outside the story that affect the reader's responses, taste is the most powerful. It is likely that as a reader reaches a better understanding of the nature of taste and of fiction, his own tastes will change.

Many kinds of environmental and educational forces converge with personal make-up to create an individual's tastes in literature. We speak of good and bad, cultivated and unformed, fine and gross, healthy and depraved or perverted (by good and bad literature), true and false, proper taste (which coincides with a consensus as to pure morality), eclectic and narrow tastes. Some groups promote the supremacy of their own tastes and attempt to arbitrate for others. When author and reader's prejudices coincide good taste is claimed. But taste, combined with other qualities, is all we have; each man must be his own final arbiter. Poe said that in the evaluation of literature taste was the arbiter between Pure Intellect and Moral Sense. Judging by the preconceived tastes of the individual critic is called the "good taste" fallacy. We should rise above our own individual feelings, our predispositions and prejudices to an objective self. The taste that is not aware of its own nature may promote a static interest in more of the same. But Henry James has said, "I am quite at a loss to imagine anything that people ought to like or dislike." He also said, "We must grant the writer his *donnee*" (the basic elements he has chosen to work with), and many readers have no taste for James' own donnee.

Critics have stayed out of the murky realms of taste, but a deeper understanding of the process whereby it is shaped will illuminate a great deal about the creative process itself. In any given era, the so-called general reader develops a taste for particular kinds of novels—trends and fashions evolve. We ought to remember that often the touchstones of the present are the tombstones of the future. If tastes are indeed formed, new tastes can be learned. But how may they be taught? More importantly, how may the horizons of the individual's tastes be broadened? Taste often prevents a person from entering new realms of the novel—a form in which everything is possible.

Because he has strong tastes of her own, each writer makes certain assumptions about his reader's tastes and morality. Unconsciously, though sometimes very deliberately, a writer writes out of certain assumptions about the kinds of reader he imagines will read his story; working out of these assumptions, he appeals, more consciously than unconsciously, to certain *attitudes* he thinks his readers have about love, violence, religion, morality, politics, education (and other institutions), sex, masculinity (heroes and villains), femininity (heroines), in a style which his readers will find acceptable. Usually, the writer shares these attitudes and assumptions with his readers and himself reads the kinds of stories that appeal to those attitudes and assumptions. In some stories the writer has assumed too much, in others too little about his readers.

A study of the novel should include a study of the way these assumptions operate. Are they implicit or explicit, and with what results, technical and otherwise? A simple way to begin is to examine very different kinds of magazines, to study their ads. These ads make certain assumptions about the readers of magazines; similar assumptions are at work in a novel. The reader will be sympathetic or hostile to the novel depending on the degree to which he senses and agrees with these assumptions. The popular writer is known to manipulate stock responses which he can assume his readers will make to stereotyped characters, situations, and themes, as in Jack Schaefer's *Shane,* James M. Cain's *Serenade,* Frank Yerby's *The Foxes of Harrow.* But in subtler ways, the more serious writers work the same way: Walter Van Tilburg Clark's *The Ox-Bow Incident,* Wright Morris' *Love Among the Cannibals,* and Robert Penn Warren's *Band of Angels.*

An area even less studied than the author–reader relationship is the reader–author transaction. The reader comes to a novel with certain expectations and when the writer's assumptions and the reader's expectations coincide, the reader has a pleasurable experience. The reader moves from anticipation to expectation to gratification. Sometimes the equilibrium is the same with a Lloyd C. Douglas religious novel as with a novel by Kurt Vonnegut. Another kind of experience is a head-on collision between the reader's expectations and the author's assumptions, resulting either in injury to the reader or in an opportunity to make the acquaintance of a writer very different from those he has known before.

The difference between the act of creation and the act of reading must be taken into account when we set about studying the novel in greater depth. How do these contrasts end up complementing each other, and what might result if some of the conflicts could be resolved? There needs to be, in other words, a psychology of reading, understood by both reader and writer, student and teacher.

To involve his reader, the writer appeals to and often manipulates the reader's response to aspects of the nature of fiction. The reader comes to the form with certain conventional expectations. If the writer is to surprise the reader, or to jolt the reader's perspective by violating these conventions, the conventions themselves must be employed. So the writer who hopes to do away with conventions entirely undercuts his relationship with the reader to that extent. Each work, of course, sets up its own peculiar expectations and anticipations, and the reader enjoys either having them realized or reversed. A major source of energy in the fictive experience is the reader's curiosity, which the writer arouses and satisfies. The reader's natural responses carry him or her through much of a novel, but the reader enjoys situations in which the writer causes him or her to reverse his or her natural response. Most writers set out to draw the reader into an emotional involvement. Although the writer may strive for a certain distance, he wants to play upon and evoke intense emotions and persuade the reader to become emotionally attached to one of the characters, at least.

How does fiction affect the reader? It affects him or her ethically, aesthetically, psychologically, politically, perhaps religiously. Judging literature by how it affects us often leads us away from the work into subjective and impressionistic responses only (the affective fallacy). Effects are relative. Thus, it is extremely difficult to judge a work by whether it has the effects the writer seems to intend. But certainly the writer wishes to move his reader, and if he fails, the work fails. The writer may persuade the reader intellectually; he may move the reader to laughter or to tears—which some critics and writers consider inauthentic responses; he may charm him; he may encourage sensory, instinctive responses; he may deliberately make the reader uncomfortable; he may offer him a "voyeuristic" experience. There is an infinite range of individual differences among readers in this realm of possible emotional and intellectual and purely literary responses. What counts is the reader's experience on personal and public levels; a synthesis of these levels intensifies the reader's experience.

The concept of "the interesting" as a vital reader experience is seldom discussed, except by David Daiches and Wayne Booth. A reader is often heard to say, "I didn't finish that novel because it wasn't very interesting," but according to Daiches, "Interestingness is a criterion no serious critic has dared to apply to art, but I can see no reason why it should not be applied." There are simple, obvious, categorical areas of interest for the reader: tragic and comic pleasure in experiencing suffering or in observing the suffering of others, commiserating with the pitiable, being in awe of the marvelous. One of the writer's main objectives is to astonish, to cause the reader to wonder.

All these experiences are vicarious, induced by illusion, with the use of abstract symbols called words, which are merely black marks on a page. Both literature and society depend heavily upon man's need to go beyond himself into the selves of others. In some forms, some types of literature, that experience is more intense than in others. If the reader fails to identify with at least one person in a novel, the experience is unsatisfying. There are many kinds of sympathy, involving degrees of intimacy; there is a difference between commiserating with a character and having compassion for him; between having sympathy and feeling empathy. In the romantic novel, we might admire the hero for his actions, his intellect, his morals. In today's fiction, we often sympathize with a person who commits evil. But because we identify in some way with the characters, we vicariously feel fear, horror, pity, terror, even hatred. When empathy rises to a certain level we might even speak of the writer's successful communication with the reader as being an act of communion in the brotherhood of man. But in some novels, the emotion reader and writer share may be scorn.

The writer has many responsibilities to the reader, but some writers insist that such responsibilities require a two-way relationship. "We ought to have readers who do as much goddamn work," said Mark Harris, "as we who write." Many readers do themselves and the writer an injustice when they say that a novel is good if it's easy to read. "Easy writing makes difficult reading," said S. J. Perelman. Other readers perhaps go too far in saying that those books are best which are most difficult. In such works, obscurity poses as profundity. The writer himself is often a victim of this delusion. A certain degree of bewilderment in the reader is necessary if an illusion is to be sustained, but bewilderment in the writer himself is a limited asset.

There needs to be training in the art of reading, not simply in the limited pleasures of deciphering codes, puzzles, and hunting symbols and motifs. "A good novel needs all the attention the reader can give it," said Ford Madox Ford. "And then some more." Appreciation, taste, and enthusiasm, says Wellek and Warren, are the province of the reader, as distinguished from the scholar or critic. The act of reading in its various aspects parallels in many ways the act of creating. It was a poet, after all, who coined the phrase "the willing suspension of disbelief" to describe the initial act of the reader that makes all else possible. And the reader's total response makes it possible for a mere character to become a "phantasm," something that leads a life of its own once the reader-writer transaction is over. "The novelist does not as a rule rely sufficiently," says Gide's protagonist in *The Counterfeiters,* "on the reader's imagination."

While objectivity in reading and studying literature can be carried too far, more readers are turned away from literature by objectivity in required study than by objectivity in their own patient reading. Submersion in self makes other selves unavailable. Objectivity is enforced by second readings of a novel. Repeated readings enable readers not only to enjoy new facets and to experience already-felt elements more deeply but to cultivate their responses, to observe and evaluate their own reading mechanisms, and thus make their responses to another work richer, more sensitive and complete. "And when the process is over," says E. M. Forster, describing the reader's experience also, "the artist, looking back on it, will wonder how on earth he did it. And indeed he did not do it on earth." Conrad said, "The demand of the individual to the artist is, in effect, the cry 'Take me out of myself!' meaning really, out of my perishable activity into the light of imperishable consciousness."

The effect of the mass media (journalism, magazines) and of electronics (radio, movies, television) on the novel has been both stimulating and threatening. There has long been a debate as to whether the novel's competition has caused a decline in its vitality, whether it is, in fact, dead, or at least dying. The novel provided the early movies with narrative content and a few techniques, and as early as the 1920s the novel was borrowing techniques from the movies. As narrative modes, the movies and novels are closer to each other than they are to plays, for both employ controlled point-of-view techniques. In the case of the movies, the camera-eye is intimately controlled by the director. Since the movies have some of the best qualities of plays and novels, they may supplant those media. For the consumer, movies are easier, more immediate, more accessible, cheaper than novels.

In the early 1960s numerous articles appeared, proclaiming the approaching death of the novel including English novelist John Wain's "The Conflict of Forms," Steven Marcus's "The Novel Again," Mary McCarthy's "The Fact in Fiction," Norman Podhoretz's "The Article as Art," and Louis Rubin's "The Curious Death of the Novel: or, What to Do About Tired Literary Critics," a defense.

John Wain sees the novel's great period of fertility and change as between 1850 and 1925. After that, with its divorce from life and its allegiance to art, it lost its prestige as a means of conveying information, as a vehicle for destroying pretense, and as a way to truth. The novel is no longer the major popular entertainment form (except, one might add, such novels as *Airport, Hotel,* and various lawyer and police novels, which do inform their readers about certain special areas of life).

Marcus despairs because of two characteristics of the current novel: it fails to deal with ideas relevant to man living in a society that may lack a future and it is written, read, and studied as if it were a poem; these characteristics suggest serious ill health. Criticism itself competes in potency with the novels it scrutinizes.

Mary McCarthy wonders whether it is still possible to write novels today, since "the staple ingredient" of all novels has been "fact." The novel is "disappearing from view" because the world we live in—a world of Buchenwald, Hiroshima, the Kennedy and King assassinations, Watergate, global pollution, moon-landings, and terrorist attacks—is unreal, unimaginable. The everyday world of common sense seems insignificant. "The novel seems to be dissolving into its component parts: the essay, the travel book, reporting . . . the 'pure' fiction of the tale. . . . We know that the real world exists but we can no longer imagine it." McCarthy, who has written several novels since, including the best-seller *The Group,* concludes with faint optimism: "Someone may be able to believe again in the reality, the factuality, of the world."

Podhoretz's thesis is not so much that the novel is dying but that it has been preempted by nonfiction. "The discursive writing of people who think of themselves as novelists turns out to be more interesting, more lively, more penetrating, more intelligent, more forceful, more original—in short, *better,* than their fiction." He continues: "And what the novel has abdicated has been taken over by discursive writers. Imagination has not died (how could it?) but it has gone into other channels," into magazine articles that reveal a "remarkable fusion of feeling and intelligence." Some excellent recent nonfiction, written in a few instances by novelists, has indeed used some of the devices of fiction: Truman Capote's *In Cold Blood,* Norman Mailer's *The Armies of the Night,* Jean Stafford's *A Mother in History,* Frank Conroy's *Stop-Time,* Willie Morris' *North Toward Home,* Annie Dillard's *Pilgrim at Tinker Creek,* Tom Wolfe's *The Electric Kool-Aid Acid Test,* Hunter S. Thompson's *Fear and Loathing in Las Vegas,* and Robert M. Pirsig's *Zen and the Art of Motorcycle Maintenance.*

The trouble with these arguments, says Rubin, is "that they are no more true now than during those past times when the novel was supposedly at its heyday." The only thing that can destroy the novel is bad novels. This is a time of transition, but when the next major phase in the novel's evolution comes we probably won't be able to recognize it. We should stop listening to those critics who hate fiction in the first place and "spend more time reading living novels."

• *Appendix* •

Critical Approaches

*W*hat follows is a list of possible critical approaches to the novel that may suggest the scope and complexity of literary criticism. Though it is very seldom that an individual critic is characterized by a single approach, at least one major critic is listed for each approach—often the originator of the approach in question. Implicitly or explicitly, all critics attempt to define the functions or purposes, aims or ends of literature: to instruct; delight; produce knowledge, insight, and criticism of men and events; show causes and effects; and produce an aesthetic object of the imagination.

LITERARY APPROACHES

Tradition, the influence of: Eliot
Value: Fuller
Norms and criteria, providing means of evaluation: Daiches
Appreciation (taste and discrimination): Pater
Aristotelian precepts from drama (unities, etc.): Crane
Origins: Scholes and Kellogg
Definitions: Beckson
Genetic (the genesis or development of a work): Steegmuller
Genre or category (generic) or modes (epic, heroic, comedy, satire, tragedy, lyric): Frye, Scholes
Kinds (realistic, naturalistic, surrealistic): Levin, Zola, Fowlie, Becker
Types: Ehrenpreis
Mimetic (imitation of reality, Stendhal's concept of the writer as a mirror in the roadway imitating whatever shows up in his mirror): Auerbach

Autonomy (the work of art as a beautiful object, art for art's sake): Rogers, Croce

Nationalism (portrayals of national types and characteristics and great moments in a nation's history or culture): Chase

Periods (in which a work is produced) or *Zeitgeist* (spirit of the times) or eras (classic, romantic): Hulme, Praz, Hansen, Bradbury

Historical, sense of the past: Kettle, Watt, Edmund Wilson, Trilling

Biographical (the author's life and literary career): Krutch

Author's moral outlook or vision of life: Gide, Hough

Moral, society's point of view: Winters, Elliott, May, Trilling, Gardner

NONLITERARY APPROACHES

Philosophical: Glicksberg, Barren

Psychological: Freudian, aspects such as stream of consciousness, and Jungian, the collective unconscious: Hoffman, Friedman

Scientific: Snow

Sociological: Fiedler, Duncan

Political: Howe (Marxian: Fox; radical: Aaron; proletarian: Madden, Rideout)

Mythological: Frye

Folk: Rourke

Archetypal: Bodkin

Impressionistic: D. H. Lawrence, Wright Morris

ASPECTS OF FICTION

Character: Max Schultz, Bayley, Gillie, Harvey

Point of view: Lubbock, Booth

Plot: Crane, O'Grady

Narrative: Hardy, Scholes, Todorov

Setting (time and place): Poulet, Mendilow, Frank

Context: Harvey

Imagination: Levi

Formalistic approaches (new criticism): Tate, Ransom

Form and structure (dialectics of form): Burke, Hardy, Rickword

Structure: Muir

Structuralism: Barthes

Techniques: Schorer, Macauley

Rhetoric: Booth

Style, language: Lodge, Harris, Martin

Semantic, linguistic, philological: Empson, Richards

Imagery: Ullmann

Symbolism: Tindall, Symons

Allegory: Honig

Comparative, with other literature, other fictional forms, other media, other countries and times: Levin, Bluestone

Eclectic (combinations of the above approaches) or pluralistic (tolerance of all approaches): Hyman, Elliott, Zabell

Experimental: Barthes, Gras

Popular: Cawelti, Madden

Creative process: Allott, Mann, Hildick, McCormack

Audience (study of reader's responses): Slatoff, Leavis, Richards

Relations between writer and reader: Gerould, Gordon, Gibson

Many of these approaches have been considered fallacious or comparatively ineffectual, sometimes implying inadequacies in certain types of novels. Among the fallacies sometimes discussed are historicist, formalist, didactic, intentional (assuming the author's intentions), communication (claiming that the purpose of literature is to communicate a message), pathetic, and a fallacy of expressive form.

A knowledge of literary norms, and their parallels with other arts and areas of knowledge, enables us to experience ways in which the best novels depart or deviate from them. The historical development of the novel is marked by the influence of other forms (drama, poetry, epic, cinema), other arts (painting, sculpture, music, architecture), and other kinds of knowledge (science, philosophy, history, psychology, religion). And other forms and media claim as their primary concern certain aspects of fiction: theme or thought is the province of philosophy, dialog of drama, fact of nonfiction, pure narrative of history, lives of biography, and image of poetry and the fine arts.

The most comprehensive volume of criticism about the novel as a form is *The Theory of the Novel*, edited by Philip Stevick. It contains seminal essays, key chapters from classical critical works, and a detailed annotated bibliography of almost every other noteworthy essay and book in the field as of 1967. Stevick's bibliography has provided the basis for my own. Another collection that is valuable for its essays and bibliography is *Critiques and Essays on Modern Fiction, 1920–1951*, edited by John W. Aldridge. (It provides a topical checklist: problems of the artist and his society, writers on their craft, the artist and the creative process, the craft of fiction: technique and style, realism and naturalism, and symbol and myth, with bibliographies for major authors.)

The Modern Tradition: Backgrounds of Modern Literature, edited by Richard Ell-mann and Charles Feidelson Jr., offers a rich and thorough selection of read-ings that help to provide an understanding of modern literature in general; concepts and terms in that work have been very suggestive in the writing of this book.

Most of the entries in the bibliography to this book are single works of criticism or collections of critical essays, dealing with all the types and tech-niques discussed in this book and demonstrating all the critical approaches al-luded to in the book and outlined above. Some entries cite works dealing with related arts. Very few periodicals deal exclusively with fiction. Here is a list of those that do:

The International Fiction Review, University of New Brunswick, New Brunswick, Canada.

Journal of Narrative Technique, English Department, Eastern Michigan University, Ypsi-lanti, Michigan, 48197.

Modern Fiction Studies, Department of English, Purdue University, Lafayette, Indiana, 47907.

Novel: A Forum on Fiction, Box 1984, Brown University, Providence, Rhode island, 02912.

Studies in American Fiction, Department of English, Northeastern University, Boston, Mass., 02115.

Studies in the Novel, P.O. Box 13706, N. T. Station, North Texas State University, Den-ton, Texas, 76203.

Studies in Short Fiction, Newberry College, Newberry, South Carolina, 29108 (see the summer bibliography issues).

Style, University of Arkansas, Fayetteville, Arkansas, 72701 (deals with all genres, includ-ing film, but as style is a neglected subject, this publication deserves special notice).

Selected Bibliography

WORKS ABOUT FICTION BY FICTION WRITERS

Allott, Miriam. *Novelists on the Novel*. NY and London: Columbia UP, 1959.

———. "The Temporal Mode: Four Kinds of Fiction," *Essays in Criticism* 8 (1958): 214–216.

Amis, Kingsley. *New Maps of Hell: A Survey of Science Fiction*. NY: Arno Press, 1975 [c 1960].

Anderson, Sherwood. *A Storyteller's Story*. NY: Viking Press, 1924.

Barth, John. *The Friday Book: Essays and Other Non-Fiction*. NY: Putnam, 1984.

———. "All Trees are Oak Tress . . ." *Poets & Writers*, 32, no. 1 (2004): 19–26.

Bellamy, Joe David, ed. *The New Fiction: Interviews with Innovative American Writers*. Urbana: U of Illinois P, 1974.

Bellow, Saul. "Deep Readers of the World, Beware" and "Facts That Put Fancy to Flight." *Opinions and Perspectives from* The New York Times Book Review. Francis Brown, ed. Boston: Houghton Mifflin, 1964.

Bennett, Arnold. *Books and Persons*. NY: G. H. Doran, 1917.

Bowen, Elizabeth. "Notes on Writing a Novel." *Myth and Method: Modern Theories of Fiction*. James E. Miller, ed. Lincoln: U of Nebraska P, 1960.

———. "Rx for a Story Worth Telling." *Opinions and Perspectives from* The New York Times Book Review. Francis Brown, ed. Boston: Houghton Mifflin, 1964.

Braine, John. *Writing a Novel*. NY: McGraw-Hill, 1974.

Breit, Harvey. *The Writer Observed*. Cleveland: World, 1956.

Brooks, Cleanth, and Robert Penn Warren. *Understanding Fiction*. NY: Appleton Century Crofts, 1943.

Brooks, Van Wyck. *Writers at Work,* Second Series. NY: Viking Press, 1963.

Buckler, William E. *Novels in the Making*. Boston: Houghton Mifflin, 1961.

Burgess, Anthony. *The Novel Now*. NY: Norton, 1967.

Calisher, Hortense. *Herself, An Autobiographical Work*. NY: Arbor House, 1972.

Camus, Albert. *Notebooks 1935–1942* and *Notebooks 1942–1951.* NY: Knopf, 1963, 1965.

Cary, Joyce. *Art and Reality: Ways of the Creative Process.* NY: Harper & Row, 1958.

———. "The Way a Novel Gets Written." *Harper's* 200 (1950): 87–93.

Cassill, R.V. *Writing Fiction.* 2nd ed. Englewood Cliffs, NJ: Prentice Hall, 1975.

Cather, Willa. *On Writing: Critical Studies on Writing as an Art.* NY: Knopf, 1949.

Chekhov, Anton. *Notebooks of Anton Chekhov.* London: Huebsch, 1921.

———. *The Personal Papers of Anton Chekhov.* NY: Lear Publications, 1948.

Coleridge, Samuel Taylor. *Biographic Literaria.* London: J.M. Dent & Sons, 1975.

Comfort, Alex. *The Novel and Our Time.* London: Dent, 1948.

Conrad, Joseph. *Joseph Conrad on Fiction.* Walter F. Wright, ed. Lincoln: U of Nebraska P, 1964.

———. *Last Essays.* London: J. M. Dent & Sons, 1921.

———. *Notes on Life and Letters.* Garden City, NY: Doubleday, 1921.

Dahlberg, Edward, and Herbert Read. *Truth is More Sacred.* NY: Horizon Press, 1964.

Dillard, Annie. *Living by Fiction.* New York: NY: Harper & Row, 1982.

Dostoevsky, F. M. *The Diary of a Writer.* NY: Scribner's, 1949.

Eco, Umberto. *Six Walks in the Fictional Woods.* Cambridge: Harvard UP, 1994.

Eisenstein, Sergei. *Film Sense.* New York: Harcourt, Brace, 1942.

———. *Film Form: Essays in Film Theory.* New York: Harcourt, Brace, 1949.

Elliott, George P. "A Defense of Fiction." *Hudson Review* 16 (1963): 9–48.

———. "The Novelist as Meddler." *Virginia Quarterly Review* 40 (1964): 96–113.

Ellison, Ralph. *Shadow and Act.* NY: Random House, 1953, 1964.

Feuchtwanger, Lion. *The House of Desdemona, or The Laurels and Limitations of Historical Fiction.* Trans. by Harold A. Basilius. Detroit: Wayne State UP, 1963.

Fitzgerald, F. Scott. *The Crack-up.* NY: New Directions, 1945.

Flaubert, Gustave. *Selected Letters.* Francis Steegmuller, trans. and ed. NY: Books for Libraries Press, 1971.

Ford, Ford Madox. *Critical Writings of Ford Madox Ford.* Frank MacShane, ed. Lincoln: U of Nebraska P, 1964.

———. *The English Novel: From the Earliest Days to the Death of Joseph Conrad.* Philadelphia and London: J. B. Lippincott, 1929.

———. *Joseph Conrad: A Personal Remembrance.* London: Duckworth & Co., 1924.

———. "Techniques." *Southern Review* 1 (1935): 205.

Forster, E. M. *Aspects of the Novel.* NY: Harcourt, Brace, 1927.

Gardner, John. *On Moral Fiction.* NY: Basic Books, 1978.

———. *The Art of Fiction: Notes on Craft for Young Writers.* NY: Vintage, 1983.

———. *On Becoming a Novelist.* NY: Norton, 1983.

Gass, William. *Fiction and the Figures of Life: Essays.* NY: Knopf, 1971.

George, Elizabeth. *Write Away: One Writer's Approach to Fiction and the Writing Life.* NY: HarperCollins, 2004.

George, W. L. *A Novelist on Novels.* London: W. Coffins & Sons, 1918.

Gerould, Gordon Hall. *How to Read Fiction.* Princeton, NJ: Princeton UP, 1937.

Gide, Andre. *The Journals of Andre Gide,* Vols. 1 and 2. Justin O'Brien, trans. and ed. NY: Knopf, 1947, 1948, 1949, 1951.

————. *Pretexts: Reflections on Literature.* Justin O'Brien, ed. NY: Meridian 1959.

Gins, Madeline. "Brief Autobiography of a Nonexistent" in David Madden's (ed.) *Creative Choices.* Glenview: Scott Foresman, 1975.

Glasgow, Ellen. *A Certain Measure: An Interpretation of Prose Fiction.* NY: Harcourt Brace, 1943.

————. "One Way to Write Novels." *Saturday Review of Literature* 2 (Dec. 8, 1934): 335, 344, 350.

Gold, Herbert. "The Lesson of Balzac's Stupidity." *Hudson Review* 7 (1954): 7–18.

————. "The Mystery of Personality in the Novel." *Partisan Review* 24 (1957), 453–462.

————. "Truth and Falsity in the Novel." *Hudson Review* 8 (1955): 410–422.

Goodman, Paul. *The Structure of Literature.* Chicago: U of Chicago P, 1954.

Gordon, Caroline. *How to Read a Novel.* NY: Viking, 1958.

————. "Some Readings and Misreadings." *Sewanee Review* 61 (1953): 384–407.

Gordon, Caroline, and Tate, Allen. *The House of Fiction.* NY: Scribner's, 1950.

Graves, Robert. *Occupation: Writer.* NY: Creative Age Press, 1950.

Graves, Robert, and Hodge, Allen, eds. *The Reader Over Your Shoulder: A Handbook for Writers of English Prose.* NY: Macmillan, 1943.

Greene, Graham. "Fiction." *The Spectator.* 1933.

Greene, Graham, Bowen, Elizabeth, and Pritchett, V. S. *Why Do I Write? An Exchange of Views.* London: Chatto & Windus, 1948.

Hale, Nancy. *The Realities of Fiction.* Boston: Little, Brown, 1962.

Hall, James B. *The Lunatic in the Lumber Room: The British and American Novel Since 1930.* Bloomington: Indiana UP, 1968.

Hartley, L.P. "The Novelist's Responsibility." *Essays and Studies* 15 n.s. (1962), 88–100.

Hersey, John, ed. *The Writer's Craft.* NY: Knopf, 1974.

Hildick, Wallace. *Word for Word: A Study of Authors' Alterations, with Excercises.* London: Faber and Faber. 1965.

————. *Writing with Care.* New York: David White, 1967.

————. *Thirteen Types of Narrative.* New York: Crown, 1970.

Hills, Rust, ed. *Writer's Choice.* NY: David McKay, 1974.

James, Henry. *The Art of the Novel,* with intro. by R. P. Blackmur. NY: Scribner's, 1934.

————. *The Future of the Novel: Essays on the Art of Fiction.* Ed. with intro. by Leon Edel. NY: Vintage Press, 1956.

————. *Literary Reviews and Essays.* Albert Mordell, ed. NY: Twayne, 1957.

Jameson, Storm. "The Craft of the Novelist." *English Review* 58 (1934): 28–43.

————. *The Novel in Contemporary Life.* Boston: The Writer, 1938.

————. *The Writer's Situation.* NY: Macmillan, 1937.

Janeway, Elizabeth. "Fiction's Place in a World Awry." In *Opinions and Perspectives from The New York Times Book Review.* Francis Brown, ed. Boston: Houghton Mifflin, 1964.

King, Stephen. *Danse Macabre.* NY: Everest House, 1981.

————. *On Writing: A Memoir of the Craft.* NY: Scribner, 2000.

Kipling, Rudyard. *Something of Myself.* NY: Macmillan, 1937.

Kostelanetz, Richard. *Twelve from the Sixties.* New York: Dell, 1967.

————. *Breakthrough Fictioneers: An Anthology*. Barton: Something Else Press, 1973.

Kronenberger, Louis, ed. *Novelists on Novelists: An Anthology*. Garden City, NY: Anchor Books, 1962.

Kuehl, John. *Creative Writing and Rewriting, Contemporary American Novelists at Work*. NY: Appleton-Century-Crofts, 1967.

L'Engle, Madeline. *Madeline L'Engle Herself: Reflections on a Writing Life*. Colorado Springs: Shaw, 2001.

Lawrence, D. H. "Morality and the Novel." *Selected Literary Criticism*. Anthony Beal, ed. NY: Viking, 1956.

————. *Selected Letters* of *D. H. Lawrence*. Diana Trilling, ed. NY: Farrar, Straus & Cudahy, 1961.

————. *Studies in Classic American Literature*. NY: Viking Press, 1923.

————. "Why the Novel Matters." *Selected Literary Criticism*. Anthony Beal, ed. NY: Viking Press, 1956.

Lewis, Wyndham. *Men Without Art*. London: Cassell, Harcourt, 1934.

————. *Time and Western Man*. NY: Harcourt, Brace, 1928.

Liddell, Robert. *Some Principles of Fiction*. London: Jonathan Cape, 1953.

————. *A Treatise on the Novel*. London: Jonathan Cape, 1947.

Lodge, David. *Language of Fiction: Essays in Criticism and Verbal Analysis of the English Novel*. London: Columbia UP, 1966.

————. *The Art of Fiction: Illustrated from Classic and Modern Texts*. NY: Penguin, 1994.

Lytle, Andrew Nelson. "The Image as Guide to Meaning in the Historical Novel." *Sewanee Review* 61 (1953): 408–426.

————. "Impressionism, the Ego, and the First Person," *Daedalus* 92 (1963): 281–296.

————. "The Working Novelist and the Mythmaking Process," *Daedalus* 88 (1959): 326–338.

Macauley, Robie, and Lanning, George. *Technique in Fiction*. NY: Harper & Row, 1964.

Madden, David, ed. *American Dreams, American Nightmares*. Carbondale: Southern Illinois UP, 1970.

————. *Creative Choices*. Glenview, IL: Scott Foresman, 1975.

————. *The Poetic Image in Six Genres*. Carbondale: Southern Illinois UP, 1969.

————. *Proletarian Writers of the Thirties*. Carbondale: Southern Illinois UP, 1968.

————. *Rediscoveries*. NY: Crown, 1971.

————. *Tough Guy Writers of the Thirties*. Carbondale: Southern Illinois UP, 1968.

————. *Revising Fiction: A Handbook for Writers*. 9th ed. NY: Barnes and Noble, 2002.

Madden, David, and Richard Powers. *Writers' Revisions: An Annotated Bibliography of Articles and Books about Writers' Revisions and Their Comments on the Creative Process*. NY: Scarecrow, 1981.

Mann, Thomas. "The Art of the Novel." In *The Creative Vision: Modern European Writers on Their Art*. Haskell M. Block and Herman Salinger, eds. NY: Grove Press, 1960.

————. *The Genesis of a Novel*. Richard and Clara Winston, trans. London: Secker & Warburg, 1961.

Mansfield, Katherine. *The Journal of Katherine Mansfield*. John Middleton Murry, ed. NY: Knopf, 1930.

Marrs, Suzanne. "The Making of *Losing Battles*: Plot Revision." *Southern Literary Journal* 18 (1985): 40–49.

Maugham, W. Somerset. *The Summing Up.* NY: Literary Guild, 1938.

———. *A Writer's Notebook.* Garden City, NY: Doubleday, 1949.

Maupassant, Guy de. "Essays on the Novel." *The Portable Maupassant.* NY: Viking Press, 1947.

Mauriac, Claude. "The 'New Novel' in France." In *Opinions and Perspectives from* The New York Times Book Review. Francis Brown ed. Boston: Houghton Mifflin, 1964.

McCarthy, Mary. "Characters in Fiction." *On the Contrary.* New York: Noonday Press, 1961.

———. "The Fact in Fiction," *Partisan Review* 27 (1960): 438–458.

McCormack, Thomas, ed. *Afterwords, Novelists on Their Novels.* NY: Harper & Row, 1969.

McHugh, Vincent. *Primer of the Novel.* NY: Random House, 1950.

Meredith, George. "An Essay on Comedy." *Comedy.* NY: Anchor Books, 1956.

Miller, Henry. *Henry Miller on Writing.* NY: New Directions, 1957, 1964.

Montague, C. E. *A Writer's Notes on His Trade.* London: Chatto & Windus, 1930.

Morris, Wright. *About Fiction.* NY: Harper & Row, 1975.

———. *Earthly Delights, Unearthly Adornments:* NY: Harper & Row: 1978.

———. *The Territory Ahead.* NY: Harcourt, Brace, 1958.

Moss, Howard. "Notes on Fiction." *Wisconsin Studies in Contemporary Literature* 7 (1966): 1–11.

Nabokov, Vladimir. *Speak, Memory: the Conclusive Evidence; An Autobiography Revisited.* NY: G.P. Putnam's Sons, 1951, 1966.

———. *Lectures on Literature.* NY: Harcourt Brace, 1980.

Nin, Anais. *The Novel of the Future.* NY: Macmillan, 1968.

Norris, Frank. "The Novel with a Purpose." *The World's Work* 4 (May 1902): 2117–2119.

———. *The Responsibilities of the Novelist.* NY: Doubleday, 1903.

Oates, Joyce Carol. *The Edge of Possiblity: Tragic Forms in Literature.* NY: Vanguard Press, 1972.

———. "In the Studio." *American Poetry Review,* 32, no. 4 (2003): 15.

———. "Where Is an Author?" *Gettysburg Review* 12.1 (1999): 58–63.

O'Connor, Flannery. *Mystery and Manners: Occasional Prose.* NY: Farrar, Straus & Giroux, 1969.

O'Connor, Frank. *The Mirror in the Roadway: A Study of the Modern Novel.* NY: Knopf, 1956.

O'Faolain, Sean. *The Short Story.* NY: Devin-Adair, 1951.

———. *The Vanishing Hero: Studies of the Hero in the Modern Novel.* NY: Atlantic Little Brown, 1956.

Pasternak, Boris. *Safe Conduct: An Autobiography and Other Writings.* NY: New Directions, 1949, 1958.

Plimpton, George, ed. *Writers at Work: The* Paris Review *Interviews.* NY: Third series, 1968, Fourth series, 1976.

Porter, Katherine Anne. *The Collected Essays and Occasional Writings of Katherine Anne Porter.* NY: Delacorte Press, 1970.

Price, Reynolds. *Learning a Trade: A Craftsman's Notebooks, 1955–1997.* Durham, NC: Duke UP, 1998.

Priestley, J.B. "Some Reflections of a Popular Novelist." *Essays and Studies* 18 (1932): 149–159.

Proust, Marcel. *On Art and Literature, 1896–1919*. Sylvia Townsend Warner, trans. NY: Meridian, 1958.

Rand, Ayn. *The Art of Fiction: A Guide for Writers and Readers*. Tore Beckman, ed. NY: Plume, 2000.

Ransom, John Crowe. "Characters and Character." *American Review* 6 (January 1936): 271–288.

———. "The Content of the Novel." *American Review* 7 (1936): 301–318.

———. "The Understanding of Fiction." *Kenyon Review* 12 (1950): 189–218.

Read, Herbert. *English Prose Style*. NY: Pantheon Books, 1952.

Robbe-Grillet, Alain. *For a New Novel, Essays on Fiction*. NY: Grove Press, 1965.

———. "From Realism to Reality." *Evergreen Review* 10 (1966): 50–53, 83.

———. "Reflections on Some Aspects of the Traditional Novel." *International Literary Annual* 1 (1958): 114–121.

Roditi, Edouard. "Trick Perspectives." *Virginia Quarterly Review* 20 (Oct. 1944): 545–549.

Rodway, A. E. "The Truth of Fiction: A Critical Dialogue." *Essays in Criticism* 8 (1958): 405–417.

Rogers, W. H. "Form in the Art-Novel." *Helicon* 2 (1939): 1–17.

Romberg, Bertil. *Studies in the Narrative Technique of the First-Person Novel*. Stockholm: Almquist & Wiksell, 1962.

Roth, Philip. *Reading Myself and Others*. NY: Farrar, Straus and Giroux, 1975.

Rovit, Earl H. "The Ambiguous Modern Novel." *Yale Review* 49 (1960): 413–424.

Rubin, Louis D., and John Rees Moore, eds. *The Idea of an American Novel*. NY: Thomas Y. Crowell, 1961.

———. *The Curious Death of the Novel: Essays in American Literature*. Baton Rouge: Louisiana State UP, 1967.

Sarraute, Nathalie. *The Age of Suspicion: Essays on the Novel*. Maria Jolas, trans. NY: George Braziller, 1963.

Sartre, Jean-Paul. *What Is Literature?* Bernard Frechtman, trans. NY: Philosophical Library, 1949.

———. *The Words*. NY: George Braziller, 1964.

Schorer, Mark. *Society and Self in the Novel: English Institute Essays, 1955*. NY: Columbia UP, 1956.

———. "Fiction and the 'Analogical Matrix.'" In *The World We Imagine*. NY: Farrar, Straus, and Giroux, 1968.

———. "Technique as Discovery." *The World We Imagine*. NY: Farrar, Straus, and Giroux, 1968.

Seaver, Richard, and Terry Southern, eds. *Writers in Revolt: An Anthology*. NY: Frederick Fell, 1963.

Simenon, Georges. *The Novel of Man*. NY: Harcourt, Brace, 1964.

Snow, C. P. "Science, Politics, and the Novelist." *Kenyon Review* 23 (1961): 1–17.

Sontag, Susan. "On Style" and "Notes on 'Camp.'" In *Against Interpretation*. NY: Farrar, Straus & Giroux, 1966.

Stafford, Jean. "The Psychological Novel." *Kenyon Review* 10 (1948): 214–227.

Steegmuller, Francis. *Flaubert and Madame Bovary: A Double Portrait*. Revised. Chicago: U of Chicago P, 1977.

Stegner, Wallace. "A Problem in Fiction." *Pacific Spectator* 3 (1949): 368–375.

Stein, Gertrude. *Narration*. Introduction by Thornton Wilder. Chicago: U of Chicago P, 1935.

Steinbeck, John. *Journal of a Novel*. NY: Viking Press, 1969, 1972.

Stephen, Leslie. *Hours in a Library*. NY: 1904.

Stevenson, Robert Louis. "A Gossip on Romance," "A Humble Remonstrance." In *Works*, XIII. NY, 1895.

Sukenick, Ronald. *The Death of the Novel*. NY: Dial Press, 1969.

———. Interview in *The Falcon* (Spring, 1971): 5–25.

———. "The New Tradition." *Partisan Review* 39 (1972): 580–588.

Swinnerton, Frank. "Variations of Form in the Novel," *Essays and Studies*, 23 (1937): 79–92.

Tate, Allen. "The Post of Observation in Fiction." *Maryland Quarterly* 2 (1944): 61–64.

———. "Techniques of Fiction." *Sewanee Review* 52 (1944): 210–225.

Tate, Allen, and Caroline Gordon. *House of Fiction*. 2nd ed. NY: Scribner's, 1950, 1960.

Trilling, Lionel. *The Liberal Imagination*. NY: Scribner, 1976 [1950].

———. *The Opposing Self*. NY: Viking Press, 1955.

Wain, John. "The Conflict of Forms in Contemporary English Literature." *Essays on Literature and Ideas*. London: Macmillan; NY: St. Martin's, 1963.

Welty, Eudora. "Words into Fiction." *Southern Review* 1 (1965): 543–553.

———. *One Writer's Beginning*. Cambridge, MA: Harvard UP, 1984.

Wescott, Glenway. *Images of Truth: Remembrances and Criticism*. NY: Harper & Row, 1962.

West, Paul *The Modern Novel*. London: Hutchinson, 1963.

———. "The Nature of Fiction." *Essays in Criticism* 13 (1963): 95–100.

West, Rebecca. *The Strange Necessity*. Garden City, NY, 1928.

Wharton, Edith, *A Backward Glance*. NY: Appleton Century, 1934.

———. *The Writing of Fiction*. NY: Scribner's, 1925.

Wilson, Angus. "The Novelist and the Narrator." *English Studies Today: Second Series; . . . Fourth Conf., Internat'l Assn. of Univ. Professors of English . . . Lausanne and Berne, August, 1959*. Berne: Francke Verlag, 1961.

Wilson, Colin. *The Outsider*. Boston: Houghton Mifflin, 1956.

Wilson, Edmund. *Axel's Castle: A Study of Imaginative Literature of 1870–1930*. NY: Scribner's, 1931.

———. "The Historical Interpretation of Literature." In *The Triple Thinkers*. NY: Oxford UP, 1948.

Wolfe, Thomas. "The Story of a Novel." *The Thomas Wolfe Reader*. C. Hugh Holman, ed. NY: Scribner's, 1962.

Woolf, Virginia. *The Common Reader*. NY: Harcourt, Brace, 1925.

———. *Granite and Rainbow*. NY: Harcourt, Brace, 1958.

———. *The Second Common Reader*. NY: Harcourt, Brace, 1932.

———. "The Workaday World that the Novelist Never Enters." *The British Imagination: A Critical Survey from the* Times Supplement. NY, 1961.

———. *A Writer's Diary*. NY: Harcourt, Brace, 1953, 1954.

Zola, Emile. *The Experimental Novel and Other Essays*. Belle M. Sherman, trans. NY: Cassell, 1893.

REFERENCE WORKS

Beckson, Karl, and Arthur Ganz. *A Reader's Guide to Literary Terms: A Dictionary.* NY: The Noonday Press, 1960.

Bell, Inglis Freeman, and Baird, Freeman. *English Novel, 1578–1956: A Checklist of Twentieth-Century Criticisms.* Denver: Swallow Press, 1958.

Brown, Francis, ed. *Highlights of Modern Literature: A Permanent Collection of Memorable Essays from* The New York Times Book Review. NY: New American Library, 1954.

Drew, Elizabeth A. *The Novel: A Modern Guide to Fifteen English Masterpieces.* NY: Dell Publishing, 1963.

Gerstenberger, Donna, and Georg Hendrick. *1789–1959: A Checklist of Twentieth Century Criticism.* Denver: Swallow Press, 1961.

———. *The American Novel, Vol. II: Criticims; Checklist of Twentieth Century Criticism 1960–1968.* Chicago: Swallow Press, 1970.

Kunitz, Stanley J. *Authors Today and Yesterday.* NY: H.W. Wilson, 1933–1934.

Kunitz, Stanley J., and Howard Haycraft, eds. *Twentieth Century Authors: A Biographical Dictionary* of Modern Literature. NY: H.W. Wilson, 1942.

Magill, Frank, ed. *Cyclopedia of World Authors.* Englewood Cliffs, NJ: Prentice Hall, 1974.

Magill, Frank, and David Madden, eds. *Survey of Contemporary Literature.* Englewood Cliffs, NJ: Prentice Hall, 1977.

Riley, Caroline, and Phyllis Carmel Mendelson, eds. *Contemporary Literary Criticism: Excerpts from Criticism of the Works of Novelists, Poets, Playwrights and Other Creative Writers.* Detroit: Gale Research, 1974–79.

Rosenheim, E. W., Jr. *What Happens in Literature: A Student's Guide to Poetry, Drama and Fiction.* Chicago: U of Chicago P, 1960.

Rubin, Louis D., ed. *A Bibliographical Guide to the Study of Southern Literature.* Baton Rouge: Louisiana State UP, 1969.

Spiller, Robert E., et al. *Literary History of the United States.* Rev. ed. NY: Macmillan, 1974.

Warfel, Harry R. *American Novelists of Today.* NY: American Book Company, 1951.

Weber, J. Sherwood. *Good Reading: Guide for Serious Readers.* NY: New American Library, 1935, 1969.

Zitner, Sheldon P., et al. *The Practice of Criticism.* Chicago: Scott, Foresman, 1966.

CRITICAL WORKS ABOUT THE NOVEL

Aaron, Daniel. *Writers on the Left.* NY: Harcourt Brace, 1961.

Abel, Elizabeth, Marianne Hirsch, and Elizabeth Langland, eds. *The Voyage In: Fictions of Female Development.* Hanover, NH: UP of New England, 1983.

Ahmad, Aijaz. "Jameson's Rhetoric of Otherness and the 'National Allegory.'" In *In Theory.* London: Verso, 1992. 95–122.

Aldridge, John W. *After the Lost Generation.* NY: Noonday Press, 1951, 1958.

————, ed. *Critiques and Essays on Modern Fiction: 1920–1951*. NY: Ronald Press, 1952.

————. *In Search of Heresy*. NY: McGraw-Hill, 1956.

————. *Time to Murder and Create: The Contemporary Novel in Crisis*. NY: David McKay, 1966.

Allen, Dick. *Science Fiction: The Future*. NY: Harcourt Brace, 1971.

Allen, Dick, and David Chacko. *Detective Fiction: Crime and Compromise*. NY: Harcourt Brace, 1974.

Allen, Walter. *The English Novel: A Short Critical History*. London: Phoenix House, 1954; NY: Dutton, 1955.

————. *The Modern Novel in Britain and the United States*. NY: Dutton, 1964.

————. *Reading a Novel*. London: Phoenix House, 1949; Denver: Swallow Press, 1949.

————. *Writers on Writing*. London: Phoenix House, 1948.

Alter, Robert. *Partial Magic: The Novel as a Self-Conscious Genre*. Berkeley: U of California P, 1975.

————. *Rogue's Progress*. Cambridge, MA: Harvard UP, 1964.

Aristotle. *The Poetics*. Translated by S. H. Butcher, in *The Great Critics*. James Harry Smith and Edd Winfield Parks, eds. NY: Norton, 1932, 1951.

Auerbach, Erich. *Mimesis: The Representation of Reality in Western Literature*. Princeton, NJ: Princeton UP, 1953.

Azim, Firdous. *The Colonial Rise of the Novel*. London: Routledge, 1993.

Bagehot, Walter. *Literary Studies*. London: Longmans Green, 1879.

Baker, Ernest A. *A History of the English Novel*. 10 vols. London: H. F. & G. Witherby, 1924–1939.

Bakhtin, M. M. *Speech Genres and Other Late Essays*. Vern W. McGee, trans. Austin: U of Texas P, 1986.

Barnes, Hazel E. "Modes of Aesthetic Consciousness in Fiction." *Bucknell Review* 12 (1964): 82–93.

Barrett, William. *Irrational Man: A Study in Existential Philosophy*. Garden City, NY: Doubleday, 1958.

Barthes, Roland. *S/Z*. Richard Miller, trans. NY: Hill & Wang, 1974.

————. *Writing Degree Zero*. NY: Hill and Wang, 1968.

Bayley, John. *The Characters of Love: A Study in the Literature of Personality*. London: Constable, 1962.

Beardsley, Monroe C. *Aesthetics: Problems in the Philosophy of Criticism*. NY: Harcourt Brace, 1958.

Beebee, Thomas O. *The Ideology of Genre: A Comparative Study of Generic Instability*. State College: Pennsylvania State UP, 1994.

Belsey, Catherine. *Critical Practice*. London: Routledge, 1980.

Bender, John. *Imagining the Penitentiary: Fiction and the Architecture of Mind in Eighteenth-Century England*. Chicago: U of Chicago P, 1987.

Bentley, Phyllis. *Some Observations on the Art of Narrative*. NY: Macmillan, 1948.

Bergson, Henri. "Laughter." *Comedy*. NY: Anchor Books, 1956.

Besant, Walter. *The Art of Fiction*. London: Brentano's, 1902.

Bhaba, Homi K., ed. *Nation and Narration*. NY: Routledge, 1990.

Booth, Bradford A. "Form and Technique in the Novel." *The Reinterpretation of Victorian Literature.* Joseph E. Baker, ed. Princeton, NJ: Princeton UP, 1950.

Booth, Wayne C. "Distance and Point-of-View: An Essay in Classification." *Essays in Criticism* 11 (1961): 60–79.

———. *The Rhetoric of Fiction.* Chicago: U of Chicago P, 1961.

Bordwell, David. *Narration in the Fiction Film.* Madison: U of Wisconsin P, 1985.

Bradbury, John M. *Renaissance in the South: A Critical History of the Literature 1920–1960.* Chapel Hill: U of North Carolina P, 1963.

Brower, R. A. *The Fields of Light: An Experiment in Critical Reading.* NY: Oxford UP, 1951.

Brown, E. K. *Rhythm in the Novel.* Toronto: U of Toronto P, 1950.

Brown, Marshall. "The Logic of Realism: A Hegelian Approach." *PMLA* 96 (1981): 224–241.

Buchan, John. *The Novel and the Fairy Tale.* Oxford: Oxford UP, 1931.

Burke, Kenneth. *The Philosophy of Literary Form.* Baton Rouge: Louisiana State UP, 1941.

Campbell, Joseph. *Hero With a Thousand Faces.* NY: Pantheon Books, 1949.

Cartey, Wilfred. *Whispers from a Continent: The Literature of Contemporary Black Africa.* NY: Random House, 1969.

Cassirer, Ernst. *Language and Myth.* NY: Harper & Bros., 1946.

Cawelti, John. *Adventure, Mystery, and Romance.* Chicago: U of Chicago P, 1976.

———. *The Six-Gun Mystique.* Bowling Green, OH: Popular Press, 1970.

Chase, Richard. *The American Novel and Its Tradition.* NY: Doubleday, 1957.

———. *Quest for Myth.* Baton Rouge: Louisiana State UP, 1949.

Cockshut, A. O. J. "Sentimentality in Fiction." *Twentieth Century* 161 (April 1957): 354–364.

Cohen, Ralph. "History and Genre." *New Literary History,* 17, no. 2 (1986), 203–218.

Cook, Albert. *The Meaning of Fiction.* Detroit: Wayne State UP, 1960.

Coste, Didier. *Narrative as Communication.* Minneapolis: U of Minnesota P, 1989.

Couturier, Maurice. *Textual Communication: A Print-Based Theory of the Novel.* London: Routledge, 1991.

Cowley, Malcolm. *The Literary Situation.* NY: Viking Press, 1954.

———. "A Natural History of Naturalism." *Critiques and Essays on Modern Fiction, 1920–1951.* John W. Aldridge, ed. NY: Ronald Press, 1972.

———. *A Second Flowering: Works and Days of the Lost Generation.* NY: Viking, 1973.

Crane, R. S., ed. *Critics and Criticism: Ancient and Modern.* Chicago: U of Chicago P, 1952.

Crary, Jonathan. *Techniques of the Observer: On Vision and Modernity in the Nineteenth Century.* Cambridge: MIT P, 1990.

Croce, Benedetto. *Aesthetics.* NY: Macmillan, 1919.

Culler, Jonathan. *Structuralist Poetics: Structuralism, Linguistics, and the Study of Literature.* Ithaca, NY: Cornell UP, 1975.

Daiches, David. *A Study of Literature.* London: Oxford UP, 1948.

Davis, Lennard J. *Factual Fictions: The Origins of the English Novel.* NY: Columbia UP, 1983.

De Voto, Bernard. *The World of Fiction.* Boston: Houghton Mifflin, 1950.

Dobree, Bonamy. *Modern Prose Style.* NY: Oxford UP, 1946.

Doody, Margaret Anne. "George Eliot and the Eighteenth-Century Novel." *Nineteenth-Century Fiction*, 35, no. 2 (1980): 265–290.

Dubrow, Heather. *Genre*. London: Methuen, 1982.

Eisinger, Charles. *Fiction of the Forties*. Chicago: U of Chicago P, 1963.

Eliot, T. S. "Tradition and the Individual Talent." *The Sacred Wood: Essays on Poetry and Criticism*. NY: Knopf, 1921.

Ellmann, Richard, and Charles Feidelson. *The Modern Tradition*. NY: Oxford UP, 1965.

Empson, William. *Seven Types of Ambiguity*. NY: New Directions, 1930.

Ermarth, Elizabeth Deeds. *Realism and Consensus in the English Novel*. Princeton, NJ: Princeton UP, 1983.

Farber, Marjorie. "Subjectivity in Modern Fiction." *Kenyon Review* 7 (1945): 645–652.

Feher, Ferenc. "Is the Novel Problematic? A Contribution to the Theory of the Novel." *Telos* 15 (Spring 1973): 47–74.

Fiedler, Leslie A. *Love and Death in the American Novel*. NY: Stein and Day, 1960.

———. *No! in Thunder*. Boston: Beacon, 1960.

Firmat, Gustavo Perez. "The Novel as Genres." *Genre* 12 (Fall 1979): 269–292.

Flores, Angel. "Magical Realism in Spanish American Fiction." *Hispania*, 38, no. 2 (1955): 187–192.

Fludernik, Monica. *The Fictions of Language and the Languages of Fiction: The Linguistic Representation of Speech and Consciousness*. London: Routledge, 1993.

Fowler, Alastair. *Kinds of Literature: An Introduction to the Theory of Genres and Modes*. Cambridge: Cambridge UP, 1982.

Fowlie, Wallace. *Age of Surrealism*. Bloomington: Indiana UP, 1960.

Fraiman, Susan. *Unbecoming Women: British Women Writers and the Novel of Development*. NY: Columbia UP, 1993.

Freedman, Ralph. *The Lyrical Novel: Studies in Hermann Hesse, Andre Gide, and Virginia Woolf*. Princeton, NJ: Princeton UP, 1963.

———. "The Possibility of a Theory of the Novel." *The Disciplines of Criticism*. Peter Demetz, Thomas Greene, and Lowry Nelson Jr., eds. New Haven, CT: Yale UP, 1968. 57–77.

Friedman, Melvin. *Stream of Consciousness: A Study in Literary Method*. New Haven, CT: Yale UP, 1955.

Friedman, Norman. "Point of View in Fiction." *PMLA* LXXX (1955).

Frohock, W. M. *The Novel of Violence*. 2nd ed. Dallas: Southern Methodist UP, 1950.

Frye, Northrop. *Anatomy of Criticism*. Princeton, NJ: Princeton UP, 1957.

———. *Fables of Identity: Studies in Poetic Mythology*. NY: Harcourt, Brace, 1963.

Geertz, Clifford. "Blurred Genres: The Refiguration of Social Thought." *Local Knowledge*. NY: Basic Books, 1983. 19–35.

Geismar, Maxwell. *American Moderns: From Rebellion to Conformity*. NY: Viking, 1946.

Gerhart, Mary. *Genre Choices: Gender Questions*. Norman: U of Oklahoma P, 1992.

Girard, Rene. *Deceit, Desire, and the Novel*. Yvonne Frecerro, trans. Baltimore: Johns Hopkins Press, 1965.

Goldmann, Lucien. *Towards a Sociology of the Novel*. Alan Sheridan, trans. London: Tavistock, 1975.

Goodman, Theodore. *The Techniques of Fiction*. NY: Liveright, 1955.

Goodstone, Tony, ed. *The Pulps: Fifty Years of American Pop Culture.* NY: Chelsea House, 1970.

Goody, Jack, and Ian Watt. "The Consequences of Literacy." *Literacy in Traditional Societies.* Jack Goody, ed. Cambridge: Cambridge UP, 1968. 27–68.

Grant, Barry Keith, ed. *Film Genre Reader.* Austin: U of Texas P, 1986.

Grant, Douglas. "The Novel and Its Critical Terms." *Essays in Criticism* 1 (1951): 421–429.

Gregor, Ian, and Brian Nichols. *The Moral and the Story.* London: Faber & Faber, 1962.

Gross, Beverly, and Richard Giannone, eds. *The Shapes of Fiction.* NY: Holt Rinehart & Winston, 1971.

Halperin, John. *The Theory of the Novel, New Essays.* NY: Oxford UP, 1974.

Harvey, W. J. *Character and the Novel.* Ithaca: Cornell UP, 1965.

Heiserman, Arthur. *The Novel Before the Novel: Essays and Discussions About the Beginnings of Prose Fiction in the West.* Chicago: U of Chicago P, 1977.

Hernadi, Paul, ed. *Beyond Genre: New Directions in Literary Classification.* Ithaca, NY: Cornell UP, 1972.

Hirsch, Marianne. *The Mother/Daughter Plot.* Bloomington: Indiana UP, 1989.

Hoffman, Frederick J. *Freudianism and the Literary Mind.* Baton Rouge: Louisiana UP, 1945.

———. *The Art of Southern Fiction.* Carbondale: Southern Illinois UP, 1967.

Hoffman, Michael J., and Patrick Murphy, eds. *Essentials of the Theory of Fiction.* 2nd ed. Durham, NC: Duke UP, 1996.

Holloway, John. *The Victorian Sage.* London: Macmillan, 1953.

Honig, Edwin. *Dark Conceit: The Making of Allegory.* Evanston, IL: Northwestern UP, 1959.

Howe, Irving. *A World More Attractive: A View of Modern Literature and Politics.* NY: Horizon Press, 1963.

———. *Politics and the Novel.* NY: Horizon Press, 1957.

Hughes, Linda K., and Michael Lund. *The Victorian Serial.* Charlottesville: UP of Virginia, 1991.

Humphrey, Robert. *Stream of Consciousness in the Modern Novel.* Berkeley: U of California P, 1954.

Jameson, Frederick. *The Prison House of Language: A Critical Account of Structuralism and Russian Formalism.* Princeton, NJ: Princeton UP, 1972.

———. "Third-World Literature in the Era of Multinational Capitalism." *Social Text* 15 (Fall 1986): 65–88.

———, ed. *Aesthetics and Politics: Adorno, Benjamin, Block, Brecht, Lukacs.* London: Verso. 1977.

Jauss, Hans Robert. *Toward an Aesthetic of Reception.* Timothy Bahti, trans. Minneapolis: U of Minnesota P, 1982.

Jehlen, Myra. "The Novel and the Middle Class in America." *Ideology and Classic American Literature.* Sacvan Bercovitch and Myra Jehlen, eds. Cambridge: Cambridge UP, 1986.

Jolas, Eugene. "Manifesto," in *Transition Stories.* NY: Walter V. McKee, 1929.

Jordan, Robert M. "The Limits of Illusion: Faulkner, Fielding, and Chaucer." *Criticism* 2 (1960): 278–305.

Kahler, Erich. *The Inward Turn of Narrative.* Richard and Clara Winstom, trans. Evanston, IL: Northwestern UP, 1973.

Karl, Frederick, and Leo Hamalian (eds.). *The Naked i: Fictions for the '70s*. Greenwich: Fawcett, 1971.

Kaufmann, Walter A., ed. *Existentialism from Dostoevsky to Sartre*. NY: Meridian Press, 1956.

Kayser, Wolfgang. *The Grotesque in Art and Literature*. Ulrich Weisstein, trans. Bloomington: U of Indiana P, 1963.

Kermode, Frank. *The Genesis of Secrecy: On the Interpretation of Narrative*. Cambridge, MA: Harvard UP, 1979.

———. *The Sense of an Ending: Studies in the Theory of Fiction*. NY: Oxford UP, 1966, 1967.

Kern, Edith. "The Romance Novel/Novella." In *The Disciplines of Criticism*. Peter Demetz, Thomas Greene, and Lowry Nelson Jr., eds. New Haven, CT: Yale UP, 1968. 511–530.

Klinkowitz, Jerome, ed. *Innovative Fiction*. NY: Dell, 1972.

Krieger, Murray. *The Tragic Vision: Variations on a Theme in Literary Interpretation*. NY: Holt, Rinehart & Winston, 1960.

Langer, Susanne K. *Feeling and Form*. NY: Scribner's, 1953.

Lanser, Susan Sniader. *Fictions of Authority: Women Writers and Narrative Voice*. Ithaca, NY: Cornell UP, 1992.

Lathrop, Henry Burrows. *The Art of the Novelist*. London: Dodd Mead, 1919.

Lawall, Sarah N. *Critics and Consciousness: The Existential Structure of Literature*. Cambridge, MA: Harvard UP, 1968.

Layoun, Mary N. *Travels of a Genre: The Modern Novel and Ideology*. Princeton, NJ: Princeton UP, 1990.

Leavis, F. R. *The Great Tradition*. London: George Stewart, 1949.

Leavis, Q. D. *Fiction and the Reading Public*. London: Chatto & Windus, 1932.

Levy, Julian. *Surrealism*. NY: Black Sun, 1936.

Lord, Albert B. *The Singer of Tales*. Cambridge, MA: Harvard UP, 1960.

Lovell, Terry. *Consuming Fiction*. London: Verso, 1987.

Lubbock, Percy. *The Craft of Fiction*. London: Jonathan Cape, 1921.

Lukacs, George. "Essay on the Novel." *International Literature* 5 (1936): 68–74.

———. *The Historical Novel*. H. and S. Mitchell, trans. London: Merlin, 1962.

———. "The Intellectual Physiognomy of Literary Characters." *International Literature* 8 (1936): 55–83.

———. *Studies in European Realism: A Sociological Survey of the Writings of Balzac, Stendhal, Zola, Tolstoy, Gorki, and Others*. Edith Bone, trans. London: Hillway, 1950.

———. *The Theory of the Novel*. Cambridge, MA: Harvard UP, 1971.

Lund, Michael. *America's Continuing Story: An Introduction to Serial Fiction, 1850–1900*. Detroit: Wayne State UP, 1993.

Man, Paul de. *Blindness and Insight: Essays in the Rhetoric of Contemporary Criticism*. NY: Oxford UP, 1971.

Martin, Wallace. *Recent Theories of Narrative*. Ithaca, NY: Cornell UP, 1986.

McCormack, Thomas, ed. *Afterwords: Novelists on Their Novels*. NY: Harper & Row, 1969.

McCormick, John. *Catastrophe and Imagination. An Interpretation of the Recent English and American Novel*. London: Longmans, Green, 1957.

McKeon, Michael. *The Origins of the English Novel, 1600–1740.* Baltimore: Johns Hopkins UP, 1987.

Mei, Huang. *Transforming the Cinderella Dream: From Frances Burney to Charlotte Bronte.* New Brunswick, NJ: Rutgers UP, 1990.

Mendilow, A. A. *Time and the Novel.* London: Nevill, 1952.

Mercier, Vivian. *A Reader's Guide to the New Novel from Queneau to Pinget.* NY: Farrar, Straus, and Giroux, 1971.

Meyerhoff, Hans. *Time in Literature.* Berkeley: U of California P, 1955.

Miller, D. A. *The Novel and the Police.* Berkeley and Los Angeles: U of California P, 1988.

Moffett, James, and Kenneth R. McElheny. *Points of View.* NY: New American Library, 1966.

Moretti, Franco. "On Literary Evolution." *Signs Taken for Wonders.* London: Veil, 1988. 262–278.

Muir, Edwin. *The Structure of the Novel.* NY: Hogarth Press, 1929.

Nevins, Francis M. *The Mystery Writer's Craft.* Bowling Green, OH: Bowling Green Popular Press, 1970.

Nye, Russel. *The Unembarrassed Muse, The Popular Arts in America.* NY: Dial Press, 1970.

O'Grady, Walter. "On Plot in Modern Fiction: Hardy, James, and Conrad." *Modern Fiction Studies* 11 (1965): 107–15.

Ortega y Gasset, Jose. "Notes on the Novel." In *The Dehumanization of Art and Other Writings on Art and Culture.* Princeton, NJ: Princeton UP, 1948.

Pater, Walter. *Appreciations: With an Essay on Style.* NY: Macmillan, 1927.

Perloff, Marjorie, ed. *Postmodern Genres.* Norman: U of Oklahoma P, 1988.

Podhoretz, Norman. "The Article as Art." In *Doings and Undoings: The Fifties and After in American Writing.* NY: Noonday Press, 1964.

Poirier, Richard. *A World Elsewhere.* NY: Oxford UP, 1966.

Praz, Mario. *The Romantic Agony.* NY: Oxford UP, 1933.

Radway, Janice A. *Reading the Romance: Women, Patriarchy, and Popular Culture.* Chapel Hill: U of North Carolina P, 1984.

Rhav, Philip. "Fiction and the Criticism of Fiction" in *The Myth and the Powerhouse.* NY: Farrar, Straus & Giroux, 1965.

Richards, I. A. *The Philosophy of Rhetoric.* NY: Oxford UP, 1936.

———. *Practical Criticism: A Study of Literary Judgment.* NY: Harcourt Brace, 1929.

Romberg, Bertil. *Studies in the Narrative Technique of the First-Person Novel.* Stockholm: Almquist & Wiksell, 1962.

Rosmarin, Adena. *The Power of Genre.* Minneapolis: U of Minnesota P, 1985.

Sale, Roger, ed. *Discussions of the Novel.* Boston: Heath, 1960.

Scholes, Robert. *Approaches to the Novel.* San Francisco: Chandler, 1961.

———. "Towards a Poetics of Fiction: An Approach Through Genre." *Novel: A Forum on the Novel.* II (Winter, 1969): 101–110.

———, and Robert Kellogg. *The Nature of Narrative.* NY: Oxford UP, 1966.

Shklovsky, Viktor. *Theory of Prose.* Benjamin Sher, trans. Elmwood Park, IL: Dalkley Archive, 1990.

Singer, Godfrey Frank. *The Epistolary Novel.* Philadelphia: U of Pennsylvania P, 1933.

Sontag, Susan. *On Photography.* NY: Farrar, Straus, and Giroux, 1977.

Spiegel, Alan. *Fiction and the Camera Eye.* Charlottesville: UP of Virginia, 1976.

Stamm, James R. *A Short History of Spanish Literature*. NY: Anchor Books, 1967.

Stang, Richard. *The Theory of the Novel in England, 1850–1870*. NY: Columbia UP, 1959.

Stevick, Philip, ed. *Anti-Story: An Anthology of Experimental Fiction*. NY: The Free Press, 1971.

———. *The Theory of the Novel*. NY: The Free Press, 1967.

———. "Fictional Chapters and Open Ends" in Davis, R. M., ed. *The Novel: Modern Essays in Criticism*. NY: Prentice-Hall, 1969.

Tanner, Tony. *Adultery in the Novel*. Baltimore: Johns Hopkins UP, 1979.

Thompson, Denys. *Reading and Discrimination*. London: Chatto & Windus, 1949.

Tillotson, Kathleen. *The Tale and the Teller*. London: R. Hart-Davis, 1959.

Tillyard, E. M. W. *The Epic Strain in the English Novel*. London: Chatto & Windus, 1958.

———. "The Novel as Literary Kind." *Essays and Studies* 9 (1956): 78–86.

Tindall, William York. *The Literary Symbol*. NY: Columbia UP, 1955.

Todorov, Tzvetan. "Structural Analysis of Narrative." *Novel: A Forum on Fiction* (Fall, 1969): 70–76.

———. *Genres in Discourse*. Catherine Porter, trans. Cambridge: Cambridge UP, 1990.

Tompkins, Jane. *Sensational Designs*. NY: Oxford UP, 1985.

Trilling, Lionel. *The Liberal Imagination*. NY: Viking, 1950.

Turnell, Martin. *The Novel in France*. NY: New Directions, 1951.

Uzzell, Thomas H. *The Technique of the Novel*. NY: Citadel, 1959.

Van Doren, Carl. *The American Novel, 1789–1939*. NY: Macmillan, 1921, 1940.

———. *Contemporary American Novelists 1900–1920*. NY: Macmillan, 1922, 1931.

Van Nostrand, Albert. *The Denatured Novel*. Indianapolis and NY: Bobbs-Merrill, 1960.

Visser, N. W. "The Generic Identity of the Novel." *Novel*, 11, no. 2 (1978): 101–114.

Vivas, Eliseo. *The Artistic Transaction and Essays on Theory of Literature*. Columbus: Ohio State UP, 1963.

———. "The Self and Its Masks." *Southern Review* 1 (1965): 317–336.

Volosinov, V. N. *Marxism and the Philosophy of Language*. Ladislav Matejka and I. R. Titunik, trans. Cambridge, MA: Harvard UP, 1986.

Watt, Ian. *The Rise of the Novel*. Berkeley: U of California P, 1957.

Webster, Harvey Curtis. *After the Trauma: Contemporary British Novelists Since 1920*. Lexington: UP of Kentucky, 1970.

Wellek, Rene, and Austin Warren. *Theory of Literature*. NY: Harcourt Brace, 1962.

Wheelwright, Philip. *The Burning Fountain*. Bloomington: U of Indiana P, 1954.

Williams, Ioan, ed. *Novel and Romance 1700–1800: A Documentary Record*. NY: Barnes & Noble, 1970.

Williams, Raymond. *Culture and Society, 1780–1950*. London: Chatto & Windus, 1958.

———. *Reading and Criticism*. London: Muller, 1950.

Wimsatt, W .K., and Monroe Beardsley. *The Verbal Icon*. Lexington: UP of Kentucky, 1954.

———, and Cleanth Brooks. *Literary Criticism: A Short History*. NY: Knopf, 1957.

Winters, Yvor. *Maule's Curse*. NY: New Directions, 1938.

Wright, Andrew. "Irony and Fiction." *Journal of Aesthetics and Art Criticism* 12 (1953): 111–118.

Zamora, Lois Parkinson, and Wendy B. Faris, eds. *Magical Realism: Theory, History, Community*. Durham, NC: Duke UP, 1995.

Chronology

The Development of the Novel

*W*ith the exception of a few popular novels, all novelists, novels, and precursors to the novel mentioned in the text are included here. Many additional publications, however, are not mentioned in the text. In most cases, publication dates are those of original publication, not of the first English translation. English titles of foreign novels are given here when the text is most often known by its English title (e.g., Proust's *A Remembrance of Things Past*); otherwise the original foreign title is used. When not obvious, the author's nationality is given.

c850 B.C.	Homer: *The Odyssey*
6th cent B.C.	Aesop: *Aesop's Fables*
4th cent B.C.	Xenophon: *Cyropaedia*
2nd cent A.D.	Heliodorus: *Aethiopica*
	Lucian: *The True History*
c150	Apuleius, Lucius: *The Golden Ass*
3rd cent	Adigal, Ilango (Indian): *The Ankle Bracelet*
	Longus: *Daphnis and Chloe*
300–500	Panchatantra (Indian): *Fables*
9th cent	Arihara No Narihira: *Tales of Ise*
1000	*Beowulf*
1001–1015	Murasaki, Shikibu: *The Tale of Genji*
11th cent	*The Finn Cycle*
c1100	*The Mabinogion*
	The Song of Roland
c1150	*Song of the Nibelungenlied*
c1100–1250	*Grettir the Strong* (Norse)

211

c1235–80	Lorris, Guillaume de, and Meung, Jean de: *Romance of the Rose*
12th cent	*Poem of the Cid*
	Reynard the Fox (Germanic)
Early 13th cent	*Prose Edda* (Icelandic)
13th cent	*Burnt Nijal Saga* (Icelandic)
	Sturluson, Snorri: *The Heimskringla*
14th cent	*Aucassin and Nicolette* (French)
	Lo Kuan-Chung: *Romance of the Three Kingdoms*
	Shih Nai-An (Chinese): *All Men Are Brothers*
1340–45	Boccaccio, Giovanni: *L'Amorosa Fiametta*
1350–1400	Pearl Poet: *Sir Gawain and the Green Knight*
1353	Boccaccio, Giovanni: *Decameron*
1393–1400	Chaucer, Geoffrey: *The Canterbury Tales*
1400–50	*Huon de Bordeaux*
15th cent	*The Arabian Nights*
	La Sale, Antoine de: *The Fifteen Comforts of Matrimony*
1485	Malory, Sir Thomas: *Le Morte d'Arthur*
c1490	*Robin Hood's Adventures*
1499	Rojas, Fernando de la: *Celestina*
1508	Lobeira, Vasco de (Portuguese): *Amadis de Gaul*
1516	More, Thomas: *Utopia*
1533–1567	Rabelais, Francois: *The Lives, Heroic Deeds, and Sayings of Gargantua and Pantagruel*
16th cent	Wu, Ch'eng-en: *Monkey* or *A Journey to the West*
1554	*La Vida de Lazarillo de Tormes*
1559	Montemayor, Jorge de (Portuguese): *La Diana*
1579	Lyly, John: *Euphues: The Anatomy of Wit*
1588	Greene, Robert: *Pandosto*
1590	Sidney, Sir Philip: *Arcadia*
1594	Nashe, Thomas: *The Unfortunate Traveller*
Late 16th cent	Li Yu: *The Golden Lotus*
1599–1604	Aleman, Mateo (Spanish): *Guzman de Alfarache*
Early 17th cent	Feng, Meng-Lung: *Lieh Kuo Chih*
1605	Cervantes, Miguel de: *Don Quixote*
1621	Barclay, John: *Argenis*
1627	Bacon, Francis: *New Atlantis*
1646–53	Scudery, Madeleine de: *Artamene*
Before 1657	Urfe, Honore d' (French): *Astree*
c1660	Quevedo, Francisco de (Spanish): *Life of the Great Rascal*
1664	Petronius: *Satyricon*
1668–94	La Fontaine, Jean de: *Fables*

1669	Grimmelshausen, H. J. C. von: *Simplicissimus the Vagabond*
1678	Bunyan, John: *Pilgrim's Progress*
	La Fayette, Madame de: *The Princess of Cleves*
c1685	Saikaku, Ihara: *Five Women Who Loved Love*
1688	Behn, Mrs. Aphra: *Oroonoko*
1715–35	Le Sage, Alain Rene: *Gil Blas of Santillane*
1719	Defoe, Daniel: *Robinson Crusoe*
1722	Defoe, Daniel: *The Journal of the Plague Year*; *Moll Flanders*
1726	Swift, Jonathan: *Gulliver's Travels*
1731	Prevost, Abbe: *Manon Lescaut*
1731–41	Marivaux, Pierre Carlet de Champlain de: *Marianne*
1740	Richardson, Samuel: *Pamela*
1741	Fielding, Henry: *Shamela*
	Holberg, Ludwig (Norwegian): *Journey of Niels Klim to the World Underground*
1747–48	Richardson, Samuel: *Clarissa*
1749	Cleland, John: *Fanny Hill*
	Fielding, Henry: *The History of Tom Jones*
1759	Johnson, Samuel: *Rasselas*
	Voltaire: *Candide*
1760	Rousseau, Jean-Jacques: *The New Heloise*
1760–67	Sterne, Laurence: *The Life and Opinions of Tristram Shandy, Gent.*
1761	Fielding, Henry: *Amelia*
1762	Rousseau, Jean-Jacques: *Emile*
1764	Walpole, Horace: *Castle of Otranto*
1766	Goldsmith, Oliver: *The Vicar of Wakefield*
	P'u Sung-Ling: *Strange Stories from a Chinese Studio*
1766–67	Wieland, Christoph Martin: *Agathon*
1767	Marmontel, Jean Francois: *Belisaire*
1768	Sterne, Laurence: *Sentimental Journey*
1771	Mackenzie, Henry: *The Man of Feeling*
	Smollett, Tobias: *The Expedition of Humphrey Clinker*
1774	Goethe, Johann Wolfgang von: *The Sorrows of Young Werther*
1782	Burney, Fanny: *Cecilia*
	Laclos, Pierre Choderlos de: *Dangerous Liaisons*
1783–89	Day, Thomas (English): *Sandford and Merton*
1786	Beckford, William (English): *The History of the Caliph Vathek*
	Raspe, Rudolph Erich: *Adventures of Baron Munchhausen*
1787	Saint Pierre, Bernardin de: *Paul and Virginia*
1789	Brown, William Hill: *The Power of Sympathy*

1790–94	Rowson, Susanna Haswell: *Charlotte Temple*
1792	Hsueh-chin, Tsao: *Dream of the Red Chamber*
1792–1815	Brackenridge, Hugh Henry: *Modern Chivalry*
1794	Godwin, William: *Caleb Williams, or Things as They Are*
	Radcliffe, Mrs. Ann: *Mysteries of Udolpho*
1795	Lewis, Matthew Gregory: *The Monk*
1795–96	Goethe, Johann Wolfgang von: *The Apprenticeship of Wilhelm Meister*
1797	Foster, Hannah Webster: *The Coquette*
	Sade, Marquis de: *Justine*
1797–99	Holderlin, Friedrich: *Hyperion; or The Hermit in Greece*
1798	Brown, Charles Brockden: *Wieland*
1800	Edgeworth, Maria (English): *Castle Rackrent*
1800–01	Richter, Jean Paul: *Titan*
1801	Chateaubriand, Francois-Rene de: *Atala*
1802	Chateaubriand, Francois-Rene de: *Rene*
	Novalis (Friedrich von Hardenberg): *Heinrich von Ofterdingen*
	Stael, Madame de: *Delphine*
1802–14	Jippensha-Ikku: *Shank's Mare*
1804	Kyoden, Santo: *Fortune's Wheel*
	Senancour, Etienne Pivert de: *Obermann*
1806	Kyoden, Santo: *Inazuma-byoshi*
1808	Goethe, Johann Wolfgang von: *Elective Affinities*
	Kleist, Heinrich von: *Michael Kohlhaas*
1811	La Motte-Fouque, Friedrich de: *Undine*
1812–13	Wyss, Johann Rudolph: *The Swiss Family Robinson*
1813	Austen, Jane: *Pride and Prejudice*
1814	Scott, Sir Walter: *Waverley*
1815	Austen, Jane: *Emma*
1815–16	Hoffman, Ernst Theodor Amadeus: *The Devil's Elixir*
1816	Constant, Benjamin (French): *Adolphe*
	Scott, Sir Walter: *The Antiquary*
1816–30	Fernandez de Lizardi, Jose Joaquin (Mexican): *The Itching Parrot*
1817	Shelley, Mary: *Frankenstein*
1818	Austen, Jane: *Northanger Abbey; Persuasion*
	Peacock, Thomas Love: *Nightmare Abbey*
	Scott, Sir Walter: *The Heart of Midlothian*
1820	Maturin, Charles (Irish): *Melmoth the Wanderer*
1824	Moller, Poul (Danish): *Adventures of a Danish Student*
1825–26	Manzoni, Alessandro: *The Betrothed*

1826	Cooper, James Fenimore: *The Last of the Mohicans*
	Disraeli, Benjamin: *Vivian Grey*
	Vigny, Alfred de (French): *Cinq Mars*
1828	Griffin, Gerald: *The Collegians*
1830	Balzac, Honore de: *The Wild Ass's Skin*
	Stendhal: *The Red and the Black*
1831	Hugo, Victor: *The Hunchback of Notre Dame*
	Peacock, Thomas Love: *Crotchet Castle*
1832	Morike, Eduard (German): *Mater Nolten*
	Sainte-Beuve, Charles Augustin: *Volupte*
1833	Balzac, Honore de: *Eugenie Grandet*
1834	Balzac, Honore de: *Pere Goriot*
	Bulwer-Lytton, Edward: *The Last Days of Pompeii*
1835	Andersen, Hans Christian: *The Improvisatore*
	Simms, William Gilmore (American): *The Yemassee*
1836	Marryat, Frederick (English): *Mr. Midshipman Easy*
	Pushkin, Alexander: *The Captain's Daughter*
1837	Bird, Robert Montgomery: *Nick of the Woods*
1837–39	Dickens, Charles: *Oliver Twist*
1838	Conscience, Hendrik (Flemish): *The Lion of Flanders*
	Immerman, Karl Liberecht: *Munchhausen*
	Poe, Edgar Allan: *The Narrative of Arthur Gordon Pym*
1839	Lermontov, Mikhail Yurievich: *A Hero of Our Time*
	Stendhal: *Charterhouse of Parma*
	Thompson, Daniel Pierce: *The Green Mountain Boys*
1841	Cooper, James Fenimore: *The Deerslayer*
1842	Gogol, Nikolai Vasilyevieh: *Dead Souls*
	Sand, George: *Consuelo*
1843	Surtees, Robert (English): *Handley Cross*
1843–44	Dickens, Charles: *Martin Chuzzlewit*
1844	Disraeli, Benjamin (English): *Coningsby*
	Dumas, Alexandre: *The Count of Monte Cristo*
1844–45	Sue, Eugene (French): *The Wandering Jew*
1845	Merimee, Prosper (French): *Carmen*
1847	Bronte, Charlotte: *Jane Eyre*
	Bronte, Emily: *Wuthering Heights*
1847–48	Thackeray, William Makepeace: *Vanity Fair*
1847–49	Murger, Henri (French): *The Bohemians of the Latin Quarter*
1849	Melville, Herman: *Mardi*
1849–50	Dickens, Charles: *David Copperfield*
1850	Hawthorne, Nathaniel: *The Scarlet Letter*

1851	Borrow, George Henry (English): *Lavengro*
	Melville, Herman: *Moby Dick*
	Ruskin, John: *The King of the Golden River*
1852	Melville, Herman: *Pierre; or The Ambiguities*
	Stowe, Harriet Beecher: *Uncle Tom's Cabin*
1853	Gaskell, Elizabeth Cleghorn: *Cranford*
	Nerval, Gerard de (Gerard Labrunie): *Sylvie*
1854	Cooke, John Esten: *The Virginia Comedians*
1854–55	Keller, Gottfried (Swiss): *The Green Henry*
1855	Freytag, Gustav: *Debit and Credit*
	Kingsley, Charles: *Westward Ho!*
1856	About, Edmond Francois: *The King of the Mountains*
1857	Borrow, George: *The Romany Rye*
	Flaubert, Gustave: *Madame Bovary*
	Hughes, Thomas: *Tom Brown's School Days*
	Trollope, Anthony: *Barchester Towers*
1858	Bjornson, Bjornstjerne (Norwegian): *Arne*
	Goncharov, Ivan Alexandrovich: *Oblomov*
1859	Dickens, Charles: *A Tale of Two Cities*
	Meredith, George: *The Ordeal of Richard Feverel*
	Rydberg, Viktor (Swedish): *The Last Athenian*
1860	Eliot, George: *The Mill on the Floss*
	Goncourt, Edmond and Jules de: *Charles Damailly*
	Multatuli (Dutch): *Max Havelaar*
1860–61	Dickens, Charles: *Great Expectations*
1861	Eliot, George: *Silas Marner*
	Reade, Charles: *The Cloister and the Hearth*
	Whyte-Melville, George J.: *Market Harborough*
1862	Fromentin, Eugene (French): *Dominique*
	Hugo, Victor: *Les Miserables*
	Turgenev, Ivan: *Fathers and Sons*
1863	Gautier, Theophile: *Le Capitaine Fracasse*
1864	Goncourt, Edmond and Jules de: *Renee Mauperin*
1865	Carroll, Lewis: *Alice in Wonderland*
	Verne, Jules: *A Trip to the Moon*
1865–69	Tolstoy, Count Leo Nikolayevich: *War and Peace*
1866	De Forest, John William: *Miss Ravenel's Conversion from Secession to Loyalty*
	Dostoyevsky, Fydor Mikhailovich: *Crime and Punishment; The Idiot*
1867	Coster, Charles de (Flemish): *The Legend of Tyl Ulenspiegel*
	Dostoyevsky, Fydor Mikhailovich: *The Possessed*

Gaboriau, Emile: *File No. 113*
Goncourt, Edmond and Jules de: *Manette Salomon*
Nievo, Ippolito: *The Castle of Fratta*
Ouida (Ramee, Marie Louise de la) (English):
    Under Two Flags

1868	Bjornson, Bjornstjerne (Norwegian): *The Fisher Maiden*
	Collins, William Wilkie: *The Moonstone*
1868–69	Alcott, Louisa May: *Little Women*
	Lautreamont: *Maldoror*
1869	Dostoyevsky, Fydor Mikhailovich: *Notes from Underground*
	Gaboriau, Emile: *Monsieur Lecop*
	Trollope, Anthony: *Phineas Finn*
1871	Carroll, Lewis: *Through the Looking Glass*
	Eggleston, Edward: *The Hoosier Schoolmaster*
1872	Butler, Samuel: *Erewhon*
	Daudet, Alphonse: *Tartarin of Tarascon*
	Jokai, Maurius: *A Modern Midas*
1873	Alger, Horatio: *Bound to Rise; or Up the Ladder*
	Twain, Mark, and Charles Dudley Warner: *The Gilded Age*
1873–77	Tolstoy, Count Leo Nikolayevich: *Anna Karenina*
1874	Alarcon, Pedro Antonio de: *The Three Cornered Hat*
	Valera, Juan: *Pepita Jimenez*
1876	De Amicis, Edmondo (Italian): *The Romance of a Schoolmaster*
	Perez Galdos, Benito: *Dona Perfecta*
	Saltykov-Shchedrin, Mikhail: *The Golovlovs*
1877	Zola, Emile: *The Dram Shop*
1878	Chatterjee, Bankim-Chandra (Indian): *Krishnakanta's Will*
	Hardy, Thomas: *Return of the Native*
1879	Daudet, Alphonse: *Kings in Exile*
	Keller, Gottfried (Swiss): *Der Grune Heinrich*
1880	Cable, George Washington: *The Grandissimes*
	Dostoyevsky, Fydor Mikhailovich: *The Brothers Karamazov*
	Jacobsen, Jens Peter (Danish): *Niels Lyhne*
	Kielland, Alexander Lange (Norwegian): *Garman and Worse*
	Machado de Assis, Joaquim Maria (Brazilian): *Epitaph of a Small Winner*
	Wallace, Lew: *Ben Hur: A Tale of the Christ*
	Zola, Emile: *Nana*
1881	James, Henry: *The Portrait of a Lady*
	Shorthouse, Joseph Henry (English): *John Inglesant*
	Verga, Giovanni (Sicilian): *House by the Medlar Tree*

1882	Barbey d'Aurevilly, Jules Amedee: *The Story without a Name*
	Halevy, Ludovic (French): *The Abbe Constantin*
1883	Howe, Edgar W.: *The Story of a Country Town*
	Lie, Jonas (Norwegian): *The Family at Gilje*
	Maupassant, Guy de: *A Woman's Life*
	Pereda, Jose Maria de: *Pedro Sanchez*
	Schreiner, Olive (S. African): *The Story of an African Farm*
1884	Daudet, Alphonse: *Sappho*
	Huysmans, Joris-Karl (French): *Against the Grain*
	Jackson, Helen Hunt: *Ramona*
	Jewett, Sarah Orne: *A Country Doctor*
	Pereda, Jose Maria de: *Sotileza*
1885	Howells, William Dean: *The Rise of Silas Lapham*
	Pater, Walter: *Marius the Epicurean*
	Twain, Mark: *The Adventures of Huckleberry Finn*
1886	Haggard, H. Rider: *King Solomon's Mines*
	Lie, Jonas (Norwegian): *The Commander's Daughter*
	Loti, Pierre (French): *An Iceland Fisherman*
	Stevenson, Robert Louis: *Dr. Jekyll and Mr. Hyde; Kidnapped*
1886–87	Perez Galdos, Benito: *Fortunata and Jacinta*
1887	Craddock, Charles Egbert: *In the Clouds*
	Dujardin, Edouard (French): *We'll to the Woods No More*
	Hardy, Thomas: *The Woodlanders*
	Strindberg, August (Swedish): *The Natives of Hamso*
	Sudermann, Herman (German): *Dame Care*
1888	Bellamy, Edward: *Looking Backward*
	Eca de Queiroz, Jose Maria de (Portuguese): *Os Maias*
1889	Bourget, Paul: *The Disciple*
	Hearn, Lafcadio: *Chita: A Memory of Last Island*
	Verga, Giovanni (Sicilian): *Mastro Don Gesualdo*
1890	Hamsun, Knut (Norwegian): *Hunger*
	Howells, William Dean: *A Hazard of New Fortunes*
	Morris, William: *News from Nowhere*
1890–91	Perez Galdos, Benito: *Angel Guerre*
1891	Diderot, Denis: *Rameau's Nephew* (composed 1761–1774)
	Freeman, Mary E. Wilkins: *A New England Nun*
	Gissing, George Robert: *The New Grub Street*
	Hardy, Thomas: *Tess of the d'Urbervilles*
	Lagerlof, Selma (Swedish): *Gosta Berlings Saga*
	Wilde, Oscar: *The Picture of Dorian Gray*
1892	Zangwill, Israel (English): *Children of the Ghetto*
1893	Crane, Stephen: *Maggie: A Girl of the Streets*

Frederic, Harold (American): *The Copperhead*

Vazov, Ivan (Bulgarian): *Under the Yoke*

1894 D'Annunzio, Gabriele (Italian): *The Triumph of Death*

Du Maurier, George (English): *Trilby*

Hardy, Thomas: *Jude the Obscure*

Hope, Anthony: *The Prisoner of Zenda*

Moore, George (Irish): *Esther Waters*

1895 Crane, Stephen: *The Red Badge of Courage*

Fontane, Theodor (Prussian): *Effi Briest*

Kipling, Rudyard: *The Jungle Book*

Mikszath, Kalman (Hungarian): *St. Peter's Umbrella*

1896 Crane, Stephen: *George's Mother*

Frederic, Harold (American): *The Damnation of Theron Ware*

Louys, Pierre (French): *Aphrodite*

Pontopiddan, Henrik (Danish): *The Promised Land*

1897 Gide, Andre: *Fruits of the Earth*

James, Henry: *The Spoils of Poynton*

Kipling, Rudyard: *Captains Courageous*

Mitchell, S. Weir (American): *Hugh Wynne, Free Quaker*

Sheldon, Charles Monroe (American): *In His Steps*

Stoker, Bram: *Dracula*

1898 Crawford, F. Marion (American): *Ave Roma Immortalis*

James, Henry: *The Turn of the Screw*

Wells, H. G.: *War of the Worlds*

Wescott, Edward Noyes (American): *David Harum*

1899 Chesnutt, Charles Waddel: *The Conjure Woman*

Chopin, Kate: *The Awakening*

Tarkington, Booth: *The Gentleman from Indiana*

Tolstoy, Count Leo Nikolayevich: *The Resurrection*

1900 Conrad, Joseph: *Lord Jim*

Dreiser, Theodore: *Sister Carrie*

Johnston, Mary: *To Have and To Hold*

Tarkington, Booth: *Monsieur Beaucaire*

1900–01 Jensen, Johannes V. (Danish): *The Fall of the King*

1901 Altamirano, Ignacio (Mexican): *The Bandit*

Brown, George Douglas: *House with Green Shutters*

Churchill, Winston: *The Crisis*

Kipling, Rudyard: *Kim*

Mann, Thomas: *Buddenbrooks*

Norris, Frank: *The Octopus*

1901–03 Couperus, Louis Marie Anne (Dutch): *The Book of the Small Souls*

1902	Doyle, Sir Arthur Conan: *The Hound of the Baskervilles*
	Gide, Andre: *The Immoralist*
	Merejkowski, Dmitri: *The Romance of Leonardo da Vinci*
	Wister, Owen: *The Virginian*
1902–06	Leautaud, Paul: *The Child of Montmartre*
1902–09	James, Henry: *The Wings of the Dove*
	Reymont, Wladyslaw (Polish): *The Peasants*
1903	Butler, Samuel: *The Way of All Flesh*
	Gissing, George Robert (English): *The Private Papers of Henry Ryecroft*
	James, Henry: *The Ambassadors*
	London, Jack: *Call of the Wild*
	Norris, Frank: *The Pit*
1904	Conrad, Joseph: *Nostromo*
	Hudson, W. H.: *Green Mansions*
	London, Jack: *The Sea Wolf*
	Pirandello, Luigi: *The Late Mattia Pascal*
	Rolfe, Frederick William (Baron Corvo; English): *Hadrian the Seventh*
	Zeromski, Stefan (Polish): *Ashes*
1904–12	Rolland, Romain: *Jean-Christophe*
1905	Fogazzaro, Antonio: *The Saint*
	Herrick, Robert: *The Memoirs of an American Citizen*
	Kuprin, Alexander: *The Duel*
	Mann, Heinrich: *Professor Unrat*
	Wells, H. G.: *A Modern Utopia*
1905–07	Heidenstam, Verner von (Swedish): *The Tree of the Folkungs*
	Sologub, Fedor (Russian): *The Petty Demon*
1906	Gourmont, Remy de: *A Night in the Luxembourg*
	Sinclair, Upton: *The Jungle*
1906–10	Nexo, Martin Anderson (Danish): *Pelle, the Conqueror*
1906–21	Galsworthy, John (English): *The Forsyte Saga*
1907	Artsybashev, Mikhail: *Sanin*
	Friedman, Isaac Kahn: *The Radical*
	Gorki, Maxim: *Mother*
	Harris, Joel Chandler: *Brer Rabbit*
	London, Jack: *The Iron Heel*
	Machen, Arthur (English): *Hill of Dreams*
1908	Andreyev, Leonid: *The Seven Who Were Hanged*
	Bennett, Arnold: *The Old Wives' Tale*
	Blasco-Ibanez, V.: *Blood and Sand*
	Chesterton, G. K.: *The Man Who Was Thursday*
	Forster, E. M.: *A Room with a View*

Fox, John: *Trail of the Lonesome Pine*

France, Anatole: *Penguin Island*

Grahame, Kenneth: *The Wind in the Willows*

Rinehart, Mary Roberts: *The Circular Staircase*

1909   Stein, Gertrude: *Three Lives*

Wells, H. G.: *Tono-Bungay*

1910   Bunin, Ivan: *The Village*

Forster, E. M.: *Howards End*

Mulford, Clarence E.: *Hopalong Cassidy*

Rilke, Rainer Maria: *The Notebook of Malte Laurids Brigge*

1911   Beerbohm, Max: *Zuleika Dobson*

Chesterton, G. K.: *The Innocence of Father Brown*

Glaspell, Susan: *The Visioning*

Norris, Kathleen: *Mother*

Romains, Jules: *Death of a Nobody*

Wright, Harold Bell: *The Winning of Barbara Worth*

1912   Grey, Zane: *Riders of the Purple Sage*

Perez de Ayala, Ramon: *The Fox's Paw*

Saki (H. H. Munro; English): *The Unbearable Bassington*

1912–13   Soseki, Natsume: *The Wayfarer*

1912–14   Gunnarsson, Gunnar (Icelandic): *Guest the One-Eyed*

1913   Alain-Fournier: *The Wanderer*

Bentley, E. C.: *Trent's Last Case*

Cather, Willa: *O Pioneers!*

Singmaster, Elsie: *A Boy at Gettysburg*

1913–16   Biely, Andrei: *Petersburg*

1913–27   Proust, Marcel: *Remembrance of Things Past*

1914   Burroughs, Edgar Rice: *Tarzan of the Apes*

Elizabeth (English): *The Pastor's Wife*

Russel, Mary Annette

Gide, Andre: *Lafcadio's Adventures*

Grey, Zane: *Light of Western Stars*

1915   Azuela, Mariano (Mexican): *The Underdogs*

Conrad, Joseph: *Victory*

Ford, Ford Madox: *The Good Soldier*

Lawrence, D. H.: *The Rainbow*

Maugham, W. Somerset: *Of Human Bondage*

Poole, Ernest: *The Harbor*

Richardson, Dorothy M.: *Pilgrimage*

1916   Barbusse, Henri: *Under Fire*

Blasco-Ibanez, V. (Spanish): *The Four Horsemen of the Apocalypse*

Bojer, John (Norwegian): *The Great Hunger*

	Hemon, Louis: *Maria Chapdelaine*
	Joyce, James: *A Portrait of the Artist as a Young Man*
	Lardner, Ring (American): *You Know Me Al*
	McFee, William (English): *Casuals of the Sea*
	Tarkington, Booth: *Seventeen*
1917	Cabell, James Branch: *Cream of the Jest*
	Cahan, Abraham: *The Rise of David Lavinsky*
	France, Anatole: *The Gods Are Athirst*
	Garland, Hamlin: *A Son of the Middle Border*
	Hamsun, Knut (Norwegian): *Growth of the Soil*
	Hergesheimer, Joseph (American): *Three Black Pennies*
	Phillips, David Graham: *Susan Lenox, Her Rise and Fall*
1917–29	Richardson, Henry Handel: *The Fortunes of Richard Mahony*
1918	Cather, Willa: *My Antonia*
	Wast, Hugo (Gustavo Martinez Zuviria; Argentinian): *Black Valley*
1918–23	Dunn, Olav (Norwegian): *The People of Juvik*
1919	Anderson, Sherwood: *Winesburg, Ohio*
	Baroja y Nessi, Pio: *Caesar or Nothing*
	Cabell, James Branch: *Jurgen*
	Gide, Andre: *Pastorale Symphony*
	Hergesheimer, Joseph (American): *Java Head*
	Maugham, W. Somerset: *Moon and Sixpence*
	Sillanpaa, Frans Eemil (Finnish): *Meek Heritage*
	Wassermann, Jacob: *The World's Illusion*
1919–41	Tolstoy, Alexey: *The Road to Calvary*
1920	Anderson, Sherwood: *Poor White*
	Colette, Sidonie Gabrielle: *Cheri*
	Deledda, Grazia (Italian): *The Mother*
	Lawrence, D. H.: *Women in Love*
	Lewis, Sinclair: *Main Street*
	Masters, Edgar Lee: *Mitch Miller*
	Wharton, Edith: *The Age of Innocence*
1920–22	Undset, Sigrid: *Kristin Lavransdatter*
1920–31	Zamyatin, Yevgeny: *We*
1921	Aragon, Louis (French): *Anicet*
	Byrne, Donn (American): *Messer Marco Polo*
	De la Mare, Walter: *Memoirs of a Midget*
	Hull, E. M.: *The Sheik*
	Macaulay, Rose: *Dangerous Ages*
	Maran, Rene (Martiniquian): *Batouala*
	Miro, Gabriel: *Our Father Daniel, Scenes of Clerical Life*

	Sabatini, Rafael (Italian): *Scaramouche*
1922	Barrios, Eduardo (Chilean): *Brother Ass*
	cummings, e.e.: *The Enormous Room*
	Garnett, David: *Lady into Fox*
	Ernst, Max: *Les Malheurs des Immortels*
	Hesse, Hermann: *Siddhartha*
	Hough, Emerson: *The Covered Wagon*
	Joyce, James: *Ulysses*
	Lewis, Sinclair: *Babbitt*
	Pilnyak, Boris: *The Naked Year*
	Van Vechten, Carl: *Peter Whiffle*
1922–29	Martin Du Gard, Roger: *The World of the Thibaults*
1923	Aldanov, Mark: *The Ninth Thermidor*
	Salten, Felix (Austrian): *Bambi*
	Svevo, Italo: *Confessions of Zeno*
	Toomer, Jean: *Cane*
1923–24	Jensen, Johannes V. (Danish): *The Long Journey*
1924	Ferber, Edna (American): *So Big*
	Forster, E. M.: *Passage to India*
	Mann, Thomas: *The Magic Mountain*
	Melville, Herman: *Billy Budd*
	Rivera, Jose Eustasio (Colombian): *The Vortex*
	Webb, Mary: *Precious Bane*
1924–26	Ford, Ford Madox: *Parade's End*
1925	Dos Passos, John: *Manhattan Transfer*
	Dreiser, Theodore: *An American Tragedy*
	Erskine, John (American): *Private Life of Helen of Troy*
	Fitzgerald, F. Scott: *The Great Gatsby*
	Gide, Andre: *The Counterfeiters*
	Glasgow, Ellen: *Barren Ground*
	Heyward, DuBose: *Porgy*
	Kafka, Franz (Czechoslovakian): *The Trial*
	Schnitzler, Arthur (Austrian): *Traumnovelle* [*Dream Story*]
	Woolf, Virginia: *Mrs. Dalloway*
1926	Christie, Agatha: *The Murder of Roger Ackroyd*
	Glasgow, Ellen: *The Romantic Comedians*
	Guiraldes, Ricardo: *Don Segundo Sombra*
	Hasek, Jaroslav (Czechoslovakian): *The Good Soldier Schweik*
	Hemingway, Ernest: *The Sun Also Rises*; *The Torrents of Spring*
	Kafka, Franz (Czechoslovakian): *The Castle*
	Lawrence, D. H.: *The Plumed Serpent*
	O'Flaherty, Liam: *The Informer*

Roberts, Elizabeth Madox (American): *The Time of Man*

1927   Aiken, Conrad: *Blue Voyage*

Cather, Willa: *Death Comes for the Archbishop*

De La Roche, Mazo (Canadian): *Jalna*

Hesse, Hermann (German): *Steppenwolf*

Katayev, Valentine (Russian): *The Embezzlers*

Leonov, Leonid: *The Thief*

Lewis, Sinclair: *Elmer Gantry*

Masters, Edgar Lee: *Kit O'Brien*

Mauriac, Francois: *Therese*

Powys, T. F.: *Mr. Weston's Good Wine*

Rolvaag, O. E. (Norwegian): *Giants in the Earth*

Traven, B. (German-American): *The Treasure of the Sierra Madre*

Van Dine, S. S.: *The Canary Murder Case*

Wescott, Glenway: *The Grandmothers*

Wilder, Thornton: *The Bridge of San Luis Rey*

Woolf, Virginia: *To the Lighthouse*

1928   Breton, Andre: *Nadja*

Del Mar, Vina: *Bad Girl*

Guzman, Martin Luis (Mexican): *The Eagle and the Serpent*

Hall, Radclyffe: *The Well of Loneliness*

Huxley, Aldous: *Point Counter Point*

Lawrence, D. H.: *Lady Chatterley's Lover*

Remarque, Erich Maria: *All Quiet on the Western Front*

Sholokhov, Mikhail: *And Quiet Flows the Don*

Waugh, Evelyn: *Decline and Fall*

Woolf, Virginia: *Orlando*

1928–29 Tanizaki, Junichiró: *Some Prefer Nettles*

1929   Burnett, W. R.: *Little Caesar*

Cocteau, Jean: *The Holy Terrors*

Ernst, Max: *La Femme 100 Tetes*

Faulkner, William: *The Sound and the Fury*

Gallegos, Romulo (Venezuelan): *Dona Barbara*

Green, Julien (American-French): *The Dark Journey*

Hemingway, Ernest: *A Farewell to Arms*

Hughes, Richard: *A High Wind in Jamaica*
    (The Innocent Voyage)

Renn, Ludwig (German): *War*

Scott, Evelyn: *The Wave*

Tarkington, Booth: *The Magnificent Ambersons*

Wolfe, Thomas: *Look Homeward, Angel*

1930	Alvaro, Corrado: *Revolt in Aspromonte*
	Baroja y Nessi, Pio: *The Restlessness of Shanti Andia*
	Baum, Vicki (Austrian): *Grand Hotel*
	Brand, Max (American): *Destry Rides Again*
	Ernst, Max: *Rêve d'une Petite Fille. . .*
	Faulkner, William: *As I Lay Dying*
	Gold, Michael: *Jews Without Money*
	Hammett, Dashiell: *The Maltese Falcon*
	Lewis, Wyndham: *The Apes of God*
	Maugham, W. Somerset: *Cakes and Ale*
	Rhys, Jean (English): *After Leaving Mr. Mackenzie*
1930–32	Broch, Hermann (German): *The Sleepwalkers*
1930–43	Musil, Robert (Austrian): *The Man without Qualities*
1931	Buck, Pearl: *The Good Earth*
	Faulkner, William: *Sanctuary*
	Miller, Henry: *Tropic of Cancer*
	Saint-Exupery, Antoine de: *Night Flight*
	Strong, L. A. G.: *The Garden*
	Uslar Pietri, Arturo (Venezuelan): *The Red Lances*
	West, Nathanael: *The Dream Life of Balso Snell*
	Woolf, Virginia: *The Waves*
1932	Brody, Catherine: *Nobody Starves*
	Caldwell, Erskine: *Tobacco Road*
	Celine, Louis Ferdinand (Louis Fuchs Destouches): *Journey to the End of the Night*
	Faulkner, William: *Light in August*
	Gibbons, Stella: *Cold Comfort Farm*
	Huxley, Aldous: *Brave New World*
	Lindsay, Norman: *The Cautious Amorist*
	Lumpkin, Grace: *To Make My Bread*
	Mauriac, Francois: *Viper's Tangle*
	Morgan, Charles: *The Fountain*
	Nordhoff, Charles, and James Norman Hall: *Mutiny on the Bounty*
	Smith, Homer: *Kamongo*
	Smith, Thorne: *Topper Takes a Trip*
1932–35	Farrell, James T.: *Studs Lonigan*
1932–46	Romains, Jules: *Men of Good Will*
1933	Aiken, Conrad: *Great Circle*
	Ayme, Marcel: *The Green Mare*
	Caldwell, Erskine: *God's Little Acre*

Conroy, Jack: *The Disinherited*
Hilton, James: *Lost Horizon*
Malraux, Andre: *Man's Fate*
March, William: *Company K*
Martin Du Gard, Roger: *The Postman*
O'Faolain, Sean: *A Nest of Simple Folk*
West, Nathanael: *Miss Lonelyhearts*

1933–34   Ernst, Max: *Une Semaine de Bon*

1934   Aragon, Louis (French): *The Bells of Basel*
Armstrong, Arnold B.: *Parched Earth*
Cain, James M.: *The Postman Always Rings Twice*
Dinesen, Isak (Danish): *Seven Gothic Tales*
Fitzgerald, F. Scott: *Tender Is the Night*
Giono, Jean (French): *Song of the World*
Graves, Robert: *I, Claudius*
Icaza, Jorge (Ecuadorian): *Huasipungo*
Montherlant, Henri de: *Perish in Their Pride*
Newhouse, Edward: *You Can't Sleep Here*
O'Hara, John: *Appointment in Samarra*
Roth, Henry: *Call It Sleep*
Smith, Thorne: *The Glorious Pool*
Stone, Irving: *Lust for Life*
Suckow, Ruth: *The Folks*
Werfel, Franz (Czech): *The Forty Days of Musa Dagh*
West, Nathanael: *A Cool Million*
Young, Stark: *So Red the Rose*

1934–35   Laxness, Halldor (Icelandic): *Independent People*
1934–37   Fuchs, Daniel: *Williamsburg Trilogy*
1935   Bishop, John Peale: *Act of Darkness*
Cobb, Humphrey: *Paths of Glory*
Kromer, Tom: Waiting for *Nothing*
McCoy, Horace: *They Shoot Horses, Don't They?*
Myers, L. H.: *The Root and the Flower*
O'Hara, John: *Butterfield 8*
Ramuz, C. F. (Franco-Swiss): *When the Mountain Fell*
Read, Herbert: *The Green Child*
Wolfe, Thomas: *Of Time and the River*

1936   Barnes, Djuna: *Nightwood*
Bowen, Elizabeth: *The House in Paris*
Canetti, Elias (Bulgarian): *Auto-da-fe*
Chevallier, Gabriel: *The Scandals of Clochemerle*

Farrell, James T.: *A World I Never Made*
Faulkner, William: *Absalom, Absalom!*
Greene, Graham: *This Gun for Hire*
Mitchell, Margaret: *Gone with the Wind*
Nin, Anais (Spanish-American): *House of Incest*
Santayana, George: *The Last Puritan*
Silone, Ignazio: *Bread and Wine*

1937   Bernanos, Georges: *The Diary of a Country Priest*
Cain, James M.: *Serenade*
Capek, Karel, (Czech): *War with the Newts*
Dos Passos, John: *U.S.A.*
Hurston, Zora Neale: *Their Eyes Were Watching God*
Kang, Younghill (Korean-American): *East Goes West*
Malraux, Andre: *Man's Hope*
Marquand, John P.: *The Late George Apley*
Prokosch, Frederic (American): *The Seven Who Fled*
Roberts, Kenneth: *Northwest Passage*
Steinbeck, John: *Of Mice and Men*
Williams, William Carlos: *White Mule*

1937–47   Kawabata, Yasunari (Japanese): *Snow Country*
1938   Alvaro, Carrado (Italian): *Man Is Strong*
Bowen, Elizabeth: *Death of the Heart*
Du Maurier, Daphne: *Rebecca*
Gombrowicz, Witold (Polish): *Feryduke*
Greene, Graham: *Brighton Rock*
Lewis, C. S.: *Out of the Silent Planet*
Rao, Raja (Indian): *Kanthapura*
Sartre, Jean-Paul: *Nausea*
Tate, Allen: *The Fathers*

1938–40   Bacchelli, Riccardo (Italian): *The Mill on the Po*
1939   Asch, Sholom (Polish): *The Nazarene*
Chandler, Raymond: *The Big Sleep*
Faulkner, William: *The Wild Palms*
Joyce, James: *Finnegans Wake*
Junger, Ernst: *On the Marble Cliffs*
Leiris, Michel: *The Age of Man*
Marquand, John P.: *Wickford Point*
Miller, Henry: *The Tropic of Capricorn*
O'Brien, Flann: *At Swim-Two-Birds*
Sarraute, Nathalie (French): *Tropisms*
Steinbeck, John: *The Grapes of Wrath*

	Trumbo, Dalton: *Johnny Got His Gun*
	Wolfe, Thomas: *The Web and the Rock*
1940	Chandler, Raymond: *Farewell, My Lovely*
	Clark, Walter Van Tilburg: *The Ox-Bow Incident*
	Costa du Rels, Adolfo (Bolivian): *Bewitched Lands*
	Greene, Graham: *The Power and the Glory*
	McCullers, Carson: *The Heart Is a Lonely Hunter*
	Mallea, Eduardo (Argentian): *The Bay of Silence*
	Simenon, Georges (French): *The Patience of Maigret*
	Snow, C. P.: *Strangers and Brothers*
	Stead, Christina (Australian): *The Man Who Loved Children*
	Wright, Richard: *Native Son*
1941	Alegria, Ciro (Peruvian): *Broad and Alien Is the World*
	Amorim, Enrique (Uruguayian): *The Horse and His Shadow*
	Cary, Joyce: *Herself Surprised*
	Gordon, Caroline: *Green Centuries*
	Koestler, Arthur (Anglo-Hungarian): *Darkness at Noon*
	McCullers, Carson: *Reflections in a Golden Eye*
	Piovene, Guido: *Letters of a Novice*
	Stewart, George R.: *Storm*
	Werfel, Franz (Czech): *The Song of Bernadette*
	Woolf, Virginia: *Between the Acts*
1942	Camus, Albert: *The Stranger*
	Cela, Camilo Jose: *The Family of Pascual Duarte*
	Chase, James Hadley: *No Orchids for Miss Blandish*
	Cozzens, James Gould: *The Just and the Unjust*
	Douglas, Lloyd C.: *The Robe*
	Fast, Howard: *The Unvanquished*
	Faulkner, William: *The Bear*
	Merritt, Abraham: *Burn, Witch, Burn!*
1943	Asch, Sholem: *The Apostle*
	Genet, Jean: *Our Lady of the Flowers*
	Greene, Graham: *The Ministry of Fear*
	Lins do Rego, Jose (Brazilian): *Dead Fires*
	Rand, Ayn (Russo-American): *The Fountainhead*
	Saroyan, William: *The Human Comedy*
	Smith, Betty: *A Tree Grows in Brooklyn*
	Stegner, Wallace: *The Big Rock Candy Mountain*
	Verissimo, Erico (Brazilian): *The Rest Is Silence*
1944	Bellow, Saul: *Dangling Man*
	Busch, Niven: *Duel in the Sun*

	Dali, Salvador: *Hidden Faces*
	Jackson, Charles: *The Lost Weekend*
	Joyce, James: *Stephen Hero*
	Kossak, Zofia (Polish): *Blessed Are the Meek*
	Maugham, W. Somerset: *The Razor's Edge*
	Smith, Lillian: *Strange Fruit*
	Williams, Ben Ames: *Leave Her to Heaven*
1945	Andric, Ivo (Yugoslavian): *The Bridge on the Drina*
	Broch, Hermann: *The Death of Virgil*
	Isherwood, Christopher: *The Berlin Stories*
	Laforet, Carmen: *Nada*
	Orwell, George: *Animal Farm*
	Williams, Charles: *All Hallows Eve*
1945–49	Sartre, Jean Paul: *Roads to Freedom*
1946	Asturias, Miguel Angel (Guatemalan): *El Senor Presidente*
	Gide, Andre: *Theseus*
	Graves, Robert: *King Jesus*
	Heggen, Thomas: *Mister Roberts*
	Kazantzakis, Nikos (Greek): *Zorba, the Greek*
	McCullers, Carson: *A Member of the Wedding*
	Peake, Mervyn: *Titus Groan*
	Vittorini, Elio (Italian): *In Sicily*
	Warren, Robert Penn: *All the King's Men*
	Welty, Eudora: *Delta Wedding*
	Yerby, Frank: *The Foxes of Harrow*
1947	Bellow, Saul (Canadian-American): *The Victim*
	Burns, John Horne: *The Gallery*
	Camus, Albert: *The Plague*
	Curtis, Jean-Louis (French): *The Forests of the Night*
	Ehrenburg, Ilya (Russian): *The Storm*
	Lowry, Malcolm (Canadian): *Under the Volcano*
	Mann, Thomas: *Doctor Faustus*
	Moravia, Alberto: *Woman of Rome*
	Motley, Willard: *Knock on Any Door*
	Schneider, Isidor (Polish-American): *The Judas Time*
	Spillane, Mickey: *I, The Jury*
	Trilling, Lionel: *The Middle of the Journey*
	Unamuno y Jugo, Miguel de: *Abel Sanchez*
	Yanez, Agustin (Mexican): *The Edge of the Storm*
1948	Bhattacharya, Bhabani (Indian): *So Many Hungers*
	Capote, Truman: *Other Voices, Other Rooms*

Dazai Osamu (Japanese): *No Longer Human*
Desani, G. V. (Indian): *All About H. Hatter*
Fedin, Konstantin (Russian): *No Ordinary Summers*
Greene, Graham: *The Heart of the Matter*
Lockridge, Ross: *Raintree County*
Mailer, Norman: *The Naked and the Dead*
Paton, Alan (South African): *Cry, the Beloved Country*
Sender, Ramon (Spanish): *The King and the Queen*
Shaw, Irwin: *The Young Lions*
Skinner, B. F.: *Walden Two*
Vidal, Gore: *The City and the Pillar*
Vittorini, Elio: *The Red Carnation*
Waugh, Evelyn: *The Loved One*

1949   Algren, Nelson: *The Man with the Golden Arm*
Aragon, Louis (French): *Les Communistes*
Bates, H. E.: *Jacaranda Tree*
Carpentier, Alejo (Cuban-Venezuelan): *The Kingdom of This World*
Lagerkvist, Par Fabian (Sweden): *Barabbas*
Morris, Wright: *The World in the Attic*
Orwell, George: *1984*
Pavese, Cesare: *The Moon and the Bonfires*
Pratolini, Vasco: *A Hero of Our Time*
Sansom, William: *The Body*
Schaefer, Jack: *Shane*

1950   Bradbury, Ray: *Martian Chronicles*
Buechner, Frederick: *A Long Day's Dying*
Hemingway, Ernest: *Across the River and into the Trees*
Howard, Robert E.: *Conan the Barbarian*
Simenon, Georges: *The Snow Was Black*
Spillane, Mickey: *My Gun Is Quick*
Warren, Robert Penn: *World Enough and Time*
Williams, Tennessee: *The Roman Spring of Mrs. Stone*

1951   Beckett, Samuel: *Malone Dies*
Cela, Camilo Jose (Spanish): *The Hive*
Diaz Lozano, Argentina (Honduran): *Mayapan*
Giono, Jean (French): *Horseman on the Roof*
Jones, James: *From Here to Eternity*
Mailer, Norman: *Barbary Shore*
Morante, Elsa (Italian): *House of Liars*
Morris, Wright: *Man and Boy*
Ooka, Shohei (Japanese): *Fires on the Plain*

Salinger, J. D.: *The Catcher in the Rye*
Spillane, Mickey: *The Big Kill*
Styron, William: *Lie Down in Darkness*
Wouk, Herman: *The Caine Mutiny*
Yourcenar, Marguerite (French): *Hadrian's Memoirs*

1952   Boulle, Pierre: *The Bridge Over the River Kwai*
Ellison, Ralph: *Invisible Man*
Hemingway, Ernest: *The Old Man and the Sea*
McCarthy, Mary: *The Groves of Academe*
MacDonald, John D.: *The Damned*
Malamud, Bernard: *The Natural*
Malaparte, Curzio (Italian): *The Skin*
Morris, Wright: *Works of Love*
Steinbeck, John: *East of Eden*
Thompson, Jim: *The Killer Inside Me*
Tutuola, Amos (Nigerian): *The Palm-Wine Drinkard*

1952–1969   Lessing, Doris: *The Children of Violence*
1953   Amis, Kingsley: *Lucky Jim*
Baldwin, James: *Go Tell It on the Mountain*
Basso, Hamilton: *The View from Pompey's Head*
Bellow, Saul: *The Adventures of Augie March*
Bradbury, Ray: *Fahrenheit 451*
Gironella, Jose Maria: *The Cypresses Believe in God*
Grubb, Davis: *Night of the Hunter*
Hyman, Mac: *No Time for Sergeants*
Morris, Wright: *The Deep Sleep*
Oldenbourg, Zoe (French): *The Cornerstone*
Wain, John: *Hurry on Down*

1954   Arnow, Harriette: *The Dollmaker*
Beauvoir, Simone de: *Les Mandarins*
Bhattacharya, Bhabani (Indian): *He Who Rides the Tiger*
Bowles, Paul: *The Sheltering Sky*
Duggan, Alfred: *Leopards and Lilies*
Faulkner, William: *A Fable*
Frisch, Max (Swiss, 1911): *I'm Not Stiller*
Galvan, Manuel de Jesus (Dominican Republican):
    The Cross and the Sword
Golding, William: *Lord of the Flies*
Jackson, Shirley: *The Bird's Nest*
Jarrell, Randall: *Pictures from an Institution*
Mann, Thomas: *Confessions of Felix Krull, Confidence Man*
March, William: *The Bad Seed*

Markandaya, Kamala (Indian): *Nectar in a Sieve*
Menen, Aubrey (Indian): *The Ramayana*
Morris, Wright: *The Huge Season*
Nin, Anais: *A Spy in the House of Love*
Sagan, Françoise (French): *Bonjour Tristesse*

1954–55   Tolkien, J. R. R.: *The Lord of the Rings*

1955   Dennis, Nigel: *Cards of Identity*
Donleavy, J. P.: *The Ginger Man*
Dratler, Jay: *The Judas Kiss*
Fulop-Miller, Rene (German): *The Night of Time*
Gaddis, William: *The Recognitions*
Millar, Margaret (Canadian): *Beast in View*
Robbe-Grillet, Alain: *The Voyeur*
Rulfo, Juan (Mexican): *Pedro Paramo*
Singh, Khushwant (Indian): *Train to Pakistan*
Warren, Robert Penn: *Band of Angels*

1956   Barth, John: *The Floating Opera*
Bastide, Francois-Regis: *Les Adieux*
Beckett, Samuel: *Malone Dies*
Bellow, Saul: *Seize the Day*
Camus, Albert: *The Fall*
Gary, Romain: *The Roots of Heaven*
Heinrich, Willi: *The Cross of Iron*
Jhabvala, R. Prawer (Indian): *Amrita*
Kawabata, Yasunari (Japanese): *Snow Country*
Metalious, Grace: *Peyton Place*
Moore, Brian (Canadian): *The Lonely Passion of Judith Hearne*
Morris, Wright: *The Field of Vision*
Renault, Mary: *The Last of the Wine*
Tanizaki, Junichiro (Japanese): *The Key*

1957   Agee, James: *A Death in the Family*
Bataille, George: *The Blue Sky*
Bjarnhof, Karl (Danish): *The Good Light*
Braine, John: *Room at the Top*
Butor, Michel (French): *A Change of Heart*
Cheever, John: *The Wapshot Chronicle*
Hedyat, Sadegh (Persian): *The Blind Owl*
Kerouac, Jack: *On the Road*
Mishima, Yukio: *The Sound of Waves*
Morris, Wright: *Love Among the Cannibals*
Nabokov, Vladimir: *Pnin*
Rand, Ayn: *Atlas Shrugged*

Robbe-Grillet, Alain: *Jealousy*
Simon, Claude: *The Wind*
Vailland, Roger: *The Law*
White, Patrick: *Voss*
1957–60   Durrell, Lawrence: *Alexandria Quartet*
1958   Amado, Jorge (Brazilian): *Gabriela, Clove, and Cinnamon*
Barth, John: *End of the Road*
Beckett, Samuel: *The Unnamable*
Burdick, Eugene, and Lederer, William: *The Ugly American*
Gordimer, Nadine (S. African): *A World of Strangers*
Lampedusa, Giuseppe di (Sicilian): *The Leopard*
Mishima, Yukio: *Confessions of a Mask*
Nabokov, Vladimir: *Lolita*
Narayan, R. K. (Indian): *The Guide*
Pasternak, Boris: *Doctor Zhivago*
Traver, Robert: *Anatomy of a Murder*
Uris, Leon: *Exodus*
White, T. H.: *The Once and Future King*
1958–59   Bellow, Saul: *Henderson the Rain King*
1959   Boll, Heinrich (German): *Billiards at Half-Past Nine*
Burroughs, William: *Naked Lunch*
Castillo, Michel del (French): *A Child of Our Time*
Drury, Allen: *Advise and Consent*
Durrenmatt, Friedrich (Swiss): *The Pledge*
Grass, Gunter (German-Polish): *The Tin Drum*
Johnson, Uwe (German): *Speculations About Jacob*
Kerouac, Jack: *The Subterraneans*
Knowles, John: *A Separate Peace*
Lafourcade, Enrique (Chilean): *King Ahali's Feast*
Mauriac, Claude: *The Dinner Party*
Menen, Aubrey (Indian): *The Fig Tree*
Michener, James: *Hawaii*
Miller, Walter M., Jr.: *A Canticle for Liebowitz*
Queneau, Raymond: *Zazie in the Metro*
Southern, Terry: *Candy; The Magic Christian*
Vale, Eugene (Swiss-American): *The Thirteenth Apostle*
1960   Barth, John: *The Sot-Weed Factor*
Bazin, Herve: *In the Name of the Son*
Ferlinghetti, Lawrence: *Her*
Lee, Harper: *To Kill a Mockingbird*
Morris, Wright: *Ceremony in Lone Tree*
O'Connor, Flannery: *The Violent Bear It Away*

	Ousmane, Sembene (Senegalian): *God's Bits of Wood*
	Theriault, Yves (French-Canadian): *Ashini*
	Updike, John: *Rabbit, Run*
1961	Hawkes, John: *The Lime Twig*
	Heinlein, Robert: *Stranger in a Strange Land*
	Heller, Joseph: *Catch-22*
	Madden, David: *The Beautiful Greed*
	Mauriac, Claude: *The Marquise Went Out at Five*
	Murdoch, Iris: *A Severed Head*
	Ngugi, James (African): *Chocolates for My Wife, Slices of My Life*
	Osaragi, Jiro: *The Journey*
	Percy, Walker: *The Moviegoer*
	Pirajno, Alberto Denti Di (Italian): *Ippolita*
	Robbins, Harold: *The Carpetbaggers*
	Stone, Irving: *The Agony and the Ecstasy*
1962	Baker, Dorothy: *Cassandra at the Wedding*
	Berger, Yves: *The Garden*
	Burgess, Anthony: *A Clockwork Orange*
	Demitriu, Petru (Romanian): *Incognito*
	Duras, Marguerite: *10:30 on a Summer Night*
	Fuentes, Carlos (Mexican): *The Death of Artemio Cruz*
	Goytisolo, Juan: *The Party's Over*
	Kelly, William Melvin: *A Different Drummer*
	Kesey, Ken: *One Flew over the Cuckoo's Nest*
	La Guma, Alex (Nigerian): *A Walk in the Night*
	Nabokov, Vladimir: *Pale Fire*
	Pinget, Robert (French): *The Inquisitory*
	Porter, Katherine Anne: *Ship of Fools*
	Singer, Isaac Bashevis (Polish): *The Slave*
	Vonnegut, Kurt: *Mother Night*
1963	Cortazar, Julio (Argentinian): *Hopscotch*
	Dayan, Yael (Israeli): *Dust*
	Donoso, Jose (Chilean): *Coronation*
	Ekwensi, Cyprian (Lagosian): *People of the City*
	Klein-Haparash, J.: *He Who Flees the Lion*
	McMurtry, Larry: *Leaving Cheyenne*
	Mandiargues, Andre Pieyre de: *The Motorcycle*
	Modisane, Bloke (African): *Blame Me on History*
	Morris, Wright: *Cause for Wonder*
	Plath, Sylvia: *The Bell Jar*

Pynchon, Thomas: *V.*

Semprun, Jorge (French): *The Long Voyage*

Sontag, Susan: *The Benefactor*

Spark, Muriel: *The Girls of Slender Means*

Tevis, Walter: *Man Who Fell to Earth*

Vonnegut, Kurt: *Cat's Cradle*

West, Morris L. (Australian): *The Shoes of the Fisherman*

1964   Abe, Kobo: *The Woman in the Dunes*

Bellow, Saul: *Herzog*

Berger, Thomas: *Little Big Man*

Kesey, Ken: *Sometimes a Great Notion*

Oates, Joyce Carol: *With Shuddering Fall*

Rawicz, Piotr (French): *Blood from the Sky*

Sarraute, Nathalie (French): *The Golden Fruits*

1965   Abrahams, Peter (African): *A Night of Their Own*

Calvino, Italo: *Cosmicomics*

Fleming, Ian: *Thunderball*

Ford, Jesse Hill: *The Liberation of Lord Byron Jones*

Fowles, John: *The Magus*

Herbert, Frank: *Dune*

Herlihy, James Leo: *Midnight Cowboy*

Jones, LeRoi: *The System of Dante's Hell*

Morris, Wright: *One Day*

Pynchon, Thomas: *The Crying of Lot 49*

Williams, John Edward: *Stoner*

1966   Achebe, Chinua (Nigerian): *A Man of the People*

Barth, John: *Giles Goat-Boy*

Capote, Truman: *In Cold Blood*

Farina, Richard (American): *Been Down So Long It Looks Like Up to Me*

Holland, Cecila: *Rokossy*

Keyes, Daniel: *Flowers for Algernon*

Rexroth, Kenneth: *An Autobiographical Novel*

Singer, Isaac Bashevis: *The Family Muskat*

Susann, Jacqueline: *Valley of the Dolls*

1966–67   Bulgakov, Milhail: *The Master and Margarita*

1967   Barthelme, Donald: *Snow White*

Callado, Antonio (Brazilian): *Quarup*

Kazan, Elia: *The Arrangement*

Levin, Ira: *Rosemary's Baby*

Macken, Walter (Irish): *Lord of the Mountain*

Mailer, Norman: *Why Are We in Vietnam?*
Molinaro, Ursule (French-American): *Green Lights Are Blue: A Pornosophic Novel*
Morris, Wright: *In Orbit*
Oates, Joyce Carol: *A Garden of Earthly Delights*
Oe, Kenzaburo (Japanese): *The Silent Cry*
Salas, Floyd (Spanish-American): *Tattoo the Wicked Cross*
Sinclair, Andrew: *Gog*
Sontag, Susan: *Death Kit*
Styron, William: *Confessions of Nat Turner*
Williams, John A.: *The Man Who Cried I Am*

1968   Armah, Ayi Kwei (Ghanian): *The Beautiful Ones Are Not Yet Born*
Beagle, Peter S.: *The Last Unicorn*
Coover, Robert: *The Universal Baseball Association, Inc., J. Henry Waugh, Prop.*
Hailey, Arthur: *Airport*
Katz, Stephen: *The Exaggerations of Peter Prince*
Kosinski, Jerzy (Polish-American): *Steps*
Momaday, N. Scott: *House Made of Dawn*
Oates, Joyce Carol: *Expensive People*
Puig, Manuel: *Betrayed by Rita Hayworth*
Richter, Mordecai (Canadian): *Cocksure*
Solzhenitsyn, Aleksandr I.: *The Cancer Ward*
Vargas Llosa, Mario (Peruvian): *The Green House*
Vidal, Gore: *Myra Breckenridge*

1969   Angelou, Maya: *I Know Why the Caged Bird Sings*
Fowles, John: *The French Lieutenant's Woman*
Fraser, George MacDonald: *Flashman*
Garcia Marquez, Gabriel: *One Hundred Years of Solitude*
LeGuin, Ursula: *The Left Hand of Darkness*
Madden, David: *Cassandra Singing*
Nabokov, Vladimir: *Ada*
Oates, Joyce Carol: *them*
Oe, Kenzaburo (Japanese): *A Personal Matter*
Puzo, Mario: *The Godfather*
Reed, Ishmael: *Yellow Back Radio Broke Down*
Roth, Philip: *Portnoy's Complaint*
Vonnegut, Kurt: *Slaughterhouse-Five*

1970   Bellow, Saul: *Mr. Sammler's Planet*

Brautigan, Richard: *The Abortion: An Historical Romance 1966*
Dickey, James: *Deliverance*
Didion, Joan: *Play It as It Lays*
Niven, Larry: *Ringworld*
O'Brian, Patrick: *Master and Commander*
Seelye, John: *The True Adventures of Huckleberry Finn*
Segal, Erich: *Love Story*
Shaw, Irwin: *Rich Man, Poor Man*
Vasquez, Richard (Mexican-American): *Chicano*
Walker, Alice: *The Color Purple*

1971   Blatty, William: *The Exorcist*
Bukowski, Charles: *Post Office*
Doctorow, E. L.: *The Book of Daniel*
Gaines, Ernest J.: *Autobiography of Miss Jane Pittman*
Macdonald, Ross: *The Underground Man*
Percy, Walker: *Love in the Ruins*
Stone, Irving: *The Passions of the Mind*
Thompson, Hunter S.: *Fear and Loathing in Las Vegas*

1972   Adams, Richard: *Watership Down*
Anaya, Rudolfo A. (Mexican-American): *Bless Me, Ultima*
Barrio, Raymond (Mexican-American): *The Plum, Plum Pickers*
Camus, Albert: *A Happy Death*
Hannah, Barry: *Geronimo Rex*
Millhauser, Steven: *Edwin Mullhouse: The Life and Death of an American Writer, 1943–1954 by Jeffrey Cartwright*
Tournier, Michel: *The Ogre*

1973   Atwood, Margaret: *Surfacing*
Faulkner, William: *Flags in the Dust*
Hillerman, Tony: *Dance Hall of the Dead*
Jong, Erica: *Fear of Flying*
McGuane, Thomas: *Ninety-Two in the Shade*
Pynchon, Thomas: *Gravity's Rainbow*
Roth, Philip: *The Great American Novel*
Sanchez, Thomas (Mexican-American): *Rabbit Boss*
Sheldon, Sidney: *The Other Side of Midnight*
Villasenor, Edmund (Mexican-American): *Machol*
Vonnegut, Kurt: *Breakfast of Champions*
Wallant, Edward Lewis: *The Human Season*
Welch, James: *Winter in the Blood*

1974	Benchey, Peter: *Jaws*
	Dick, Philip K.: *Flow My Tears, the Policeman Said*
	Jakes, John: *The Bastards*
	King, Stephen: *Carrie*
	Madden, David: *Bijou*
	Welch, James: *Winter in the Blood*
1975	Clavell, James: *Shogun*
	Doctorow, E. L.: *Ragtime*
	Gaddis, William: *JR*
	Williams, Tennessee: *Moise and the World of Reason*
1976	DeLillo, Don: *Ratner's Star*
	Fuentes, Carlos: *Terra Nostra*
	Gardner, John: *October Light*
	Guest, Judith: *Ordinary People*
	Maclean, Norman: *A River Runs Through It*
	Sharpe, Tom: *Wilt*
	Theroux, Paul: *The Family Arsenal*
	Walker, Alice: *Meridian*
1977	Cheever, John: *Falconer*
	Handke, Peter (German): *A Moment of True Feeling*
	McCullough, Colleen (Australian): *The Thorn Birds*
	Morrison, Toni: *Song of Solomon*
	Nin, Anais: *Delta of Venus*
	Silko, Leslie Marmon: *Ceremony*
	Tyler, Anne: *Earthly Possessions*
	Voinovich, Vladimir: *The Life and Extraordinary Adventures of Private Ivan Chonkin*
	Wolitzer, Hilma (American): *In the Flesh*
1978	Barthes, Roland: *Lover's Discourse: Fragments*
	Carroll, James: *Mortal Friends*
	Chih-yen, Hsia: *The Coldest Winter in Peking*
	Irving, John: *The World According to Garp*
	McEwan, Ian: *The Cement Garden*
	Madden, David: *The Suicide's Wife*
	Piercy, Marge: *The High Cost of Living*
	Price, Richard: *Ladies Man*
	Ribeiro, Ubaldo Joao: *Sergeant Getulio*
	Schulz, Bruno (Polish): *Sanatorium Under the Sign of the Hour Glass*
	Selby, Hubert, Jr.: *Requiem for a Dream*
	Yehosha, A. B. (Israeli): *The Lover*
1979	Adams, Douglas: *The Hitchhiker's Guide to the Galaxy*
	Ballard, J. G.: *The Unlimited Dream Company*

Barth, John: *Letters*
Calvino, Italo: *If on a Winter's Night a Traveler*
McCarthy, Cormac: *Suttree*
Madden, David: *Pleasure-Dome*
Mailer, Norman: *The Executioner's Song*
Styron, William: *Sophie's Choice*

1980   Adams, Douglas: *The Restaurant at the End of the Universe*
Auel, Jean: *Clan of the Cave Bear*
Burgess, Anthony: *Earthly Powers*
Doctorow, E. L.: *Loon Lake*
Heinlein, Robert A.: *The Number of the Beast*
Ludlum, Robert: *The Bourne Identity*
Madden, David: *On the Big Wind*
Oba, Minako (Japanese): *A Journey through the Mist*
Rushdie, Salman (Indian): *Midnight's Children*
Toole, John Kennedy: *A Confederacy of Dunces*

1981   Clavell, James: *Noble House*
Dick, Philip K.: *Valis*
Marquez, Gabriel Garcia (Columbian): *Chronicle of a Death Foretold*
Morrison, Toni: *Tar Baby*
Roth, Philip: *Zuckerman Unbound*
Smith, Martin Cruz: *Gorky Park*
Updike, John: *Rabbit Is Rich*

1982   Adams, Douglas: *Life, the Universe, and Everything*
Allende, Isabel: *The House of the Spirits*
Burgess, Anthony: *The End of the World News*
Dick, Philip K.: *The Transmigration of Timothy Archer*
Kineally, Thomas: *Schindler's List*
King, Stephen (as Richard Bachman): *The Running Man*
Marsh, Ngaio: *Light Thickens*
Oates, Joyce Carol: *A Bloodsmoor Romance*
Weir, Allen: *Departing as Air*

1983   Ackroyd, Peter: *The Last Testament of Oscar Wilde*
Coetzee, J. M.: (South African): *The Life & Times of Michael K*
Collins, Jackie: *Hollywood Wives*
Eco, Umberto (Italian): *The Name of the Rose*
Grafton, Sue: *"A" is for Alibi*
Kincaid, Jamaica (Antiguan): *At the Bottom of the River*
Oates, Joyce Carol: *Luxury of Sin*
Wilcox, James: *Modern Baptists*

1984   Bainbridge, Beryl: *English Journey*
Barker, Clive: *The Books of Blood*

Cisneros, Sandra: *The House on Mango Street*

Clancy, Tom: *The Hunt for Red October*

DeLillo, Don: *White Noise*

Gibson, William: *Neuromancer*

Heinlein, Robert A.: *Job: A Comedy of Justice*

Kundera, Milan: *The Unbearable Lightness of Being*

Lodge, David: *Small World: An Academic Romance*

Naipaul, V. S. (Indian): *Finding the Centre*

Updike, John: *The Witches of Eastwick*

Vargas Llosa, Mario (Peruvian): *The War at the End of the World*

1985   Adams, Douglas: *So Long and Thanks for All the Fish*

Atwood, Margaret: *The Handmaid's Tale*

Burgess, Anthony: *The Kingdom of the Wicked*

Dick, Philip K.: *Radio Free Albemuth*

Innes, Michael: *Lament for a Maker*

Irving, John: *The Cider House Rules*

Keillor, Garrison: *Lake Wobegon Days*

Kincaid, Jamaica (Antiguan): *Annie John*

McCarthy, Cormac: *Blood Meridian, or The Evening Redness in the West*

Marquez, Gabriel Garcia (Columbian): *Love in the Time of Cholera*

Michener, James A.: *Texas*

Roth, Philip: *Zuckerman Bound*

Sagan, Carl: *Contact*

Winterson, Jeanette: *Oranges Are Not the Only Fruit*

1985–87   Kay, Guy Gavriel: *The Fionavar Tapestry*

1986   Conroy, Pat: *The Prince of Tides*

Daitch, Susan: *L.C.*

Doctorow, E. L.: *World's Fair*

Gibson, William: *Count Zero*

Hillerman, Tony: *Skinwalkers*

King, Stephen: *It*

Kinsella, W. P.: *The Iowa Baseball Confederacy*

Murray, Doug, and Michael Golden: *The 'Nam*

Sayers, Dorothy L.: *Murder Must Advertise*

1987   Achebe, Chinua (Nigerian): *Anthills of the Savannah*

Clancy, Tom: *Patriot Games*

Heinlein, Robert A.: *To Sail Beyond the Sunset*

King, Stephen: *Misery*

McMurtry, Larry: *Lonesome Dove*

Morrison, Toni: *Beloved*

Naipaul, V. S. (Indian): *The Enigma of Arrival*
Oates, Joyce Carol: *You Must Remember This*
Rankin, Ian: *Knots and Crosses*
Wallace, David Foster: *The Broom of the System*
Winterson, Jeanette: *The Passion*
Wolfe, Tom: *The Bonfire of the Vanities*

1988 Bach, Richard: *One: A Novel*
DeLillo, Don: *Libra*
Eco, Umberto (Italian): *Foucault's Pendulum*
Gibson, William: *Mona Lisa Overdrive*
Kingsolver, Barbara: *The Bean Trees*
Kincaid, Jamaica (Antiguan): *A Small Place*
Miller, Frank: *Batman: Year One*
Rushdie, Salman: *The Satanic Verses*
Uris, Leon: *Mitla Pass*

1989 Doctorow, E. L.: *Billy Bathgate*
Francis, Dick: *The Edge*
Golding, William: *Fire Down Below*
Grisham, John: *A Time to Kill*
Hannah, Barry: *Boomerang*
Ishiguro, Kazuo: *The Remains of the Day*
Kenan, Randall: *A Visitation of Spirits*
Oates, Joyce Carol: *American Appetites*
Preston, Richard: *The Hot Zone*
Saramago, Jose (Portuguese): *The History of the Siege of Lisbon*
Tan, Amy (Chinese-American): *The Joy Luck Club*
Winterson, Jeanette: *Sexing the Cherry*

1990 Burke, James Lee: *Heaven's Prisoners*
Gear, W. Michael, and Kathleen O'Neal: *People of the Wolf*
Oates, Joyce Carol: *Because It Is Bitter, and Because It Is My Heart*
Oe, Kenzaburo (Japanese): *A Quiet Life*
Pynchon, Thomas: *Vineland*
Rice, Anne: *The Witching Hour*
Turow, Scott: *The Burden of Proof*
Updike, John: *Rabbit at Rest*

1991 Bainbridge, Beryl: *The Birthday Boys*
Cook, Robin: *Vital Signs*
Ellis, Bret Easton: *American Psycho*
Grisham, John: *The Firm*
Hannah, Barry: *Never Die*
Nersesian, Arthur: *The Fuck-Up*

Saramago, Jose (Portuguese): *The Gospel According to Jesus Christ*

Silko, Leslie Marmon: *Almanac of the Dead*

Wilcox, James: *Polite Sex*

1992   Adams, Douglas: *Mostly Harmless*

Allen, Edward: *Mustang Sally*

Allison, Dorothy: *Bastard Out of Carolina*

Connelly, Michael: *The Black Echo*

King, Stephen: *Gerald's Game*

McCarthy, Cormac: *All the Pretty Horses*

McMillan, Terry: *Waiting to Exhale*

Marquez, Gabriel Garcia (Colombian): *Strange Pilgrims*

Morrison, Toni: *Jazz*

Oates, Joyce Carol: *Black Water*

Spiegelman, Art: *Maus: A Survivor's Tale*

Stephenson, Neal: *Snow Crash*

Waller, Robert James: *The Bridges of Madison County*

1993   Bainbridge, Beryl: *Something Happened Yesterday*

Burgess, Anthony: *A Dead Man in Deptford*

Clowes, Daniel: *Ghost World*

Esquivel, Laura: *Like Water for Chocolate*

Eugenides, Jeffrey: *The Virgin Suicides*

Gaiman, Neil: *Sandman*

Kingsolver, Barbara: *Pigs in Heaven*

Nordan, Lewis: *Wolf Whistle*

Sacco, Joe: *Palestine*

Welsh, Irvine (Scottish): *Trainspotting*

Yan, Mo (Chinese): *Red Sorghum: A Novel of China*

1994   Connelly, Michael: *The Concrete Blonde*

Doss, James D.: *Shaman Sings*

Lowry, Lois: *The Giver*

McCarthy, Cormac: *The Crossing*

Naipaul, V. S. (Indian): *A Way in the World*

Redfield, James: *The Celestine Prophecy*

1995   Chabon, Michael: *Wonder Boys*

Eco, Umberto (Italian): *The Island of the Day Before*

Evans, Nicholas: *The Horse Whisperer*

Hornby, Nick: *High Fidelity*

Moore, Alan, and Eddie Campbell: *From Hell*

Oates, Joyce Carol: *Zombie*

Rushdie, Salman (Indian): *The Moor's Last Sigh*

Stahl, Jerry: *Permanent Midnight: A Memoir*

Stephenson, Neal: *The Diamond Age: or A Young Lady's Illustrated Primer*

1996   Anonymous (Joe Klein): *Primary Colors*

Gibson, William: *Idoru*

King, Stephen: *Desperation*

King, Stephen (as Richard Bachman): *The Regulators*

Madden, David: *Sharpshooter: A Novel of the Civil War*

Oates, Joyce Carol: *We Were the Mulvaneys*

Palahniuk, Chuck: *Fight Club*

Schlink, Bernhard: *The Reader*

Wallace, David Foster: *Infinite Jest*

1997   DeLillo, Don: *Underworld*

Frazier, Charles: *Cold Mountain*

Golden, Arthur: *Memoirs of a Geisha*

Junger, Sebastian: *The Perfect Storm*

Morrison, Toni: *Paradise*

Pynchon, Thomas: *Mason & Dixon*

Roth, Philip: *American Pastoral*

1998   Bainbridge, Beryl: *Master Georgie*

Collins, Max Allan: *Road to Perdition*

Kingsolver, Barbara: *The Poisonwood Bible*

McCarthy, Cormac: *Cities of the Plain*

Perrotta, Tom: *Election*

Roth, Philip: *I Married a Communist*

Rowling, J. K.: *Harry Potter and the Sorcerer's Stone*

Welsh, Irvine (Scottish): *Filth*

Wolfe, Tom: *A Man in Full*

Yu, Miri (Korean): *Gold Rush*

1999   Allison, Dorothy: *Cavedweller*

Bowden, Mark: *Black Hawk Down*

Coetzee, J.M. (South African): *Disgrace*

Escandón, Maria Amparo: *Esperanza's Box of Saints: A Novel*

Kenji, Nakagami (Japanese): *The Cape*

Oe, Kenzaburo (Japanese): *Somersault*

Palahniuk, Chuck: *Survivor*

Rushdie, Salman (Indian): *The Ground Beneath Her Feet*

Saramago, Jose (Portuguese): *The Tale of the Unknown Island*

Stephenson, Neal: *Cryptonomicon*

2000   Chabon, Michael: *The Amazing Adventures of Kavalier & Clay*

Danielewski, Mark Z.: *House of Leaves*

Eco, Umberto (Italian): *Baudolino*

Oates, Joyce Carol: *Blonde*

	Roth, Philip: *The Human Stain*
	Updike, John: *Gertrude and Claudius*
2001	Bainbridge, Beryl: *According to Queeney*
	DeLillo, Don: *The Body Artist*
	Franzen, Jonathan: *The Corrections*
	Palahniuk, Chuck: *Choke*
	Tan, Amy (Chinese-American): *The Bonesetter's Daughter*
2002	Barris, Chuck: *Confessions of a Dangerous Mind*
	Coetzee, J. M. (South African): *Youth*
	Eugenides, Jeffrey: *Middlesex*
	Faber, Michel: *The Crimson Petal and the White*
	Goodman, Carol: *The Lake of Dead Languages*
	Kingsolver, Barbara: *Small Wonder*
	Kincaid, Jamaica (Antiguan): *Mr. Potter*
	Marquez, Gabriel Garcia (Colombian): *Living to Tell the Tale*
	Palahniuk, Chuck: *Lullaby*
2003	Baker, Nicholson: *A Box of Matches*
	Boyd, William: *Any Human Heart*
	Brown, Dan: *The Da Vinci Code*
	DeLillo, Don: *Cosmopolis*
	Gibson, William: *Pattern Recognition*
	Lahiri, Jhumpa: *The Namesake*
	Lethem, Jonathan: *The Fortress of Solitude*
2003–04	Stephenson, Neal: *The Baroque Cycle*; *Quicksilver*
2004	Clarke, Susanna: *Jonathan Strange & Mr. Norrell*
	Kretser, Michelle de: *The Hamilton Case*
	Locke, Vince, and John Wagner: *A History of Violence*
	Marquez, Gabriel Garcia (Colombian): *Memories of My Sad Whores*
	Munro, Alice: *Runaway*
	Patterson, James: *Sam's Letters to Jennifer*
	Robinson, Marilynne: *Gilead*
	Roth, Philip: *The Plot Against America*
	Spiegelman, Art: *In the Shadow of No Towers*
	Toibin, Colm: *The Master*
	Winterson, Jeanette: *Lighthousekeeping*
2005	Doctorow, E. L.: *The March*
	Ishiguro, Kazuo: *Never Let Me Go*
	McEwan, Ian: *Saturday*
	Rushdie, Salman: *Shalimar the Clown*
2006	Wier, Allen: *Tehano*

Author and Title Index

Abe, Kobo, 155
Abrahams, Peter, 63
Absalom, Absalom! 108, 117, 128, 132, 140
Achebe, Chinua, 63, 118
Ackroyd, Peter, 15
Ada, 141
Adams, Douglas, 5
Adams, Richard, 26, 34
Adolphe, 72
The Adventures of Augie March, 5, 126
Advise and Consent, 63
Against Nature, 118
Against the Grain, 28, 61, 72
The Age of Innocence, 21, 50
Agee, James, 130, 140, 149
The Agony and the Ecstasy, 14
Aiken, Conrad, 73, 78
Airport, 189
AlainFournier, 27, 72
Alcott, Louisa May, 19
Alder Gulch, 38
Aleman, Mateo, 4
Alexandria Quartet, 29, 108
Alexeiyevich (Ivan Bunin), 64
Al Filo del Aqua, 63
Alger, Horatio, 23
Algren, Nelson, 50, 151
Allen, Edward, 58
Allende, Isabel, 55

All Hallows Eve, 116
Allison, Dorothy, 18, 33
All Men Are Brothers, 6
All the King's Men, 63, 84, 108, 110, 123;
    pace in, 129; story-within-a-story in,
    124
All the Pretty Horses, 38
Almanac of the Dead, 60
Alvaro, Corrado, 64
Amado, Jorge, 46
The Ambassadors, 73, 91, 95
Amelia, 50
American Psycho, 13
An American Tragedy, 54, 117, 128, 141,
    144
Amis, Kingsley, 2, 150
Anatomy of a Murder, 41
Anaya, Rudolfo A., 60
Anderson, Poul, 36
Anderson, Sherwood, 32, 84, 139; *Poor
    White*, 51, 57, 90; on raw materials,
    84; on tone, 85
Andrea, 27
Andric, Ivo, 63
Angel Guerra, 63
Angelou, Maya, 12
Anicet, 168, 169
Animal Farm, 26, 65–66
Anna Karenina, 66, 89–90, 92, 123, 124

AntiStory, 173–74

The Apostle, 27

Appointment in Samarra, 54, 90, 117, 139

The Apprenticeship of Wilhelm Meister, 17

Apuleius, Lucius, 4

Aquinas, St. Thomas, 77, 162

Aragon, Louis, 168, 169

A Rebours, 28

Argenis, xviii

Aristotle, 84, 122

Armah, Ayi Kwei, 65

Armies of the Night, 190

Armstrong, Arnold B., 68

Arnow, Harriette, 56, 117, 125, 147

The Arrangement, 41

Artamene, 22

"Article as Art," 189

Artsybashev, Mikhail, 62

Atwood, Margaret, 69

Asch, Sholem, 27

Ashenden, 41

Ashes, 46

As I Lay Dying, 5, 73, 92

Asimov, Isaac, 36

l'Assomoir (The Dram Shop), 52

Asturias, Miguel Angel, 6

Atala, 28

Atlas Shrugged, 62

At Swim-Two-Birds, 55

Auel, Jean M., 47

Austen, Jane, 7, 20–21, 123, 127; character
    contrast in, 131; style of, 140

An Autobiographical Novel, 13

The Autobiography of an Ex-colored Man, 59

Autobiography of Miss Jane Pittman, 12

Azuela, Mariano, 47

Babbitt, 7, 57, 141

Bacchelli, Riccardo, 46

Bacon, Francis, 69

Bad Girl, 42

Bainbridge, Beryl, 15, 46

Baldwin, Faith, 22

Baldwin, James, 59

Ballard, J. G., 34

Balzac, Honore de, xix, 62, 90, 148

Bambi, xviii–xix

Band of Angels, 186

Banning, Margaret Culkin

Barabbas, 26

Barbary Shore, 67

Barchester Towers, 6, 21, 90, 92

Barclay, John, xviii

Barnes, Djuna, 13, 97, 115, 140, 166, 167

Baroja y Nessi, Pio, 6, 57

Barren Ground, 58

Barrio, Raymond, 60

Barrios, Eduardo, 12

Barris, Chuck, 13

Barth, John, 4, 154–55; *Giles Goat-Boy*,
    12, 81, 175; *The Floating Opera*, 155;
    The Sot-Weed Factor, 170

Barthelme, Donald, 37, 169

Bastard Out of Carolina, 18, 33

Batman: Year One, 43

Baudelaire, Charles, 150, 168

The Bear, 118

Beardsley, Monroe, 120

Beast in View, 32

The Beautiful Ones Are Not Yet Born, 65

Beauvoir, Simon de, 24, 62, 119

Beckett, Samuel, 24, 111, 170, 171, 175

*Been Down So Long It Looks Like Up to
    Me*, 24, 150

Beerbohm, Max, 6

Being and Nothingness, 119

Bellamy, Edward, 69

Bellem, Robert Leslie, 41

The Bell Jar, 12

Bellow, Saul, 182; *The Adventures of Augie
    March*, 5, 126; *The Dangling Man*, 9;
    Henderson the Rain King, 182; *Herzog*,
    xvi, 9, 58, 62; *Seize the Day*, 119; *The
    Victim*, 117

Beloved, 59

The Benefactor, 62, 167

Ben Hur, 27

Bennett, Arnold, 53

Bentley, E. C., 40

Bernanos, George, 73

Bernstein, Carl, 65
Between the Acts, 26
Beyle, Marie-Henri. *See* Stendhal
The Big Rock Candy Mountain, 57
The Big Sky, 38
The Big Sleep, 39
Bijou, 81
Bird, Robert Montgomery, 28
The Birthday Boys, 15, 46
The Birth of Tragedy, 75
The Black Echo, 39
Black Hawk Down, 65
Black Valley, 57
Blame Me on History, 66
Blasco-Ibanez, V., 53
Blatty, William, 36
Bleak House, 91, 103, 120, 124, 169;
    expressionism in, 131–32; styles in,
    141
Bless Me, Ultima, 60
Bloch, Robert, 36
Blood and Sand, 53
Blood Meridian, 62
Blue Murder, 41
Blue Voyage, 73
Boccaccio, Giovanni, 72
Bodenheim, Maxwell, 68
The Body Artist, 55
Beowulf, xvii
Bone, 59
Bonfire of the Vanities, 7, 51
The Book of Daniel, 46
Books of Blood, 36
Booth, Wayne C., 81–82, 93, 96, 186,
    187; *The Nature of Narrative*, 97;
    Rhetoric of Fiction, 82, 96, 184
Borrow, George, 12
Bottled in Blonde, 41
Bottom Dogs, 68
Boulle, Pierre, 69
Bound To Rise, 23
Bowden, Mark, 65
Bowen, Elizabeth, 73, 122
A Boy at Gettysburg, 56
Bradbury, Ray, 35–36, 69

Brand, Max, 38
Brave New World, 7, 69
Bread and Wine, 63
Breakfast of Champions, 150
Breton, Andre, 166, 169
The Bridge of San Luis Rey, 62
The Bridge on the Drina, 63
Bridges of Madison County, 22
Brighton Rock, 139
Broch, Hermann, 27, 62
Brody, Catherine, 68
Bronte, Charlotte, 28, 98
Bronte, Emily, 13, 28, 72, 90–91
Brother Ass, 12
The Brothers Karamazov, 73, 116, 118,
    120, 124
Brown, Charles Brockden, 31
Bruen, Ken, 40
Buck, Pearl, 58
Bucky Follows a Cold Trail, 38
Buddenbrooks, 47
Buechner, Frederick, 91, 140
Buffalo Bill's Fair Square Deal
Bukowski, Charles, 5
Bulgakov, Mikhail, 55
Bulwer-Lytton, Edward, 46
Bunin, Ivan (Alexeiyevich), 64
Bunyan, John, 23, 25, 26
Burgess, Anthony, 27, 35, 48, 69
Burke, Fielding (Olive Tilford Dargan),
    68
Burke, James Lee, 41
Burnett, W. R., 41
Burney, Fanny, 22
Burroughs, William, 125, 127, 132–33,
    167, 169
Butler, Samuel, 18–19, 69, 116, 126
Butor, Michel, 170
Butterfield 8, 41
Byrne, Dorm, 28
Byron, George Gordon, 27

Cabell, James Branch, 6, 23, 150
Cable, George Washington, 56, 58
Cabot Wright Begins, 170

Cage, John, 133

Cahan, Abraham, 58–59

Cain, James M., 39, 120, 129, 141, 151;
   The Postman Always Rings Twice, 39,
   76–77, 94, 110, 169; *Serenade*, 186; on
   symbolism, 154; use of motif, 151

Cakes and Ale, 7

Calder (series), 42

Caldwell, Erskine, 58, 66, 141, 149

Caleb Williams; or, Things as They Are, xx

Call Her Savage, 42

Call It Sleep, 68, 131

Calvino, Italo, 55

Campbell, Eddie, 43

Campbell, Joseph, 3

Camus, Albert, 24, 73, 119; *The Fall*, 62,
   88, 94, 116; *A Happy Death*, 181; *The
   Plague*, 117, 155; *The Stranger*, 119,
   124, 169 (anti-hero in, 24, 116;
   charged image in, 158; epiphany in,
   159; and *A Happy Death*, 181;
   imagery in, 159; as novella, xv; pace
   in, 129; setting, lack of, in, 111;
   symbolism in, 158, 159)

The Canary Murder Case, 40

Candide, 6

Candy, 42

Cane, 59

The Cannibal, 111, 135, 167

A Canticle for Leibowitz, 36

Cantwell, Robert, 68

Capek, Karel, 35

Capote, Truman, xx, 88; *In Cold Blood*,
   65, 190; *Other Voices, Other Rooms*,
   32–33, 91, 112–113

Captains Courageous, 28

Carrie, 36

Carroll, Lewis, 34, 144

Cary, Joyce, 121

The Case of Mr. Crump, 119

Casino Royale, 40

Cassandra Singing, 56, 103–4, 110

Cassirer, Ernst, 156

The Castle, xx, 27

The Castle of Fratta, 47

The Castle of Otranto, 31

Casuals of the Sea, 50

The Catcher in the Rye, 10, 44, 119

Catch-22, 6, 150, 169–70, 175; repetition
   in, 140, 143–44

Cather, Willa, 51, 57, 141

Cat's Cradle, 35, 69, 126

Cause for Wonder, 91

The Cautious Amorist, 42

Cave, Hugh B., 41

Cecilia, 22

Cela, Camilo Jose, 53, 124

Celine, Louis Ferdinand, 5, 24, 86, 126

The Cement Garden, 32

Ceremony, 55

Ceremony in Lone Tree, 124

Cervantes, Miguel de, 4, 7, 127

Cezanne, Paul, 133

Chagall, Marc, 168

Challans, Mary, 46

Champion, D. L., 41

Chandler, Raymond, 38, 39, 120

"Character and the Context of Things,"
   102

The Charterhouse of Parma, 112

Chateaubriand, Francois-Rene de, 28

Cheever, John, 91

Chekhov, Anton, 126, 147, 162

Cheri, 73

Chesnutt, Charles Waddell, 56

Chesterton, G. K., 26, 40, 150, 151

Chicano, 60

Children of Violence (series), 18

Chirico, Giorgio di, 168

Chita: A Memory of Last Island, 28

Chocolates for My Wife, Slices of My Life,
   67

Chopin, Kate, 58

Christie, Agatha, 41

Churchill, Winston, 46

The Cider House Rules, 50

The Circular Staircase, 40

Cisneros, Sandra, 60

Cities of the Plain, 38

Clancy, Tom, 41

The Clan of the Cave Bear, 47
Clarissa, xx, 21, 23
Clark, Donald Henderson, 42
Clark, Walter Van Tilburg, 26, 57, 186
Clavell, James, 47
Cleland, John, 42
A Clockwork Orange, 35, 6
The Cloister and the Hearth, 46
Clowes, Daniel, 74
Cocteau, Jean, 88, 141, 153, 169
Cold Mountain, 47
Coleridge, Samuel, 27
Colette, Sidonie Gabrielle, 73
The Collegians, 50
Collins, Jackie, 41–42
Collins, Max Allan, 43
Collins, William Wilkie, 40
The Color Purple, 59
The Commander's Daughter, 50
The Company, 68
Company K, 97, 127
Compton-Burnett, Ivy, 109, 122, 146, 148
Conan the Barbarian, 34
The Concrete Blonde, 39
La Condition Humaine, 49
A Confederacy of Dunces, 24, 56
Confessions (Rousseau), 13
Confessions (St. Augustine), 13
Confessions of a Dangerous Mind, 13
Confessions of a Mask, 13
Confessions of an English Opium Eater, 13
The Confessions of Felix Krull, 61, 116
The Confessions of Zeno (*La Coscienza di Zeno*), 12–13
"The Conflict of Forms," 189
Coningsby, 63
Conjure Woman, 56
Connell, Evan S., 126
Connelly, John, 40
Connelly, Michael, 39
Conrad, Joseph, 41, 80, 120, 178, 189; *Lord Jim*, 84, 114, 135; *Victory*, 72, 113, 117, 154
Conroy, Frank, 13, 190

Conroy, Jack, 68
Constant, Benjamin, 72
A Contract with God, 43
Cook, Robin, 39–40
Cooke, John Esten, 22
Cooper, James Fenimore, 46
Cop Hater, 41
Corbiere, Tristan, 168
Cortazar, Julio, 125, 127, 163, 169
The Counterfeiters, 9, 73, 76, 165, 188
The Count of Monte Cristo, 46
A Country Doctor, 56
The Covered Wagon, 38
Cowboys Don't Cry, 37
Cozzens, James Gould, 141, 147
Craddock, Charles Egbert, 56
The Craft of Fiction, 97, 126–27
Cramer, Jan, 13
Crane, R. S., 122
Crane, Stephen, 53, 73, 149, 154
Cream of the Jest, 6
Crime and Punishment, 73, 116
The Crimson Petal and the White, 48
The Crisis, 46
Croce, Benedetto, 157
The Crossing, 38
Cry, the Beloved Country, 65
cummings, e. e., 13, 78
The Cunning of the Dove, 46
"The Curious Death of the Novel," 189
The Cypresses Believe in God, 67
Cyropaedia, 14

Dahlberg, Edward, 68
Daiches, David, 187
Dailey, Janet, 42
Daitch, Susan, 63, 74
Dali, Salvador, 168
Daly, Carroll John, 41
The Damnation of Theron Ware, 64
The Damned, 41
Dance Hall of the Dead, 40
A Dancer in Darkness, 46
Dangerous Acquaintances (*Les Liaisons Dangereuses*), 73

Danielewski, Mark Z., 32
D'Annunzio, Gabriele, 72
Daphnis and Chloe, xviii
Dargan, Olive Tilford (Fielding Burke), 68
The Dark Journey, 73
Darkness at Noon, 62–63
A Darkness More than Night, 39
Daudet, Alphonse, 6, 63
David Copperfield, 18
Davis, L. J., 37
The Day of the Jackal, 41
Dazai Osamu, 12
Dead I Well May Be, 40
A Dead Man in Deptford, 48
Dead Fires, 64
Dead Souls, 6, 90
De Amicis, Edmondo, 67
Death Comes for the Archbishop, 51
A Death in the Family, 130, 140, 148
Death of a Nobody, 24
Death of the Fox, 46
Death of the Heart, 73
The Death of the Novel, 172
The Death of Virgil, 27
Debit and Credit, 50
Debussy, Claude, 133
Decline and Fall, 7
The Decline of the West, 71
The Deep Sleep, 107
The Deerslayer, 46
Defoe, Daniel, 5, 10, 12, 90; *Journal of the Plague Year*, xx, 9, 95
Degas, Edgar, 133
Deidre, xix
De la Mare, Walter, 10
De la Roche, Mazo, 51
Deledda, Grazia, 73
Delillo, Don, 55
Deliverance, 33, 54
Delmar, Vina, 42
Delta Wedding, 56
De Quincey, Thomas, 13
Derleth, August, 36
Destry Rides Again, 38

De Voto, Bernard, 178
The Diary of a Country Priest, 73
Dick, Phillip K. 36
The Dick Gibson Show, 150
Dickens, Charles, 12, 90, 123, 147; *Bleak House*, 91, 103, 120, 124, 169 (expressionism in, 131–32); *David Copperfield*, 125; *Great Expectations*, 17–18, 128, 146; portmanteau words in, 144
Dickey, James, 33, 54
Diderot, Denis, 109
Didion, Joan, 126
Dillard, Annie, 190
The Disinherited, 68
Disraeli, Benjamin, 63
"Distance and Point-of-View," 97
Do and Dare, 23
Doctor Faustus, 61
Dr. Jekyll and Mr. Hyde, 31
Doctorow, E. L., 46
The Dollmaker, 117, 125
Dominique, 72
Dona Barbara, 57
Dona Perfecta, 27
Don Quixote, 4, 7, 84, 127, 157
Don Segundo Sombra, 57
Donleavy, J. P., 2, 24, 118, 141, 170
Dorothea (Anonymous), 42
Dos Passos, John, 47, 73, 124, 153
Doss, James D., 40
Dostoyevsky, Fyodor, 24, 82; *The Brothers Karamazov*, 73, 116, 118, 120, 124
Douglas, Lloyd C., 7, 27, 186
Doyle, Arthur Conan, 38, 40
Dracula, 9, 31
The Dram Shop (*L'Assomoir*), 52
Dratler, Jay, 41
The Dream Life of Balso Snell, 167
Dreiser, Theodore, 54, 117, 128, 141
Drury, Allen, 63
du Maurier, Daphne, 31–32
Ducasse, Isidore Lucien. *See* Lautreamont
Duggan, Alfred, 46
Dujardin, Edouard, 73, 94, 169

Dumas, Alexandre, 46

Dune, 36

Dunn, Olav, 47

Duras, Marguerite, 135, 171

Durrell, Lawrence, 29, 108

Eco, Umberto, 10, 55, 62

The Edge, 41

Eca de Queiroz, Jose Maria de, 66

Edwin Mullhouse, 15

Effi Briest, 62

Eggleston, Edward, 56–57

Eisenstein, Sergei, 134–35

Ekwensi, Cyprian, 63

Election, 7

Elective Affinities, 62

The Electric Kool-Aid Acid Test, 190

Eliot, George, 122, 123, 126, 127; *The Mill on the Floss*, 19–20, 50, 90

Eliot, T. S., 131

Elkin, Stanley, 150

Ellis, Bret Easton, 13

Ellison, Harlan, 36

Ellison, Ralph, 59, 87, 88, 113, 159

Elmer Gantry, 116

Emile, 64

Emma, 20, 140

The Emperor Jones, 131

The End of the Line, 40

The Enormous Room, 13, 78

Epitaph of a Small Winner, 62, 128

Erewhon, 69

Ernst, Max, 168

Escandon, Maria Amparo, 74

Esperanza's Box of Saints, 74

Esther Waters, 53

Euphues, 145

Every Dead Thing, 40

The Exaggerations of Peter Prince, 125, 176

The Executioner's Song, 65

The Exorcist, 36

The Expedition of Humphrey Clinker, xx, 8

Faber, Michael, 48

A Fable, 26, 127

"The Fact in Fiction," 189

Fahrenheit 451, 69

Falconer, 91

The Fall, 62, 88, 94, 116

The Family at Gilje, 50

The Family Moskat, 51

The Family of Pascual Duarte, 53

Fanny Hill, 42

A Farewell to Arms, 73, 139

Farigoule, Louis. *See* Romains, Jules

Farina, Richard, 24, 150

Farrell, James T., 66, 68, 117, 139, 141; detail use by, 148; style of, 149; symbolism, lack of, 153

Fast, Howard, 67

Fathers and Sons, 73, 90, 129, 160

Faulkner, William, 88, 115, 153; *Absalom, Absalom!* 108, 110, 128, 132, 140; *As I Lay Dying*, 5, 73, 92; *The Bear*, 118; *A Fable*, 26, 127; *Flags in the Dust*, 181; *The Hamlet*, 56; influences on, 84; juxtaposition in, 136; *Light in August*, 87, 120; motif use by, 151; *Sanctuary*, 33, 72, 135; *Sartoris*, 181; *The Sound and the Fury*, 73, 91, 97, 108, 120 (dissonance in, 161; form of, 162; time-shifts in, 109, 110, 130); *The Wild Palms*, 124

Les Faux Monnayeurs. See *The Counterfeiters*

Fear and Loathing in Las Vegas, 7, 65, 190

La Femme 100 Tetes, 43

Ferber, Edna, 66

Ferlinghetti, Lawrence, 78

Fernandez de Lizardi, Jose Joaquin, 6

"Fictional Chapters and Open Ends," 126

"Fiction and the 'Analogical Matrix,'" 138, 152

Fiedler, Leslie, 114

The Field of Vision, 84, 97, 109, 152

Fielding, Henry, 82, 90, 93, 127, 138; *Amelia*, 50; humor of, xvii, 2–3, 7; *Shamela*, 7

Fight Club, 74

Filth, 24

Finnegans Wake, 4, 144
The Fionavar Tapestry, 34
Firbank, Ronald, 142, 150
Fire Down Below, 46
Fires on the Plain, 66
The Firm, 39
Fitzgerald, F. Scott, 84, 184; juxtaposition
    in, 136; *The Great Gatsby*, xv, 51, 79,
    81, 151 (descriptive detail in, 148,
    150; epiphanies in, 159; hero-witness
    relationship in, 84, 96; myths
    conflicting in, 117, 118; point of view
    in, 90; symbolism in, 155, 157); *Tender
    Is the Night*, 181
Five Women Who Loved Love, 22
Flags in the Dust, 181
Flashman (series), 46
Flaubert, Gustave, 19, 76, 77, 78, 96; on
    distance, 85, 96; on style, 138, 145–46,
    151; on writing, 84, 99
Fleming, Ian, 40
Flowers for Algernon, 9
Flow My Tears, the Policeman Said, 36
Fogazzaro, Antonio, 27
The Folks, 57
Fontamara, 63
Fontane, Theodor, 50–51
Foote, Shelby, 97
Footprints on a Brain, 41
For a New Novel, 170
Ford, Ford Madox, 47, 73, 90, 126, 159,
    161; irony in, 150, 151
Forster, E. M., 50, 90, 150, 188–89; on
    characterization, 102; *Howards End*,
    110, 141; *A Passage to India*, 144; on
    plotting, 109, 125; *A Room with a
    View*, 21, 129
Forsyth, Frederick, 41
Fortunate and Jacinta, 47
Foucault's Pendulum, 62
The Foundry, 68
The Fountainhead, 62
Four Eves, 42
The Four Horseman of the Apocalypse, 53
Fowles, John, 48, 62, 147, 181
The Foxes of Harrow, 186

France, Anatole, 6, 69
Francis, Dick, 41
Frankenstein, 31, 34
Fraser, George MacDonald, 46
Frazer, James, 71
Frazier, Charles, 47
Frederic, Harold, 64
Freeman, Joseph, 67
Freeman, Mary E. Wilkins, 56
French Symbolist poets, 153, 165, 168
Freud, Sigmund, 14, 29
Freudianism and the Literary Mind, 71
The French Lieutenant's Woman, 48
Freytag, Gustav, 50
Friedman, Bruce Jay, 169, 170
Friedman, Isaac Kahn, 67
Friedman, Norman, 97
Fromentin, Eugene, 72
From Hell, 43
From Here to Eternity, 144, 185
Frost, 41
Fruits of the Earth, 13
Fuchs, Daniel, 68
The Fuck-Up, 5

Gaboriau, Emile, 40
Gaddis, William, 27, 74, 94, 119, 124
Gaiman, Neil, 43
Gaines, Ernest, 12
Gallegos, Romulo, 57
Garcia Marquez, Gabriel, 55, 84, 110–11
The Garden, 73
A Garden of Earthly Delights, 33
Gargantua and Pantegruel, 3, 7
Garland, Hamlin, 57
Garnett, David, 34
Garrett, George P., 46
Gauguin, Paul, 14
Gautier, Theophile, 85
Gear, W. Michael and Kathleen O'Neal,
    47
Genet, Jean, 175
The Gentleman from Indiana, 57
Gerald's Game, 74
Germinal, 117,
Ghost World, 74

Giants in the Earth, 117
Gibson, William, 36
Gide, Andre, 13, 78, 118, 174–75; *The
    Counterfeiters*, 9, 73, 76, 165, 188; *The
    Immoralist*, 129; *Theseus*, 62, 118
Giles Goat-Boy, 12, 81
The Ginger Man, 24, 118, 170
Giono, Jean, 72
Gironella, Jose Maria, 67
Gissing, George, 62
The Giver, 69
Glasgow, Ellen, 6, 58
Glaspell, Susan, 67
The Glorious Pool, 42
A God and His Gifts, 146
The Gods Are Athirst, 6
God's Bits of Wood, 68
God's Little Acre, 66
Godwin, William, xx
Goethe, Johann Wolfgang von, 9, 13, 17,
    22, 27, 62
Gog, 34
Gogol, Nikolai, 6, 90
Gold, Herbert, 142–43, 147
Gold, Michael, 58, 67–68
Golden, Arthur, 10–11
Golden, Michael, 43
The Golden Ass, 4
The Golden Bough, 71
Golding, William, xvii, 44, 46, 87, 117;
    Lord of the Flies as philosophical novel,
    67, 69
Goldsmith, Oliver, 21–22
Goncharov, Ivan, 66
Gone with the Wind, 46
The Good Earth, 58
The Good Soldier, 73, 90, 151, 159
The Good Soldier Schweik, 6
Gorki, Maxim, 53
Gosse, Edmund, 85
Gosta Berlings Saga, 5
Go Tell it on the Mountain, 59
Gourmont, Remy de, 27
Goyen, William, 13
Goytisolo, Juan, 50
Grafton, Sue, 41

Grahame, Kenneth, 34
The Grandissimes, 56
Le Grand Meaulnes, 28
The Grandmothers, 57
The Grapes of Wrath, 141
Grass, Gunter, 5, 54, 169
Graves, Robert, 27, 46
Gravity's Rainbow, 55, 81, 163
The Great Circle, 78
Great Expectations, 17–18, 128, 146
The Great Gatsby, xv, 51, 79, 81, 151;
    descriptive detail in, 148, 150;
    epiphanies in, 159; hero-witness
    relationship in, 84, 96; myths
    conflicting in, 117, 118; symbolism
    in, 155, 157
Green, Gerald, 63
Green, Henry, 146
Green, Julien, 73
The Green Child, 69, 140
Greene, Graham, xx, 39, 41, 72, 83, 129;
    Brighton Rock, 139; *The Heart of the
    Matter*, 27, 39, 91, 106, 139, 148; *The
    Power and the Glory*, 116
Green Mansions, 34
Grey, Zane, 38
Griffin, Gerald, 50
Der Grune Heinrich, 12
Grimmelshausen, H. J. C. von, 5
Grisham, John, 39
The Group, 190
The Groves of Academe, 7, 140
Growth of the Soil, 58, 117
Grubb, Davis, 33
The Guards, 40
The Guide, 2
Guiraldes, Ricardo, 57
The Gulag Archipelago, 159–60
Gulliver's Travels, xx, xxi, 4, 6, 64, 69
Guthrie, A. B., 38

Hadrian's Memoirs, 10
Haggard, H. Rider, 28
"Haircut," 96
Halper, Albert, 68
Hammett, Dashiell, 39, 41, 120

Hamsun, Knut, 58, 73, 117

Handley Cross, 6

The Handmaiden's Tale, 69

Hannah, Barry, 33

A Happy Death, 181

Hardcase, 28

Hardy, Thomas, 62, 78, 110, 115, 147

Harris, Joel Chandler, 58

Harris, Mark, 9, 188

Harry Potter (series), 44

Harte, Bret, 58

Harvey, W. J., 102

Hasek, Jaroslav, 6

The Haunting of Hill House, 32

Hawkes, John, 33, 115; *The Cannibal*,
    111, 135, 167

Hawthorne, Nathaniel, xxi, 58, 72, 116,
    154

Haycox, Ernest, 38

A Hazard of New Fortunes, 21, 51

Hearn, Lafcadio, 28

The Heart Is a Lonely Hunter, 33, 73, 84,
    97, 113; irony in, 150–51; symbolism
    in, 157; texture in, 144

The Heart of Midlothian, 28, 87

The Heart of the Matter, 27, 39, 91, 106,
    139, 148

The Heart Remembers, 22

Heaven's Prisoners, 41

Heinlein, Robert, 36

Heinrich von Ofterdingen, 13

Heller, Joseph, 115, 170, 175; *Catch-22*,
    6, 140, 143–44, 150, 169, 175;
    Something Happened, 175

Hemingway, Ernest, 26, 39; *A Farewell to
    Arms*, 73, 139; style of, 136–38, 139,
    142, 146–47; *The Sun Also Rises*, 15,
    51, 90, 92, 130, 152 (dialogue in,
    146–47; objective correlative in, 131)

Hemon, Louis, 57

Henderson the Rain King, 182

Her, 78

Herbert, Frank, 36

Hergesheimer, Joseph, 46

A Hero of Our Time (Pratolini), 50

A Hero of Our Time (Lermontov), 72

The Hero with a Thousand Faces, 3

Hersey, John, 65

Herzog, xvi, 58, 62

Hesse, Hermann, 26–27, 62, 72

High Fidelity, 74

A High Wind in Jamaica, 87

Hildick, Wallace, 97

Hillerman, Tony, 40

Hill of Dreams, 28

Hilton, James, 69

Hiroshima, Mon Amour, 135

A History of Violence, 43

Hitchhiker's Guide to the Galaxy, 5

The Hive, 124

Hoffmann, Frederick J., 71

Hofmannsthal, Hugo von,

Holberg, Ludwig, 34

Holderlin, Friedrich, 13

Holland, Cecelia, 46

Hollywood Wives, 41–42

The Home Place, 57, 151

Homer, xvi, xvii

Les Hommes de Bonne Volonté, 47

A Hoosier School Master, 56–57

Hopalong Cassidy, 38

Hope, Anthony, 46

Hopscotch, 125, 127, 163

Hornby, Nick, 74

Hotel, 189

The Hot Zone, 65

Hough, Emerson, 38

The Hound of the Baskervilles, 40

House Made of Dawn, 60

House of Breath, 13

House of Incest, 166–67

House of Leaves, 32

The House of the Seven Gables, xxi

The House of the Spirits, 55

The House on Mango Street, 60

Howard, Robert E., 34

Howards End, 50, 90, 110, 141

Howe, E. W., 57, 66

Howells, William Dean, 21, 51

Huasipungo, 66

Huckleberry Finn, 5, 6, 10, 48, 51, 126; symbolism in, 157
Hudson, W. H., 34
Hughes, Richard, 87
Hughes, Thomas, 23
Hugo, Victor, 31, 46, 85, 127
Hull, E. M., 41
Hulme, T. E., 75, 82
The Human Comedy (Saroyan), 151
The Human Season, 58
The Hunchback of Notre Dame, 31
Hunger, 73
Hunter's Horn, 56
The Hunt for Red October, 41
Hurston, Zora Neale, 59
Huxley, Aldous, 7, 69, 97, 151
Huysmans, Joris-Karl, 28, 61, 72, 118, 142
Hyman, Mac, 66–67
Hyperion; or, The Hermit in Greece, 13

Icaza, Jorge, 66
An Iceland Fisherman, 28
I, Claudius, 46
The Idiot, 73
If on a Winter's Night a Traveler, 55
Ihara Saikaku, 22
I, Jan Cramer, 13
I Know Why the Caged Bird Sings, 12
L'Ile Des Pinguoins, 69
The Immoralist, 129
In Cold Blood, 65, 190
Infinite Jest, 81
The Informer, 72
Innes, Michael, 41
The Innocence of Father Brown, 40
In Orbit, 147
Interview with the Vampire, 36
In the Shadow of No Towers, 43
In Sicily, 50
In the Clouds, 56
Invisible Man, 59, 87, 88, 113, 159
An Irish Solution, 40
The Iron Heel, 67
Irving, John, 50
Ishiguro, Kazuo, 46

Islandia, 69
Island of Women, 50

JR, 74, 124
Jackson, Charles, 72
Jackson, Helen Hunt, 57
Jackson, Shirley, 32
Jake Home, 67
Jalna, 51
James, Henry, xvi, 81, 99–100, 116, 159; *The Ambassadors*, 73, 91, 95; on form, 162, 163; juxtaposition in, 136; narrative technique in, 127; on plotting, 99; *The Spoils of Poynton*, 21; style of, 139, 149; symbolism in, 166; on taste, 185; time reversals in, 130–31; *The Turn of the Screw*, 32, 116; *The Wings of the Dove*, 130–31, 139
Jane Eyre, 28, 31, 98
Jarrell, Randall, 7
Java Head, 46
Jealousy, 51, 170
Jenkins, Jerry B., 27
Jensen, Johannes V., xvii
Jewett, Sarah, Orne, 56, 58
Jews Without Money, 58, 67–68
John Inglesant, 62
Johnny Got His Gun, 68
Johnson, James Weldon, 59
Johnson, Josephine, 68
Johnson, Samuel, 62
Johnston, Mary, 46
Jolas, Eugene, 167
Jones, James, 144, 185
Jones, LeRoi, 59
Jordanstown, 68
The Journal of Albion Moonlight, 10, 167
Journal of a Novel: The East of Eden Letters, 181
Journey of Neils Klim to the World Underground, 34
Journal of the Plague Year, xx, 9
Journey to the End of the Night, 5, 24, 126
Joyce, James, 85, 115, 166–67; allusion in, 88; field of consciousness in, 79, 85;

epiphany use by, 158–59; *Finnegans Wake*, 144; language of, 144, 169; motif use by, 151; obscurity of, 115; sense of place in, 79; *Stephen Hero*, 158–59, 181; stream of consciousness in, 94–95, 169; style of, 141, 144, 145; *Ulysses*, 85, 109, 155, 159 (aesthetic pattern in, 124; free association in, 73, 167; humor in, 4, 7; interior monologue in, 73, 94–95; mythical style in, 98, 118; plotting of, 124; style in, 141); use of time by, 109
The Joy Luck Club, 59
The Judas Kiss, 41
The Judas Time, 67
Jude the Obscure, 62
Junger, Sebastian, 65
The Jungle, 54, 64
Jurgen, 6, 23
The Just and the Unjust, 141
Justine, 42

Kafka, Franz, 119; *The Castle*, xx, 27; *The Trial*, xx, 24, 34, 55, 105, 119
Kanthapura, 63
Katz, Steve, 125, 176
Kawabata, Yasunari, 157
Kay, Guy Gavriel, 34
Kazan, Elia, 41
Kazantzakis, Nikos, 118
Keats, John, 27, 183
Keillor, Garrison, 10
Keller, Gottfried, 12
Kellogg, Robert, 97
Kerouac, Jack, 5, 21, 86, 116, 133–34
Kesey, Ken, 86
The Key, 73
Keyes, Daniel, 9
Kidnapped, 28
The Killer Inside Me, 41
"The Killers," 39
Kim, 28
Kineally, Thomas, 15
King, Stephen, 30, 69, 74
The King and the Queen, 50

The Kingdom of the Wicked, 27
King Jesus, 27
The King of the Golden River, 34
Kings in Exile, 63
Kingsley, Charles, 46
King Solomon's Mines, 28
Kingston, Maxine Hong, 59–60
Kipling, Rudyard, 28
Kiss Me, Deadly, 41
Kit O'Brien, 57
Klee, Paul, 168
Klein, Joe, 15–16
Knock on Any Door, 66, 106
Knots and Crosses, 40
Koestler, Arthur, 62–63
Kosinski, Jerzy, 125, 127
Kristin Lavransdatter, 46
Kromer, Tom, 68
Kundera, Milan, 62
Kyle, Richard, 43

Laclos, Pierre Choderlos de, 8–9, 73
Lady into Fox, 34
La Fayette, Madame de, xviii, 22
Laforet, Carmen, 27
Lagerkvist, Par Fabian, 26
Lagerlof, Selma, 5
La Guma, Alex, 66
Lahaye, Tim, 27
Lake Wobegon Days, 10
Lamartine, Alphonse de, 85
Lament for a Maker, 41
L'Amorosa Fiametta, 72
L'Amour, Louis, 38
Lampedusa, Giuseppe Tomasi di, 48
La Mer, 133
La Motte-Fouque, Friedrich de, 26
The Land of Plenty, 68
Langer, Susanne K., 162
Langus, xviii
Lardner, Ring, 6, 96
The Last Angry Man, 63
The Last Days of Pompeii, 46
The Last of the Wine, 46
The Last Testament of Oscar Wilde, 15

The Late George Apley, 15, 21
The Late Mattia Pascal, 73
Lautreamont, 78, 169
Lavengro, 12
Lawrence, D. H., 104, 118, 125, 140, 151;
  epiphanies in *The Rainbow*, 159;
  symbolism in, 153–54
Lazarillo de Tormes, 4
L. C., 63, 73
Le Carre, John, 41
Lee, Harper, 22
Left Behind (series), 27
The Left Hand of Darkness, 36
Le Guin, Ursula, 36
The Leopard, 47
Leopards and Lilies, 46
Lermontov, Mikhail Yurievich, 72
Lessing, Doris, 18, 72
Letters of a Novice, 9
Levin, Ira, 36
Lewis, C. S., 35
Lewis, Matthew Gregory, 31
Lewis, Sinclair, 7, 57, 116, 141
Lewisohn, Ludwig, 119
Les Liaisons Dangereuses, 8–9
Lie, Jonas, 50
Lie Down in Darkness, 73, 128, 155
Life of the Great Rascal, 4–5
Light in August, 87, 120
Light of Western Stars, 38
Light Thickens, 41
The Lime Twig, 33
Lindsay, Norman, 42
Lins do Rego, Jose, 64
Lish, James, 36
Little Caesar, 41
Little Women, 19
Locke, Vince, 43
Lockridge, Ross, Jr., 57, 98, 128
Lodge, David, 7, 15, 58
Lolita, 13
London, Jack, 67
Lonesome Dove, 38
A Long Day's Dying, 91, 140
The Long Journey, xvii

The Long Voyage, 108
Look Homeward, Angel, 11, 29, 56, 73,
  123–24; epiphanies in, 159; metaphor
  in, 149; style in, 140
Looking Backward, 69
Lord Jim, 84, 114, 135
Lord of the Flies, xvii, 44, 67, 69, 87, 117
The Lord of the Rings, 34
Lost Horizon, 69
The Lost Weekend, 72
Loti, Pierre, 28
Love Among the Cannibals, 186
Lovecraft, H. P., 36
Love in the Ruins, 62
Love in the Time of Cholera, 55
Love Story, 22, 41
Loving, 146
Lowry, Lois, 69
Lowry, Malcolm, 12, 141
Lubbock, Percy, 97, 126–27
Lucky Jim, 2
Lust for Life, 14
Lyly, John, 145

McBain, Ed, 41
McCarthy, Cormac, 33, 38, 62
McCarthy, Mary, 140, 150, 189–90
McCoy, Horace, 39, 120, 129
McCullers, Carson: *Heart Is a Lonely
  Hunter*, 33, 73, 84, 97, 113 (irony in,
  150–51; isolation theme in, 117; style
  of, 140, 144; symbolism in, 157); *A
  Member of the Wedding*, 18, 119
McDermid, Val, 40
MacDonald, John D., 41
Macdonald, Ross, 41
McElheny, Kenneth R., 97
McEwan, Ian, 32
McFee, William, 50
McGuane, Thomas, 118
Machado de Assis, Joaquim Maria, 62,
  128
Machen, Arthur, 28
Macho! 60
McKenney, Ruth, 67

Mackenzie, Henry, 21
McKinty, Adrian, 40
MacLean, Norman, 58
MacLeish, Archibald, 77, 120
Madame Bovary, 96, 141
Madden, David: *Bijou*, 81; *Cassandra Singing*, 56, 103–4, 110; *Pleasure-Dome*, 116; *Poetic Image in Six Genres*, 87; *Sharpshooter*, 46
Maggie: A Girl of the Streets, 53
The Magic Christian, 170
The Magic Mountain, 17, 61–62, 120, 154
The Magnificent Ambersons, 27
Magritte, Rene, 168
The Magus, 62, 181
Os Maias, 66
Mailer, Norman, 23, 63, 67, 144; imaginative nonfiction by, xx, 65, 190
Main Street, 7, 57
Malamud, Bernard, 51, 58
Malaparte, Curzio, 169
Malcolm, 33
Maldoror, 78
Les Malheurs des Immortels, 43
Mallarme, Stephen, 168
Malraux, Andre, 49, 117
The Maltese Falcon, 39
Maltz, Albert, 67
Man and Boy, 179–81
The Mandarins, 24, 62, 119
Manhattan Transfer, 73
A Man in Full, 50
Man Is Strong, 64
Mann, Thomas, 17, 47, 61–62, 116, 120; narrative technique in, 127; symbolism in, 153, 154
The Man of Feeling, 21
A Man of the People, 63
Mano Majra, 57
Manon Lescaut, 22
Man's Fate, 49, 117
Man's Hope, 117
Mansfield, Katherine, 137
The Man Who Fell to Earth, 36
The Man Who Loved Children, 50

The Man Who Was Thursday, 26, 151
The Man with the Golden Arm, 50
March, William, 97, 127
Marching! Marching! 68
Marcus, Steven, 189
Mardi, 26
Maria Chapdelaine, 57
Marianne, 21
Marius the Epicurean, 62
Marivaux, Pierre Carlet de Chamblain de, 21
Markandaya Kamala, 57
Marquand, John P., 7, 15, 21, 185
Marquise Went Out at Five, 136, 170
Marsh, Ngaio, 41
The Martian Chronicles, 35–36
Martin du Gard, Roger, 47
Mason & Dixon, 47
Master and Commander (series), 46
Masters, Edgar Lee, 57
Mastro Don Gesnaldo, 53
Maturin, Charles, 31
Maugham, W. Somerset, 7, 14, 41, 90, 127
Maupassant, Guy de, 79
Mauriac, Claude, 136, 170
Mauriac, Francois, 27, 73, 99, 116
Maus: A Survivor's Tale, 26, 43
Max Havelaar, 6
Max Jamison, 150
Mayer, Robert, 37
Melmoth the Wanderer, 31
Melville, Herman, 10, 62, 84, 127, 141; symbolism used by, 25–26, 166
A Member of the Wedding, 18, 119
Memoirs of a Geisha, 10–11
Memoirs of a Midget, 10
Mendilow, A. A., 109
Men of Good Will, 47
Meredith, George, 18, 90, 120
Merejkowski, Dmitri, 14
Messer Marco Polo, 28
Metalious, Grace, 42
Michelangelo, 14
Michener, James, 47

The Mill on the Floss, 19–20, 50, 90
The Mill on the Po, 46
Millar, Cormac, 40
Millar, Margaret, 32
Miller, Frank, 43
Miller, Henry, 11, 29, 86, 167
Miller, Walter M., Jr., 36
Millhauser, Steven, 15
Millie's Daughter, 42
The Ministry of Fear, 41, 72
Miriam, 42
Miro, Gabriel, 141, 168
Les Miserables, 46, 127
Mishima, Yukio, 13
"Miss Brill," 137
Miss Lonelyhearts, 7
Mitchell, Margaret, 46
Mitch Miller, 57
Moby Dick, 10, 25–26, 84, 127, 166; styles in, 141
Modern Baptists, 21
A Modern Utopia, 69
The Modification, 170
Modisane, Bloke, 66
Moffett, James, 97
Moise and the World of Reason, 78
Moll Flanders, 5, 10, 12, 90
Momaday, N. Scott, 60
Monet, Claude, 133
The Monk, 31
Monkey, 34
Monsieur Beaucaire, 46
Monsieur Lecoq, 40
The Moon and Sixpence, 14
The Moon and the Bonfires, 128
The Moonstone, 40
Moore, Alan, 43
Moore, George, 53
Moore, Marianne, 79
Moravia, Alberto, 53
More, Thomas, 68
Morris, William, 69
Morris, Willie, 190
Morris, Wright, 32, 83–84, 116, 184, 186; action in, 136; black humor in,

119; *Cause for Wonder*, 91; *Ceremony in Lone Tree*, 124, 141; cliche use by, 145; *The Deep Sleep*, 107; *The Field of Vision*, 84, 97, 109, 152; *The Home Place*, 57, 151; *The Huge Season*, 91; *In Orbit*, 147; juxtaposition in, 136; *Love Among the Cannibals*, 186; *Man and Boy*, 145, 179–81; *One Day*, 124; parallelism in, 152; point of view in, 84, 91, 97; "The Ram in the Thicket," 179–81; sense of place in, 112; and style, 139, 141, 142, 145–47, 148, 151; *Works of Love*, 140; *The World in the Attic*, 57
Morrison, Toni, 55, 59
The Mother (Deledda), 73
Mother (Gorki), 22, 53
A Mother in History, 190
Mother Night, 170
A Mother's Kisses, 170
Motley, Willard, 66, 106
The Moviegoer, 88, 109
Mr. Sammler's Planet, 62
Mr. Weston's Good Wine, 27
Mrs. Bridge, 126
Mrs. Dalloway, 73
Mulford, Clarence E., 38
Multatuli, 6
Munro, H. H. *See* Saki
Murder Must Advertise, 41
Murder on the Orient Express, 41
Murdoch, Iris, 24, 62
Murphy, 24
Murray, Doug, 43
Mustang Sally, 58
My Antonia, 57
Myra Breckenridge, 2
My Secret Life, 42
The Mysteries of Udolpho, 31

Nabokov, Vladimir, 7, 13, 58, 141, 150
Nada, 27
Nadja, 166
The Naked and the Dead, 144
Naked Lunch, 127, 132–33, 167

The Naked Year, 49, 57
The 'Nam, 43
The Name of the Rose, 10, 55
Nana, 52
Nashe, Thomas, 5
Native Son, 59, 68
The Natural, 51
The Nature of Narrative, 97
Nausea, 9, 24, 62, 104–5, 119
The Nazarene, 27
Nectar in a Sieve, 57
Nersesian, Arthur, 5
Nerval, Gerard de, 168
A Nest of Gentle Folk, 57
Neuromancer, 36
Never Call Retreat, 67
Never Die, 33
The New Atlantis, 69
A New England Nun, 56
New Heloise, 62
Newhouse, Edward, 68
News from Nowhere, 69
Ng, Mae Myenne, 59
Ngugi, James, 67
Nick of the Woods, 28
Nietzsche, Friedrich, 75
Nievo, Ippolito, 47
Night Flight, 73
A Night in the Luxembourg, 27
Nightmare Abbey, 6
Night of the Hunter, 33
A Night of Their Own, 63
Nightwood, 13, 97, 115, 140, 166, 167
Nin, Anais, 9, 118, 166–67
1984, 35, 69
Ninety-two in the Shade, 118
Nobody Starves, 68
No Longer Human, 12
Nordan, Lewis, 33
Norris, Frank, 54, 117
Norris, Kathleen, 22
Northanger Abbey, 7
North Toward Home, 190
Northwest Passage, 46
Nostromo, 120

The Notebooks of Malte Laurids Brigge 13
Notes from Underground, 24
"Notes on 'Camp,'" 36
No Time for Sergeants, 66–67
Nourritures Terrestres, 13
Nova Express, 125, 169
Novalis, 13
"The Novel Again," 89

Oates, Joyce Carol, 33, 54, 117, 148
Oblomov, 66
O'Brian, Patrick, 46
O'Brien, Flann, 55
O'Connor, Flannery, 33
The Octopus, 54, 117
The Odyssey, xvi, xvii
O'Faolain, Sean, 57, 76, 178
Of Human Bondage, 127
O'Flaherty, Liam, 72
Of Mice and Men, 22, 58
Of Time and the River, 73
O'Grady, Walter, 123, 125
The Ogre, 154
O'Hara, John, 41, 54, 90, 117; style of, 139, 151
The Old Man and the Sea, 26
The Old Wives' Tale, 53
The Once and Future King, 46
One Flew over the Cuckoo's Nest, 84
One Hundred Years of Solitude, 110–11
O'Neill, Eugene, 131
"On Plot," 125
On the Road, 5, 21, 116
Ooka, Shohei, 66
O Pioneers! 57
Oranges Are Not the Only Fruit, 10, 12
The Ordeal of Richard Feverel, 18, 90, 120
Orlando, 111, 158
Orwell, George, 26, 35, 65–66, 69
The Other, 35
The Other Side of Midnight, 41
Other Voices, Other Rooms, 32–33, 91, 112–13
Ouida, 46
Our Lady of the Flowers, 175

Ousmane, Sembene, 68
Out, 172
Out of the Silent Planet, 35
The Ox-Bow Incident, 57, 186

Palahiuk, Chuck, 74
Pale Fire, 7
Palestine, 43
The Palm-Wine Drinkard, 118
Pamela (Anonymous), 42
Pamela (Richardson), xx, 7, 8, 10, 21
Parade's End, 47
Parched Earth, 68
The Party's Over, 50
The Passions of the Mind, 14
Pastoral Symphony, 9
La Pata de la Raposa, 5
Patchen, Kenneth, 10, 167, 169
Pater, Walter, 62, 77, 142
The Patience of Maigret, 41
Paton, Alan, 64–65
Patterson, James, 9
Pavese, Cesare, 128
Peacock, Thomas Love, 6
Pedro Sanchez, 5
Penguin Island, 69
The People of Juvik, 47
People of the City, 63
People of the Wolf, 47
Pepita Jimenez, 73
Pepys, Samuel, 9
Percy, Walker, 62, 87, 109
Pereda, Jose Maria de, 5, 57
Pere Goriot, 90, 148
Perelman, S. J., 188
Perez de Ayala, Ramón, 5
Perez Galdos, Benito, 27, 47, 63
The Perfect Storm, 65
El Periquillo Sarniento, 6
Permanent Midnight: A Memoir, 10
Perrotta, Tom, 7
Persuasion, 20
Peter Whiffle, 15
Petronius, 4, 6
The Petty Demon, 66

Peyton Place, 42
Phineas Finn, 63
The Picture of Dorian Gray, 34, 61, 118
Pictures from an Institution, 7
Pierre; or, The Ambiguities, 62
Pilgrimage, 95
Pilgrim at Tinker Creek, 190
Pilgrim's Progress, 23, 25, 26, 116
Pilnyak, Boris, 50, 57
Pingaud, Bernard, 170
Piovene, Guido, 9
Pirandello, Luigi, 73
Pirsig, Robert M., 190
The Pit, 54
A Place of Execution, 40
The Plague, 62, 73, 117, 155
Planet of the Apes, 69
Plath, Sylvia, 12
Plato, 68–69
Play It as It Lays, 126
Pleasure-Dome, 116
The Plum, Plum Pickers, 60
Pnin, 58
Podhoretz, Norman, 189, 190
Poe, Edgar Allan, 29, 38
The Poetic Image in Six Genres, 87
Pohl, Frederick, 36
Point Counter Point, 97, 151
"Point of View in Fiction," 97
Points of View, 97
Poor White, 51, 57, 90
Portnoy's Complaint, 6, 58
Portrait of the Artist as a Young Man, 10,
    19, 73, 119, 181; estrangement in,
    119; juxtaposition in, 134; as
    Kunstlerroman, 19; plotting of, 124;
    point of view in, 91; statements on art
    in, 77, 134, 163; style in, 141
The Possessed, 73
The Postman Always Rings Twice, 39,
    76–77, 94, 110, 169
Post Office, 5
Pound, Ezra, 87, 143, 154, 157
The Power and the Glory, 116
Powys, T. F., 27

Pratolini, Vasco, 50
Precious Bane, 57
Preston, Richard, 65
Prevost, Abbe, 22
Pride and Prejudice, 19–20, 123, 131
Primary Colors, 15–16
The Princess of Cleves, xviii, 22
The Prisoner of Zenda, 46
The Private Papers of Henry Ryecroft, 62
Prokosch, Frederic, 28
Proust, Marcel, 11, 73, 74, 82, 118, 151;
    symbolism in, 154, 166
Pumpkin Seed Massacre, 40
Purdy, James, 33, 170
Pusig, Robert M., 190
Pynchon, Thomas, 26, 47, 115; *Gravity's Rainbow*, 55, 81, 163

Queen, Ellery, 41
Quevedo Villegas, Francisco Gomez de, 4–5
Quo Vadis, 27

Rabbit Boss, 60
Rabbit, Run, 73
Rabelais, Francois, 3, 7
Radcliffe, Ann, 31
The Radical, 67
Radigan, 38
Rahv, Philip, 82
The Rainbow, 118, 125, 140, 153–54, 159
Raine, William MacLeod, 38
Raintree County, 57, 98, 128, 159
Rameau's Nephew, 109
"The Ram in the Thicket," 179–81
Ramona, 57
Ramuz, Charles-Ferdinand, 57
Rand, Ayn, 62
Rankin, Ian, 40
Ransom, John Crowe, 143
Rao, Raja, 63
Raped on the Railway, 42
Rasselas, 62
The Razor's Edge, 90
Read, Herbert, 69, 137, 140

Reade, Charles, 46
Rebecca, 31–32
The Recognitions, 27, 94, 119, 124
The Red and the Black, 116
The Red Badge of Courage, 73, 148, 154
The Red Carnation, 50
Red Harvest, 41
Reed, Ishmael, 145
Reflections in a Golden Eye, 33
The Remains of the Day, 46
Remembrance of Things Past, 11, 73
Renault, Mary, 46
Rene, 28
Renoir, Pierre, 133
Republic, 68–69
The Restlessness of Shanti Andia, 57
Restored Youth, 50
Return of the Native, 110
Reve d'une Petite Fille, 43
Rexroth, Kenneth, 13
The Rhetoric of Fiction, 81–82, 96
Rhodes, Eugene Manlove,
Rice, Anne, 36, 42
Richardson, Dorothy, 95
Richardson, Samuel: *Clarissa*, xx, 21, 23;
    Pamela, xvi, xx, 7, 8, 10, 21, 99
Rilke, Rainer Maria, 13
Rimbaud, Arthur, 168
Rinehart, Mary Roberts, 40
The Rise of David Lavinsky, 58–59
The Rise of Silas Lapham, 51
The Rise of the Novel, xix
River of Earth, 56
A River Runs Through It, 58
Road to Perdition, 43
Robbe-Grillet, Alain, xix, 51, 136, 162, 168, 170–71
The Robe, 27
Roberts, Kenneth, 46
Roberts, Nora, 41
Robinson Crusoe, 9
The Rogue, 4
Rokóssy, 46
Rolvaag, Ole E., 57–58, 117
Romains, Jules, 24, 47

The Romance of a Schoolmaster, 67
The Romance of Leonardo da Vinci, 14
The Romance of the Rose, xvi
The Roman Hat Mystery, 41
The Roman Spring of Mrs. Stone, 78
The Romantic Comedians, 6
The Romany Rye, 12
A Room with a View, 21
Roquelaure, A. N., 42
Rosemary's Baby, 36
Roth, Henry, 68, 131
Roth, Philip, 6, 58
Rousseau, Jean-Jacques, 13, 57, 62, 64
Rowling, J. K., 44
Rubin, Louis D., 189
The Running Man, 69
Rushdie, Salman, 5, 7, 55
Ruskin, John, 34, 143

Sacco, Joe, 43
Sade, Marquis de, 42
The Saint, 27
St. Augustine, 13
Sainte-Beuve, Augustin Charles, 72
Saint-Exupery, Antoine de, 73
Saki, 7
Salinger, J. D., 10, 44, 118
Salt, 142–43
Salten, Felix, xviii–xix
Sam's Letters to Jennifer, 9
Sanchez, Thomas, 60
Sanctuary, 33, 72, 135
Sandman, 43
Sanin, 62
Saroyan, William, 151
Sarraute, Nathalie, 117, 136, 162, 170
Sartoris, 181
Sartre, Jean-Paul, 9, 24, 62, 104–5, 119
The Satanic Verses, 7, 55
Satyricon, 4, 6
Sayers, Dorothy, 41
The Scarlet Letter, 72, 116, 154
Schaefer, Jack, 38, 186
Schindler's List, 15
Die Schlafwandler, 62

Schneider, Isidor, 67
Scholes, Robert, 97
Schorer, Mark, 82, 138, 151, 152
Schreiner, Olive, 64
Scott, Walter, 28, 45, 87
Scudery, Georges de 75–76
Scudery, Madeleine de, 22
Search for Love, 41
Season of Passion, 42
Seaver, Edwin, 68
The Secret Agent, 41
The Secret Sharer, xv
Seelye, John, 48
Segal, Erich, 22, 41
Seize the Day, 119
Une Semaine de Bon, 43
Semprun, Jorge, 108
Sender, Ramon, 50
El Senor Presidente, 6
Sentimental Journey, 12
A Separate Peace, 84
Seven Who Fled, 28
A Severed Head, 24, 62
Shaman (series), 40
Shamela, 7
Shane, 38, 186
Sharpe, Tom, 7, 58
Sharpshooter, 46
Shaw, Irwin, 66, 124
Sheed, Wilfred, 150
The Sheik, 41
Sheldon, Sidney, 41
Shelley, Mary, 31, 34
Shelley, Percy Bysshe, 27–28
Shih Nai-an, 6
Shiloh, 97
Shogun, 47
Short, Luke, 38
Shorthouse, Joseph Henry, 62
Shuji Tsushima, 12
The Shuttered Houses of Paris, 42
Siddhartha, 26–27, 62
Sienkiewicz, Henryk, 27
Silas Marner, 50
Silko, Leslie Marmon, 55, 60

Silone, Ignazio, 63
Silverberg, Robert, 36
Simenon, Georges, 39, 41, 76
Simms, William Gilmore, 56
Simon, Claude, 162
Simplicissimus the Vagabond, 5
Sinclair, Andrew, 34
Sinclair, Upton, 54, 64
Singer, Isaac Bashevis, 51, 98
Singh, Khushwant, 57
Singmaster, Elsie, 56
Sister Carrie, 54
The Skin, 169
Skinner, B. F., 69
Skinwalkers, 40
Slater, Susan, 40
Slaughterhouse-Five, 6, 35
Sleeping Beauty Trilogy, 42
The Sleepwalkers, 62
Small World: An Academic Romance, 7, 15, 58
Smith, Betty 22
Smith, Thorne, 42
Smollett, Tobias, xx, 8
Snow, C. P., 48, 147
Snow Country, 157
Snowcrash, 69
The Snow Was Black, 39
Snow White, 37
So Big, 66
"The Solitary Reaper," 57
Sologub, Fedor, 66
Solzhenitsyn, Alexander, 159–60
Sometimes a Great Notion, 86
The Song of Bernadette, 27
Song of Solomon, 55
Song of the Lark, 141
Song of the World, 72
Sontag, Susan, 36, 62, 167, 171
So Red the Rose, 46
The Sorrows of Young Werther, 9, 13, 17, 28
Sotileza, 57
The Sot-Weed Factor, 4
The Sound and the Fury, 73, 91, 97, 120; dissonance in, 161; organic form of, 161, 162; time-shifts in, 108–10 passim, 130
Southern, Terry, 42, 170
South Wind, 7
Spark, Muriel, 150
Spengler, Oswald, 71
Spiegelman, Art, 26, 43
Spillane, Mickey, 41
The Spoils of Poynton, 21
The Spy Who Came in from the Cold, 41
Stacton, David, 46
Stafford, Jean, xx, 190
Stahl, Jerry, 10
Stead, Christina, 50
Steele, Danielle, 42
Stegner, Wallace, 57
Stein, Gertrude, 95, 139, 167, 169
Steinbeck, John, 112, 149, 153, 181; *The Grapes of Wrath*, 141; *Of Mice and Men*, 22, 58; *The Pearl*, xv
Stendhal, 63, 112, 116
Stephen Hero, 158–59, 181
Stephens, James, xx
Stephenson, Neal, 36, 69
Steppenwolf, 62, 72, 102
Steps, 125, 127
Sternberg, Meir, 128–29
Sterne, Laurence, 4, 12, 73, 90, 126, 176
Stevenson, Robert Louis, 28, 31, 159
Stevick, Philip, 126, 173–74
Still, James 56
Stoker, Bram, 9, 31
Stone, Irving, 14
A Stone Came Rolling, 68
Stop-time, 13, 190
The Story of a Country Town, 57, 66
The Story of an African Farm, 64
Stowe, Harriet Beecher, 22, 65
Strange Fruit, 64
The Stranger, 119, 124, 169; anti-hero in, 24, 116; charged image in, 158; epiphany in, 159; and *A Happy Death*, 181; imagery in, 159; as novella, xv; pace in, 129; setting, lack of, in, 111; symbolism in, 158, 159

Stranger in a Strange Land, 36
Strangers and Brothers (series), 48
Strike! 68
Strong, L. A. G., 73
Studs Lonigan (trilogy), 66, 109, 117, 139
A Study in Scarlet, 38
Sturgeon, Theodore, 36
Styron, William, 73, 128, 155
The Subterraneans, 86, 133–34
Suckow, Ruth, 57
Sukenick, Ronald, 172–73, 175
The Sun Also Rises, 15, 51, 90, 92, 130,
  152;
dialogue in, 146–47
Superfolk, 37
Surtees, Robert Smith, 6
Susann, Jacqueline, 41
Suttree, 33
Svevo, Italo, 12–13
Swift, Jonathan, xx, xxi, 4, 6, 64, 69
Swinburne, Algernon, 78, 85
The System of Dante's Hell, 59

The Tag Murders, 41
A Tale of Two Cities, 90
Tan, Amy, 59
Tanguy, Yves, 168
Tanizaki, Junichiro, 73
Tarkington, Booth, 27, 46, 57
Tartarin of Tarascon, 6
Tehano, 90
The Tenants, 58
Tender Is the Night, 181
Tevis, Walter, 36
Texas, 47
Thackeray, William, 90, 93
Thayer, Tiffany, 42
Their Eyes Were Watching God, 59
them, 54, 117
Therese, 73
Theseus, 62, 118
They Shoot Horses, Don't They? 39, 129
Les Thibaults, 47
Things Fall Apart, 118
The Third Man, 39

The Thirteenth Apostle, 27
Thirteen Types of Narrative, 97
Thompson, Hunter S., 7, 65, 190
Thompson, Jim, 41
Three Black Pennies, 46
The Three-Cornered Hat, 2
Three Lives, 169
Through the Looking Glass, 34
Thunderball, 40
Thunderbird, 40
A Time to Kill, 39
The Tin Drum, 5, 54, 169
"Title" (Barth), 172
Tobacco Road, 58, 66, 141
To Have and To Hold, 46
To Kill a Mockingbird, 22
Tolkien, J. R. R., 34
Tolstoy, Leo, 127, 147; *Anna Karenina*, 66,
  89–90, 92, 123, 124; *War and Peace*,
  46, 98
To Make My Bread, 68
Tom Brown's School Days, 23
Tom Jones, 90, 93, 126, 127; as comic
  epic, xvii, 2, 4
Tono-Bungay, 6–7
Toole, John Kennedy, 24, 56
Toomer, Jean, 59
Topper Takes a Trip, 42
To the Lighthouse, 74, 97, 109, 151;
  structure in, 125, 126, 133
Tournier, Michel, 154
The Track of the Cat, 26
Tracy, Honor, 150
Trainspotting, 5
Train to Pakistan, 57
transition magazine, 167
Traven, B., 41, 120
Traver, Robert, 41
The Treasure of the Sierra Madre, 41
A Tree Grows in Brooklyn, 22
Trent's Last Case, 40
The Trial, xx, 24, 34, 55, 105, 119
A Trip to the Moon, 34
Tristram Shandy, 4, 12, 73, 90, 126, 176
The Triumph of Death, 72

Trollope, Anthony, 23, 63; *Barchester Towers*, 6, 21, 90, 92; point of view in, 92

Tropic of Cancer, 11

Tropic of Capricorn, 11, 167

Tropisms, 117, 136, 170

The True Adventures of Huckleberry Finn (Seelye), 48

Trumbo, Dalton, 68

Try and Trust, 23

Tryon, Thomas, 36

Turgenev, Ivan, 73, 90, 129, 160

The Turn of the Screw, 32, 116

Tutuola, Amos, 118

Twain, Mark, 58; *Huckleberry Finn*, 5, 6, 10, 48, 51, 126 (symbolism in, 157)

Ulysses, 85, 109, 155, 159; aesthetic pattern in, 124; free association in, 73, 167; humor in, 4, 7; interior monologue in, 73, 94–95; mythical style in, 98, 118; plotting of, 124; style in, 141

The Unbearable Bassington, 7

The Unbearable Lightness of Being, 62

Uncle Tom's Cabin, 22, 65

The Underdogs, 47

The Underground Man, 41

The Underground Stream, 67

Under the Volcano, 12

Under Two Flags, 46

Undine, 26

Undset, Sigrid, 46

The Unfortunate Traveller, 5

The Unnamable, 111, 171

The Unvanquished, 67

Updike, John, 73, 150

Up the Ladder, 23

U.S.A., 47, 124

Utopia, 68

V., 26

Vale, Eugene, 26

Valera, Juan, 73

Valery, Paul, 30, 77, 81, 168

Van Dine, S. S., 40

Van Gogh, Vincent, 14

Vanity Fair, 90, 93

Van Vechten, Carl, 15

Van Vogt, A. E., 36

Vargas Llosa, Mario, 26

Vasquez, Richard, 60

The Verbal Icon, 120

Verga, Giovanni, 53

Verlaine, Paul, 77, 168

Verne, Jules, 34

Viaud, Julian, 28

The Vicar of Wakefield, 21–22

Vicky (Anonymous), 42

The Victim, 117

Victory, 72, 113, 117, 154

La Vida del Buscon, 4–5

Vidal, Gore, 2

La Vida y Hechos del Picaro Guzman de Alfarache, 4

Vigny, Alfred de, 85

The Village, 64

Villasensor, Edmund, 60

The Violent Bear It Away, 33

The Violent Land, 46

Viper's Tangle, 116

The Virginia Comedians, 22

The Virginian, 37–38, 57

The Visioning, 67

Vital Signs, 39–40

Vittorini, Elio, 50

Voltaire, 6

Volupte, 72

Vonnegut, Kurt, 169, 186; *Breakfast of Champions*, 150; *Cat's Cradle*, 35, 69, 136; *Mother Night*, 170; *Slaughter-House Five*, 6, 35

Vorse, Mary Heaton, 68

The Voyeur, 51, 136

Wagner, John, 43

Wain, John, 189

Waiting for Nothing, 68

Wake Up, Stupid, 9

Walden Two, 69

A Walk in the Night, 66
Walker, Alice, 59
The Wall, 65
Wallace, David Foster, 81
Wallace, Lew, 27
Wallant, Edward, 58
Waller, Robert James 22
Walpole, Horace, 31
The Wanderer, 28, 72
Wandrei, Donald, 41
War and Peace, 46, 98
The War at the End of the World, 26–27
Warhol, Andy, 133
The War of the Worlds, 34
Warren, Robert Penn, 46, 62, 63, 108,
     123, 186
War with the Newts, 35
Wast, Hugo, 57
Watership Down, 26, 34
Watt, 175
Watt, Ian, xix
Waugh, Evelyn, 7, 150
Waverley (series), 45
The Waves, 13, 78, 125–26
The Way of All Flesh, 18–19, 116, 126
We, 69
Weatherwax, Clara, 68
Webb, Mary, 57
Weinbaum, Stanley, 36
Welch, James, 60
We'll to the Woods No More, 73, 94
Wells, H. G., 6–7, 34–35, 69
Welsh, Irvine, 5, 24
Welty, Eudora, 56, 110
Werfel, Franz, 27
Wescott, Glenway, 57
West, Nathanael, 7, 167
Westward Ho! 46
Wharton, Edith, 21, 50, 156
"What Is Exposition?" 128–29
When the Mountain Fell, 57
White, T. H., 46
White Mule, 78
Why Are We in Vietnam? 23, 63
Wickford Point, 7

Wieland, 31
Wier, Allen, 90
Wilcox, James, 21
The Wild Ass's Skin, 62
Wilde, Oscar, 23, 78, 142, 143;
     The Picture of Dorian Gray, 34, 61, 118
Wilder, Thornton, 62
The Wild Palms, 124
Williams, Charles, 116
Williams, Tennessee, 78
Williams, William Carlos, 78
Williamsburg Trilogy, 68
Wilt, 7, 58
Wimsatt, William K., Jr., 120
The Wind in the Willows, 34
Winesburg, Ohio, 57
The Wings of the Dove, 130–31, 139
The Winning of Barbara Worth, 23
Winter in the Blood, 60
Winterson, Jeanette, 10, 12
Wister, Owen, 37–38, 57
Wolfe, Thomas, 11, 29, 78, 83, 86, 181;
     descriptive detail in, 147; inspiration
     and, 86; *Look Homeward, Angel*, 11, 29,
     56, 73, 86, 123–24 (epiphanies in,
     159; metaphor in, 149; style in, 140,
     142); *You Can't Go Home Again*, 142
Wolfe, Tom, 7, 50, 51, 190
Wolf Whistle, 33
The Woman in the Dunes, 155
Woman of Rome, 53
The Woman Warrior, 59–60
Women in Love, 118
Woodford, Jack, 42
Woodward, Bob, 65
Woolf, Virginia, 136, 141, 162, 167, 181;
     Between the Acts, 26; *Mrs. Dalloway*, 73;
     Orlando, 111, 158; *To the Lighthouse*,
     74, 97, 109, 151 (structure in, 125,
     126, 133); *The Waves*, 13, 78, 125–26
Wordsworth, William, 27, 57
Work and Win, 23
World Enough and Time, 46, 62
A World I Never Made, 68
The World in the Attic, 57

The World of the Thibaults, 47
Wright, Austin Tappan, 69
Wright, Harold Bell, 23
Wright, Richard, 59, 68
Wu, Ch'eng-en, 34
Wuthering Heights, 13, 28, 72, 90–91
Wylie, Philip, 126

Xenophon, 14

Yamassee, 56
Yanez, Agustin, 63
Yeats, William Butler, 157
Yellow Back Radio Broke-down, 145
Yerby, Frank, 186
You Can't Go Home Again, 142

You Can't Sleep Here, 68
You Know Me Al, 6
Young, Stark, 46
The Young Lions, 66, 124
Yourcenar, Marguerite, 10

Zamyatin, Yevgeny, 69
Der Zauberberg, 17
Zen and the Art of Motorcycle Maintenance,
    190
Zeromski, Stefan, 46
Zola, Emile, 52, 117, 138, 142
Zorba the Greek, 118
Zoshchenko, Mikhail, 49
Zuleika Dobson, 6
Zuviria, Gustavo Martinez, 57

Type and Technique Index

Note: To both encourage their use and stress their importance, some terms are included in this index that are often used in literary discussions but seldom given the status of literary terms, and thus often omitted from indexes.

abstraction: in allegorical novel, 25; in description, 149; images embodying, 156–57; and innovative fiction, 169–70, 174, 175; language as, 79, 142–43, 149, 187; in novel of ideas, 62

the absurd, 119; in innovation fiction, 24, 119, 169–70, 174. *See also* humor, black

academia. *See* campus novel

action, 136, 138, 150; extreme, 143; in innovative fiction, 174; misplaced emphasis on, 160; in mystery novel, 40; in philosophical novel, 61, 62; and plot, 93, 122–23, 128–29; in psychological novel, 72

adjectives, 145, 149

adolescent novel, 44

adolescent perception novel, 18

adventure novel, romantic, 28

aesthetes, 78–79

aesthetic(s), 82–83, 134, 174; absolute, 79–80, 145; anti-, 168; of camp, 36–37; criticism, 138; distance, 85, 88; existential, 39; experience, 61, 163, 169, 184, 187; misuse of term, 52;

with moral dimension, 79–80; mysticism, 80; pattern, as opposed to plot, 124; pleasure, 114; resolution, 107; and structure, 162

affective fallacy, 120–21

African American heritage novel, 59

alienation themes, 117–20

aliterature, 170

allegorical novel, 25–26, 34

allegory, xviii, 4, 12; characters as, 102; in didactic novel, 22–23; satire and, 4

allusion, 88; literary, 88

alogical structure, 135–36, 171

amalgam structure, 164

ambience, 31, 112, 162

ambiguity, 87

American dream/nightmare, 51, 53, 116–17, 155

anovel, 170

ante-novel, 170

anticlimax, 123

anti-hero, 23–24, 175

anti-novel, 168, 170, 175

anti-religious theme, 116

antiquarian novel, 47–48

anti-thesis, 164

anxiety theme, 118

Apollonian (classical) approach, 78, 162–63, 119, 162; concept of literature, xviii, 30; Nietzsche's concept of, 115; principles of, 75–76, 79, 82, 99–100; and vorticism, 75

appearance vs. reality, 115

archaic language, 142, 145

archetypes, 71, 104

architectonics, 163

architecture: compared to fiction, 77, 85, 163

art: for art's sake, 78–79; autonomy of, 115–16; and biographical novel, 14; coherence in, 159; content and, 99; of fiction, 81–88; imitating life, 116, 189; innovative techniques and, 165–76; novel as, 19, 30, 43, 56, 74–80, 137; and organic form, 162–63; process of, 189; purpose of, 30, 184; of reading, 188; revision and, 178; style and, 145

artist: as con man, 116, 173; control and, 83–84, 87, 96, 168; and creative process, 189; *donnee* of, 100; in *kunstlerroman*, 18–19, 119; romantic, 28

atmosphere, 111–13

author: addressing reader, 9, 93, 184; attitude toward work, 9, 79, 85, 96, 112, 184 (shared with reader, 186; and theme, 114, 15, 119–20); narrative voice of, 85, 89, 91–93 passim, 95, 96; and raw material, 81–85 passim, 100, 120, 138, 165; reader and, 52, 81–97 passim, 183–90 (author educating reader, 19, 30, 64, 71); vision of, 119–20

autobiographical novel, 11–12; lyrical, 13–14

automatic writing, 167–69 passim

avant garde fiction. *See* innovative techniques

bathos, 85

bildungsroman, 17–18, 119

biographical novel, 14–15

burlesque novel, 3, 7

camp, defined 36. *See also* pop novel

campus novel, 58

Celtic Twilight movement, xix

central intelligence. *See* point of view

chaos, imitation of, 124, 125, 174

chapter, 126

character, novel of, 19–20

character(s), 101–5; action and, 101–2; as allegory, 102; anti-hero, 23–24, 105; archetypal, 71, 104; card, 103; development of, 123; exemplary, 23; flat, 102; fragrant, 103–4; heroic, 24; motivation of, 104, 105; narrator as, 90, 96, 103; pawn, 103; protatic, 103; romantic, 28; round, 102; stereotypical, 30, 102–3; stock, 102; types, 103

charged image, 84, 131, 153, 157–58

Chinese American heritage novel, 59–60

chronicle novel, 46–47

claims fallacy, 160

clarity/obscurity technique, 114–15, 142

classical approach. *See* Apollonian approach

cliche, 144–45, 171

climax in plot, 106, 123

coincidence, in plot, 124

collage, 132–33, 169

collective unconscious, 71

colloquial language, 145

comic novel, 2–7; black, 2, 35, 118, 169–70; burlesque, 3, 7; epic, 2; of intrigue, 2; literary satire, 7; parody, 7; picaresque, 3–5; satirical, 5–7; social satire in, 6–7. *See also* humor

comic relief, 2

commercial fiction, 30, 122

communication, difficulty of, 33, 119

communication fallacy, 120

compassion, experience of, 2

complication, in plot, 106–7, 122–23

compression, in structure, 135

condensation technique, 135, 157

confessional novel, 12–13

conflict: as theme, 117; types of, 106–7

con man, artist as, 116, 173

connotation, use of, 138, 141–42
consciousness, novel of, 20
context, in plotless novel, 162
contrast, in structure, 131
control, 83–87, 175
cute-tone fallacy, 143
cyber fiction, 37

Dadaism, 133, 167–70 passim, 173
dance: compared to fiction, 77, 172–73
dehumanization theme, 24, 61, 117, 171
denotation, use of, 141–42
denouement, 106–7, 123
description, 137, 142, 146–50; detail in,
    148–50; vs. dialogue, 147–48;
    exposition as, 110; in omniscient
    point of view, 92–93
design. *See* pattern
detail, in description, 148–50
detective novel, 38–40
determinism: in anti-hero novel, 24; -
    choice conflict theme, 106–7; in
    naturalistic novel, 52, 117; in realistic
    novel, 47
development novel, 17–24
dialogue, 145–47
diaries, published, 9. *See also* journal-
    form novel
didactic novel, 22–23, 26–27; illustrative,
    23; and novel of realism, 49;
    representational, 23
dime novel, 30
Dionysian approach, 75–76, 79, 115, 119,
    162
dissonance, in support of unity, 161
distance, author's, 84–88, 112
domestic realism novel, 50–51
donnee, 81, 185
doppelganger device, 118
dramatic present tense, 109
dream(s): American, 116–17; as narrative
    device, 118
dystopian novel, 35, 69–70

eclecticism, 81, 164, 175
empathy, 2, 101, 188

emphasis technique, 135
Enlightenment, xix
environment: in naturalistic novel, 52; of
    southern gothic novel, 32–33
epic novel, xvii–xviii, 63, 98, 127,
    163–64; comic, xvii
epics, national, xvii, xviii
epic synthesis structure, 164
epigrammatic chapters, 128
epiphany, 72, 158–59
episodic structure, 125–26, 127–28
epistolary novel, xvi, 1, 8–9
erotic novel, 42
erziehungsroman, 18
escape fiction, 30
espionage. *See* spy novel
ethnic novel, 58–60
euphemism, 145
exaggeration technique, 131–32, 139,
    175
exemplary characters, 23
existential novel, 23–24, 119, 169–70;
    mystery novel as, 39
experimental fiction. *See* innovative
    techniques
exposition, 110, 128–29, 147–48
expressionism, 72, 131–33, 173
expressive: form, 162–63; fallacy, 86

fable, xvi–xvii, 22, 27
fallacies: affective, 120–21, 187; claims,
    160; communication, 120; cute-tone,
    143; didactic, 120; expressive form,
    86; hysterical discovery of the
    obvious, 86; imitation, 87, 163;
    inspiration, 85; it-really-happened, 86;
    lighting a cigarette, 160; moral, 120;
    pathetic, 143; point of view, 92;
    propaganda, 120; sentimentality, 143;
    thesis, 120; trivia, 160; unintentional
    hyperbole, 143; writer on rack, 85–86
fantasy novel, 33–34; compared to
    magical realism, 54
farce, 2
ficelle, 103
field of consciousness, 85

first person. *See* point of view
flashback, 109, 135
focus, in structure, 135
folklore: in picaresque novels, 3; as style, 118
foreshadowing, 107, 124
form: anti-mimetic, 173–75 passim; expressive, 162–63; imitative, 162; mimetic, 162; musical analogies for, 163; organic, 162–63; spatial, 162; unity of, 161–64
formal realism novel, 51–52, 170
formation novel. *See bildungsroman*
frame, in structure, 128
French Symbolists, 71, 153, 165–66

gestalt, 72–73, 84, 126, 161
gothic novel, 7, 31–32; southern, 32–33
graphic novel, 43
Great American Novel, xvii
the grotesque: gothic fiction and, 31; in romantic novel, 27; southern gothic fiction and, 32–33

hard-boiled mystery novel, 38–40
heritage, novel of, 58–60
hero-witness technique, 84, 94, 95–96
historical novel, 45–48; antiquarian, 47–48; biographical, 14–15; chronicle, 46–47
historic present tense, 109
horror novel, 30, 31, 36
humor, 2, 120, 150; black, 2, 35, 118, 169–70; ironic, 5–6, 150–51; wit, 150
hyperbole, 139, 143
hysterical discovery of the obvious fallacy, 86

identity-search theme, 118–19
illusion vs. reality theme, 115, 118
imagery, 138, 149–50, 156–60; charged image, 84, 131, 153, 157–58; epiphany, 158–59; metaphor, 156; pattern and, 159–60; selectivity of, 159–60; simile, 156; stylized, 167
imagination, 181–82

imagist movement, 173
imitation fallacy, 87, 163
imitative form, 162
impingement, 97, 135–36, 174
impressionism, in structure, 133–34, 173
incongruity device, 2
inevitability, 52, 92, 123, 128, 161
innovative techniques, 30, 163–77; assimilation of, 81, 131; black humor, 2, 35, 119, 169–70; of Dadaists, 168–69; exaggeration and, 169; free association, 167; of French Symbolists, 153, 165–66; goals of, 174–75; limitations of, 175–76; of surrealists, 166–69
insight, 2
inspiration, 75–76, 85–86, 283
interesting concept of the, 187
interior monologue, 73, 94–95
intuition, 85, 86, 182
Irish Renaissance movement, xix
irony, 5–6, 12, 150–51
isolation theme, 117
it-really-happened fallacy, 86

Jewish heritage novel, 58–59
journal-form novel, 9–10
journalism novel. *See* nonfiction novel; muck-racking novel
journey, novel of, 4
juxtaposition, 105, 134–35

kinetic devices, 132
kunstlerroman, 18–19

language: archaic, 142; cliche, 144–45; colloquial, 145; in dialogue, 145–47; euphemism, 145; innovative fiction and, 169, 171, 173; invented, 144; "literary," 142; portmanteau, 144; plastic, 171
Latin American heritage novel, 60
legends, xvi–xvii, xix, 3–4, 98–99
letters. *See* epistolary novel
leitmotif, 151
life-based novel, 11–16

life imitating art, 116, 189
lighting a cigarette fallacy, 160
local color novel, 58
lyrical: attitude, 85; autobiographical
    novel, 13–14; form, 77, 163
lyricism, 32, 85–86, 139–42; misuse of,
    139, 142

magical realism novel, 54–55
manga, 43
manners, novel of, 20–21
the marvelous, 28
Marxian triad structure, 164
material. *See* raw material of fiction
memoir novel, 10
metaphor, 138, 156
mimetic form, 162, 173
mock-heroic writing, 4
modernist movement, 73–74
monologue, interior, 73, 94–95
monomyth, 3–4
montage, 105, 134–35, 169
mood, 112
moral concern in fiction, 6, 79–80, 183
motif/motive, 151–52
motivation of character, 101, 105
muck-raking novel, 54
music: as analogy to fiction, 77, 78, 85,
    163, 172; and poetry, 153
mystery novel, 38–41; hard-boiled, 38–40
mystification, deliberate, 114–15
myth(s), 3-4, 71, 88, 98

narrative, 99–100
narrator, 93–94; as character, 90, 96, 103
Native American heritage novel, 60
natural determinism, 52
naturalistic novel, 52–54, 87, 88, 170
neo-romanticism, 29
nihilism, 120
nonfiction: with fictional qualities, 13;
    novel, 65
notion, compared to concept, 84
nouveau roman, 170
novel: defined, xxi; development of,
    xv–xxi, 211–44; revising, 178–82;

types of, 2–80; writing techniques in,
    81–177
novella, xv, 1, 169, 172

objective correlative, 131
objectivism, 170
objectivity, 85–87
obscurity, 115, 174
occult novel, 36
omniscient author. *See* point of view
Open Theater, 133
optimism, 119, 120
organic form, 162–63
over-/underwriting, 142

pace, in structure, 128–29
panorama, as structural element, 126–27
paradox, 151
parallel, as technique, 98, 151–52
Parnassians, 85
parody, literary, 7
pastiche novel, 133
pastoral romance, xviii
pathetic fallacy, 143
pathos, 85, 101, 143
pattern: in imagery, 156, 159; mythic, 3,
    98, 118, 154; instead of plot, 123–24;
    spatial or temporal, 108; in structure,
    77, 108, 126, 129; in style, 137,
    150–52; in symbolism, 153–54
personal history novel, 12
personal-writing novel, 8–10
pessimism, 119, 120
phenomenalism, 170
philosophical novel, 1, 61–62, 88
picaresque novel, 3–5
place, 110–12
plant device, 107
plot, 93, 98–100, 122–24; aesthetic
    pattern in, 124; anticipation in, 124;
    anti-climax in, 123; climax in, 106,
    123; coincidence in, 124; definitions
    of, 122; development within, 122–23;
    double, 124; episodic, 107, 124;
    foreshadowing in, 107, 124; key
    moment in, 124; lack of, 161–62;

multiple, 124; resolution in, 107, 123;
  rhythm of, 123; story compared to,
  93, 125; story-within-a-story in, 124;
  structure compared to, 125; subplot
  in, 123–24; suspense in, 107
plotless novel, 161–62
poetic novel, 78
point of view, 89–97, 108; central
  intelligence (*see herein* third person);
  fallacy, 92; first person, 90–97 passim,
  148; multiple, 91, 92, 97, 141;
  omniscient, 89–90, 92; third person,
  89, 91–94 passim, 148
political approach to fiction, 170
political novel, 54, 62–63, 67
pop novel, 36–37, 169
popular novel, 30–44; as influence on
  avant garde, 30–31
portmanteau words, 144
postmodern novel, 37
present tense, 109; dramatic, 109;
  historic, 109
problem novel, 63–65
process, in plotless novel, 98, 161–63
proletarian novel, 23, 35, 37, 67–68, 120,
  168–69
propaganda novel, 65–66
protest novel, 67–68
psyche, 145
psychological analysis novel, 20
psychological novel, xviii, 71–74
pure novel, 75–80
Puritanism, xix, 23
purple prose, 142

rack, author on the, fallacy, 85–86
radical novel, 23
randomness, in structure, 125
raw material of fiction, xx, 81–85 passim,
  120, 138, 165
reader: author and, 52, 81–97 passim,
  183–90; author educating the, 19, 30,
  64, 71; vicarious experience of, 12,
  57, 76, 105
realism, novel of, 49–55; domestic,
  50–51; formal *r.*, novel of, 51–52, 170;

historical determinism subgenre, 47,
  88; magical *r.*, novel of, 54–55; Soviet,
  50
realistic: as honorific, 51–52; portrayal of
  psychological processes, 71, 73–74,
  133; style, 3–4, 51–52, 57–58;
realistic formalism, 51–52, 170
reality *vs.* illusion theme, 115, 118
regional novel, 56–60
relativity of values, 119
relevance in fiction, 87, 175, 183–84, 189
religious novel, 26–27, 88, 116; anti-,
  116; chronicle, 27; mystical, 27, 88
repetition: of imagery, 159; forming
  structure, 125; stylistic use of, 143–44,
  152, 161
reshaping imagination, 182
resolution, in plot, 107, 123, 173
reversal, in structure, 130–31
revision, 76, 178–82
rhythm: of plot, 123; in prose style, 144;
  in structure, 129–31, 134
roman a clef, xviii, 15–16
romance, xv–xvi, xvii–xix, xx, 3, 6, 7;
  pastoral, xviii
romance novel (modern), 41–42
romantic novel, 27–29; autobiographical
  nature of, 28, 29; adventure, 28–29;
  burlesque of, 3; gothic, 29, 31
  (southern gothic, 32–33); grotesque,
  32–33; impressionistic, 28;
  philosophical, 28; psychological, 29,
  72; sentimental, 21–22

saga, xvii
satire: and the grotesque, 31; pop novel
  and, 37; in science fiction 35; social,
  4, 6–7; tone of, 85
satirical novel, 5–7
scene, 82; to advance plot, 82; in
  Dostoevsky, 82; in omniscient point
  of view, 92–93; in structure, 126–27
science fiction novel, 34–36
scop, 99
selectivity, of imagery, 159–60
self, divided, as theme 118–19

sensibility: novel of, 21–22; in Proust, 82

sentimental novel, 21–22

sentimentality: fallacy, 143; inverted, 170

setting, 111–12; exotic, xv, xvii, xviii, xx, 27, 28–29

sexual mores theme, 119

short story, 1, 38, 39, 88, 96, 172; revision into novel, 179–81

simile, 156

sincerity of author, xviii, 96–97

situation, in structure, 128

social criticism novel, 35, 66–67; satirical, 6–7

socialist novel, 67

soil, novel of, 57–58

soliloquy, 94

southern gothic novel, 32–33

Soviet realism, 50

space (spatial) organization, 108, 162

spontaneity, 86–87. *See also* automatic writing

spy novel, 40, 41

story, 91–93, 98–100; compared to plot and structure, 93, 125

stream of consciousness, 73, 95, 169

structure, 125–36; action in, 128–30, 136; alogical, 135–36, 171; amalgam, 164; anti-structure, 162–64; chapters in, 126; chronological, 125, 135, 173; compression in, 135; contrast in, 131; digressions in, 127; emphasis in, 135; epic synthesis, 164; episodic, 24, 39, 124–26, 127–28; exposition in, 110, 128–29, 147–48; expressionism in, 131–33; focus in, 135; and form, 162–64; frame types in, 128; in hard-boiled novels, 39; impressionistic, 133–34; in innovative fiction, 171, 173, 174; juxtaposition in, 134–35; Marxian triad form, 164; montage in, 134–35; "musical," in fiction, 78; organic, 162–63; pace in, 128–29; panoramic method in, 126–27; plot compared to, 125; reversal in, 130–31; rhythm in, 129–30; scenic method in, 126–27; situation in, 128; story compared to,

98, 125; symbolic, 153–54; transition in, 130. *See also* unity

sturm und drang, 27

style, 82, 113, 137–52; as absolute, 78–79, 145; abstract language in, 142–43; complex, 139–40; connotative words in, 141–42; contrast in, 131; denotative words in, 141–42; description in, 110, 147–50; in dialogue, 145–47; mannered 138–39; metaphor in, 138; mid-, 140–41; mixed, 141; over-/underwriting, 142; parallel in, 151, 152; repetition in, 143–44, 152, 161; rhythm in, 144; simple, 138–39; suggestion in, 149–50; texture in, 144. *See also* description; language

stylistic imagination, 182

subjectivity, 85–87, 131; in nonfiction novel, 65; in psychological novel, 71, 73, 74; and romantic temperament, 28, 78

subplot, 123–24

suggestion, in style, 149–50

supernatural theme, 116

surrealism, 9–10, 133, 166–69, 173

suspense, 106–7, 130

symbol-hunting, 151, 154

symbolic novel, 25–29

symbolism, 82, 153–55, 157, 165–66, 168, 173; allegorical novel and, 25–26; misuse of term, 151; in structure, 153–54

symbolists. *See* French Symbolists

synthesis, 164

tale, xvi, xviii, 3–4, 32, 34 98–99; tall, 3, 99

tale-telling voice, 85

taste, as criterion, 185–86

tear-jerker novel, 22

technical imagination, 182

technique(s): defined, 81–88; innovative, 163–77; point of view and, 89–97. *See also* language, style

tempo, 130

tense, 109; and style, 141, 145–46
tension, 107, 113
texture, 138, 144
theme(s), 114–21; absurdity, 119;
    alienation (of individual, 117–19; of
    society from nature, 117–18);
    American dream/nightmare, 116–17;
    anti-religious, 116; anxiety, 118;
    dehumanization in mass society, 117,
    171; determinism-choice conflict,
    117; domination of, 115; existential,
    119; identity search, 118; isolation,
    117; mythic patterns, 118;
    reality/illusion, 115, 118; religious,
    116; self, divided, 118; sexual mores,
    119; supernatural, 116
theme-mongering, 115
thesis, 164
thesis novel, 63–65
thingism, 170, 171
third person. *See* point of view
time in fiction: dramatic/historical
    present, 108, 109; reader's perception
    of, 108
time and space patterns, 108–13;
    atmosphere, 112; chronological, 109;
    disorientation, 111; exposition, 110,

147–48; flashbacks, 109, 135;
    foreshadowing, 107, 124; setting,
    111–12
tone, 84–85, 112–13
tough-guy mystery novel, 38–39, 41, 120
transition, in structure, 130
travel novel, 4–5
trivia fallacy, 160
truth, metaphysical, 114

under-/overwriting, 142
underplot, 123
unintentional hyperbole fallacy, 143
unity, 159, 161–64; dissonance and, 161;
    types of, 162
universality, 115
utopian novel, 68–69

verisimilitude, 49
visionary novel, 53
Volksgeist, xvii
vorticism, 75

western novel, 37–38
wit, 150
witness. *See* hero-witness technique
writer. *See* author

About the Authors

Born in Knoxville, Tennessee, in 1933, **David Madden** graduated from the University of Tennessee, served in the army, earned an M.A. at San Francisco State, and attended Yale Drama School on a John Golden Fellowship. Writer-in-residence at LSU from 1968 to 1992, director of the Creative Writing Program from 1992 to 1994, founding director of the United States Civil War Center from 1992 to 1999, he is now Donald and Velvia Crumbley Professor of Creative Writing at LSU.

In 1961, Random House published his first novel, *The Beautiful Greed*, based on his merchant seaman experiences. For Warner Bros., he adapted his second novel, *Cassandra Singing*, to the screen (not yet produced). *The Shadow Knows*, a book of stories, won a National Council on the Arts award, judged by Hortense Calisher and Walker Percy. His second collection, *The New Orleans of Possibilities*, appeared in 1982. His stories have been reprinted in numerous college textbooks and twice in *Best American Short Stories*. A Rockefeller Grant, recommended by Robert Penn Warren and Saul Bellow, enabled him to work in Venice and Yugoslavia on his third novel, *Bijou*, a 1974 Book-of-the-Month Club alternate selection. His best-known novel, *The Suicide's Wife*, was nominated for the Pulitzer Prize and made into a CBS movie. *Pleasure-Dome, On the Big Wind*, and *Sharpshooter: A Novel of the Civil War* are his most recent novels. He has finished a novel, *Abducted by Circumstance*, and is finishing *London Bridge Is Falling Down*, an epic novel set in London, 1665–1666, in plague and fire.

His poems and short stories have appeared in a wide variety of publications, from *Redbook* and *Playboy* to *The Southern Review* and *Botteghe Oscure*. His plays have won many state and national contests; several have been published.

Among his works of literary criticism are: *Touching the Web of Southern Novelists, A Primer of the Novel, Wright Morris, Harlequin's Stick, Charlie's Cane,*

277

James M. Cain, Revising Fiction, and *The Poetic Image in Six Genres.* He has published essays on Albert Camus, James Joyce, William Faulkner, Katherine Anne Porter, Katherine Mansfield, Michel Tournier, William Gaddis, Jules Romains, Emily Bronte, Edward Albee, Graham Greene, Richard Wilbur, Tennessee Williams, Carson McCullers, Joseph Conrad, Eugene O'Neill, Ross Macdonald, Flannery O'Connor, Thomas Wolfe, James Dickey, Ingmar Bergman, and Ikira Kurasawa. Best known of the many books of original critical essays he has edited are *Tough Guy Writers of the Thirties, Proletarian Writers of the Thirties, Remembering James Agee, Nathanael West: The Cheaters and the Cheated, Rediscoveries* [*I* and *II*], *Classics of Civil War Fiction, Thomas Wolfe's Civil War,* and *Loss of the Sultana and Reminiscences of the Survivors.*

Madden has also edited several innovative textbooks: *The Popular Culture Explosion, Creative Choices, The World of Fiction, A Pocketful of Prose,* eight other titles in the *Pocketful* series from Harcourt Brace, and *Studies in the Short Story.*

He is a former assistant editor of *The Kenyon Review* and has served on the advisory board of several other literary magazines.

He has given lectures at many conferences and dramatic readings from his fiction at more than 100 colleges and universities. He has been writer-in-residence at UNC–Chapel Hill, Clark University, and Lynchburg College, among others, and distinguished visiting scholar at the University of Delaware. He has also held the Chair of Excellence at Austin Peay State University. *David Madden: A Writer for All Genres* is a forthcoming book about Madden's works.

Charles Bane, a Ph.D. candidate in twentieth-century literature at Louisiana State University, is assistant professor at the University of Central Arkansas, Conroy, Arkansas.

Sean Flory is a Ph.D. candidate in Renaissance studies at Louisiana State University.